SOLDIER AND SOCIETY IN
ROMAN EGYPT

SOLDIER AND SOCIETY IN ROMAN EGYPT

A social history

Richard Alston

London and New York

First published 1995
by Routledge
11 New Fetter Lane, London EC4P 4EE

Simultaneously published in the USA and Canada
by Routledge
29 West 35th Street, New York, NY 10001

First published in paperback 1998

© 1995 Richard Alston

Typeset in Bembo by Florencetype Ltd, Stoodleigh, Devon

Printed and bound in Great Britain by
Mackays of Chatham PLC, Chatham, Kent

British Library Cataloguing in Publication Data
A catalogue record for this book is available from the British Library

Library of Congress Cataloguing in Publication Data
A catalogue record for this book is available from the Library of Congress

ISBN 0–415–12270–8 (hbk)
ISBN 0–415–18606–4 (pbk)

CONTENTS

LIST OF MAPS, TABLES
AND FIGURES

PREFACE

This book is very largely based on my University of London Ph.D. thesis completed in 1990. For various reasons, publication has been delayed and the final version of this book has been written while I was enjoying a British Academy Post-doctoral fellowship. I thank the British Academy for their support. I benefited greatly from the knowledge and enthusiasm of the staff of the relevant London university departments and have been greatly helped by the staff of the Institute of Classical Studies. There are, of course, some people who have been more directly involved in my work. I must especially thank Dominic Rathbone who supervised my thesis and guided the transformation from thesis to book. I shudder to think how many times he has read sections of this work, has corrected my errors, restrained my wilder ideas and pointed me in the right direction. I would also like to thank my external examiners, Tim Cornell and Alan Bowman, whose help and detailed criticism have been invaluable, Jane Rowlandson, Margaret Roxan, Lin Foxhall, Averil Cameron, and Donald Bailey. I owe a great debt also to Kate Gilliver upon whose skills and knowledge I have had frequently to call. I must also thank Sally Tsoukaris for the drawings. My greatest debt though is to my family and to Sara who has put up with my obsessions and enthusiasms with unfailing patience and support. Any failings or errors in the work are, however, my own.

Richard Alston
Department of Classics,
Royal Holloway, University of London

ABBREVIATIONS

Throughout this book standard abbreviations have been used in references to editions of papyri and ostraka and to journals. These are listed in J.F. Oates, *Checklist of Editions of Greek Papyri and Ostraka* (*BASP* suppl. 4), Atlanta, 1985, and *L'Année Philologique*. In addition to these standard abbreviations, the following have been used to refer to the major collections of inscriptions from Egypt:

I. Fayoum = E. Bernand, *Recueil des inscriptions grecques du Fayoum*, vols I–III, Leiden, Brill, 1975–84.

I. Koptos = A. Bernand, *De Koptos à Kosseir*, Leiden, Brill, 1972.

I. Memnon = A. Bernand and E. Bernand, *Les inscriptions grecques et latines du colosse de Memnon*, Cairo, IFAO, 1960.

I. Pan. = A. Bernand, *Pan du Désert*, Leiden, Brill, 1977.

I. Portes = A. Bernand, *Les portes du désert: recueil des inscriptions grecques d'Antinooupolis, Tentyris, Koptos, Apollonopolis Parva et Apollonopolis Magna*, Paris, CNRS, 1984.

1

INTRODUCTION

There is an image of the Roman imperial army embedded in the popular consciousness and in the minds of many Roman military historians. It is an image with which all who read this book will be familiar. The Roman army is frequently portrayed and described as the first modern, professional army. The achievements of the soldiery in maintaining the frontiers of a vast empire almost unchanged for four centuries are lauded and the credit is given to the quality of the troops and Roman military organisation. Yet this vast empire, stretching from the south of Scotland to Arabia and from the deserts of Africa to the lands beyond the Danube, was mostly not acquired by this professionalised force. The Roman army of the early Republic was, like the armies of many other ancient city states, a citizen militia, gathered every summer to fight the enemies of the state in wars which sometimes appear more like extended bandit raids. Gradually, for reasons that are still hotly disputed, this army conquered Italy, defeated the superpower in the Western Mediterranean basin, Carthage, and then extended her power to the East, conquering first one and then the rest of the Hellenistic kingdoms created by the successors of Alexander the Great. In the meantime, the armies went West and North, establishing control of Southern Gaul, Spain and the North Balkans. In surges of conquest, Rome came to rule the lands around the Western Mediterranean and exercise hegemony over those encircling the Eastern Mediterranean. In the last great explosion of conquering energy at the end of the Republic, the armies of Pompey completed the conquest of the Hellenistic kingdoms, only Egypt maintaining a fragile independence under the last Ptolemies, and Caesar conquered Gaul and threatened the remote, semi-mythical island of Britain.

These massive conquests were made by an army which remained institutionally a citizen militia. Armies were recruited for single campaigns and served with the generals appointed for those campaigns. To a large extent, the armies that fought the campaigns of Pompey and Caesar were the armies of Pompey and Caesar and not the armies of the Roman

1

state. The army had changed from the time of the early Republic. The ideal soldier had been the soldier-peasant who left his plough to fight in the spring and returned to harvest in the autumn, but no longer could peasants farm and fight. There was no pretence that the soldiers could return home at the end of a year's campaigning. Originally, the very poorest of Roman society had been excluded from the army and only those with property had fought; by the late Republic, service was open to all Roman citizens and, with Roman citizenship extended throughout most of the peninsula of Italy, many Roman legionaries may have had only the most tenuous connections with the city itself. Inevitably, the demands of maintaining a vast empire meant that the army of the late Republic came to differ more and more from the citizen militia, and the soldiers, who had received some pay since the early Republic, became not peasants fighting only for the summer but 'career soldiers' enlisting and re-enlisting in the campaigns of the great generals.

The gradual professionalisation of the Roman army created great political problems for the Roman senate and state. After Sulla had shown that a charismatic general could march his troops on Rome itself and hence win political battles, powerful politicians commanding the large armies necessary for the great wars of conquest would always be a threat to political stability. When tensions within the ruling elite became open conflict, the conflict could escalate into violence and, further, into civil war. After the wars of Sulla and the Marians, the violence of political struggle in the late Republic, a further outbreak of civil wars between Caesar and Pompey, the Caesarian faction and the assassins of Caesar, Octavian and Antony, it seemed that political stability could only be assured by the prominence of an individual who would retain control over the army. Octavian's final victory at Actium in 31 BC gave him temporary dominance and vast political, military and financial resources. Octavian's political settlement laid the foundation of the imperial system of government and provides a convenient divide in the history of Rome between the Republican and imperial periods.

One of the most important tasks of Octavian, or Augustus as he was known after 27 BC, was to establish his control over the army. This, over time, he achieved by a number of reforms. He improved the finances of the army. He made provision for retirement allowances. He set terms and conditions of service. Although there were adjustments in the reigns of his successors, the Roman imperial army can reasonably be said to have come into being with Augustus. Service in the legions was no longer for a single campaign and no longer with an individual general. Legionaries served for twenty years, later extended to twenty-five, and, in a society where life expectancy was probably under 30, many who joined the army would have died in service even without the threat of enemy action. Military service became a career. The army was no longer

institutionally amateur but, apart from the senior officers, was a professional body and Augustus did all he could to ensure that this new model
army from the lowliest infantryman to the highest of generals was personally loyal to the emperor. The legions were no longer founded for
individual campaigns and disbanded when not needed, but continued
to recruit soldiers over generations. The imperial army maintained the
frontiers and repelled the barbarians. This army conquered Britain, drove
deep into Germany and across the Euphrates into Parthia, besieged
Masada and destroyed the Temple at Jerusalem. The military system
created under Augustus was still recognisable three centuries later and
elements of the Augustan military system can be perceived in the armies
of the Christian emperors of the fourth century.

Understandably political leaders and historians have, since the Renaissance, been impressed by the achievements of the Roman army and
the tenacity with which it maintained the territorial integrity of the
Roman empire. Some of the former group have even tried to emulate
the army in order to obtain similar political influence and power. Many
scholars have been fascinated by the army and have devoted their lives
to an attempt at understanding it. It may seem a little perverse then to
burden the already groaning shelves with another book on the Roman
army but I offer no apology. Roman imperial military history has evolved
over the last generation into almost a separate sub-discipline of ancient
history. In a recent survey of the work of the previous forty years,
M.P. Speidel, one of the leading practitioners of imperial military history,
called on his colleagues to isolate themselves further from mainstream
ancient history by setting up separate journals, possibly separate academic
posts and a separate literature on the Roman imperial army. Speidel asks
of the work of his generation of Roman military historians,

> where is the unifying thread? I believe that we do have such a
> thread and a clear overall vision in what we are doing, and that is
> the past itself, which, of course, is just another way of saying that
> our sources are rich and clear, that our methods are mostly sound,
> that our accounts of the Roman army are informed by our various
> lives' experience rather than by ideology or outside forces.[1]

Rarely in the last twenty years can any historian have written with such
confidence or produced so explicit a statement of Rankean positivism
and amongst ancient historians especially, such confidence is shocking.

The root of Speidel's confidence is the general agreement amongst
military historians about the methodologies to be used and the context
of their study. Roman military history has been dominated by the two
disciplines of epigraphy and archaeology and, in the Anglo-Saxon world,
by the scholars who have come to be known as the 'Durham school',

3

many of whom were trained by Prof. E. Birley in whose honour Speidel wrote the paper from which I have just quoted. Birley has produced the most explicit and informative statements of the ideology of this school. He served in British military intelligence during the second world war, devoting his energies to understanding the German army and its officer corps, and, after the war, transferred the skills developed in military intelligence to the study of the Roman army. Birley and his followers set out to interpret the evidence concerning the Roman army using methodologies and assumptions developed to understand modern armies.[2] The perceived success of this approach has encouraged military historians to understand the Roman army as if it were a force analogous to modern armies, though allowing for the obvious differences in technology.

This modernising view has given the Roman army the patina of modern Western European military forces and it is this model which has dominated Roman military studies. It is no coincidence that Speidel laid out a plan of research on the Roman army for the next generation under the title 'Work to be done on the Organization of the Roman army'. We should concentrate on those aspects of research that have most concerned modern military intelligence: ranks and career structures, the officer corps, logistics, equipment and tactics. The modernising tendency was taken to its logical conclusion by Luttwak who brought his skills as a Pentagon strategist to the analysis of the Roman army in his book *The Grand Strategy of the Roman Empire*. For Luttwak, the German threat in Roman Europe was analogous to the Russian threat and the essay was as much about the strategy of NATO as it was about the Roman empire.[3] Luttwak's view may be radical but it does not run contrary to the prevailing intellectual assumptions of Roman military historians. It did, however, cause some disquiet amongst other historians of the Roman empire. Writers such as Millar, Mann and, at most length, Isaac have questioned Luttwak's fundamental assumptions. These writers doubt whether there was any strategy in the modern sense. Millar especially casts great doubt on the policy-making capabilities of the Roman emperor and the quality of information available to him in order that sensible strategic decisions could be taken.[4]

Mainstream Roman history has itself adopted a position of broad consensus in the last twenty years, a consensus that is fundamentally opposed to that in Roman military history. Historians have come to lay great stress on the ancient aspects of the ancient world. This is no tautology. Historians have concentrated not on political history, to which previous generations devoted most of their attention, but on social history, in an attempt to create a kind of sociology of ancient society, emphasising such elements as the economy, status divisions, the relationship between state and individual and the institutions of everyday life. Historians have found that the technology available to the ancients was, in many ways, primitive and that social organisation differed greatly from modern, Western expectations. Life in the ancient world was very different from modern life and the institutions which shaped that life also differed greatly. There is, then, an incongruity between mainstream ancient history and military history which necessitates a re-examination of the assumptions brought to both aspects of what should be a single discipline of ancient history.

We have already noted Speidel's confidence in the quality of the sources available and the comparative ease with which these can be interpreted. This may lead us to believe that there is a strong empirical case for believing in the modernist view of the Roman army. The interpretation of the sources is often, however, dependent upon the basic assumption of a modernist view. Three groups of sources can be singled out: the military treatises, archaeological remains and inscriptions.

The military treatises are far from simple texts. Frequently based on Hellenistic precursors, they usually deal with specific aspects of Roman military life such as the construction of camps and the organisation of units. Though sometimes based upon the reality of Roman military life, the treatises at best present a text-book version of reality. They single out specific aspects of the Roman military for comment and these tend to be the more technical aspects like trench design or order of march. At worst, the treatises are arguments for reform to be discussed in the political salons of Roman society and their connection with any military reality is, to say the least, tenuous.[5]

Archaeology may offer a certain concrete reality but even here there are problems of interpretation. As we shall see when we look at the forts of Roman Egypt, dating criteria can be decidedly loose and even the century of construction can be a matter of debate. Also, the presence of a fort tells us very little about the military disposition of the troops at the site. We may know that there were troops present and, judging from the size of the fort, we may be able to establish that there were quite a large number of troops there, but we can establish neither what the troops did while they were there nor for how long many of the troops were present. A large fort might have been built for six or seven thousand men but who can tell from the archaeological evidence whether that number of troops remained in garrison for the lifetime of the fort or what their duties and roles were while they were in garrison? Even a seemingly simple structure of linear defence such as Hadrian's Wall has been the subject of much scholarly debate as to its purpose.[6] Did the Roman army spend its time training for major conflicts or policing or terrorising the local inhabitants? We may assume that where there were forts there were soldiers but we cannot assume that where there were soldiers there were forts. Quite large numbers of soldiers could have been billeted on civilians or have requisitioned houses and not left any archaeological trace.

The archaeological data can be supplemented with inscriptions but a brief foray through any collection of military inscriptions will demonstrate the weaknesses of these sources. Inscription on stone was an expensive, very formal and permanent record. Like our inscriptions, the inscriptions of the Romans tended to be highly standardised. The inscriptions emphasise career structures, length of service and names. They serve to identify but no one would expect to be able to reconstruct modern society merely by noting the inscriptions in stone and even allowing for the fact that ancient inscriptions are much fuller and varied than modern inscriptions, the problems with the evidence are clear. Let us take a hypothetical example: the tombstone of a Roman legionary at some town in Middle Egypt. What does this tell us? It tells us precisely what the tombstone says: that the soldier of the legion was buried at this spot. We do not know whether the entire legion was situated nearby, why the soldier was in the area, nor why the soldier died. If there was a fort nearby we might assume that the soldier was stationed at the fort at the time of his death but if the fort was small, we might assume that he was visiting the garrison of a smaller unit. If there was no nearby extant military installation, do we assume that he was on campaign, police duties or home on leave? As soon as we try to interpret the death of the soldier, we have to make certain suppositions and assumptions which, to a greater or lesser extent, are constructions separate from the actual text on the stone. I would not argue that such constructions are necessarily wrong, only that the evidence is problematic and our sources are far from the perfection attributed to them. If we were to change the context in which we interpret the inscription, the meaning of that inscription would change as well. The view that the sources are unproblematic springs from the basic assumption that the Roman army behaved in a manner similar to a modern army.

This assumption is, of course, not necessarily incorrect since the institutional arrangements of a modern army are not totally dependent upon industrial technology, allowing for the absence of telecommunications, nor would I wish this book to be seen in a negative light, as an attack on the traditional forms of military history, though I believe that the traditional forms are deeply flawed. By discussing the work of these scholars, I seek merely to clear the field of analysis and to sweep aside previous convictions that discourage the raising of big issues such as what the army was for, what the soldiers did, who the soldiers were and how the army related to the civilian population. If the context is assumed, the answers are also obvious: the Roman army acted in the way modern armies act and performed the same functions. We cannot simply assume that the Roman army existed as a modern-type army.

The modern army is ideally seen as having a very limited function in Western society. The prime function of the army is to defend their societies against threats from external powers or, in more aggressive states, to pose threats to external powers. The army is, therefore, trained for war and whenever the army becomes involved in activities which do not involve fighting a war, these are regarded as extraordinary or aberrations. Thus, the recent involvement of armies in the distribution of humanitarian aid is seen as an extreme measure, only to be undertaken when the civilian agencies are unable to act because of violence. Again, the involvement of the army in anti-terrorist activities frequently causes unease and is excused as part of the extraordinary measures needed to combat terrorism. The ideology of non-involvement is highly developed in certain Western democracies but in many other modern societies the military is far more pervasive and, given the general development of ancient political institutions, such as the judiciary and bureaucracy, one might expect that the army would have been far more integrated into the political and social structures of ancient Rome than in modern Western democracies.

During the Republic, the army had been the people in arms and one would assume a priori that there was no real difference between the social structures of the army and civilian life. Political and military power were inextricably intertwined. Rome's political leaders commanded her armies and this conjunction of powers, together with the pervasiveness of patronage in Roman social and political life, partially explain the involvement of the Roman army in the political struggles of the late Republic. During the imperial period, there was, until the third century, no division between political and military leaders. Governors administered provinces, heard legal cases and conducted military campaigns. Emperors themselves occasionally led troops into battle. The army, on various occasions, intervened in politics to appoint their general as emperor. At a more local level, although the soldiery fought wars, they were also involved in matters which we might class as civilian. There is at least a prima facie case for assuming that there was no great divide between civilian and soldier. The problematic relationship between soldier and civilian is one of the major themes of this study.

Discussion of the nature of the soldier–civilian relationship raises many questions concerning Roman imperialism. The Roman army was the largest single institution in the Roman empire. If the army was tucked away on the frontiers, in forts, preparing itself assiduously for the day when it would be called to defend the empire, then the army would be remote from civilians and, one suspects, the Roman empire itself might be far distant. However, an army intimately involved in the everyday life of a Roman province would not only be a very visible presence, but would also bring Roman imperial power to the cities and villages of the province. The army would provide a means for the imperial power becoming a real and intrusive element in the life of a provincial.

When considering the relationship between the Roman state, through its representatives, and civilians, we should not lose sight of the soldiers themselves. After all, they started as civilians and those who survived retired into civilian life. The soldiers were themselves an element of society whose lives were deeply affected by the institution of the army. A major element of this study will concern itself with how the army treated its soldiers, a problem which has obvious implications for the issue of military–civilian relations. Patterns of recruitment and settlement and the rewards, both financial and legal, given to the soldiers affected their standing in society. Chapters on the economic and legal status of soldiers and veterans and the impact of veterans on the communities in which they settled create a picture of the soldier and veteran in their economic, social and cultural context allowing us to consider such issues as the 'Romanity' of the Roman troops and the extent to which they formed a separate and privileged group in provincial society.

This book aims to explore the relationship between the army and the soldiers of the army and the people and society of an individual province. It thus differs radically from the institutional military history which has been the dominant form of military history in recent years. This is a series of studies of aspects of the Roman army written from the bottom up: from the level of personal interaction between villagers and soldiers and the relationship of provincials to the power represented by the army. It is by looking at the host of individual incidents and interactions that we can gain an understanding of the role played by the Roman army in the society of the Roman empire and the imposition of Roman imperial rule.

The province of Egypt selects itself for such a study for although one could examine the archaeological evidence from other provinces to try and answer the kinds of questions posed here, Egypt provides the ancient historian with an invaluable resource, papyri. Papyrus, paper made from a marsh reed native to Lower Egypt, indeed the symbol of Lower Egypt in the Pharaonic period, can, in very dry climates, be preserved. Many towns and villages of Ptolemaic and Roman Egypt had a precarious existence, dependent upon irrigation canals to provide the fields with water. If these canals failed, the settlements died and since the settlements became desiccated, the papyri in those settlements were preserved. Papyri deposits were preserved in various forms. In the city of Oxyrhynchus, most of the papyri were discovered in the rubbish mounds of the city. At other sites, papyri are found not discarded but carefully stored in sealed jars, obviously archives of documents. At other sites, papyrus-finds come from mummies; the Egyptians sometimes used papyrus bandages to wrap the body. At Karanis, as at some other sites, many papyri were found in excavations of houses, sometimes discarded, sometimes carefully stored.

A vast number of papyri were preserved in these different contexts and once the possibilities of papyri were recognised and the Egyptian peasantry discovered that there was a market for these artefacts, the antiquities' market was flooded with ancient documents. There are now at least 30,000 published texts dating from the third century BC to the sixth century AD.

There is, of course, considerable variation within this huge body of texts but many of the texts illuminate for us a level of society unattested in other sources. Documents detail the lives of the lower orders, the peasantry and the villagers of the Roman world, when virtually all non-papyrological sources concentrate on the richest members of urban communities. The papyri detail everyday life. There are marriage contracts, house sales, land leases, business contracts, tax receipts and schedules, private accounts, notices of birth and death, documents to establish legal status, private letters and the documentation of litigation. Most of the documents concern the public life of Egyptians and a high proportion of documents deal with the interaction of individuals and official agents. Those who had more contact with officialdom or who had more extensive business dealings will have produced more documentation and have had a greater chance of their records being preserved. The documentation is still, therefore, biased towards the officially active and the wealthier sectors of Egyptian society but, nevertheless, illuminates society further down the social scale than any other form of ancient documentation.

The disadvantages of papyri as source material are, however, equally as clear as their advantages. These documents, frequently only partially preserved, frequently very difficult to read, make up only a small proportion of the documentation which must have been produced in antiquity. The peculiar conditions necessary for the preservation of papyri mean that documents are only preserved from specific sites, virtually all in Middle Egypt, and the irregular process by which many of the documents ended up in the scholarly institutions of Europe and America means that the archaeological provenance of documents is often obscure. In essence, we cannot establish the context of many of the surviving texts. The very nature of the documents also presents us with considerable difficulties. Each document illuminates a specific event. Someone may appear in one text leasing land and never appear again in our documentation. We may have documentation concerning a divorce without any other documentation concerning the relationship. What is the historical significance of these incidents? Papyri do not provide context. Rarely can we establish the socio-economic profile of an individual and even more rarely does a text allow us to generalise about a village. The nature of the texts allows certain assumptions to be made and conclusions to be reached concerning administrative history, but as sources for social history papyri are far more problematic. The historian must exercise caution and, looking at the snippets of available information, slowly construct a picture of the community being studied. The historian who works with papyri must be a detective, sifting the available material for clues, attempting to use the evidence for a reconstruction of events. At times in this investigation, we must immerse ourselves in this detail, notably in the chapter on Karanis, for it is from an understanding of this detail, laboriously reconstructed, that we can comprehend Egyptian society not from the position of the elite Romans and Greeks who have left us our literary sources, but from the position of the ordinary provincials, those at the sharp end, so to speak, of Roman imperialism.

Although the papyrological sources make Egypt a natural choice for this kind of examination, there are certain disadvantages in dealing with the province. Egypt was the last of the Hellenistic kingdoms to fall to the armies of Rome and was, in many ways, the most distinctive. Alexander the Great had conquered Egypt and founded the city which still bears his name today. In the squabbling that followed the death of Alexander, Egypt came to be controlled by the Ptolemies, a Macedonian dynasty who used the new city of Alexandria as their capital. During the Ptolemaic period, there were three 'Greek cities' in Egypt, Alexandria, Ptolemais and Naukratis, but individual Greeks settled throughout the country. It would, however, be a mistake to see the Greek settlers as an in-coming aristocracy. The Ptolemies very quickly adopted traditional methods in the governance of Egypt. In most areas of Egypt, with the possible exception of Alexandria, the Greek communities were heavily influenced by Egyptian culture.

Rome had been involved in Egyptian affairs for some considerable time before Octavian's final victory over Antony and Cleopatra. From at least 55 BC, Roman troops had supported the Ptolemaic dynasty in Egypt, though from long before the Ptolemies had relied upon Roman support to deter the expansionist and militarily powerful Seleucids of Syria. This acknowledged dependence of the Ptolemies meant that they provided no threat to Rome and they were maintained in power for a generation after the last of the other Hellenistic kingdoms had been dissolved. Cleopatra's energetic part in the alliance with Antony against Octavian and the portrayal of the struggle by Octavian as a war against an Egyptian queen and not a civil war, necessitated that Octavian's victory would see the end of the Ptolemaic dynasty. Cleopatra had ruled Egypt in the manner of her ancestors, though possibly more efficiently, with some political support from Rome. Octavian would rule Egypt as a Roman province.

Egypt differed from many other areas of the Levant. The normal Greek pattern of a patchwork of semi-autonomous Greek cities controlling large rural hinterlands did not apply to Egypt. Egypt itself was the hinterland, or *chora*, of Alexandria and this *chora* was controlled by various officials appointed by the government in Alexandria. Octavian retained many of the features of the old Ptolemaic system of government and Egypt itself retained a distinctive culture, still recognisably unique in the Mediterranean world. These features, together with the radically different nature of the historical evidence available, have encouraged ancient historians to emphasise the peculiarities of Egyptian society and to deny the applicability of any model derived from study of Roman Egypt to the rest of the empire. It is, of course, rather distressing if the one body of substantial data available is ruled irrelevant for the general history of the Roman empire. There is, however, a general current of opinion that emphasises the 'Romanity' of Roman Egypt, noting that although there were some differences between Egypt and other provinces, there were also very great similarities.[7] In an attempt to combat the alleged peculiarity of Roman Egypt, reference will be made to similar cases and supporting fragments of evidence from elsewhere in the Roman world in the Conclusion to this book. The problem is, however, less pressing for a study of the Roman army. Although the pattern of interaction between the army and civilians will have varied between provinces, we can assume certain broad similarities since the army in Egypt was not fundamentally different from the army elsewhere. The institutions of the army will not have differed greatly. The soldiers were rewarded with similar pay and conditions. They are likely to have been recruited in the same way in different provinces. Soldiers came from abroad to serve in the army in Egypt and units were transferred into and out of the province. The officer corps will have served in other provinces and it seems unlikely that they will have modified their practices radically in each province. The army in Egypt was commanded by a senior Roman official, though not a senator, who will have brought all the preconceptions developed in his education and training to the task of military command and governance. There were certain peculiarities in Roman Egypt and in the army but there were probably also differences between all the provinces of the empire. All the provinces had distinct histories, cultures and geographies which will have meant that the task of governing them was very slightly different in each case, but the differences are not sufficient to conceal broad similarities. We can write a history of the Roman empire and do not need to treat each province as an entirely separate entity and, equally, the Roman army in each different province must have been broadly similar. The history of the Roman army in Egypt is a suitable test case for the history of the Roman army in all other provinces. I claim a general applicability for my study.

Before turning to a more detailed analysis of the institutional aspects of military life, we must construct a frame for our study. The next chapter establishes certain important points of reference, exploring the physical and human geography of Egypt in Roman times and establishing the military problems facing the Roman government. We will also consider the approximate size and nature of the garrison and the dispersal of the troops across the country. We will establish the basic information necessary for an understanding of the Roman army in Egypt.

2

THE ARMY AND THE PROVINCE

Egypt is, in geographical terms, a long river valley cut into a limestone plateau. On either side of this valley is desert. Only those areas that can be watered by the Nile are capable of supporting substantial populations. In Upper Egypt, there is very little rainfall: the average annual rainfall at Luxor is around 1 mm. The temperature may rise to over 60° C at midday in the summer and fall to below freezing point in the winter nights. Further north, at Cairo, the annual rainfall is usually less than 24 mm, normally falling in a few days in winter. The temperature in summer ranges between the noon high of 35° C and a night-time low of 22° C whilst in winter the corresponding range is 20° C to 10° C. Alexandria benefits from being a coastal city and has a more Mediterranean weather pattern with an average annual rainfall, concentrated between October and April, of 190 mm. It has less of a variation in temperature with a summer high of around 30° C at noon and a winter night-time low of around 10° C. The climate in most of Egypt is characteristic of desert regions. Nowhere is the rainfall great enough to support intensive agricultural activities.[1]

The Western Desert is extremely arid, and has been so for 30,000 to 50,000 years, having a small number of oases, notably El-Khargeh, Dakhla, Siwa, Farafra and Bahariya, which are created by depressions in the desert plateau reaching down to the level of the desert springs.[2] The desert supports a small population at these oases. Dakhla, the most populous of these, is situated approximately 270 km from the Nile valley and has a population of around 20,000.[3] In the 1882 census, the whole of the Western Desert had 30,687 inhabitants and in the 1927 census 35,514 by which time artesian wells had improved agricultural productivity.[4] The Eastern Desert is slightly more habitable since moisture blown from the Red Sea and Indian Ocean sometimes forms storm clouds over the mountain range. These infrequent rains supply a significant number of water points across the desert which made the mineral exploitation of the area possible in ancient times and has supported a small Bedouin population.[5] The only centres of population, however, are on the Red

13

Sea littoral. Even here, the shortage of fresh water severely limits population and such population there is, which is now dependent on mineral exploitation or tourism, was, in earlier times, mainly involved with the Red Sea trade from India. The main sites are Berenike, built by Ptolemy Philadelpus, Quseir, the ancient Leukos Limen, Bur Safaga (Philoteras?), Abu Sha'r (Myos Hormos), and Suez (Klysma or Arsinoe). Suez is nowadays by far the most important site for the Eastern trade but in pre-steam days the Gulf of Suez was very difficult to navigate, due to the prevailing northerly winds, and so shipping was concentrated in harbours to the south.[6] The desert rains which, when they come, are very intense, have cut a series of wadis between the hills. These tend to run east to west and form convenient points of access into the hills of the desert. The main routes exploited in the Graeco-Roman period ran from Qift (Koptos) virtually due east through the Wadi Hammamat to Quseir, from Qift (Koptos) along the Wadi Zaidun and on to Berenike, and from Qena (Kaenepolis) running along the Wadi Qena north-east to Abu Sha'r (Myos Hormos). There were many other possible routes through the desert.[7]

Egypt always has been, and still is today, dependent upon the Nile for its very existence and we must talk about the physical and human geography of Egypt primarily in terms of the river valley. This means that topographically Egypt is very easy to describe. From Aswan to Cairo, a distance of 950 km, the river runs between two parallel lines of hills, in places only a few hundred metres apart but often separated by a number of kilometres. After Cairo, the Nile splits into different streams to form the characteristic Delta shape that is the flood plain of Lower Egypt.

The great peculiarity of the Nile is its annual inundation. This is caused by monsoon rains falling over the mountains of Ethiopia which wash large quantities of soil and mud into the Blue Nile. Nowadays the flood is controlled by the Aswan dams but in the ancient period these waters, rich in nutrients, would overflow the banks of the river and spread a thin layer of mud over the valley. By judicious use of dams and reservoirs the waters could be collected to irrigate the land and the mud itself acted as a fertiliser. Egypt was dependent upon this flood. Wherever the waters reached, the land would become fertile, but if the flood was too great, there would be disaster as dams were breached and villages flooded. In Lower Egypt, especially, the flood could change the landscape, placing vast expanses of land under water and seriously disrupting land communications and agricultural activities. At such times the countryside resembled a vast lake dotted with many village-islands which were situated on rises known as turtle-backs. These disadvantages, however, were far outweighed by the benefits of the flood which was responsible for the miraculous fecundity of Egypt which amazed ancient and even early modern writers.[8]

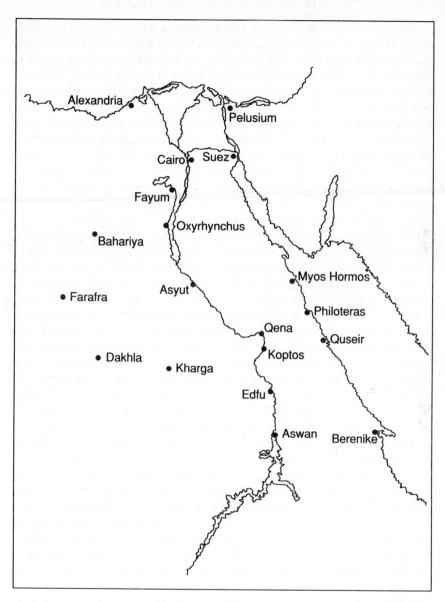

Map 1 Roman Egypt

From the First Cataract, just south of Aswan (Syene), the Nile flows northwards in a single main stream until just to the north of Cairo. The principal settlements of Upper Egypt were dotted along both banks of the Nile and although main settlements might be on one side or the other, the Nile was sufficiently easy to cross to allow 'suburbs' to develop on the bank opposite a main settlement. The Nile valley was comparatively highly urbanised during the Pharaonic and Hellenistic periods but since the vast majority of the population was engaged in agricultural labour and each city was dependent for its food on its immediate agricultural hinterland, such an assertion is of only limited significance. Large urban sites in a pre-industrialised economy can only exist if they have a political and economic structure capable of drawing surpluses from great distances and only then will the population distribution of the area not be related to the agricultural capacity of the immediate hinterland. In Pharaonic Egypt, Thebes, Amarna and Memphis, as political and religious centres, were able to control surpluses from the rest of Egypt. The Ptolemaic period saw the emergence of Alexandria, which had a very small agricultural hinterland, as the political centre, though Memphis remained important. Once the political will to maintain a city had passed then these sites could go into quite rapid decline as happened at El Amarna, Thebes, and perhaps Memphis. It is virtually impossible to describe the main centres of population for any single period from the surviving archaeological remains and we are rather dependent upon the geographical writers whose criteria for the inclusion and exclusion of sites were probably not that scientific. It is best, for my purposes, to generalise.

Virtually every major Pharaonic site seems to have been formed around a large cult centre but these urban centres did not develop in the same manner as the great cities of the Mesopotamian river valleys or the *polis* cities of Greece. Villages continued to contain the vast majority of the population and political authority was exercised on a regional or national basis but not necessarily centred on the cities. There were a number of quarries in the Eastern Desert which probably provided a certain amount of non-agricultural employment and the Eastern trade would support a number of people in the area of Koptos. It is, however, clear that any large variation in population must have been due to differences in agricultural production. Butzer has pointed to quite large variations in population densities in the Pharaonic period between different nomes (administrative districts), the cause of which was variations in the width of the flood valley. Population tended to concentrate where the valley is narrowest. In these areas the natural flood basins are less extensive and thus more manageable, needing less laborious irrigation work. The slight preference for siting nome capitals on the east bank can thus be explained since the basins are slightly smaller and easier to exploit on that bank. The extensive irrigation works of the Ptolemies in the Fayum suggest, however, that by their period the management of water was sophisticated enough to exploit very large flood basins and the necessary labour organisation is, of course, a feature of very early Egyptian history. Although the picture is complicated by some concentration of non-agricultural workers and the Nile allowed cheap transportation of bulky food stuffs, creating the conditions for extensive urban settlements, it seems likely that population density in Upper Egypt was fairly uniform in the later periods.[9]

The river feeds various small branches as it proceeds towards the Mediterranean. The most notable of these is the Bahr Yusef which flows from Asyut into a large depression to the west of the Nile known as the Fayum to form the Birket Qarun (Lake Moeris). This lake, with its abundant perennial water supply, allows intensive agricultural exploitation of the Fayum which makes this a very fertile and populous region of about 1,729 km^2. The main centre of the region is Medinet El-Fayum which was the Greek Ptolemais Euergetis or Crocodilopolis, the latter name deriving from the cult of Souchos, the crocodile god, the dominant cult in the region. The site is normally known in modern literature as Arsinoe since it was the centre of the Arsinoite nome, the administrative district. The Arsinoite was divided into three districts, the Herakleides, the Themistes and the Polemon, and the latter two were administered as one unit. Strabo notes that the area was in his day

> most noteworthy of all because of its appearance, its excellence and its development for it alone is planted with olives, of which there are many large trees bearing fine fruit . . . and it produces not a little wine, and grain and pulses and many other types of plants.[10]

Lower Egypt starts near the ancient capital of Egypt, Memphis, fourteen miles south of Cairo. North of Cairo, the single stream of the Nile breaks up to form the Delta. Today, the Delta consists of two main branches, the Rosetta and the Damietta, but in antiquity there were seven branches: the Pelusiac, Tanitic, Mendesian, the Bucolic or Phatnitic, the Sebennytic, the Bolbitine and the Canopic. Even with modern engineering and land reclamation projects, large parts of the Northern Delta are still saline marshes, unsuitable for large-scale agricultural activities. In 1978, the Delta contained about two-thirds of the Egyptian population and comprised about two-thirds of the available land.[11] In the ancient period, flooding and marsh land were probably far more serious problems and the area is frequently associated with pastoralist agriculture.[12] This suggests that the whole area was less densely populated than Upper Egypt in the ancient period, though overall population was probably larger. The major settlements were Memphis, a Pharaonic capital of Egypt, and Alexandria and these two cities were the largest in Egypt in the Graeco-Roman period.[13]

17

From a defensive point of view, Egypt is fortunate in having only very limited lines of access. The Nile is not navigable south of Aswan, which has always tended to form a southern frontier for Egypt, but the desert roads between Upper Egypt and Northern Sudan were relatively easily negotiated. Northern Sudan, however, was not a very populous region, with its settlements dispersed along the Nile valley, and, historically, the region has always been heavily influenced by its northern neighbour, without being much of a military threat, provided that the Egyptian state was unified. Another major route is the Arbain road which runs from Asyut, through the Khargeh oasis, then south into the Sudanese hills of Darfur and from there into equatorial Africa. It is a caravan road passing through desolate regions and could not support a large number of travellers.[14] To the west, there are very few routes. From Khargeh and Dakhla oases, there are routes to the south-west, to Tibetsi in Chad, but the route crosses the heart of the Sahara and can never have been a major communications channel. Directly to the west of Dakhla is the Great Sand Sea which does not seem to have had any route across it. From Siwa, there are tracks leading to Tubruq and the Gulf of Sirte but even getting to Siwa was difficult and dangerous as Alexander the Great discovered when he lost his way coming from the Nile valley. The cultivated regions of Cyrenaica probably extended far further south than they do today but the major route west from Egypt must have been along the Mediterranean littoral, a route which was probably followed by the Jewish rebels of 116–17 and, in more recent times, was the route for the invasion by the German forces under Rommel. Roads across the Eastern Desert have already been discussed. The wadis provide relatively easy access to Egypt and there are numerous water points, but this is still extremely inhospitable territory and it is difficult to imagine any large-scale military expedition coming along these routes.[15] Further north, there are two main easterly routes out of Egypt. The Wadi Tumilat runs from the Delta to Ismailiya. This is the biblical route of *Exodus* and at Ismailiya the traveller could turn south towards Suez and the Sinai peninsula, as Moses presumably did, or north to Port Said along the route of the Suez canal. In the Pharaonic and later periods, this route seems to have been popular and a canal was built from Cairo (Babylon) along the wadi to connect with the Red Sea. This should have been a great aid to trade but does not seem to have been fully developed until the reign of Trajan and before then was mainly used for irrigation purposes. The wadi was a major point of access for Nabataeans and Bedouin from the Sinai. The most important route is the road along the coast via Tell El-Farama (Pelusium) and El-Arish (Rhinocolura) to Gaza. This is the most vulnerable corridor in Egypt's natural defences. It connects Egypt by land to the cities of the Levant which have always been a major cultural influence on Lower Egypt. It is by this route that successive conquerors of Egypt have travelled and the Egyptian armies gained access to the East during periods of imperial expansion. Although from the map the easiest method of reaching Egyptian territory would seem to be via the Mediterranean, the coast is treacherous with many sand banks, caused by the deposits of the Nile, and few harbours. Alexandria owes its ancient success to being the one decent harbour on the Mediterranean coast. Egypt was then surprisingly well fortified from all directions and has very few natural invasion corridors.

For movement within Egypt, the Nile provides a very simple means of transport. Unless the Nile was in flood, when navigation became more dangerous, it was a natural highway through Egypt and since all Egyptian settlements were dependent upon the waters of the Nile for their survival, all major sites could easily be reached from the Nile. The main land routes connecting the towns of Upper Egypt ran, unsurprisingly, alongside the Nile. The Fayum was also within easy reach of the Nile valley proper with roads running east from the Fayum into the Herakleopolite nome and north-east across a short stretch of desert to Memphis. In the Delta, communications were considerably more difficult. The network of canals, marshes, lakes, and branches of the Nile made communication from east to west very difficult. Kees, writing in 1951–2, commented that to

> cross the Delta from east to west is, even today, a complicated business because of its scarcity of sound bridges. The best way to travel from Fakus or Tanis in the north-east to Alexandria in the north-west is to go the round-about route south to the level of Mit-Ghamr-Ziftah or even as far as Benha.[16]

Benha is less than thirty miles north of Cairo. The late Roman traveller, entering Egypt at Pelusium, would have been forced to skirt the marshes to the west of Pelusium, pass Qantara, Daphnae, and then pass Tanis and Thmouis (Tema El-Amdid), heading towards Kynopolis, near Busiris (Abu Sir Bana). From there, the route went to Taba (Taua), Hermopolis and, finally, Alexandria. The road went slightly further north than Kees' preferred route.[17] The main roads of the Delta, however, in Pharaonic and Ptolemaic times probably concentrated at Memphis and Babylon (Cairo) and communications within the Delta, especially during the inundation, might have been quite difficult. The centre of communications for the Delta region was at its apex, which also, obviously, controlled all routes to Upper Egypt, and it cannot be a coincidence that the administrative and religious centre of Egypt has for long periods been situated in the area. On the basis of this, it would seem that the natural defensive points for Egypt would have been Alexandria, Pelusium or Qantara or another point along the coastal route towards Gaza, the Wadi Tumilat, and Syene. There was no serious threat of invasion from east or west of Upper Egypt.

19

Egypt may have had certain natural defensive advantages as well as considerable resources of wealth and manpower, but these were never enough to resist the might of Rome. Following the catastrophic defeat at Actium, Antony and Cleopatra fled, probably hoping to recoup their losses and to meet Octavian once more on more favourable terms. But the alliance of client kings, which Antony had created through which to rule the East, collapsed as each ruler, observing the likely outcome of the war, attempted to secure his position with Octavian. Antony and Cleopatra were left without allies in Alexandria, awaiting inevitable defeat. After Octavian defeated Antony outside Alexandria in 30 BC, Octavian was left to preside over the final confused days of Ptolemaic rule. Any thought that Cleopatra might have secured herself a settlement which would have allowed her to remain in power, a client of Octavian as she had been of Caesar and Antony, was soon dispelled. Octavian had painted Cleopatra as the arch-enemy of Rome and all civilised values and he could not, even if he had wished, have maintained her in power. Egypt was to be absorbed into the Roman empire and ruled directly by Roman officials. It was also to be given a substantial garrison which would provide the governor with the means to assert Roman authority and deal with any revolts, such as the one which sprang up almost immediately in the Thebaid and was crushed with considerable comfort, if we are to believe his self-congratulatory inscription, by the prefect Cornelius Gallus.[18]

The army that defeated Antony and provided the garrison which crushed this revolt was a strange amalgam of the old style Republican army and the new imperial army. Some of the soldiers were professionals who had been serving with Octavian, or with other generals, for some time and who had seen an extended period of continuous service. Others had been recruited for the campaign against Antony and may have hoped for discharge at the end of the war. Octavian paid off some of his soldiers immediately the war was over but others he retained for an extended period of service and it was these men who became the first generation of professional soldiers in the developing Roman imperial army.

Caesar's armies had been composed of two elements, the legionary troops from Italy who formed the backbone of his army and were the heavy infantry, and irregulars recruited from allied tribes or provinces who supplemented the infantry and provided most of the cavalry and perhaps other specialist troops. By the end of the first century AD, when our sources improve, we can still perceive this division. On the one hand, there was the legionary infantry, still technically composed of Roman citizens, and, on the other, the auxiliaries. Auxiliary units were given regional or tribal designations, suggesting that they were still fundamentally units of non-citizens, levied in theory or originally from a particular group of allies or subjects.

It would seem probable that the legions changed little from Caesar's day to the time of the fully developed imperial army. Each legion was composed of approximately 5,000 men, usually commanded by a legate, and was divided into ten cohorts, the first cohort being double strength.[19] The cohorts were further divided into centuries and the centuries into *contubernia*, a tent of eight men. There were ten *contubernia* to a century (80 men) and six centuries to a cohort (480 men). Nine cohorts plus a double strength first cohort comprised a legion with a paper strength of 5,280 men. There were a number of junior officers in each century who received one and a half times or twice ordinary pay, and each century was commanded by a centurion. Ranking above the centurions were the tribunes, six to a legion. In addition, in some periods, there was a small body of cavalry, probably about 120 men, attached to each legion.

There was more variety in auxiliary organisation. There were two main types of unit, the cohorts (infantry units) and the *alae* (cavalry units). The organisation of auxiliary cohorts mirrored that of the legionary cohorts with the cohort being made up of six centuries of eighty men. The cohorts thus have a paper strength of about 480 men, though with officers and various specialists the paper strength is conventionally estimated at 500. Cohorts were commanded by prefects. The *alae* are also conventionally reckoned at a strength of 500 and were commanded by prefects, but their internal organisation differed slightly. Instead of being organised into six centuries, *alae* were subdivided into sixteen *turmae* of about thirty men, each commanded by a decurion. Some cohorts, *cohortes equitatae*, had a small number of cavalry, perhaps four *turmae*, in addition to the six centuries. Also, it was possible to have a unit of double strength known as a *cohors* or *ala milliaria*, conventionally estimated as having a strength of 1,000 men, though their actual strength may have been less than that. In the late second century *numeri* are attested. This unit was probably initially an irregular unit with little formal organisation but later evolved into a more established part of the military forces. Little is known even about the theoretical organisation of these units or their strength. They were levied from allied communities and may have maintained distinct local origins which, by the late second century, the auxiliaries had lost in all but name.

It is difficult to assess just how regular and systematic the organisation of the Augustan army was. Caesar's auxiliaries were irregular levies with terms of service differing from unit to unit and the number of troops in each unit may well have varied considerably. Units served under native commanders or under the officer who recruited them. Eventually, terms and conditions of service were regularised but our evidence for a regular system of auxiliary recruitment and reward comes only from the period after AD 69, though it is possible that Claudius introduced systematic reforms of auxiliary units together with his reform of the officer career structure.

Although auxiliary units were an important part of the army, we need not believe that Augustus organised and recruited the auxiliaries any more systematically than the generals of the Republic. The fact that auxiliary infantry units were called cohorts from the Augustan period would suggest that their internal organisation was similar to that of the legionary cohorts and one would assume that service became extended and that units could continue in existence for considerable lengths of time, even if recruited for a specific campaign or purpose. We cannot, however, simply retroject the established system of the post-69 period onto the Augustan and Julio-Claudian army.[20]

The armies of Caesar were meant to return home with their general and be disbanded like most armies of the Republic, though some did serve with different generals if the campaign was extended or the general suddenly replaced. After 30 BC, however, most armies were under the nominal or actual command of a single general who did not retire, the emperor, and these armies were retained when their immediate commanders, the legates of Augustus, were replaced. We cannot know whether the standing army was created by accident or by design but the institutional implications of the creation of that army do not appear to have been immediately understood, even if the political implications were obvious to all. The leaders in each of the various civil wars at the end of the Republic had felt constrained to offer their troops considerable material benefits for their loyal service. These promises, however, did not cause the establishment of systematic retirement bonuses which had to wait until the foundation of the *aerarium militare* in AD 6, though many and perhaps most veterans will have received some grant of land before this. It took Augustus thirty-five years to establish systematic rewards for military service. Even such a basic area of military organisation and one of considerable political importance evolved over thirty-five years rather than being established as part of a package of measures designed to create a standing army.

The paper strengths of the auxiliary units may be tested against documentary evidence. A strength report of the *cohors* I *Hispanorum veteranorum* from Stobii on the Danube, dating to AD 105, gives the strength of the unit as 546 men of whom 119 were cavalry.[21] A similar type of document relating to the I *Augusta Praetoria Lusitanorum equitata* gives a total strength of 505 men of whom 114 were horsemen and 19 camel riders.[22] P. *Brooklyn* 24 of AD 215 gives the strength of an unknown unit as 457 men. There is more evidence concerning the *cohors* XX *Palmyrenorum* stationed at Dura-Europos in Syria. In 239, the unit contained 781 troops, including infantry, cavalry and camel riders, but another text, dating from 223 to 235, gives the strength of that unit as 923 soldiers of whom 223 were cavalry.[23] The unit was not milliary. A text from Vindolanda in Britain gives the strength of the *cohors* I *Tungrorum* as 752 soldiers in *c.* AD 90.[24] The combination of these texts is indeed worrying. Three of the units are at strengths close to 500 men but the Tungrian and Palmyran cohorts had substantially higher numbers of troops. These texts show that even as late as the third century, auxiliary units preserved a certain flexibility of organisation, though in terms of service for troops and in the nomenclature of the units the auxiliaries had displayed a certain regularity since at least AD 69.

Although we should be aware of the possibilities of development and institutional change over the period and that there may have been certain organisational irregularities, the following assumes that the units attested in Egypt broadly conformed in manpower and organisation to the model units described above. This assumption allows us to reconstruct the nature of the garrison of Egypt, the number of troops stationed in the province, and how that garrison changed over time. There are two main types of information available: documentary texts and literary accounts of the Egyptian garrison.

Documentary texts normally only attest the presence of individual units or even individual members of units. In order to gain an overall picture of the garrison, we must examine and assess a large number of texts mostly of little general interest. The data available have been collected in Tables 2.1 and 2.2 which show the units attested in Egypt in specific periods. These texts are discussed in Appendix 1. What follows is a brief discussion of the salient features of the history of each unit, concentrating on the period of service in Egypt and the stationing of each unit, as far as this can be ascertained. Following this discussion of individual documents, we shall look at an inscription which allows us to estimate the total size of the garrison and at the literary sources, before reaching some conclusions.

The legionary garrison and the changes therein have been well known since Lesquier's *L'armée romaine de l'Égypte d'Auguste à Dioclétien* and there has been little change in the picture he drew.[25] In the early Augustan period, there had been three legions stationed in Egypt but only two appear in the documentary evidence: the XXII *Deiotariana* and the III *Cyrenaica*. The latter legion is one of the legions which had been placed in Cyrenaica by Antony but which, after Actium, when Antony was in desperate need of troops, remained in Cyrenaica and, in effect, defected to Octavian. The title of *Cyrenaica* was granted to the legion to honour this act.[26] The name *Deiotariana* was a reference to the King of Galatia who had created a force armed and trained after the Roman fashion.[27] By AD 23, the garrison had been reduced to two legions and both these legions were based in Nikopolis, outside Alexandria. There was no change in the first-century picture until the reigns of Trajan and Hadrian when the whole of the East was thrown into confusion by the military effort of an expedition into Parthia and various other disturbances in the East.

Table 2.1 Attestations of auxiliary units by unit

Unit	First date	Last date	Diplomata				Notitia Dignitatum	Other dates
			1	2	3	4		
Apriana	41–68	268–270	★	★		★	Hippones	48, 77, 120, 153, 170 179/80, 213, 268–70.
Augusta	1–50	105	★	★				55, 57, 103.
Commagenorum	48	165	★					
Veterana Gallica	130	242–244			★	★	Rhinocolura	131, 140, 143, 153, 154, 157–61, 161, 179, 191, 199, 201, 201/2, 216/17, 225–50.
Heracliana	185	202						185, 185/6, 186, 188.
Thracum Mauretana	159	288				★		173/4, 199, 205, 206–11.
Vocontiorum	41–68	179	★	★	★			55, 59, 116, 122, 122/3, 134, 149, 156, 165, 177.
Xoitana	41–68							
Paullini	27							
Ulpia Afrorum eq.	159	179		★	★			177
I Apamenor	144	298			★	★	Silili	151, 159/60, 163, III, c.245.
I Augusta Praetoria Lusitanorum eq.	105	288		★	★	★	Hieracon	110, 111, 98–117, 117, 117, 156, 180–92.
I Flavia Cilicia eq.	81–96	III	★	★		★		118, 124, 117–38, 140, 156, 158, 161, 162, 166, c. 216, 217/18.
I Hispanorum eq.	83	105	★	★				85, 99, 104.
II Ituraeorum eq.	28?	224	★	★	★	★	Aiy	75/6, 99, 135, 136, 144, 146/7, 188, 218.
III Ituraeorum	83	243–4	★	★	★	★		90, 103, III.
I Pannoniorum	83	III	★	★	★	★		
scutata civium Romanorum	I	143/4					Mutheos	
I Thebaeorum eq.	83	115	★	★				
II Thebaeorum eq.	83	179	★	★	★	★		92, 131, 176/7.

Table 2.1 cont.

Unit	First date	Last date	Diplomata 1 2 3 4	Notitia Dignitatum	Other dates
I Thracum eq.	127				
II Thracum	84–96	179	★ ? ★	Muson	131, 143, 167.
Nigri	19	15–36			
Facundi	28				
Flori	I				
Aelii Habeti	27				
Numerus Cataphracti	267				
Numerus Hemesenorum	II/III				
Numerus Orientalium	II/III				
Hadrianorum Palmyrenorum Sagittarorum	216	271			
Numerus Salaratorum Peregrinae	267				

Note: Diploma 1: AD 83. Diploma 2: AD 105. Diploma 3: AD 156. Diploma 4: AD 179.

At some point a new legion, the II *Traiana*, was stationed in Egypt. This may have restored the forces in Egypt to three legions but if so, the increase in the establishment was only temporary since the III *Cyrenaica* was dispatched to the new province of Arabia and the XXII *Deiotariana* disappeared, probably during the Bar-Kochba revolt.[28] From this point, there was only one legion in Egypt, based in Nikopolis.

Turning to the auxiliary units, there are four documents preserved which list all the auxiliary units, with one exception, stationed in Egypt. These documents are auxiliary diplomas, documents which attest the grant of privileges at discharge to veterans of the auxiliary units and which, rather conveniently for us, list all the auxiliary units in a particular command. The four texts are *CIL* XVI 29 of AD 83, *RMD* 9 of 105, *CIL* XVI 184 of 156–61 and a text recently published by Römer dating to 179.[29] Although there has been considerable dispute over the reading of *CIL* XVI 184, Römer's diploma has clarified the reading and we thus have four almost complete lists of the auxiliary garrison in different years. In addition to these texts, there is a plethora of other documents attesting members of individual units.

Table 2.1 collects the data concerning auxiliary units from Appendix 1. Table 2.2 allows us to see more easily which units were in the country

Table 2.2 Attestations of auxiliary units by period

Unit	1–82	83	84–104	105	106–49	150–78	179	180–220	Post-220
Alae									
Apriana	★	★	?	★	★	★	★	★	★
Augusta	★	★	★	★					
Commagenorum	★	★				★			
veterana Gallica					★	★	★	★	★
Heracliana								★	★
Thracum Mauretana						★	★	★	★
Vocontiorum	★			★	★	★	★		
Xoitana	★								
Paullini	★								
Totals	**6**	**3**	**1–2**	**3**	**3**	**5**	**4**	**4**	**4**
Cohorts									
Ulpia Afrorum eq.					★	★			
I Apamenor					★	★	★	?	★
I Aug. Pr. Lusitanorum eq.				★	★	★	★	★	★
I Flavia Cilicia eq.	?	★	★	★	★	★	★	★	★
I Hispanorum eq.		★	★	★					
II Ituraeorum eq.	★	★	★	★	★	★	★	★	★
III Ituraeorum		★	★	★	?	★	★	?	★
I Pannoniorum		★	?	★	?	★	★	?	★
scutata civium Romanorum				★				★	
I Thebaeorum eq.		★	★	★	★				
II Thebaeorum		★	★	★	★	★	?		
I Thracum eq.					★				
II Thracum eq.			★	★	★	★	★	?	★
Nigri	★								
Facundi	★								
Flori	?								
Aelii Habeti	★								
Totals	**4–6**	**7**	**7–8**	**10**	**9–11**	**9**	**7–8**	**4–8**	**7**
Numeri									
Cataphracti									★
Hadrianorum								★	★
Palmyrorum									
Sagittarorum									

★ = Positive attestation of presence.
? = Probably in Egypt.
All dates are AD.

in which periods. The division of the table into periods reflects the availability and quality of the evidence. The three most complete diplomas provide some of the chronological breaks as they give a complete, or almost complete, list of the auxiliaries. The *ala Commagenorum* and *cohors scutata civium Romanorum* apart, there are few worrying blanks in the record. There are some problems in establishing the auxiliary garrison of the third century since there are comparatively few references and there are no diplomas from this period. To compensate for this, for the final column of Table 2.2 attestation in any document later than AD 220 is taken as proving the presence of the unit in Egypt during the period AD 220–85. Several units appear for the first time in the fourth century but units which make a first appearance in the documentary evidence later than AD 285 are not included in the tables, though they may have arrived in Egypt prior to that date.

Large numbers of units attested in a single period would suggest either a large garrison or a large turnover of units. This undoubtedly happened amongst the *alae* in the period from AD 1 to 82, three of which, we must presume, ceased to be part of the garrison during that time. The same picture does not emerge from the cohorts for which there are comparatively few attestations in that period. Four of these units again ceased to be part of the garrison by 83. Apart from the period AD 1–82, there is a high level of continuity. Although there is some change in absolute numbers, there is no discernible period of radical change in the auxiliary garrison.

One may suggest some cases of units being replaced but a table such as this does give a slightly deceptive feeling of confidence since although the numbers of dated attestations for units in Egypt are probably higher than for any other province, the evidence is still rather patchy and some of my chronological divisions rather broad.[30] The evidence is simply not good enough to allow strong chronological correlations between dates of departure and fresh arrivals.

There is quite a lot of good literary material for the garrison of first-century Egypt, although the sources for the second and third centuries are exiguous. The great advantage of literary material is that it tends to give a view of the general situation in a given context, while the documentary evidence tends to illuminate one unit at a particular moment. The accuracy of the context provided and the quality of the information available to the various sources is more problematic.

The first major source on the Roman garrison is Strabo who visited Egypt during the tenure of the second prefect of the province, Aelius Gallus. He was well informed about the activities of the next prefect, Petronius, particularly his dealings with the Nubians. He is, therefore, especially useful for the situation immediately following annexation. He details the garrison of Egypt thus:

There are three legions of soldiers, one in the city and the others in the *chora*. In addition there are nine Roman cohorts, three in the city, three on the border with Ethiopia at Syene, as a guard for those places, and three elsewhere in the *chora*. There are three horse-units which are likewise positioned in the important places.[31]

During his description of particular sites in Egypt, Strabo also says that one of the legions was based at Babylon and alludes to a guard of some kind of the Hermopolite and another guard of the Thebaid.[32] This gives a fairly clear picture of the positioning of the Roman units in the late first century BC. The garrison consisted of three legions, three *alae* and nine cohorts. One of these legions and three cohorts were just outside Alexandria, at Nikopolis, another legion was at Babylon and the third legion's station remains unknown. The other known garrison is Syene where three cohorts were stationed. This leaves three *alae*, three cohorts and a legion unaccounted for. There are, however, two garrisons whose troops we know nothing about, the Thebaid and the Hermopolite. It is likely that the third legion was based in the Thebaid.[33]

The next literary source that gives any details of the situation in Egypt is the famous summary of the military situation of AD 23 which, Tacitus tells us, Tiberius delivered to the Senate. Egypt was held down by two legions, the same number as held Africa. The auxiliary forces for the entire empire were *neque multo secus in iis virium* (not much less in their strength) though he does not detail the distribution of the auxiliaries.[34]

Tacitus' attention was focused on the military situation in the East in his account of the civil wars of 69. Nero, in the face of a growing crisis in the West, concentrated his forces and recalled the *ala Siliana* which had been sent to Egypt from Africa. The unit may never have arrived in Egypt or have been in Egypt for a very short time and it left no trace in the documentary material.[35] The transfer of the *ala Siliana* was part of a general reinforcement of the Egyptian garrison in preparation for a major campaign and this concentration of forces encouraged Nero, in the panic at the end of his reign, to look to Egypt as a possible place to retreat.[36] In adding up the potential of the Flavian forces in 69, Tacitus points to the two legions in Egypt but again makes no mention of the auxiliary units.[37]

Josephus takes very little notice of cohorts. He is interested in the legions and talks about the legions as if they were all the army. Yet, the order of battle provided by Josephus shows that the legions provided only about a third of the army sent to put down the Jewish rebellion of AD 66.[38] When Agrippa spoke to the Jews in order to persuade them of the futility of revolt, a topic dear to Josephus' heart, he detailed the wealth and the population of Egypt, stating that 7,500,000 Egyptians were held down by just two legions stationed in Alexandria. Ignoring the auxiliary forces aided the rhetorical position of Agrippa, but it is significant that Josephus did not feel constrained to include the auxiliary units as part of the force controlling Egypt, though both Josephus and the audience for the speech must have known that the auxiliary units accounted for a significant proportion of the military forces stationed in Egypt.[39] At the end of the war, Josephus details the dispersal of the legions to various stations, whilst the auxiliaries are almost ignored.[40]

Strabo is the only one of these writers who stresses the place of the auxiliaries. He describes the forces sent out against the Arabs under Aelius Gallus as 10,000 foot-soldiers drawn from the Romans of Egypt and, in addition, there were the allies: the Jews and the Nabataeans. This force appears to be two legions and auxiliaries do not, at first sight, appear to have had any place in the expedition.[41] When this force of two legions was away, however, Upper Egypt was invaded by Ethiopians. The invaders were repulsed by 10,000 foot-soldiers and 800 cavalry, not counting the troops in Syene.[42] The combination of these forces suggests a total garrison of about 22,000 troops.

There are no other literary sources on the garrison of Egypt as a whole but the diplomas and one inscription allow us to estimate the size of the garrison. The inscription is from Koptos and was published as *CIL* III 6627 with extensive commentary. At first sight, it seems to be little more than a fragmentary list of names of soldiers by centuries who had been involved in the repair of forts in the Eastern Desert along the roads between Koptos and Berenike and Koptos and Myos Hormos. There is a list of soldiers, one from each century of two fourth cohorts, two fifth and two sixth cohorts, and the beginnings of the list of two seventh cohorts, arranged in two columns. Without doubt, originally each column contained the soldiers from one legion, showing that two legions contributed troops. The end of the stone has also survived. This contains a summary of previously provided information. The first column details the number of horsemen on the expedition. There were 424 horsemen, 5 decurions, 1 *duplicarius* (an officer on double ordinary pay), and 4 *sesquiplicarii* (officers paid one and a half times ordinary pay) drawn from three *alae*. Column two starts by mentioning the *cohors* I *Thebaeorum* and continues by listing three centurions of the cohort, one of whom was in command. It then summarises the contribution of the cohorts to the expedition as being 10 centurions, 61 cavalry and 782 soldiers drawn from seven cohorts. The stone had been set up to honour the soldiery who had taken part in the rebuilding of the roads through the Eastern Desert.[43]

It is of great importance to establish the date of the inscription since it is probable that the seven cohorts, three *alae* and two legions represent the whole garrison of the province. From Strabo, we know that there were three legions in the province in the early Augustan period

29

and from Tacitus we know that by AD 23, the number of legions had been reduced to two. This provides us with a *terminus post quem* of the late Augustan period for the inscription. We know also that the legionary garrison was reduced to a single legion in the first decades of the second century, providing us with a *terminus ante quem*.

The names of the legionaries might give a clue to the date. There are no *cognomina*, the final element of the Roman name, included in the lists which suggests an earlier dating for the inscription since *cognomina* were, in general, used after Claudius. Yet, this can only be used as a rule of thumb. Such general rules presume a level of standardisation which is improbable and this type of honorific inscription might have been inscribed in a conservative fashion. All the patronymics given show that the father had possessed the same *praenomen* as the son, but normally only the first-born son took the paternal *praenomen*. In the thirty-six cases here this is a remarkable coincidence, suggesting that patronymics were artificial and that the fathers of these soldiers had not been Roman citizens. Not too much can be made of this since Egyptian inscriptions containing Roman names frequently simply give the Roman son and father the same *praenomen*, but the origins of the legionaries are also given and only one appears to have come from Italy. It is, therefore, unlikely that these men were Roman citizens before enlistment and many of the filiations are almost certainly fictive. If this was the case, then the names of the legionaries would have been adopted only at entry into the legion and since it was common practice for new citizens to take the *gentilicium* (family name) of the reigning emperor, the inscription could be dated from the imperial *gentilicia*. The inscription contains three Iulii, one Flavius and one Antonius, but a T. Antonius not a M. Antonius. The evidence from the nomenclature is slight but would suggest a Flavian date.

Mommsen dated the inscription in the Augustan period because of the high number of legionaries of Galatian origins in one of the legions and since the XXII *Deiotariana* must have been more or less solely composed of Galatians in the early Augustan period, Mommsen thought the inscription could not have been erected long after the conquest of Egypt. This does not, however, persuade since although over 40 per cent of the troops came from Asia Minor and many of them from Galatia, both legions had a sizeable element drawn from Asia Minor. The Asia Minor connection was maintained in recruitment to the army so that in 117, an auxiliary unit with no obvious connection with the region received a very substantial reinforcement from Asia.[44] The legionaries were not drawn exclusively from Asia Minor with the Egyptian element forming about 20 per cent of the troops, 25 per cent if those born in camp are assumed to have been Egyptian, and three soldiers came from the West, two from Lyon, and one from Italy.

Archaeology can provide no firm date for the forts along the desert roads.[45] Literary sources mention two routes across the desert, the Koptos–Myos Hormos route and the Koptos–Berenike route, both of which were improved by the work party. For Strabo, the most important port seems to have been Myos Hormos, while Pliny stresses the importance of the Berenike road which might suggest that the Berenike road was developed after Strabo but before Pliny's time.[46] But the difference is more apparent than real. The discussion in Strabo makes quite clear that although the harbour at Berenike was inferior to the harbour at Myos Hormos, a road went to Berenike, and it was from Berenike that the fleet sailed for India. The road to Berenike was built by Ptolemy Philadelphus and was an established route.[47] A description of the Eastern trade routes, the *Periplus of the Erythraean Sea*, probably dating from AD 40–80, lays equal emphasis on both ports, as does the slightly earlier archive of Nikanor, dealing with transport across the desert.[48]

There is no good evidence for an Augustan date for the inscription, as proposed in *CIL*, but there is no very good evidence to accept any other date. The most persuasive evidence is the use of the *gentilicium* 'Flavius' but obviously there were some Flavii before the accession of Flavius Vespasianus to the imperial purple. One would suggest, therefore, very tentatively, that the inscription dated to the last decades of the first century AD.

The diplomas provide us with another guide to the Roman army's total force. The first two give Egypt a garrison of three *alae* and seven cohorts in 83 and of three *alae* and nine cohorts in 105. The 179 diploma gives Egypt a garrison of four *alae* and nine cohorts.

The information collected allows us to make some estimates, as collected in Table 2.3, of the numbers of troops in Egypt in different periods using the standard paper strengths of units of 5,000 for the legions and 500 for the auxiliaries.

Strabo estimates the forces available to Petronius and Aelius Gallus from the Egyptian garrison to have been about 22,000. The garrison was three

Table 2.3 Numbers of troops in Egypt

Date	Numbers of men	% of c. AD 23 garrison
c. 25 BC	21,000	131.25
c. AD 23	16,000	100.00
83	15,000	93.75
105	16,500	103.13
Early II century	11,000	68.75
179	12,000	75.00
Late II century	11,500	71.88
220 – c. 285	12,000	75.00

legions (15,000 men), three *alae* (1,500 men) and nine cohorts (4,500 men). With a certain neatness, this gives us a total of 21,000 men. Before AD 23, the number of legions was reduced to two. In 83, the garrison consisted of two legions (10,000 men), three *alae* (1,500 men) and seven cohorts (3,500 men), the same garrison as in *CIL* III 6627, which gives us a total of 15,000. In 105, just before the reordering of the East due to the expeditions of Trajan, there were two legions (10,000 men), three *alae* (1,500 men), and nine cohorts and, if we include the cohort of Roman citizens, ten cohorts (5,000 men) which would give a total of 16,500. Two of the cohorts were in Judaea. Although there may have been a brief raising of the garrison to three legions during the last years of Trajan, the second-century province normally had one legion. The early second-century garrison probably consisted of three *alae* (1,500 men), nine, or possibly ten, cohorts (4,500–5,000 men), and one legion (5,000 men). This gives a total of 11,000 to 11,500 men. From the diploma of 179 we can get a picture of four *alae* (2,000 men), ten cohorts (5,000 men) and one legion (5,000 men) making a total force of 12,000 men. The situation remained relatively constant into the third century: one cohort does appear to leave the garrison but this was probably compensated for by the arrival of the *numeri*. One can estimate the garrison at one legion, four *alae*, seven cohorts and two *numeri* but there is some evidence to suggest that the numbers in each unit fell during the third century. It is, then, rather difficult to estimate the number of troops in the third century but I would suggest that numbers were not greatly above 12,000 men.

There is, therefore, a clear change in the manpower levels of the garrison between the beginning of the first century and the late second century. This is not surprising since Strabo writes of a time when the province had recently been conquered and was the base for further military adventures to the south of Egypt. It would be unrealistic to compare the levels of the garrisons at the two extremes of the period. A better base for calculations would be the situation after the withdrawal of the third legion. I assume that the auxiliary units remained the same in 23 as they were in Strabo's day, though there is no evidence for this.

After *c.* AD 23, the variation in the levels of the garrison during the first century was quite small. In the second century, however, there was a significant reduction in the numbers of troops due to the withdrawal of one of the two legions. The loss of the legion was not compensated for by an increase in the number of auxiliaries which seems to have remained relatively constant throughout the period. After the withdrawal of the legion, the numbers of troops in the province varied little. The garrison declined by between a quarter and a third during the second century but the period was not especially peaceful. The revolt of the Jews in 115–17 and the revolt of the Boukoloi in the 170s threatened

Roman control of Egypt but neither revolt caused an increase in the size of the garrison. Indeed, the withdrawal of the second legion may well have occurred soon after the revolt of 115–17. The evidence for the third century is very patchy but the numbers probably did not decline and there may have been a slight increase in the number of troops in the period because of the introduction of *numeri*.

It is quite difficult to establish the disposition of units throughout Egypt. The information that we have is rather sketchy and comes from different periods. The archaeological data for the first three centuries of Roman rule tells us little more than can be discerned from literary sources or papyri.[49] We know, for instance, that there was a fort at Nikopolis and the archaeological evidence, such as it is, confirms this. The fort was evidently large, as we would expect a double legionary camp to be, but little else of historical note can be derived from the description of the remains. There were forts in the Eastern Desert from the beginning of Roman rule but many of these hardly merit the name at all, being extremely small structures, clearly intended as way stations which would provide some shelter and security and a supply of water. They could not have contained a large number of troops. More information can be gained from the scientific excavation of larger forts such as Mons Claudianus, a fort which was attached to the quarry and which was in use throughout the Roman period. Not all the forts in the Desert had such an extended life and many of the extant fortifications probably date from the late third or early fourth century. Abu Sha'r, for instance, was built on a virgin site in the early fourth century and there appears to have been no earlier military installation in the area. At Pelusium, there were at least two forts, presumably of different periods. It is probable that there was a Roman military presence there throughout the period. Another fort on this eastern frontier, at Qantara, however, was not built until 288. Other forts on this frontier lack firm dates but the evidence tends to point to a very late third or early fourth century date for them, as for many other forts. In the valley proper, at Babylon, our textual evidence has pointed to a substantial military presence from the Augustan period but the remains of the fort in Old Cairo are probably of a fifth-century date. The fort at Dionysias in the Fayum is very late third or early fourth century. There were probably two forts at El Amarna, an early and a late, but the published archaeological evidence is woefully meagre. The fort at Nag el-Hagar dates to the third or fourth century. We can be more precise with the fort at Hierakonpolis, which dates to 288, and the fort at Luxor, dating to 301. In the Western Desert, nearly all the military sites date to the late empire, probably the fourth or fifth centuries, though the camp at Dush may date as early as 280. On the borders of Upper Egypt, the camp at Syene, which was probably the main military station in the area, has not been discovered. Further south, the camp at

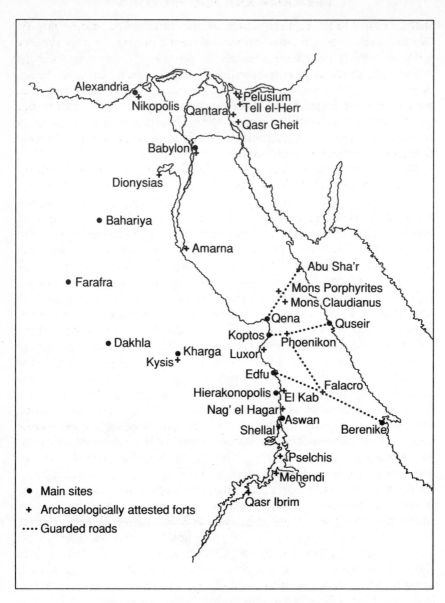

Map 2 Forts in Roman Egypt

Shellal, near Philae, probably dates to the first two centuries AD. At Pselchis, there was a Roman military presence during the first century and probably later, attested principally by ostraka. The surviving description of the camp at Mehendi is insufficient to allow accurate dating, though again, on typological grounds, it appears to be rather late. The outpost at Qasr Ibrim had a military presence in the first century but no military installation has been excavated. For the first three centuries of Roman rule, the archaeological material is very meagre, merely confirming the presence of soldiers at a few key sites.

The texts attest the stationing of soldiers in a large number of different cities and villages. There is a list of soldiers serving at Berenike from the second century[50] and a document of the third century lists horsemen stationed at Babylon, Aphrodito and Kerkesdite, the last being near Babylon.[51] The centurion Aurelius Agatho was stationed at Akoris in the third century.[52] In 174 a camp, probably in the environs of Alexandria (Nikopolis?), was rebuilt.[53] There was a camp at Euniko.[54] Two dedications from AD 288 show the construction of camps probably as part of a package of reforms at Qantara and Hierakonpolis.[55] An account of AD 180 appears to list stations of service which include Rhinocolura, Heliopolis and Babylon.[56] In AD 27 a contract between members of the *ala Paullini* and the *cohors Aelii Habeti* was executed at Alexandria.[57] There was an *ala* stationed at Koptos in the third century.[58] Two undated letters, probably of the second century, show soldiers stationed at Koptos and Pselchis.[59] Several ostraka attest the presence of soldiers at Pselchis.[60] The fort at El Amarna, where there were large alabaster quarries, may be attested in the papyri.[61] The survey of units in Appendix 1 shows that troops were stationed at Syene and in Lower Nubia, at Thebes, Koptos, the Eastern Desert, Berenike, Contrapollonospolis Magna, Akoris, Aphrodito, Ptolemais Hormou, Philadelphia perhaps, the Arsinoite, Small Oasis, Babylon, Heliopolis, Taposiris, Boukolia, Mareotis, Nikopolis, Pelusium, Rhinocolura, Klysma, Laura and the various Skenai. Quite clearly this does not list all the places where troops were stationed. Our evidence is biased by papyrological preservation, epigraphic activity and preservation and by archaeological exploration. Many other stations must have existed. This only tells part of the story since we cannot know how many troops were stationed in these places. Numbers could feasibly range from 10,000 at Nikopolis to 10 at Philadelphia. The evidence of *P. Hamb.* I 39 shows that troops from one unit could be dispersed over a considerable area, though the unit had a single base camp. Other attestations of units seem to concentrate within regions. Thus, members of a unit may be attested at Syene and at Talmis and at Koptos within quite a short space of time but it is rare for members of the same unit to appear in Lower Egypt during the same period. Although the *ala veterana Gallica* sent troops all over the Delta and Lower Egypt, none of the detachments were sent into Upper Egypt. Thus, although units seem to have a central camp from which they dispersed quite large numbers of troops and although the area these troops covered was very large, they do seem to have had some limitations on their dispersal.

Our documentary sources emphasise the pattern of dispersal since a single attestation proves merely the presence of a single soldier at a single moment and, in theory, a very large number of the troops may have been concentrated elsewhere. Nevertheless, documents such as *P. Hamb.* I 39 and *P. Brooklyn* 24 suggest that at any moment significant numbers of troops will have been away from the base camp of the unit, a picture that will be supported when we come to look at the activities of the army. In addition, it was not just individual soldiers who were dispersed but also the camps themselves. We can point to several main centres of military activity, Alexandria, Syene and Babylon, but also Koptos or its immediate surrounds, Thebes, Pelusium and the Hermopolite had camps. An army of 11,000–16,500 was divided between at least seven or more main camps, without considering the army's activities in the Eastern Desert and elsewhere.

It is rather difficult to discern any rational strategic plan behind the emplacement of military units. Our geographical survey identified several key routes. Of these the road from Palestine seems to have been well guarded at Pelusium and Rhinocolura, the coastal route from the west was watched by the garrison at Nikopolis which also controlled the port, and some forces were out at Taposiris. The route from the south was also controlled by the forces in Lower Nubia and at Syene. Forces at Koptos and Contrapollonospolis Magna together with those actually stationed in the Eastern Desert would be able to exercise control over those routes. The Western Desert seems to have been relatively lightly garrisoned. The key apex of the Delta was adequately held by units at Babylon. However, the level of dispersal of units and troops was such that the holding of these key points seems somewhat irrelevant. The dominant pattern appears to be one of an omnipresent military spread very thinly across virtually the whole of the country.

The only possible strategic concentration of forces was at Nikopolis. At first sight, this seems to be a logical place to station such a force, just outside the capital of the province, but the city of Alexander was not the geographical centre of the province. Control of Alexandria itself was, as we shall see, something of a problem for the Roman authorities, but the stationing of two legions and several auxiliary units just outside the city was hardly necessary merely to control the unruly Alexandrian mob. The centre of Egyptian communications was at Babylon from where there was easy access to Upper and Lower Egypt as well as to the east along the Wadi Tumilat. Communication across the Delta from Alexandria must have been virtually impossible during the inundation and difficult in normal times. Alexandria's strategic importance was that it was the main route of communication from Egypt to the Mediterranean. For a Mediterranean power, loss of Alexandria would have cut off their forces in Egypt from reinforcement. But Rome was not just a Mediterranean power. Rome also controlled Palestine and Syria and Rome could have marched armies to or from Egypt through Gaza and past Pelusium. The strategic centre of Egypt was at the apex of the Delta, Babylon, from where there were good routes of communication with Upper and Lower Egypt, the East and relatively easy access to Alexandria, if there should be a need.

We must not simply assume that modern strategic principles governed military dispositions and the obvious reasons for the concentration of troops at Nikopolis are not strategic but political. Alexandria was an important political and cultural centre in the Mediterranean which Antony and Cleopatra had turned into an alternative Mediterranean capital. Due to its size, geographical position and cultural importance, Alexandria had some claim to be the second city of the Mediterranean and the capital of the Greek East. It certainly served this purpose for Vespasian in 69 who chose Alexandria as the base for his attempt on the purple. It was important politically for Rome to maintain tight control over the city. More importantly, however, Alexandria was the political centre of Egypt under the Ptolemies and continued in this role during the Roman period. Political authority was concentrated in the city. The prefect was not just in charge of the civil administration of Roman Egypt but was also a military leader. The association of the prefect with the army gave the soldiers who were sent across the country a certain political authority so that they became in some sense representatives of the prefect and of Roman power. The prefect acquired additional power and authority through his association with a powerful coercive force. The concentration of military forces at Alexandria reinforced the position of the prefect since his power was ultimately dependent upon his ability to coerce the provincials, an ability the provincials tested several times. The politics of Egypt had centred on Alexandria for three centuries of Ptolemaic rule and this did not change with the advent of the Romans. Alexandria remained the seat of the government of Egypt. The army was not situated at the strategic centre of the country, Babylon/Memphis, but at the political centre and the army reinforced and secured the existing political geography. The dispositions of the troops show a certain geographical awareness and a desire to control routes of ingress and egress but this does not appear to have been the prime factor behind the garrisoning of the country. The Roman garrison represented a political force within Egypt, reinforcing the power of the Roman authorities.

It is, however, possible that strategic factors governed the size of the garrison stationed within the province even if they had little influence over the disposition of the troops. The annexation of Arabia and the wars in Parthia and Palestine during the reigns of Trajan and his imme- diate successors may have led to a reconsideration of first-century strategy in the East and a decision not to replace the legion lost from Egypt. There was, however, no thorough demilitarisation of the province, nor was there any attempt to compensate for the loss of a legion with an increase in the number of auxiliary units. It is more likely that the changes in the garrison in the early second century were not the result of strategic thinking but of an absence of policy in which the loss of a legion, prob- ably destroyed in battle, was simply accepted without any reconsidera- tion of the garrisoning of Egypt. The fundamental stability of the garrison throughout the first three centuries of Roman rule suggests an absence of strategic thinking, an absence which can be observed at a lower level in the dispositions of the troops within Egypt.

The soldiers did not merely maintain order and defend Egypt from external threats, such as they were. They also represented the political authority and power of the prefect and, through him, of the Roman empire. We cannot and should not ignore the political role of the army within Egypt. The soldiers, as we shall see, represented the conquering power, the government, as well as defending the country against poten- tial invaders and suppressing major revolts. They were thus representa- tives of the ruling power and representatives who brought that power into contact with the civilian population. Immediately, we can see that the relationship between the soldiery and the civilian Egyptian popula- tion could be extremely problematic and study of this relationship could offer us great insights into the nature of Roman imperialism. Much of this study is devoted to various aspects of the soldier-civilian relationship and the book draws towards a close with a consideration of that relation- ship in the context of an extraordinarily well-attested community, Karanis. The next two chapters consider more formal aspects of the way in which the soldier-civilian relationship was organised: the second being a study of the legal status of soldiers and veterans; the first concerning the begin- ning and the end of the soldiers' careers, the recruitment of soldiers and settlement of veterans. From there we shall consider what the soldiers actually did before tracing the economic, social and cultural integration of soldiers into Romano-Egyptian society.

3

RECRUITMENT AND VETERAN SETTLEMENT

As we shall see, the first veterans arrived in Karanis in the Domitianic period and from then until the first decades of the third century, veterans and their families formed a significant proportion of the population of the village and of the region as well. It is, however, apparent that the scale of the Roman presence in the North-East Fayum was not representative of the situation in Egypt as a whole. There are very few veterans or even Romans attested at Oxyrhynchus, though the number of papyri from that city is greater than that from Karanis and Philadelphia combined. In the second century, the percentage of the population of the Oxyrhynchite who had military connections was between a tenth and a twentieth of that at Karanis. In the same period, less than 5 per cent of the population of the Oxyrhynchite was Roman. Recent work on the material from Soknopaiou Nesos has shown that that village also had a very small Roman element.[1] The veterans of the army were not evenly dispersed across Egypt and although some veterans lived separately from any veteran community, the distinct concentration of veterans requires explanation.

The existence of veteran communities is generally accepted in the modern literature following detailed studies, principally by Forni and Mann, of soldiers' *origines* and the pattern of settlement of veterans.[2] These studies emphasise how the army gradually came to look to veteran communities for recruits so that many of the legionaries gave not a city or province as an *origo* but a camp, the *origo castris*. This development, together with a perceptible shift towards local recruiting from the early imperial period onwards, has led some scholars to consider that the army became a caste, with son following father into the army.[3] By the very late third century or the fourth century, the sons of soldiers were, to a certain extent, tied to their fathers' profession, but the evidence for the army as caste in the first three centuries of the Roman empire is less persuasive. The logic behind the theory is, however, clear. Mann and Forni based their conclusions on a detailed survey of epigraphic attestations of soldiers and veterans from each province. They were able to use these texts to show that veterans tended to remain in the areas in which they had served and that there was an increasing tendency to draw legionary recruits from the local population so that troops drawn from outside the province were increasingly rare by the time of Trajan. The explanatory model is very simple: the soldiers served for twenty-five years at a specific camp. They formed liaisons with women who are thought to have lived in civilian settlements known as *canabae* which, in the West at least, grew up outside the gates of the camps. Soldiers would, on retirement, settle close to the camp where they had spent so much time, had so many associates and, perhaps, had already founded a home. Veterans remained in the military zone and, naturally, the children of these soldiers, designated *castris*, followed their fathers into military service. The camp thus becomes an island of Roman military power containing in its vicinity the military force of the army plus the former soldiers, future recruits, and their families. Interaction with the native population would have been minimal.

It is, of course, true that the Roman state did exploit the tendency of some veterans to remain close to the camp, especially in the early imperial period, and when a substantial military force was moved from an area, the defence of that area was often secured by the foundation of a veteran colony. It may, however, be worth noting that the settlement of veterans in the area of a colony was frequently secured by the distribution of land. Colonies started as semi-military organisations but it is far from clear that the new cities had an exclusively veteran population or even an exclusively Roman population. The new cities probably formed new centres of population and trade for natives as well. It is apparent that colonies might not reflect the normal pattern of veteran settlement but rather an unusual intervention by the state for political and military reasons.

We may also take a critical attitude to the primary source material attesting settlement elsewhere in the empire. The preservation and erection of inscriptions were not random matters. It has long been noted by ancient historians that inscriptions from a particular site or area will tend to cluster chronologically into one period when the site is known to have flourished over a far longer period. Also, historians have suspected that the erection of inscriptions was the preserve of some social groups while others, for cultural, social or financial reasons, did not bother with these expensive stone monuments. If we add to the equation the vagaries of archaeological excavation and the preservation of sites, then we can see that the evidence provided by inscriptions may be severely biased. Since archaeologists have tended to concentrate on sites where there were large remains, such as cities or military installations, areas where the epigraphic habit may well have been particularly strong, our evidence may considerably underrepresent those veterans who settled in the countryside or in villages, precisely the group we see at Karanis.

Not only does the attestation of comparatively large numbers of veterans at Karanis put into question the established model of veteran settlement, but our study of those veterans would encourage us to reject this model without further analysis. The veterans of Karanis did not form a military caste and were not separated from the rest of society. The chapters on Karanis and the issue of legal privilege will emphasise the integration of veterans into the civilian community and this seems impossible to reconcile with the 'caste model'. We must, therefore, embark on a thorough re-examination of the evidence in order to understand the processes of recruitment and veteran settlement. We need to establish the factors which encouraged soldiers to move from the vicinity of their camps, the push factors, and those which encouraged them to settle in a particular area, the pull factors.

The evidence we have for Egypt is not entirely satisfactory. We have a little epigraphic material which can be used to establish the origins of legionaries, and some papyrological material. Most of the material for recruitment deals with legionaries and not auxiliaries but it is probable that auxiliary recruitment followed similar patterns to that of legionaries. The processes of recruitment were similar and similar factors will have encouraged similar developments in recruiting practice. When we come to settlement, we are almost entirely reliant upon papyrological material and this evidence has considerable disadvantages. Most importantly, papyri, like inscriptions, are preserved only for specific periods and from a small number of sites. We cannot, therefore, establish a complete picture of the province. Also, papyri tend to illuminate the particular and not the general so that our texts do not allow quantification of the veteran element of the population in any settlement. They do, however, provide an invaluable illustration of processes and it is through analysis of the small number of texts attesting the process of veteran settlement that we can make some progress. We turn first, however, to the large inscriptions of the first and second century (we have no equivalent data for the third century) concerning the recruitment of legionaries to the Roman army in Egypt.

CIL III 6627, fully discussed in the previous chapter, lists the origins of thirty-six legionaries from both legions.[4] This can be supplemented by the papyrus *BGU* IV 1083 = *RMR* 36, a list of names of Roman citizens with origins. It is not certain that the names are legionaries, or even soldiers, but it is probable that the list is a military record. The document is undated but is part of a find of papyri dating from the late Augustan period. *AE* (1955) No. 238 + *AE* (1969) No. 633 is an inscription housed in the Alexandrian Museum recording a dedication in AD 157 by soldiers of II *Traiana* who were being discharged. They had been recruited in 132 and 133. A fragmentary inscription, *CIL* III 6580, records the origins of legionaries discharged from *legio* II *Traiana* in 194 who

41

had been recruited in 168.[5] To these inscriptions we can add a number of other inscriptions, mostly funerary, which give the origins of individual soldiers. See Tables 3.1 and 3.2.

One of the main features of the data is the relative importance of Galatia as a recruiting ground in the first century. It alone provided 44 per cent of the legionaries. *Legio* XXII *Deiotariana* had been originally formed by King Dejotarus of Galatia and it is probable that the early connection with the area was maintained for some considerable time. The rest of Asia Minor provided between 6 per cent and 8 per cent of recruits. The contribution of the Western provinces, including Africa, was quite substantial, at around 18 per cent of recruits, more than Egypt herself provided. The position changed in the second century. The provinces of Asia Minor now provided 6 per cent of the total number of recruits which still outnumbered the recruits from Egypt. The West provided a large number of recruits amounting to 10 per cent, excluding Africa which provided more than half the forces. Syria's contribution increased slightly and there was a significant rise in the number who had the status of *castris*. This latter group does not, however, predominate. The tables show that although there were changes in the pattern of recruitment from the first to the third century, the logic of the change is far from clear. The West continued to make a significant contribution to the second-century legions and Egypt did not move towards a system of local recruitment until perhaps the end of the second century. The

Table 3.1 Origins of legionaries 30 BC – *c.* AD 110[1]

Province	CIL III 6627	BGU IV 1083	Others[2]	Total	%
Egypt	7(19)[3]	–	1	8	13
Africa	–	2	2	4	7
Bithynia	1(3)	1	–	2	3
Cyprus	1(3)	–	–	1	2
Cyrene	2(6)	–	–	2	3
Galatia	17(47)	5	5	27	44
Gaul	2(6)	–	–	2	3
Italy	1(3)	2	2	5	8
Palestine or Pamphylia	1(3)	–	–	1	2
Pisidia	2(6)	–	–	2	3
Syria	–	3	2	5	8
Castris	2(6)	–	–	2	3
Totals	**36**	**13**	**12**	**61**	

1. All inscriptions which deal with III *Cyrenaica* and XXII *Deiotariana* have been dated to this period. It is unclear precisely when the legions left Egypt.
2. Other sources are *CIL* III 6598, 6599, 6602, 6603, 6606, 6607, 12059, 14138[3], *AE* (1986) No.700 and *P. Mich.* XII 637.
3. The figures in brackets are percentages of the total for that particular document.

evidence represents a change in recruiting grounds and not a localisation of recruitment. Although Africa had become the most important area for recruitment, many other provinces were represented and the legions were still manned by a mix of soldiers from different parts of the empire. The later evidence shows a distinct increase in the number of soldiers with the *origo castris* and it has normally been assumed that these troops were recruited in the province in which they served, even from a settlement near the camp. If this was the case, it would represent a considerable increase in the numbers of troops recruited locally towards the end of the second century but since the *origo* probably only means 'born in the environs of a camp', presumably to a soldier, we need not assume that the recruit came from a camp near to the one in which he served. This unusual status did not represent a specific locality so that the soldier could have been born near a camp in any province of the empire. In any case, the evidence does not suggest that the Roman legions were completely reliant upon local resources of manpower during the second century AD.

Table 3.2 Origins of legionaries serving after *c*. AD 110[1]

Province	AE (1969) 633[2]	CIL III 6580	Others[3]	Total	%
Egypt	1(1)[4]	8(21)	–	9	5
Africa	84(66)	1(3)	2	87	50
Asia	1(1)	1(3)	–	2	1
Bithynia	2(2)	1(3)	–	3	2
Cilicia	1(1)	–	–	1	1
Commagene	–	1(3)	–	1	1
Dacia	1(1)	–	–	1	1
Dalmatia	2(2)	–	–	2	1
Galatia	2(2)	–	–	2	1
Germania	1(1)	–	–	1	1
Italy	15(12)	–	1[5]	16	9
Macedonia	–	–	1[5]	1	1
Pannonia	–	–	1	1	1
Pamphylia	1(1)	–	–	1	1
Syria	16(13)	3(8)	1	20	12
Tripolitania	1(1)	–	–	1	1
Castris	–	24(62)	–	24	14
Totals	**128**	**39**	**6**	**173**	

1. All references to II *Traiana* were dated to this period.
2. This inscription was republished in two parts. *AE* (1955) No. 238 contained only the introduction to the list.
3. The other inscriptions used are *CIL* III 6593, 6596, 6611, 6592, 12056, 12057.
4. Numbers in brackets refer to the percentage of recruits in the one document.
5. This figure includes one centurion.

Doubts have been raised about the representative nature of one of our inscriptions. *AE* (1969) No. 633 provides us with the majority of the origins for the period. This document contains nearly all the Africans and Italians. By contrast, there is only one Egyptian and no one who had the origin *castris*. Egyptian and *castrenses* origins dominate the later inscription. The veterans of *AE* (1969) No. 633 enlisted in 132 or 133 and it has been suggested that this group was an extraordinary reinforcement of the legion during the Bar-Kochba revolt in Judaea.[6] This revolt may have led to fears that the Jews of the Diaspora might also rebel, leading to a general conflagration, and these fears may have led to an extraordinary reinforcement of the Egyptian garrison since Egypt had been the scene of a major Jewish revolt in 115–17. There is also a possibility that the legion was strengthened before use in Judaea. Nevertheless, apart from a natural reluctance to discard a major source of data, it is the case that an unusual event is also of significance for the nature of recruitment to the army. We may also doubt whether the perceived abnormal character of the recruits to the legion in 132–3 can be explained by events in Judaea. The brunt of the war effort in the province was borne by the legions of the army in Syria and we might have expected those legions to have been reinforced or to have increased their recruitment but we find sixteen Syrians serving with the Egyptian legion. Furthermore, we have no evidence to suggest that the II *Traiana* was involved in any of the fighting in Judaea. There is also, as we shall see below, statistical evidence which makes it very unlikely that the legion received a massive reinforcement in this period and we must, therefore, accept that the pattern of recruitment attested in this inscription is broadly representative of normal patterns.

AE (1955) No. 238 + *AE* (1969) No. 633 and *CIL* III 6580 were erected to honour the emperor by those discharged in the years 157 and 194. They conform to a specific type of inscription found in several other provinces of the empire and which are collected in Table 3.3.[7]

We can see from these figures that there was a considerable variation in the numbers of veterans discharged for each year of recruitment. This varies from about 67 per year to an estimated 370. In themselves, these figures

Table 3.3 Discharge inscriptions

Inscription	Years of recruitment	Veteran numbers
CIL III 6178	*c.* 109/110	198
AE (1955) 238/(1969) 633	132/133	133
CIL III 8110	134/135	239
CIL VIII 18067	140/141	90+
CIL III 6580	168	*c.* 100
CIL III 14507	169	*c.* 220
CIL VIII 18068	173	*c.* 370

tell us only about those discharged from the legion, but if we knew what proportion of the troops died during service, we could not only calculate the number of troops recruited from a specific number of veterans but would also have a reasonable chance of estimating the number of soldiers in the legion. Methodologically, this poses a certain number of difficulties. Soldiers did not die at uniform rates and mortality patterns may vary considerably between generations. Our number of inscriptions is too small to allow any confidence that the size of the sample would iron out these difficulties. It is also rather difficult to assess mortality patterns in the ancient world since there are few reliable demographic statistics. In spite of these problems, the analysis does produce rather interesting results which suggest, but do not prove, a general pattern. Because of the problems in assessing mortality patterns in the ancient world, several figures drawn from several different sources and models are presented Table 3.4.[8] Of the seven categories of evidence, four fall within approximately similar ranges, Pannonia, Africa, Coale-Demeny and Egypt. These figures give us a possible and workable series of hypothetical figures which can be related to the demographic structure of a Roman legion.

Since we know the survival rate for any batch of recruits, it is possible to estimate how many recruits and veterans would be needed to man a legion of 5,000, assuming a standard death rate. For the purposes of calculation, I use four figures only: the Coale-Demeny, Pannonian and Egyptian survival rates for ages 20–45 and, for comparison, the Coale-Demeny figure for ages 15–40 (See Table 3.5). These figures show, unsurprisingly, that the higher the survival rate, the smaller the number of soldiers who needed to be recruited and the higher the number of veterans discharged. It is also notable how close these figures are. The small variations in survival rate lead to even smaller variations in numbers of recruits and veterans each year. For most years, therefore, there would be about 250 recruits and 150 veterans.

From the discharge inscriptions, we can calculate the average number of veterans discharged each year to be 140, only slightly less than the

Table 3.4 Mortality patterns: percentage of the male population surviving after a given twenty-five year period[9]

Ages	Source of Data						
	Rome	Italy[1]	Pannonia	Africa	Lambaesis[2]	Coale–Demeny[3]	Egypt
15–40	29	40	67.4	64.5	59.7	64.0	65.9
20–45	28.4	37.5	61.2	62.5	49	60.6	60.4
25–50	30.1	37.9	49.3	62.1	40.6	57.8	55.5

1. Excludes Rome.
2. Lambaesis, Africa. This material is drawn exclusively from military forces.
3. A modern life-table.

Table 3.5 Hypothetical average annual numbers of recruits and veterans for a legion of 5,000 men

Source of Figures	Recruits	Veterans
Coale–Demeny 20–45	247	151
Pannonia 20–45	248	152
Egypt 20–45	249	151
Coale–Demeny 15–40	244	156

ideal 150 figure. We can use the four model survival rates to calculate the probable size of a legion discharging 140 men per year at 4,638 on the Coale-Demeny 20–45 model, 4,612 on the Pannonian 20–45 model, 4,645 on the Egyptian 20–45 model and 4,483 on the Coale-Demeny 15–40 model. A higher survival rate produces a smaller legion. The models are fairly pessimistic, presuming a low life expectancy.[10] It would have been very difficult for a population with a higher mortality rate to have reproduced itself. Any variation from these models must assume a lower mortality rate and, therefore, a smaller legion.

These calculations do not prove that the legions were undermanned because of the rather slight evidential base on which they are made. The average number of veterans discharged each year conceals considerable variation in the number of veterans in each inscription. The 220 veterans in *CIL* III 14507 probably represent about 360 recruits, a significant reinforcement of the legion in 169. In that year, Rome launched a campaign against the Danubian tribes and, since it was based in Moesia, this legion was almost certainly involved. The estimated 370 veterans, possibly representing as many as 610 recruits, of *CIL* III 18068 joined the African legion, III *Augusta*, in 173, a year in which war may have broken out in Africa. It is also possible that troops were recruited to make up for a vexillation which had been sent to Moesia.[11] In contrast, in other years, numbers of about 100 to 110, representing less than 200 recruits, were discharged. We have, therefore, a combination of 'big' and 'small' years for recruitment and some of the 'big' years can be tied to crises. A crisis seems to have led to a rapid increase in the number of troops in a legion which is, in itself, informative. Although the legion represents a large standing force, capable of quelling major disturbances, it was not always on a 'war-footing' and was forced to rely upon rapidly raised levies in times of crisis, recruiting troops who cannot have undergone any of the training by which the legionaries had been prepared for war. To a certain extent, this information erodes the image of well-prepared professionalism which many historians have propagated.

Furthermore, there is other evidence to suggest that the *legio* II *Traiana* was significantly under strength in 194. About one-third of the centuries

in the legion appear in the inscription. Centuries were normally identified by the centurion in the genitive case so that a soldier would belong
to 'the century of Valerius Crispus'. This was a perfectly sensible system
for identifying units until the centurion either died or moved when the
name of the unit would change. In the interim between a death or
promotion and the appointment of a new centurion, the century would
be known by the adjectival form of the centurion's name, 'the century
Valeriana'. Of the twenty-two named centuries, eight are identified by
the adjectival forms of names. This delay in replacing centurions suggests
that there was no pressure to keep the unit up to full paper strength.

Crisis recruiting to the legions must have had ramifications in later
years. The discharge of a large number of troops after their twenty-five
years will have necessitated a similarly large batch of recruits to maintain the numbers of the legion. Although it is probable that the peak in
recruitment caused by a crisis would be diminished in the subsequent
replacement of that group, the legion would need another large batch
of recruits every twenty-five years after the crisis. To compensate for
the sudden increase in the number of troops, it is likely that recruitment would fall off in years subsequent to a crisis so that the differences
in recruitment from one year to the next would be enhanced.
Recruitment could probably sink to quite low levels in certain years
so the combination of high and low numbers of veterans, and hence
recruits, attested in our discharge inscriptions may well represent the
actual pattern of recruitment to the army. If anything, the attestation of
two crisis years from the ten for which we have inscriptions may mean
that we are slightly overestimating the average number of veterans per
year. It is, however, apparent that the very low number of veterans attested
in *AE* (1955) No. 238 + *AE* (1969) No. 633 makes it very unlikely
that these were years of crisis recruitment. This could only be accepted
if the legion had suffered extremely heavy losses in the wars of the period
and there is no evidence that these troops were involved in any significant conflicts.

The evidence for recruitment to the legions suggests an irregularity
about Roman practice. The legions were probably maintained at a level
below 5,000 men but, when there was the threat of a major conflict,
the legion was strengthened by the addition of large numbers of new
recruits, probably raising the fighting force of the legion to at least 5,000.
This irregularity in procedures is mirrored in the origins of the troops.
There was a distinct change from the first to the second century with
a decline in the importance of the provinces of Asia Minor as recruiting
grounds and a shift to Africa as the major source of recruits. It is not
apparent to me why this change should have occurred. In addition,
towards the end of the second century, there was an increase in the
number of soldiers who had been born in the vicinity of a camp. It may

well be that the number of Egyptians also increased in the later second century, suggesting a move towards more local recruiting. The pattern is, however, far from clear and throughout the first and second centuries soldiers were drawn from a comparatively large number of provinces and from both the East and West of the empire. Recruits were not drawn exclusively from the sons of veterans or from Egypt. The groups from which the army in Egypt recruited troops remained fairly disparate.

The first element of the view that the army was a closed community, recruited from veterans' sons living close to the camp, has been shown not to apply in the Egyptian case and we may now turn to the second element of the argument, the settlement of veterans.

The Roman government was fully aware of the possible advantages of creating distinct veteran communities, civilian groups who could be relied upon in times of emergency to control an area and remain loyal to the Roman authorities. In addition, veterans could form centres of economic and political authority of great importance when establishing the political infrastructure of a Roman province. The practice of the Republic and early Principate was to settle veterans on plots of land. The communities that then came into existence were given the status of *coloniae* which meant that they were self-regulating city states on the Roman model and were a means by which an area could be controlled and administered. These settlements were created as cultural bastions in the provinces.[12] Hadrian's Antinoopolis was created for very similar purposes. The city was a centre of Hellenism in Middle Egypt, an imposition on the economy and political and social structure of the area which provided a focus for various Greek cultural interests and, one suspects, had a political role as a loyal, privileged centre in Middle Egypt. Antinoopolis was not, however, a veteran colony.[13]

There is no evidence of a colony in Egypt but the word *koloneia* does appear in the papyri. The first extant use of *koloneia* comes in a land register from the village of Naboo in the Apollonopolite Heptakomias and dates from AD 118. The key part of the text is lost but it appears that there was a subdivision of klerouchic land (a type of private land) classed as colonial land.[14] The amount of land under this heading is not known but it cannot have been a large amount and Naboo was only a village. The next appearance of the word comes in a Fayum papyrus which is too badly damaged to make much sense. The *koloneia* may be a topographical reference point.[15] In 200–3, Iulius Valerius, veteran, complained to the prefect about the behaviour of another veteran, M. Aurelius Neferatus. On discharge from the army, Valerius had received, thanks to the generosity of the emperors, some land near the village of Kerkesoucha in the Herakleides district of the Arsinoite. After considerable labour and expense, he dug an irrigation channel to this land. Neferatus seems then to have denied him access to the water and the whole episode came to blows in the *kolonia*.[16] In this case *kolonia* is used as a topographical reference point but is also associated with marginal land granted by the emperors to soldiers. Kerkesoucha was a comparatively small village near Karanis. Two documents from the Oxyrhynchite nome make use of the word. The first is dated to 162–3 and is an account of a trial resulting from a mortgage on property of Iulius Voltinus which was seized by Sempronius Orestinus. The seizure may also have occurred in the *koloneia*.[17] The final document is probably second century and refers to marginal land purchased by M. Iulius Valerianus in the *koloneia* near the village of Senepta. There is a list of land purchases made from the state by Graeco-Egyptians on the verso of the document.[18] The combination of a topographical reference point and marginal land in all these documents suggests that far from referring to a self-governing urban settlement, *koloneia* refers to a small, concentrated area of marginal land made available to veterans at little or no cost by the state in the hope that they would bring the land into production. It is possible that a proportion of the land of these 'colonies' was sold to non-veterans as well.

There is, in fact, little evidence to suggest that the state controlled veteran settlement.[19] *Epikrisis* documents, the legal implications of which will be discussed in the next chapter, are the only documents which suggest supervision of veteran settlement.[20] These are statements to a judge, normally a senior military official, which established the status of the person involved, gave the names of witnesses to that status, and provided a statement either of residence or intended residence. The examination was crucial for establishing citizenship status and related privileges prior to entry into civilian society and all male members of privileged groups within Egypt underwent some sort of examination process, normally prior to entry on the poll-tax lists at the age of 14. Auxiliary veterans underwent a change of status with the grant of Roman citizenship necessitating a further examination. Such an examination could be held if there were doubts about someone's exact status. The statement of intended residence need not reflect the ability or desire of the state to control veteran settlement but may be a means of identification or of ensuring that the paperwork of the case would be passed to officials of the correct nome. Veterans had to register their residence, as did the rest of the Egyptian population, but although the administration was probably capable of calculating the number of veterans in an area or even of forcibly settling veterans in a particular area, it does not appear to have done so.

The available documentation, inadequate though it may be, does not suggest that the Roman authorities normally controlled the process of veteran settlement in Egypt. The veterans seem to have been allowed to settle where they wished. In the rhetoric of population shift, it seems that the push factors regulating the settlement of veterans were negligible. It remains to consider the pull factors which must have determined settlement patterns. Our principal problem is that these pull factors are not obvious. There is no straightforward reason why the North-East Fayum should have attracted a large number of veterans. There was no camp at or near Karanis and although Strabo notes the prosperity of the Fayum generally, it is rather difficult to believe that the North-East Fayum was sufficiently different from the rest of Egypt, or indeed the rest of the Fayum, to attract veteran settlers.[21] The economic development of the area was well advanced by the Flavian period and so the veterans were not exploiting new territory. There seems to be little reason why veterans congregated in this area.

A letter requesting that a soldier's brother offer help and hospitality to a veteran thinking of moving to Karanis may provide a part of our solution.[22] The veteran's reasons for moving to the village do not appear to have been due to any particularly strong attraction to the village. He had to settle somewhere and he had connections he was able to exploit in Karanis. He may also have been aware that other veterans had settled in the area. Thus, once a connection had been established between soldiers and a particular area, more soldiers may well have been tempted to settle in that area. This kind of process can explain why a second wave of veteran settlement could occur but not why the connection was developed with the village in the first place.

A solution to the problem of settlement lies in the pattern of recruitment. In the first century, many legionaries came from the provinces of Asia Minor which may well have been a popular recruiting ground because of the history of the *Legio* XXII *Deiotariana*. It is unfortunate that most of our first-century sources are undated but it is certainly possible, indeed likely, that the connection was maintained for some considerable time, though there was no perceptible advantage to the Roman government in recruiting from that region. In the early second century, African recruits formed a very large proportion of the legion but again there appears little of concrete benefit to the Roman authorities in this. In 117, admittedly a time of war in Egypt, the *cohors* I *Lusitanorum*, a cohort of Spanish origin, received 126 recruits from Asia though the cohort can hardly have had historic or other connections with the province.[23] The logic of the recruitment policy is elusive and one guesses that tradition and, to a certain extent, the random preferences of the recruiting officer played a significant role in recruiting policy. The army recruited some troops every year but in times of emergency there was a greatly increased demand. In such a crisis, the officer in charge of recruiting troops could turn to the traditional recruiting grounds of the unit or of the army as a whole, or he could look for sources closer to home. I suspect that this is what happened in the North-East

Fayum, situated as it was comparatively close to the military base at Babylon. Once the army had started recruiting from a particular area, that area would become an established source of recruits and once the recruited soldiers acquired their veteran status and accompanying privileges, the area would become a place of settlement for veterans. The soldier who wrote to his brother in Karanis is very likely to have been a native of the village, as were many of the veterans of the village.

At the level of the individual, personal connections were important for a successful military career and even access to the army was considerably eased by prior military connections.[24] Soldiers recruited from a community might retire home and friends from the army might also settle in that community. The next generation of soldiers would seek out connections amongst their neighbours and family to ease their entry into the army and so a single recruiting drive could create a community with strong connections to the military for several generations. We need not search for any complex geographical, historical or political reason for the creation of the veteran community of the North-East Fayum; we need only look to individuals.

Our analysis of the patterns of recruitment and discharge suggested that about 150 men per 5,000 troops would be discharged every year. On average, therefore, the army in Egypt would discharge about 450 per year in the first century and 360 men per year in the second and third centuries. Presuming that all these veterans would remain in the province, it would seem unlikely that at any time there were more than 5,000–6,000 veterans in Egypt. Since privileges were also granted to children, whom one might expect to live longer than their veteran fathers, a maximum of 30,000 may have been in receipt of privileges or status resultant from military service. This high estimate is less than 1 per cent of the population of Egypt.[25] Karanis alone may have absorbed 2–3 per cent of the Roman veteran population and if we estimate that other villages in the area absorbed a similar proportion of veterans, then the North-East Fayum will have contained 6–10 per cent of the veteran population. We do not know of any other similar concentrations of veterans but there may have been clusters of veterans in other areas of Egypt and, of course, in the immediate vicinity of the more established military camps. The concentration of veterans probably means that many communities will have had few veterans settled amongst them and many ordinary Egyptians may never have encountered a veteran. It is very difficult to believe that such a small number of people could have had any significant cultural or economic impact on Egyptian society.

The clustering of veterans together in the Fayum villages was not a result of any government policy or of any desire of the soldiers to remain together once discharged. It was a result of the lack of a consistent policy for recruitment and, for that matter, for settlement. There is little sign

51

of official interest in veteran settlement or of any attempt to manage such settlement. When the government did intervene in the process, it was for brief periods and for very specific purposes. With the possible exception of the foundation of Antinoopolis which, as we shall see in the next chapter, had a significant veteran element in its initial population, all attempts to manage settlement, with offers of land, were very small scale and limited to minor economic rejuvenation. Otherwise, recruitment and settlement were organised in a fairly haphazard manner. The patterns of recruitment and settlement were not a result of a consistent, considered policy but rather of the workings of a system which relied upon personal contact and personal recommendations.

4

THE LEGAL STATUS OF
SOLDIERS AND VETERANS

Literary texts of the imperial period portray the soldier as a bully. In Apuleius' novel, the soldier assaults a peasant farmer, beating him with a stick and seizing his ass. The peasant turns on the soldier, surprises him, knocks him unconscious and escapes with the ass. The revenge of the soldier, however, brings the full power of the Roman state down on the head of the peasant.[1] Juvenal's *Satire XVI* starts with a long complaint about the difficulties of gaining redress following an assault by a soldier. Even attempting to bring a case against a soldier was foolhardy, if not suicidal. More examples could be found without difficulty; complaints against the soldiery were common and Campbell wonders whether

> the widespread oppression of civilians by soldiers [was] a symptom of the general inability of emperors to control any of their servants ... or did it at least in part result from the difficulties of prosecuting soldiers in court and a deliberate reluctance by officials and governors, who took their guidance from the emperors, to proceed against the soldiers on behalf of the civilians, who were not as important to the welfare of the empire and its ruler?[2]

The soldiers are seen as being beyond the normal workings of the law, a privileged group, protected by the emperor and their own political power. The swaggering, bullying soldier could do what he liked, confident that behind his actions was the power of the emperor.

It was the close relationship and mutual interdependence of the soldiery and the emperor that led to the grant to the soldiers of legal privileges designed to improve their status and to deal with the special problems of the soldier's career. Campbell's assessment stresses these two factors:

> The exceptionally exacting nature of the professional soldier's career and the special problems created by long absence from home in the service of the State demanded a relaxation in some areas of the law. Obviously the need to keep the army relatively contented with its lot was of great importance to an efficient military establishment.

This leads to the second explanation of the army's legal privileges. The soldiers comprised the largest group of people who were performing a vital service for the State and whose loyalty was essential to the emperor.[3]

He explains testamentary privileges 'as a means by which emperors attempted to avoid discontent within the army, provide some protection from the rigours of military life, and perhaps assist recruitment'.[4] The picture is of a more and more powerful soldiery, enjoying greater and greater privileges. The rise of the soldiery culminates in the reforms of Septimius Severus. Among many other privileges, the soldiers were, from 197, allowed to wear a gold ring, symbol of the equestrian order.[5] The legal position of the soldiers reflects the gradual militarisation of Roman politics. The emperors were coming to rely more heavily upon their troops and less upon the good will of the senatorial order and the old aristocracy of the empire. The legal status of the soldiers was closely related to their political status and, under Septimius Severus, symbolically at least, the soldiers joined the aristocracy.

This generally accepted view of the legal status of soldiers rests primarily upon the interpretation of literary texts, texts, in the main, produced by the elite of the Roman empire, who were, by their very nature, sympathetic to aristocratic government and hostile to any group that threatened or that they perceived to threaten aristocratic power. The army, the ultimate source of imperial power, represented the greatest threat to aristocratic government since the emperors could threaten to rule through the army, intimidating the aristocrats with the threat of military violence. The elevation of the soldiery could, therefore, be seen as a symptom of the decline of the aristocracy and, therefore, the inexorable rise in privileges granted to soldiers and veterans was condemned. The hostility of the literary elite shapes our sources and influences the modern view. It is, however, a view from the centre, a macro-political view, in which the links between soldier and emperor dominate, but for the increase in legal status to be effective it must have benefited the soldiers at the micro-political level, in their daily transactions with their fellow villagers, in their dealings with local administrators and at the level at which normal life was conducted. We must establish the theoretical legal position of soldiers and veterans but we are able, by using papyri, to observe the effect and implementation of these privileges in Egypt. We have an opportunity to escape the rhetoric of the literary and legal elite and to observe the law and legal privilege in action.

Perhaps the best-known peculiarity of the legal position of a Roman soldier was that he was not allowed to enter a legal marriage. This does not mean that the soldiers were chaste or even that any attempt was made to enforce chastity. Nor did it prevent soldiers from becoming involved in long term relationships with women which looked, to uninformed eyes, like marriages. The Romans even came to admit the existence of the relationship between the soldier and woman and that the children of that relationship had a claim on their father's estate, as we shall see later. The relationship could not, however, legally be a marriage. The law runs contrary to the general thrust of Roman imperial legislation which encouraged marriage and the procreation of children.[6] The ban created a number of problems, the most notable of which involved the status of the children of the non-lawful liaisons. Claudius removed the anomaly that Roman soldiers were treated as unmarried men, a status which carried legal penalties, even though they did not have the right to marry.[7] Although various measures were passed to alleviate the problems caused, the ban on marriage was not lifted until 197.[8]

There are three judgments concerned with the legal implications of the ban on marriage preserved on one papyrus.[9] These judgments range in date from AD 115 to 142 and were almost certainly collected prior to another hearing on the same issue. The second and third judgments are very similar, both cases being concerned with Alexandrian citizenship. All Alexandrians had to have both an Alexandrian father and mother. In these cases, both natural parents were of Alexandrian status but, since there was no marriage between the couple, the children of their relationship were illegitimate and, as the children had no legal father, they could not be registered as Alexandrians. The papyrus has preserved the reaction of the father of the affected children: 'If I am able to go abroad, will you [the prefect] sign my petition so I can get my rights through a legal representative? What crime have the children committed?' The prefect refused. The first case involved the estate of the soldier Antonius Germanus. Lucia Macrina tried to reclaim property from his estate which had been deposited with him. The prefect ruled that the deposit was, in fact, a dowry but since it was illegal for soldiers to marry and, therefore, receive dowries, he disallowed her claim. The judgment is very harsh since, although Macrina was, presumably, attempting to circumvent the law, the fact that she had deposited property with Germanus was not, in itself, illegal. The prefect understood the deposit to be a dowry, which could only be given in the case of a marriage, but, since marriage did not exist, there could be no dowry. Macrina's claim that the property was a deposit, therefore, seems the most sensible legal description of the exchange. The prefect, however, judged that if he accepted that the money was merely a deposit, something very like a dowry, then he would make the relationship between the soldier and woman appear to have been something very like a marriage and, therefore, he would have condoned a circumvention of the law. Thus, on what appears to be extraordinary legal reasoning, he disallowed the claim. On both these occasions the supposed conspiracy of generosity between officials and soldiers clearly did not apply.

In the second case, concerning the rights of the son of a soldier to be his father's heir, the prefect ruled that the soldier, Martialis, in spite of the fact that his son was illegitimate, made his son heir lawfully. This judgment stemmed from the special status of soldiers in testamentary law. They were exempted from all the normal regulations governing the form of the will.[10] Indeed, the will did not even have to be written to be valid. The clear expression of a bequest was enough for the bequest to be legally acceptable. From the time of Trajan the meeting of the witnesses had to be arranged formally and it is probable that the meeting had to be called for this specific purpose so that a man present at the death of a soldier who stated that the soldier had granted him his estate would have no valid claim.[11] Before Trajan's ruling, there may not even have been the necessity to hold a formal gathering: Josephus tells the faintly ironic story of a soldier trapped on a burning platform during the siege of Jerusalem who called out to his colleague that if he came forward to catch the leaping soldier, he would be appointed his heir. The soldier succeeded in saving the life of his leaping comrade but was himself crushed to death.[12]

Normally, making a will was a fairly difficult matter, requiring specialist legal knowledge. It was comparatively easy to make a mistake and to invalidate the whole will. There were complicated rules as to who could inherit what and what proportion of the estate could be given to whom. There was also a general principle limiting inheritance to those of the same citizenship status as the testator. All these rules were waived. The first such privileges we know of were granted by Julius Caesar who allowed all the bequests of his soldiers to stand. The procedure was probably followed by generals both before and after Caesar but Trajan felt it necessary to reinforce the ruling.[13] Gaius states that soldiers were also permitted to institute *peregrini*, foreigners, as heirs, and the privilege was extended by Hadrian in AD 119 so that a soldier was not only able to bequeath his property to a *peregrinus* but also a peregrine child could establish a legal claim to the property of the soldier-father even if the father had died intestate.[14] The kin of the soldier were also able to claim his property. The *Gnomon of the Idios Logos*, a series of administrative and legal rules from Egypt collected as a reminder of procedures, contains clauses to do with the military will.[15] In our earliest version, dating from the mid-first century AD, Clause 34 appears to allow intestate succession to relatives and children, provided they were of the same group, and if there were no claimants, the property would revert to the camp. The clause is extremely lacunose and the restoration is speculative, though quite persuasive, but if the restoration is correct, Hadrian's regulation reinforced an existing privilege. In a mid-second-century version, Clause 34 allows those in the army to dispose of their property in either Roman or Greek form and to use whatever words they wish, provided that the property goes to someone who was *homophylos* (of the same tribe, people, or family) and Clause 35 states that children and kinsmen of soldiers who die intestate are permitted to inherit, provided they are of the same *genos* (type or family). Both *homophylos* and *genos* are rather difficult to translate precisely but it seems probable that *genos* means family, regulating intestate succession to only those most closely related to the soldier, whilst *homophylos*, governing testate succession, should have a broader meaning, perhaps 'of the same people'. This latter translation would suggest that the soldier was only allowed to make heir someone of the same citizenship status which is directly contrary to the rule as stated by the jurist Gaius. Given that intestate succession was allowed to those who might be of a different citizenship status, such a limitation on testate succession appears illogical, not always a problem in legal matters. I am, therefore, persuaded that the *homophyloi* would also include those who were originally of the same status as the soldier as well as those now of the same citizenship status. The rule would seem to prevent those soldiers born Roman citizens from bequeathing property to non-Romans, a severe limitation on the privileges envisaged by the jurists. If the edict of Hadrian can be taken as reinforcing or re-establishing certain testamentary privileges of the soldiers, the evidence would seem to point not to a gradual increase in the privileges granted to soldiers, but to a steady erosion of those privileges. In the *Digest*, testamentary privileges are limited to the period of service and the year after discharge.

In addition to the rules relating to the bequests of soldiers, there were also special privileges granted to soldiers with regard to receiving inherited property. The *pater familias*, the head of the family, was not allowed to disinherit a son serving away from home in the time of Augustus.[16] After Augustus, the ruling was rescinded. The property that the soldier accumulated during military service was his *castrense peculium*. This property was not within the *potestas*, jurisdiction, of his father. Normally, all the property of a son whose father was alive technically belonged to the father, so the son could not bequeath the property or dispose of it in any other way.

The legal status of soldiers, with regard to their civilian commitments, was that of being away on state business.[17] They enjoyed the rights of a *restitutio in integrum*, which meant that their property had to be left untouched until they returned from service. Creditors were allowed to seize property but that property was to remain unsold. This privilege was to remain in force until a year after discharge and this was, in the later empire, extended to include the property of the wife of the soldier.[18]

Soldiers were not allowed to own land in the provinces in which they were serving.[19] This was modified slightly by the ruling that if complaints were received whilst a soldier was in service, the property was confiscated by the *fiscus*, but if the soldier avoided detection until discharge, his property was to be left untouched. Also, a soldier was allowed to intervene if the property had previously belonged to the family of the soldier but, because of difficulties paying taxes etc., the property had been put up for sale by the *fiscus*. They were allowed to conserve their family estates but not to add to them. Soldiers could accumulate property but it was counted as their *castrense peculium* which was held separately from their ancestral holdings. Goods could be accumulated by bequest or by the everyday activities of the soldiers.

The state had an interest in keeping soldiers free of civilian commitments and, therefore, soldiers were exempted from all liturgies (compulsory public services). In cases of complaint against them, the soldiers could not be summoned away from the camp. A civilian would have to brave the camp and the colleagues of the soldier in order to press a complaint. The system was open to abuse and must have intimidated many prospective litigants. Soldiers were, as representatives of the state, occasionally given sweeping powers. This was, of course, most obvious in times of war when individual soldiers must have had considerable freedom in their dealings with civilians. Soldiers also had rights to requisition supplies and shelter for themselves and transport for their goods. This could even involve the requisitioning of persons to help them move goods. The government made frequent efforts to stamp out abuses but they must have been commonplace.[20]

The peculiarities of a military existence were reflected in the laws concerning it. The risk of sudden death accounts for the lack of formality in the making of wills, a privilege which was excused on the grounds of the ignorance of the soldiery. It is easy to see that it might be difficult to get competent legal advice on campaign. Other privileges were granted since many soldiers lived amongst *peregrini* or had been *peregrini* themselves. A soldier could not be expected to deal with civilian business if he was away on military service and so his civilian business was frozen. The right of *restitutio* in *integrum* meant that creditors could not seize his property when he was unable to defend his case in court. It was a necessary and just defence of his property.

Other aspects of the soldiers' legal position are more complex. Roman citizens were not allowed to form legal marriages with persons who were not Roman citizens unless the non-citizen involved came from a community with the *ius conubii* or the citizen involved had the right of *conubium* which meant that the children of the marriage would be granted Roman citizenship. The former privilege did not apply to any Egyptian community; the latter was a personal privilege, held by comparatively few people. In the provinces, however, Roman citizen soldiers would come into contact with a relatively small number of citizen women and the chances were that any liaisons formed would be with non-citizens. If the soldier changed citizenship status on entry to or during service, then it would be possible that liaisons had already been formed with non-citizen women and thus that the children would be of a different citizenship status from the father. The laws which permitted intestate succession by illegitimate children and the soldier to bequeath his property to peregrines allowed the family of the soldier to escape from these problems of clashing status. Auxiliaries, receiving the citizenship at discharge, would have had fewer problems with clashes of citizenship status while serving and, as we shall see, auxiliary veterans were granted *conubium* which solved most of the potential problems of clashing status facing veterans and their families. The ban on marriage, however, created many difficulties for soldiers from all units. It is difficult to think of any justification for the ban sufficient to compensate for the problems caused. When Hadrian allowed the illegitimate children of these liaisons to inherit, he commented that the liaisons were contrary to military *disciplina*.[21]

On any view of the ancient economy the land was by far the most important investment and the greatest source of political and social prestige. There are two possible explanations for the limitations on soldiers' rights to own land. First, the government did not wish the soldiers to be distracted from their duties by private business activities. Second, the rule could act as a check on any soldier who wished to use his position for corrupt purposes. The Egyptian evidence very frequently shows soldiers owning land and property, such as houses, but it is usually impossible to assess how they came to own the land. The land may have been passed on to them from their families. Augustus interfered with the testamentary rights of fathers and introduced the privilege of *peculium castrense*. Both these privileges reduced the power of a soldier's father over him even though the *patria potestas* was one of the more important principles of Roman law.

We may seek to explain these oddities in the legal position of the soldier in terms of each individual issue and seek to find some practical reason for the regulations, such as a desire that the troops would not be encumbered by their women in a baggage train or that troops might remain mobile and flexible, not tied to a particular province, but none of these explanations seems sufficient or altogether credible. Instead of seeking to explain the laws separately, we may regard them as a package defining the status of a soldier. Augustus took the crucial step of recognising that the army had evolved into a professional body and he took steps to create a formal standing army, establishing fixed terms of service and reorganising its finances. It is likely that the measures which created the legal status of the soldier evolved over a considerable period of time in a similar way to the gradual evolution of a systematic method of financing the army, yet the legal reforms do show a definite view of the army and its relationship to civilian society, a view perhaps reflected in Aelius Aristides' description of Romans 'isolating their fighting force'.[22] The three key legal measures were the ban on the contracting of marriages, the ban on the holding of land in the province in which the soldier was serving and the interference with the rights of the father over the soldier. In this way, the soldier was separated from three areas of life: the economy, his father and paternal family, and any new family unit he might wish to create.

This response to the new circumstances of the soldiers of Augustus' army was born in the specific political circumstances of the Augustan period. During the civil wars, the army developed a political personality, partly due to the *esprit de corps* of Caesar's legions, and, in the Perusine war, the demands of the legions were opposed to the rights of the Italian aristocracy. After Actium, the legions were mainly stationed in the provinces under Augustus' personal command, well away from Rome and Italy. They were Roman citizens in a foreign land. With the troops physically removed from their homes, society and the political arena for twenty or twenty-five years, the rules governing their legal status recognised and enhanced this separation. It may also be that the separation was politically desirable: the legions had identified their own political needs and loyalties and brought Octavian to power as the heir to Caesar, continuing to support him after the heir of Caesar was transformed into Augustus. The continued separation of the troops from civilian society may have prevented new ties of loyalty developing or the ties to the emperor becoming confused by new local requirements. This very separation encouraged the identification of the political interests of the soldiery with those of the ruling dynasty and although there were various attempts to modify the position of the soldier, the general principle was maintained for at least two centuries and possibly more.

Soldiers, however, underwent a transformation at the end of their twenty-five years in service: they became veterans. No longer were these men separated from civilian society but they were now part of society and their legal status with regard to that society changed drastically. They were now in a position to be rewarded for those long years of military service and they were granted significant privileges, to which we shall turn below. The legally distinct soldier became a veteran whose status was also legally defined. The privileged status of veterans must have been a factor in the regular use of the designation 'veteran' in the Karanis texts, especially in legal matters or when dealing with the administration. Although modern writers and, to a certain extent, ancient writers perceive a status differential between the soldiers of the legions and those of auxiliary units, the use of the term 'veteran' without any specification of the unit with which the soldier had served suggests that there was no great status differential between the veterans of different units and a detailed survey of the evidence fails to produce any significant legal difference between the veterans of the various units.[23]

In Roman Egypt, as elsewhere in the empire, legal privilege was linked to citizenship status. In Egypt, the primary division between Roman citizens and the rest was complicated since Rome's conquest was preceded by Greek occupation. Rome inherited a diverse population and enhanced divisions, strengthening the legal differences between various groups in Egyptian society. The most privileged non-Romans were the citizens of the Greek city of Alexandria. It is significant that this group was included in the *epikrisis* documents drawn from the daybook of the prefect, showing that the prefects took personal responsibility for their citizenship rolls, even if they usually acted through an intermediary. We know from a letter of Pliny that when an Egyptian was given the Roman citizenship, he had to register as an Alexandrian.[24] Below these groups were groups of Greek settlers or urbanised Greeks of lesser status and varying privileges. Lewis sums up the general view of the structure of Egyptian society:

> The diagram of that structure takes the form of a pyramid. The tip, flaunting the height of privilege, comprises of a small group of Roman citizens residing in the province; below them is a larger segment of lesser privilege, the urban Greeks and – till their fall from favour – the Jews ... The barrier against advancement from a lower status to a higher one was impenetrable except by special dispensation of the emperor.[25]

Roman veterans, of course, were, as Roman citizens, at the pinnacle of the pyramid. Citizens enjoyed certain concrete privileges such as immunity from poll tax. They also enjoyed rights of exemption with regard to the *potestas* (legal power) of Roman magistrates and, in case of force being used against them, they could claim redress under the *Lex Iulia de vi publica*, common to all Roman citizens, wherever they were. Egyptian officials had either limited or no jurisdiction over them though they were subject to the control of the equestrian *epistrategos*. Roman citizens had to register their property for direct taxation and were liable to perform civic duties in their home towns. The *epikrisis* documents show that they had to register their residence. There was a close connection between Roman citizenship status and that of Alexandria.

The various privileged groups were added to by Hadrian when he created the city of Antinoopolis. This city was founded in 130 after the drowning of Antinoos, Hadrian's favourite, during the emperor's visit to Egypt. The youth drowned near Hermopolis Magna and Hadrian built a new city on the opposite bank of the Nile to Hermopolis on the site of a Pharaonic town.[26] The city was known as Antinoopolis of the New Hellenes and enrolled the most fiercely Greek groups in the whole of Egypt, a practice that accords with Hadrian's well-known philhellenic tendencies.[27] Antinoopolites were exempted from performing compulsory public services in other areas.[28] They had the privilege of being judged amongst their fellow citizens in cases of legal dispute.[29] They were exempted from property purchase tax. Hadrian set up a fund to provide for the children of citizens.[30] Citizens were also given the privilege of *epigamia*, a right identical to the Roman *conubium*, which no other Greek foundation enjoyed.[31] They therefore enjoyed substantial privileges.[32]

We come across Antinoopolites quite often within the papyrological material. A large number of them had been recruited from the Arsinoite and they continued to own land there. Many veterans were also Antinoopolites and the designation 'veteran and Antinoite' is common. Bell argued that veterans were not admitted into the citizenship until the reign of Antoninus Pius but it is more likely that veterans formed part of the initial population of the town. It is possible that particular veterans belonged to the Greek groups who formed the basis of Hadrian's new city but the number of veterans who had Antinoopolite citizenship in the second century makes it unlikely that all of these were of those special status groups. In any case, large numbers of veterans were enrolled as Antinoopolite citizens and came to enjoy increased legal privileges as a result. The relationship between veteran and Antinoopolite status was a short term phenomenon. Roman veterans in later periods do not appear to have been Antinoopolites. The citizenship rolls were probably closed when a certain number of citizens had been reached.[33]

Veterans were also granted specific privileges because of their military service. They enjoyed a privileged status when it came to the criminal law. Veterans could not be condemned to the beasts or beaten with rods. Like decurions, neither they nor their children were to be condemned to the mines nor to work on public schemes since this was beneath their dignity.[34] This is a sure sign that soldiers and veterans were of the higher status group which developed about the time of Hadrian: the *honestiores*.[35] There is a papyrus which deals with the complaint of a veteran who had been beaten by the *strategos* who ignored his status.[36]

Veterans were exempted from customs duties by Octavian's and Domitian's edicts. Nero also, in his reform of taxation, seems to have continued the exemption of soldiers from these duties.[37] I have found no mention of these privileges in the *Digest* or the other law codes of later periods.

Exemption from *munera* which demanded labour for such tasks as guard duties or clearing and repairing canals, was granted to all veterans by Octavian and Domitian.[38] This *immunitas* was extended to the parents, wife, and children of the veteran. The jurists distinguished between *munera* from which the veteran and his family were exempted, and *honores* or patrimonial liturgies charged on the wealth of a person and which could involve substantial administrative labour. Patrimonial liturgies were charges on property and analogous to taxation for which a veteran was liable. There was a third category which required both. Ulpian believed that veterans were exempted from most liturgies, although he did accept that veterans were obliged to pay the taxes and other usual obligations that went along with their estates. The principle was interpreted by other jurists to mean that the veterans were liable for all liturgies which required expenditure, unless specifically exempted.[39] The regulations did not prevent a veteran undertaking a liturgy out of the goodness of his heart. Some liturgies did carry a certain amount of prestige, such as the holding of a municipal office, or provide an opportunity for profit, such as tax-collecting offices, though these tended to be patrimonial liturgies, and the good will generated by voluntarily accepting a burdensome liturgy was probably worth something to the veteran.[40]

Liturgies were a source of great contention in Roman Egypt and we have several documents which concern veterans.[41]

(i) M. Anthestius Gemellus was nominated to a liturgy in a neighbouring nome some time between 117 and 138 (*P. Mich.* IX 568–9), and he is attested as a serving soldier *c.* 90 (*P.Fam.Tebt* 18).

(ii) *BGU* I 256 is in such a poor condition as to make it almost unreadable. It seems to be a dispute between Anthestius Gemellus and Sabinus over a liturgy. Anthestius Gemellus may have been a veteran. Sabinus became a soldier. The papyrus is dated to the reign of Antoninus Pius.

(iii) *P. Wurz.* 9 is a collection of rulings on the exemption of Antinoopolites from liturgies in areas other than the city. The document is undated but was collated some time after 156. The collation was made in connection with the appeal of a veteran for exemption from liturgy. He seems not to have used his veteran status.

(iv) *BGU* I 180 is an appeal made by C. Iulius Apollinarius in AD 172 against enforced liturgy. This man was a veteran and had been pressed into continual service in a liturgical post. He claimed that the length of his service was in excess of that allowed for 'natives' and so it was even more iniquitous that he was forced to perform it. As a veteran, he enjoyed the legal right to five years in peace, before he could be called upon to perform liturgies. Also, he was too old for the task. The many grounds stated by the veteran do not suggest that Apollinarius doubted the validity of his military exemption; it was common practice to appeal on as many grounds as possible and not just the most cogent. The five-year rule appears only once in the documentation and is not attested in the *Digest*. In this document, military service was being treated as a form of liturgy since performance of liturgy always gave a period of exemption. It may be that the liturgy involved was patrimonial, in which case the veteran was liable.

(v)   *P. Oxy.* XXXVI 2760, from 179/80, is a petition addressed to the prefect of Egypt from Dionysius Amyntianus, a discharged veteran of the *ala Apriana*, complaining that he had brought blankets from the Oxyrhynchite to Alexandria for delivery to the legion but was unable to find anyone to receive the blankets. He had waited for forty days but had run out of provisions and now wanted to go home. He did not complain that he had been illegally forced into the liturgy.

(vi)   *BGU* VIII 1634 is a list of groups of people drawn up by those administering the corvée on the dykes in AD 229/30 at Philadelphia. Amongst the categories of men listed were the sons of veterans and cattle-keeping men. Cattle-keeping men were exempted from liturgies which suggests that the list is of those exempted not of those liable for service.[42] Veterans are not included on the list but if the sons of veterans had lost their immunity, they would not have been defined as a specific group. The document must be a list of immune groups.

The traditional view of the evidence is that it shows a gradual erosion of the privileges of the veterans. The evidence does have certain limitations, however, in that it only highlights individual incidents. It does not generally deal with the principles that lie behind these. One veteran delivering blankets on behalf of Oxyrhynchus does not invalidate a general principle and the non-performance of liturgy inevitably leaves little evidence. The document from 229/30 shows conclusively that the privileges of veterans and their families were maintained.

The documents also demonstrate the clash of interests between the veterans and the nome authorities. It was in the interests of the nome and village authorities to have as many people as possible available to perform liturgical duties. It was in the interest of the veterans to preserve their privileges. The evidence shows that the veterans were able to preserve their rights in law but, in reality, they found it difficult to avoid liturgies. The nome authorities, as in the case of the *strategos* who publicly beat a veteran, were able to ignore the privileges of individuals. This comes as something of a surprise since the model we have of Roman Egypt shows that veterans had a high status as Romans. If any group would have been expected to be able to use their influence with the authorities in order to preserve privileges, we would have expected the highest status group to do so.

The identification of Roman citizens used to be thought a relatively easy task but there is an increasing lack of confidence in the equation of Roman name and citizenship. Several apparent Romans in the Karanis registers appear not to have had citizenship.[43] Apion wrote to his father to say that he had joined the fleet and had changed his name to a Roman one.[44] The surviving fleet diplomas, however, suggest that citizenship was granted upon completion of service. The recruits to the *cohors* III *Ituraeorum* noted in *P.Oxy.* VII 1022 all had Roman names. *M.Chr.* 372 shows that an Alexandrian changed his name while serving in an auxiliary unit. This assumption of a Roman name on entry to a military unit was not, however, automatic and there are numerous examples of auxiliaries still using Graeco-Egyptian names, suggesting perhaps that some soldiers adopted Roman names before receiving the citizenship. The archive of Iulius Niger shows that the family was immensely conscious of its legal status but the variety of names that Gemellus Horion uses suggests that he was of confused status.[45] The confusion surrounding Roman names shows that there was a certain confusion over Roman status. Since Roman status was legally defined, however, and the use of a Roman name by a non-Roman was a serious offence it is difficult to understand how such confusion could arise.[46] The answer lies in the position of Romans at village level. Many people, such as the wives of veterans who had not been granted citizenship and the technically illegitimate children of soldiers, may have felt that they were Roman even though they were legally of a different status. The confusion does not show that Roman citizenship was not valued, indeed quite the opposite: Latin birth certificates suggest that some care was taken over records, probably with a view to claiming citizenship, and at Karanis families claimed citizenship and preserved their status over several generations, though citizenship was not the dominant factor in arranging marriages.[47] Nevertheless, the divisions between Roman citizens and non-Roman citizens became blurred in the second century.

The emergence of a new privileged group from 130 is very significant. Antinoopolites had many similar privileges to veterans. Importantly, the Antinoopolites had institutions which would defend their privileges and look after the interests of individual Antinoopolites. It gave the Antinoopolites a certain political power which the veterans never had. Veteran Antinoopolites began to rely more upon their Antinoopolite status to defend their position than their veteran or Roman status. Veterans were able to secure access to these privileges, initially, and thus preserve their high legal status, but it can hardly be a coincidence that the privileges of individual veterans seem to come under greater threat when some veterans came to rely upon a different source of privilege. The veteran whose claim for five years of rest after service was ignored and the collection of petitions related to Antinoopolite status and liturgies strongly suggest that veteran status was no longer a powerful claim on the authorities.

The position of soldiers and veterans cannot be understood as one of gradually increasing privileges. From the beginning of the Principate, when Augustus organised his new army as a standing army, far removed from the political world of Italy where most of his soldiers were born, the connections of the troops with civilian society were strictly limited. The troops were not greatly privileged. As the centuries progressed, modifications were made to the soldiers' position but the general principle was maintained. The *disciplina* of the Roman forces demanded the continuation of rules which were perceived as grossly unfair and unreasonable but the authorities strictly enforced the legal principle. Veterans were, on the other hand, not subject to military *disciplina* and were rewarded by the grant of extensive privileges. As Roman citizens who enjoyed privileges in addition to those of other Roman citizens, the veterans were, in law, an elite group from the first century onwards. In law, the position of the soldier or veteran was not notably improved from AD 69 until the very end of the second century.

The Egyptian material casts some light on the real situation of the veterans within their communities and this is noticeably different. Veterans were part of the legally elite group of the nomes together with other Romans and Alexandrians but they were in continual conflict with the nome authorities who were interested in suppressing veteran privileges. From 130 onwards, a new status group began to influence the position of veterans. Initially, as the state looked to populate the new city, veterans were admitted to the citizen rolls, thus gaining access to new privileges. After a short period, this process stopped. Antinoopolites had the political power, through their civic institutions, to force the nome authorities to respect their privileges, a political authority the veterans never had. We see the continual reinforcement of rules by emperors and officials concerning such issues as the military will, especially if Hadrian's statement was a restoration of the position of the mid-first century. In nearly all areas the rights and privileges of veterans were challenged by individuals and authorities and veterans had continually to reassert their rights. Inevitably, *strategoi* could exert their authority and some veterans were forced into tasks from which they were exempt, but this does not mean that their position had been legally weakened. By the 170s, Roman status, as reflected in nomenclature, was becoming increasingly confused. The distinction between Roman and non-Roman was becoming blurred with non-Romans carrying Roman names and the children of Roman soldiers not being Roman. The problem must have been increased when, around 140, the diploma changed so that children born in service were no longer granted citizenship when the soldier was discharged, but would remain technically illegitimate. Thus, a Roman veteran and his wife may have had three children, two of whom were Roman and the other Graeco-Egyptian. Since, as we shall see, there was little or no social or economic difference between Roman veterans and their families and other groups, there was little justification for a special legal status for veterans. They had no common institutions to defend their privileges. The actual status of veterans was in decline in the second century and those who had secured Antinoopolite citizenship found this a more effective weapon in the running battle with the nome authorities. As some, perhaps more powerful, veterans used Antinoopolite status to secure privilege, so veteran status itself became less important. The story of veteran privileges shows that it was not the law itself but the ability to influence the administration which was the most important factor in enforcing legal privilege. Status was maintained in law but not in fact.

Augustus created the professional army and probably also the legal framework of military life. The later developments were piecemeal, showing a marked reluctance to break away from the established tenets even when the social situation the laws referred to no longer existed. The laws were divorced from social reality, a reflection of specific social and political circumstances as seen by the elite, in this case by Augustus, modified and altered sometimes for social reasons but sometimes for rhetorical purposes, over time and causing problems only when someone actually applied them.[48] The Fayum was a long way away from the halls of Rome in which the Roman jurists debated. In the Fayum, soldiers behaved like other members of society, marrying, setting up families, inheriting property. The lack of mobility of the army of the first century and the gradual move to local recruitment meant that the soldiers developed strong ties to their local communities. The soldiers' position was a legal fiction, divorced from social and economic reality, a fiction that worked to the considerable disadvantage of the soldier and his family.

So what of the soldier-bully we started with? Quite clearly there was friction between the civilian population and the troops even after the initial conquest of territory. The soldiers continued to perform important policing duties which must have given individual soldiers considerable power and responsibility and I have no doubt that these powers were abused in Egypt as elsewhere. What is open to doubt is the tacit consent given to such abuses by the imperial government; efforts to clamp down on these abuses are commonly attested, suggesting that the authorities took some interest in the activities of their soldiers. The evidence of the cases concerning the status of children born to soldiers during their period of service and the marriage of soldiers does not suggest that the authorities were constrained by their political dependence on the soldiery, either directly or indirectly through the emperor, to give favourable judgments to soldiers, or were even particularly sensitive to the needs of the soldiers. Administratively, the measures governing the trial of soldiers were not unusual. It would have been more unusual if the case were heard amongst the friends of the prosecutor than the defence. The litigant who was not satisfied with the treatment meted out to him could always appeal to higher authorities. The standards of justice were probably not high but we should not expect them to be so. It seems unlikely that any modern body, in a similar position to the Roman army, as an occupying power, administrative agency, and state representative, would be able to maintain high levels of decency and honesty. Accepting this, it is a giant step to say that the violence and corruption were approved of by the authorities or that the soldiers were out of control.

In Egypt at least the soldiers were not the powerful elite they are often portrayed as. The gradual modification of the laws affecting soldiers was not a sign of their political power. A politically powerful group would have removed the legal afflictions of the ban on owning land and on marriage before 197. In 197, the position changed. The Severan dynasty was far more dependent upon the military than any emperors before them. These political changes led to an improvement in the soldiery's position but the soldiery did not enjoy greatly increased privileges in the third century, even with the immense political problems of the era, than they had in the first two centuries AD. Indeed, one of the major privileges of veterans, the citizenship, ceased to be such a privilege with the grant of Roman citizenship to all inhabitants of the empire in 212. In Egypt, the legal position of the veterans was not one of increasing legal power but decreasing influence. The soldiers and veterans could not exercise influence over the authorities, even though they were a primary resource for the government and an essential part of their security system, as we shall see in the next chapter. Veterans and, to a slightly lesser extent, soldiers, were integrated into civilian life. They were not outsiders. They were not an elite.

5

THE ARMY IN ACTION

INTRODUCTION

In this chapter, we will consider the variety of different roles performed by the army from two perspectives. First, we seek to understand the position of the army from the point of view of the emperor and prefect. We can compile a list of the tasks performed by the army in order to try and ascertain the army's purpose. Was the army, for instance, a force in training to fight prolonged foreign campaigns against well-organised enemies, a strategic reserve poised to help out in any region of the East in which there might be trouble? Was the army rather concentrating on maintaining security in Egypt, either by holding itself in readiness to cope with a major uprising in any part of the province, with units organised to mobilise quickly to suppress rebellions, or by maintaining security by the dispersal of the army across the province, observing the Egyptians and stamping out trouble before it escalated into a major crisis? We shall look at what other roles the army performed since, as a force of over 10,000 men, soldiers were a valuable source of manpower. Second, we shall try and ascertain what the soldiers actually did and how the soldiers related to the civilian community. Were the soldiers, for instance, normally separated from civilians, having little contact with them unless suppressing their revolts, or were they in contact, co-operating with civilian authorities to ensure the smooth working of government? Were the soldiers an elite, exercising influence over the civilian community by virtue of their power or was there co-operation and interaction? In other provinces, the evidence is simply insufficient to allow us even to approach an answer to these questions since any answer must rely upon detailed knowledge of the actions of individual soldiers, actions which could not be reflected in the archaeological record. Although other areas of the empire produced literary texts which comment on the relationship between soldier and civilian and the role of the army in the empire, these are very often produced by the elite and many reflect strong ideological prejudices, often hostile to the soldiery. One would not wish to deny the validity of the insights of our literary sources into the

69

relationship between soldier and civilian and it is extremely probable that there was regularly some friction in the relationship, but these sources will frequently stress the extremes of behaviour when we search for generality.[1] Let us start, however, with wars.

EXTERNAL WARS

The Romans knew little of the peoples south-east of Egypt. Strabo, in Book Sixteen of his Geography, peopled the area with nomads, named after their eating habits, with the exception of a few groups who had been able to establish stable bases on the coast.[2] Pliny the Elder thought that accounts of the area were liberally laced with fictions but had no good source to work with.[3] The main non-mythical peoples who lived south of Egypt were the Blemmyes, the Nubians, the Aethiopians and the Axumites, further to the south. The most prominent polity in the area during the early Roman period was Meroe.[4] The first contact of the Romans with the peoples of the area occurred during the prefecture of Cornelius Gallus, the first prefect of Egypt, who, having defeated a rebellion in the Thebaid in fifteen days, campaigned to the south, progressing beyond where Roman forces had previously gone, and defeated the Aethiopian king.[5] The victories of Gallus brought only a temporary peace to the frontier. His successor, Aelius Gallus, gathered troops for a campaign into Arabia. He collected Nabataean and Jewish troops as well as 10,000 from the garrison in Egypt. These forces, having sailed down the Red Sea, were eventually defeated not by force of arms but by the climate and disease. Aelius Gallus was forced to retreat in some disarray, blaming the Nabataean Syllaeus for the defeat.[6] Whilst Gallus was away in the distant regions with sizeable numbers of the Egyptian garrison, the Aethiopians of Meroe attacked Egypt. They took Syene, Elephantine and Philae, defeating the Roman garrison. Petronius, the prefect, gathered together his forces and marched to meet the threat. Facing vastly superior numbers, according to Strabo at least, Petronius defeated the invaders and forced them to retreat. Queen Candace was defeated and the town of Pselchis fell. The Romans continued their march capturing Premnis and the capital Napata, garrisoning the first two towns but destroying Napata. Petronius was then forced by the season to return to the milder climate of Alexandria. Candace, thinking that the Roman general's strength had been drawn, gathered her forces and marched against the garrisons of Nubia. Petronius returned in time to save his men. Candace sued for peace and ambassadors were sent to Augustus.[7] These campaigns were the high-water mark of Rome's expansion southwards and, although ultimately unsuccessful, were significant enough to be mentioned in the *Res Gestae*.[8]

Nero was attracted by the prospect of conquest in the area and there is considerable evidence of a build up of forces in Egypt. We know that the *legio* XV *Apollinaris*, the *ala Siliana* and 2,000 Libyan troops were moved to Egypt in the late 60s.[9] Nero was intending to visit Egypt to lead the expedition himself before the Jewish rebellion and the collapse of Nero's power brought an end to his plans.[10] The only military action was the sending of troops across the border as a pseudo-scientific expedition to discover the source of the Nile. Seneca wrote, 'I indeed heard the two centurions, sent by Nero, who loves dearly all virtues but especially truth, to discover the source of the Nile.'[11] Pliny the Elder took a more sanguine view of proceedings saying that the expedition took place at a time when Nero was considering war against the Aethiopians.[12]

There are no further reports of major expeditions or disputes until the third century. The only record of trouble in the area is an inscription erected under Hadrian recording the success of a pursuit of raiding *agriophagoi* who were chased for two days and then cut down by Roman forces.[13] This illustrates the nature of the military threat posed by the peoples across the Egyptian frontier. Strabo described them as 'neither numerous nor warlike, although they were once thought to be so since they often attacked the unguarded as bandits'.[14] Aelius Aristeides' mid-second-century oration in praise of the imperial city mentions the trouble spots of the Roman empire: Mauretania, Dacia, and the Red Sea.[15] This last comes as something of a surprise but both Strabo and Pliny point to the Red Sea as being a centre of pirate activity, suggesting that Aristeides was referring to banditry or piracy rather than the threat of large scale invasion.[16] There is some evidence to suggest that the Romans withdrew from their most southerly outpost at Qasr Ibrim *c.* AD 100 but this withdrawal cannot be linked to any other evidence of increased military difficulties on the frontier.[17] It is possible that the withdrawal was related to the reduction in the size of the Egyptian garrison in the first decades of the second century but it is perhaps more likely that the Roman forces came under pressure and it was decided not to maintain a military presence at the site. Probably only a very small number of troops had been stationed in the town. The threat to the security of Egypt was not an invading army but a *razzia* and the Roman forces were probably kept reasonably active dealing with such incursions throughout the period.

There appears to have been a change in the intensity of the threat in the middle of the third century though the events of this period are fairly obscure. Aurelian celebrated triumphs over the Arabs, Blemmyes and Axumites, suggesting perhaps that tribes well beyond the border region were involved in raiding the empire.[18] Probus also campaigned against invaders near Koptos and Ptolemais but the frontier seems to have remained in turmoil until Diocletian gave the Nobatae land and paid a subsidy to the Blemmyes.[19] These events suggest a collapse of the frontier which may be a result of either increased pressure from the barbarian tribes or weaker defences. The same period sees an increase in problems on the frontiers of Arabia and it may have been that the region of Arabia and East Africa was in flux, leading to a movement of populations northwards towards the Roman empire. The period is also, however, one of tremendous military, economic and political difficulty in the Roman empire with a collapse of political order due to a series of civil wars and economic problems caused by rapid inflation. In such conditions, the defences may well have been temporarily weakened and it is notable that the return of relatively stable government under Diocletian and his successors appears to end the problems on the frontiers. One guesses, therefore, that the campaigns of the third century against these tribes were relatively minor affairs in which the Roman forces, once organised, were easily victorious.

The army in Egypt played its part in most of the major military expeditions in the eastern half of the empire. The main events were the campaigns of Corbulo to the East, AD 58–63, the Jewish revolts of AD 66–70, 115–17, 132–5, the annexation of Arabia in 106 and the Parthian war of Trajan, 116–17. The sources are much poorer for the later second century but, in 163–5, Verus went East and Septimius Severus led forces against Parthia in 194–5 and 197–9. His son, Caracalla, probably attempting to emulate the success of his hero Alexander the Great, led troops on the frontier and was, in fact, assassinated while on campaign in 216–17. Severus Alexander used Egyptian troops in his invasion of Parthia in 232–3. There were further troubles on the frontier in 243 and in the reign of Valerian which culminated in his disastrous capture by the Persians in 260. Carus invaded Persia in 283 and relations with the Persians remained strained throughout the later Roman empire. In addition to these problems, in an extraordinary period from c. 267 to 272, large parts of the Eastern Mediterranean, including Egypt, came under the control of Queen Zenobia of the city of Palmyra. Our knowledge of many of these events is insufficient to allow a detailed reconstruction of the military campaigns. In many cases, we simply do not know whether Egyptian troops were involved. It is, however, apparent from the better-attested campaigns that the forces stationed in Egypt did have an important role to play in at least some of these wars.

For his campaigns, Corbulo collected the *legiones* XV *Apollinaris* and III *Augusta* together with vexillations (detachments) from Illyricum and from Egypt, with cavalry and infantry auxiliaries.[20] The conclusion of these campaigns with the disgrace of Corbulo led to the dispersal of the army.[21] The XV *Apollinaris* did not return to the Danube, where it had come from, but went to Egypt from where Titus collected it in 66. Titus does not seem to have gathered other troops from the garrison before joining his father's expedition to suppress the rebellion in Judaea.

After Vespasian's victory in the civil wars, Titus took control of the three legions in Judaea and to these he added *legio* XII from Syria and vexillations of legions III and XXII from Alexandria which he collected from Nikopolis.[22] Following his victory, Titus disbanded his armies leading the bulk of his forces back to Alexandria. *Legiones* V and XV went back with him but, on arrival in Alexandria, Titus decided that they were surplus to requirements and sent them back to their old stations, Moesia and Pannonia.[23]

Under Trajan and Hadrian there was considerable military activity in the East and both legions in Egypt left to be replaced by the *legio* II *Traiana*.[24] In 105, several auxiliary units were sent to Judaea though there is little other evidence of trouble in that province in this period and neither of the legions seems to have been involved in the campaign.[25] *Legio* III *Cyrenaica* left Egypt in 106/7 for the new province of Arabia, though there was probably little fighting involved in the annexation of the province.[26] The legion was involved in Trajan's Eastern campaign but was back at Nikopolis with *legio* XXII in 119.[27] It then went to fight the Parthians in 123 though war was averted on this occasion.[28] An officer of the legion was rewarded by Hadrian for his valour during the Jewish war.[29] The legion then reappeared in Bostra, Arabia, from 140 and remained in Arabia until well beyond our period of study.[30]

The evidence of this series of campaigns fought in by the III *Cyrenaica* is in remarkable contrast to the evidence concerning the XXII *Deiotariana* which simply disappears after 119, a disappearance which may be connected with the Bar-Kochba revolt.[31]

Egyptian forces of the later second century do not appear in any of the accounts of the campaigns in the East. This may be because of the reduction in the legionary garrison to one legion but we should take into account the decline in the quantity and quality of the source material. *P.Coll.Youtie* I 53 details the movements of troops to Mauretania. The *ala* I *Thracum Mauretana* was being sent and at least one other auxiliary unit. The sending of reinforcements to Mauretania was probably in response to a fresh outbreak of hostilities, possibly *c.* 145.[32] In 232, Severus Alexander once more marched Roman forces against the empire's eastern neighbour. His biographer tells us that he suffered a mutiny at Antioch from members of a legion. The legionaries had been misbehaving and raiding the women's baths. The emperor's attempt to restore order was not received well by the troops concerned. Herodian, in a shorter report of the incident, tells us merely that there was a mutiny by Egyptian and Syrian troops.[33] The *legio* II *Traiana* must have been brought from Egypt to take part in the expedition.

In the later third century, we hear little of the army in Egypt. The most important event which involved the army was the invasion of Egypt by the forces of Zenobia. The events of the conflict are not entirely clear but it appears that an army estimated at 50,000 was defeated by Zenobia's forces though this invasion may have been eventually repulsed.[34] The Palmyrenes did, however, take control of Egypt and remained in control until after the defeat of Zenobia by Aurelian.[35] Order may not have been fully restored until the Diocletianic settlement and reorganisation of the garrison of the province.

The army in Egypt was involved in most, but perhaps not all, of the major military expeditions of the Eastern armies. The army was not, however, merely used on external campaigns. One of its major strategic roles was to secure Alexandria and to prevent revolt in the *chora*.

INTERNAL REVOLTS

Alexandria was Egypt's major port and the point of egress for the important corn supplies from the Egyptian *chora*. It was also the centre of communications between Egypt and the Mediterranean world and it was vital for a Mediterranean power to control the port. Alexandria was the second city of the Mediterranean and was only surpassed by Rome in population and grandeur. As the city of Alexander the Great, the Ptolemies and Cleopatra and a city that had been the most influential cultural centre in the Hellenistic world, Alexandria could pose as the capital of the Greek East and could compete with Rome as a centre of power in times of strife, as during the civil wars between Antony and Octavian and Vitellius and Vespasian. It was a city renowned for its volatility and the mob had frequently caused its Ptolemaic rulers considerable problems, even driving them from the city. This unruliness continued into the Roman period and the first disturbance we hear about is under Augustus when the bodyguard of the prefect Petronius held off a stone throwing mob of countless numbers.[36] Vespasian had similar problems though the details of the events are unknown.[37]

The major disturbances in Alexandria in the first century involved ethnic violence between the Greek and Jewish communities. The first outbreak occurred between AD 38 and 41. When the King of Judaea, Agrippa, passed through Alexandria on his return journey from Rome, the Jewish community welcomed him by processing through the streets of the city.[38] The Alexandrians staged a mock procession with an idiot, Karabas, taking the place of the king. The prefect did not exert his authority and there was a pogrom, involving the desecration of synagogues and the public beating of the members of the Jewish *gerousia*, the council of elders which governed the community.[39] The army did not play a major role in events. A centurion and some troops disarmed the Jews and a centurion arrested Flaccus, the prefect, on the orders of Gaius.[40] In AD 66, with the outbreak of revolt in Judaea, there was further rioting in Alexandria. The prefect Tiberius Julius Alexander tried to calm the situation, but when this failed, he ordered his two legions and 2,000 troops who had been transferred to Alexandria from Libya, to attack the Jewish area.[41]

The Jewish revolt of 115–17 is not so well served by the ancient literary sources. The revolt sprang from the Cyrenaican Jewish community and was part of the general unrest sweeping the area in the aftermath of an earthquake in Antioch and the disturbances caused by Trajan's campaigns in Parthia.[42] Eusebius tells us that

> In the eighteenth year of Trajan the Jews of Alexandria, Cyrene and Egypt rose up and in the next year caused a large war when Lupus was Prefect of all Egypt. In the first battle the Jews were victorious but the retreating Greeks fell upon the Jews of Alexandria and killed them all. The Cyrene Jews, deprived of their allies, fell upon the *chora* of Egypt and laid waste the nomes led by Loukouas. Against these the emperor sent Marcius Turbo with foot and fleet and also cavalry. These men, in many battles and over a long period of time, slew many thousands of Jews, not only those from Cyrene but also those from Egypt who had taken up with them, together with their King, Loukouas.[43]

Cassius Dio details the savagery of the revolt: 'Also, at this time, the Jews of Cyrene appointed Andreas as their leader and killed both Romans and Greeks, eating the flesh of their victims and making belts with their entrails.'[44] Orosius devoted most of his narrative for the reign of Trajan to events in Cyrenaica:

> At once, it is incredible to say, the Jews, as if afflicted by madness, rose up in different parts of the world and fought a most terrible war against the natives throughout the whole of Libya which was so damaged, and so many farmers killed, that if Hadrian had not collected and placed there colonies, the land would have remained desert, cleared of habitation.[45]

Appian was in Egypt at the time and mentions the revolt when discussing Caesar's arrangements for the body of Pompey which was placed in a temple of Nemesis. This temple was destroyed in the uprising, 'when Trajan was destroying the Jewish race in Egypt'. Appian himself had a fortunate escape from Pelusium just before the Jews established control over the waterways.[46] We have papyrological evidence for the scale of the revolt in the *chora*. There is evidence of damage in the Fayum during the revolt.[47] Damage occurred in the Lykopolite nome and in the Oxyrhynchite where the population was still celebrating the victory over the Jews eighty-three years later.[48] The Hermopolite nome was also attacked.[49] The disappearance of the Jewish community at Edfu after 116 is probably connected with the revolt.[50]

The military effort against the Jews is illuminated by an archive belonging to the *strategos* Apollonios who was given forces, probably local levies, to secure the nome of Apollonospolis-Heptakomias in Upper Egypt. The exact date of each document is obscure since the year in which the letter was written is not given. One letter, from September, urges Apollonios to follow the example of the *strategos* of the Hermopolite who went everywhere with a strong guard, looking to his personal safety before all else.[51] Another letter urges him not to let the rebels roast him, recalling the horror stories in Dio's account.[52] A fragmentary letter actually describes the course of a battle somewhere south of Memphis. The Roman forces, probably a legionary group, had been defeated and the one hope left was a force of villagers conscripted from the surrounding area, but these too were defeated with heavy losses. The writer, possibly Apollonios, did not despair since he had news of the arrival of another legion of Rutilius at Memphis.[53] Another letter from the archive deals with private business in a rather cryptic fashion. The letter also informed the recipient of the local gossip: if the troops moved up in sufficient numbers the *basilikoi g[eorgoi]* would be moved by Apion. The appearance of these royal farmers in a military context is very unusual and nearly all other references to them date to the Ptolemaic period. The restoration is probably incorrect.[54] The next letter shifts the scene. Servants of Apollonios rejoice at the news of their master's success at Memphis and the victory of the Roman forces.[55] In the aftermath of the revolt, another letter from the archive complains of the difficulties and dangers of travelling through the *chora* between Alexandria and Hermopolis.[56] Throughout these letters the Jews are called 'impious'.

The evidence gives a vivid picture of the troubles. The rebels spread destruction from the Delta, though failing to capture Alexandria, to Middle and Upper Egypt. Their progress appears to have been uncontrolled. Appian's escape from Pelusium before the arrival of the rebels does not suggest that there was to be any organised resistance and the tactical situation following the defeat of the Roman forces and their retreat to Alexandria suggests that the *chora* was left open to the rebels. The resistance from the authorities gradually gathered strength but the Egyptian garrison was unable to deal with the problem and forces were dispatched by Trajan. Eusebius stresses the difficulties of the campaign and the papyrological evidence points to defeats suffered by the Roman forces. Indeed, after the defeat of the Romans mentioned by Apollonios and the defeat of the levied forces, the situation was desperate with the Jews controlling the field.

The rebels proved more than a match for the highly trained legions of ancient and modern legend even when supplemented by local levies. The eventual defeat of the rebels was inevitable, given superior Roman resources. The war itself was not just one of a few set-piece battles but was more complex. The security problems, both during and after the revolt, were great. Officials had to go around with armed guards and it was unsafe to travel. The spread of the revolt and the testimony of the ancient sources show that the large Jewish community of Egypt became involved, perhaps faced with an antisemitic reaction to the Cyrenaican invasion, and we may envisage several separate risings of the Jewish population. Not only were the authorities faced with the army in the field but also with guerrilla warfare and, once the army had broken up, many rebels, and probably many displaced persons, roamed the countryside, surviving as best they could. It was an anarchic situation which would take some time to correct. The fate of the Alexandrian community is not in doubt. The retreating Romans fell upon the community and rabbinic sources note the destruction of the main synagogue.[57]

Under Hadrian, after the suppression of the Jewish revolt, there is a reference to disturbances within Alexandria but no mention of any military involvement.[58] There are suggestions of conflicts under Antoninus Pius. John Malalas, by no means an expert on Egyptian matters, reports that Antoninus Pius began a campaign against the Egyptians who had rebelled and killed the *Augustalios deinarchos*. The passage is obviously difficult to interpret since the account of the killing of this official, who must surely represent the prefect, does not appear in any other source. There is some supporting evidence of a major disturbance to be found in the edict of the prefect Sempronius Liberalis and the *Historia Augusta*, but the disturbances mentioned in both these sources do not appear to have been as serious as the killing of a prefect.[59]

In about 171/2, the Boukoloi revolted. Cassius Dio's account reads:

And those called the Boukoloi created a revolt in Egypt and joined with the other Egyptians led by a priest, Isidoros. First, dressed as women, they tricked the Roman centurion, since they seemed to be the women of the Boukoloi approaching to give him money on behalf of the men, and struck him down. They sacrificed his companion, swearing an oath on the entrails and then eating them. Of these men, Isidoros was the bravest of all. Then, when they conquered those Romans in Egypt in a full battle, they advanced nearly to Alexandria and would have got there if Cassius had not been sent against them from Syria and contrived to upset their unity, dividing them from each other, since, because of their desperation and numbers, he did not dare to come against them all and so he subdued them as they divided.[60]

The revolt is also mentioned in the biography of Marcus Aurelius: 'And when the soldiers of the Bucolici did many terrible things throughout Egypt, they were put down by Avidius Cassius.'[61]

The next attested disturbance was an assault on Alexandria by the

Emperor Caracalla in 215. Caracalla approached Alexandria with his army but after all the leading men had left the city to meet him on the road, as was the custom when the emperor or other important person came to visit, he welcomed them into his camp. Only when he reached the city was this impression of cordiality dispelled. Caracalla set the troops on the city and retired to the Serapeum to commune with the gods. Outsiders and foreigners were expelled from the city. The city itself was divided by a cross-wall to prevent freedom of movement and was patrolled by soldiers of the guard. All the public messes were abolished as were the games and processions. The ceremonial of Greek civic life was ended.[62] Three years later there was an outbreak of violence at Alexandria between the troops and the civilian population as to which contender to the throne to support. There was large-scale bloodshed with both troops and civilians being killed. The situation became so serious that the prefect Basilianus had to flee the country.[63] Later, under Valerian, the various factions in the city fought running battles through the streets. There is no mention of any military intervention.[64]

Alexandria caused the Romans serious problems but those problems have been well publicised in our literary evidence due to the peculiarities of the culture of Alexandria. Although it is a temptation to assume that these disturbances conceal a much larger number which the literary sources did not record, we cannot, in fact, do so. We know about these events because they were extraordinary. We cannot safely surmise the normal role of the army from this extraordinary evidence. Although Alexandria did present special problems for the Roman authorities, it is not clear that the Romans were heavily involved in the everyday security of the city. Indeed, the authorities seem to show a reluctance to commit large numbers of troops to the policing of the city and seem to have been slow to react to major outbreaks of violence.

The army fought two wars in the *chora* during the second century. On both occasions the army was defeated. The Boukoloi and the Jews were able to defeat trained Roman forces and, against the Jews, the army appears to have been supplemented by large numbers of levies. The army in Egypt was unable to deal effectively with these major rebellions.

Taken together with the campaigns outside Egypt, a Roman soldier was likely to spend at least some of his career involved in warfare. Indeed, for the average Roman soldier fighting street battles against mobs, even lightly armed mobs, or fighting guerrilla wars against rebels might have been considerably more dangerous than fighting set-piece battles. A soldier would not, however, spend a great deal of time at war, though we must make some allowances for the imperfection of the source material. The soldier could expect to fight at some point in his career but it seems unlikely that many of the soldiers of the Egyptian army were killed while on active service or that, in terms of time, war was a major part of the life of the soldier.

THE ARMY AS LABOUR FORCE

As the soldiers were not continually involved in fighting, the Roman authorities had over 10,000 men available for other tasks. Their use as a convenient manual labour force is, however, comparatively rarely attested outside a context which could be classed as military. On arrival in Egypt, Augustus is said to have set his soldiers to work on the canals, clearing them out and repairing them, to improve the economy of Egypt.[65] There is, however, no parallel for soldiers being used in this way in Egypt for the next five centuries.[66] The canals were constructed and maintained by corvées levied on the local population and not by soldiers. It is possible that there was some major reconstruction work to be done in the aftermath of the wars, but it is far more likely that Augustus was merely publicising his good management of Egypt's resources in contrast to that of his immediate predecessor. In any case, if soldiers were ever involved, it was exceptional. The more usual role of the soldiers is shown in a document from 7 BC. Bassus wrote to Herakleides and Tryphon about the failure of the people from the hamlets to perform some task relating to the canals. The two were instructed to take a soldier and seize the crop of the villagers. Soldiers did not do the work. They merely ensured that the work would be done.[67]

The association of soldiers and tax collectors is, in part, to be related to the unpopularity of the activities of these officials. The scope for corruption and extortion would be increased if a soldier were present during the collection of the taxes to guarantee the safety of the tax man. The literary evidence shows us a centurion being paid taxes, or at least some money, in the company of a companion of some kind, by the people of the Boukolia. In AD 75, in the Fayum, a soldier was associated with the *sitologos* in a rather obscure context related to taxes on grain.[68] In the village of Komas, *c.* 15 BC, the ferry-man who was operating the only ferry across a newly built canal had his books examined by the tax collector Apollos. This man was accompanied by a soldier and they stole two cloaks from the ferry-man's house.[69] In the third-century Oxyrhynchite, the collection of taxes got out of hand since the collector, although not doing anything illegal, seemed to be a little too enthusiastic about his task. Soldiers had to be sent to protect him.[70] Evidence for the more direct involvement of soldiers comes from a very badly damaged account of the taxes paid on salt. The account comes from Oxyrhynchus but is a cumulative total of taxes collected by soldiers from several units which suggests that the account covered the taxes from a substantial area. There were at least four cohorts involved and three of the names are readable: I *Flavia Cilicia*, II *Ituraeorum*, and I *Lusitanorum*. One *ala* is mentioned which is probably the *ala Vocontiorum*. All these units were attested in Egypt throughout the second century. The money and the accounts were dispatched to the appropriate authority, who may have been Irenaeus, imperial freedman, by two centurions, Valerius Perpetuus and Livius.[71]

Soldiers were also involved in the supervision of the grain boats down the Nile. In AD 42, a centurion accompanied a shipload of grain down the Nile as *epiploos*, a ship's guard.[72] In AD 13, the *epiploos* on a shipment was an ordinary soldier and in an undated document of the first century the *epiploos* was a soldier of *legio* XXII.[73] By the second century, the duty was liturgic, imposed on the local population. There was still, however, military involvement and a second-century document from the Oxyrhynchite attests payments made to soldiers during the shipping of grain. We are not told why the soldiers were paid.[74] The *epiploos* guaranteed that the grain arrived in Alexandria in the same state that it had left the *chora*. The presence of a soldier ensured this but it was equally efficient to make it a liturgic post so that the *epiploos* personally guaranteed the good condition of the grain. It is possible that both methods were used simultaneously.

One letter, probably from the reign of Gaius Caligula, attests the use of soldiers to hunt and capture wild beasts on the order of the prefect. The beasts were presumably intended for the games in Rome.[75]

Soldiers supervised and guarded the state's economic assets in the Eastern Desert, the quarries. In AD 19, the quarries were under the control of Tiberius Poplius Iuventius Rufus. This official was aided by Mammogais, son of Bataios, of *cohors Nigri*.[76] At the marble quarry of Mons Claudianus, the centurion Annius Rufus from the *legio* XV *Apollinaris* was in charge under Trajan.[77] Under the same emperor, an altar was erected to Helios-Sarapis when Encolpios was procurator and Q. Accius Optatus centurion, by Apollonios, son of Ammonios, Alexandrian architect.[78] In 118, the chain of command put Chresimos, an imperial freedman, in charge, but military authority rested with Avitus, centurion of *cohors I Flavia Cilicia equitata*.[79] A contract of 143 from Thebes between Semphasies, daughter of Boucheos, from Thmorbos of the Upselite nome, mother and heir of Ammonios, son of Ammonios, and Iulius Silvanus, *optio* of the century of Claudius, records the receipt of the worldly goods of Ammonios. The deceased had been a soldier and quarry man of *cohors* II *Thracum*.[80]

These desert quarries had to be supplied and the garrisons that watched the supply routes were, in the main, also able to supervise the caravans, loaded with luxuries imported from India, which travelled from the Red Sea ports to Koptos and on to the Mediterranean. An inscription from Koptos records the repair of the forts across the desert by legionaries and auxiliary units drawn from the whole garrison of Egypt.[81] A further road was built across the desert in AD 137 in order to connect Antinoopolis to the Red Sea ports. The road was well fortified with many garrisons and resting points.[82] In AD 90, men of *legio* III *Cyrenaica* built a bridge at Koptos.[83] Probus apparently put the soldiers to work on an extensive scheme of public building including temples, bridges and porticoes.[84]

The army was also involved in the erection of honorary monuments. *Cohors* I *Flavia Cilicia* erected two obelisks in honour of the emperors at Syene in 166.[85] The army also put up inscriptions celebrating the rebuilding of camps. In 150–2, the camp at Euniko was rebuilt by the *cohors* III *Ituraeorum*.[86] In 174 a camp, probably Nikopolis, was renovated.[87] Forts at Qantara and Hierakonpolis were built in 288 and one must presume that the army built or renovated forts across the whole province of Egypt throughout this period.[88]

POLICING

The involvement of soldiers in policing Egypt and maintaining a security system is attested by several collections of ostraka, pieces of pot which were written on. Three collections of second-century ostraka come from the same source; the original pot has been reconstructed, and recent evidence has suggested that the ostraka refer to places near the camp of Tell el-Zerqa, a fort in the Eastern Desert.[89] Other ostraka come from Esna (Latopolis) and there is a first-century collection from the Wadi Fawakhir, half way between Qift (Koptos) and Quseir, on the road through the Wadi Hammamat.[90] All these collections attest the lives of the soldiers in garrison in the Eastern Desert and the workings of the desert security system.

Several ostraka list the guards of watchtowers.[91] Two guards worked together, alternating daily with another pair. Each day one of the guards was up and the other was down. The archaeology of the desert roads provides us with a context for these texts. The Romans fortified water points along the roads and, in addition to these fortifications, stone watchtowers were built along one road. The towers are not preserved to their full height but were clearly quite substantial structures, though the lack of a door suggests that they were merely platforms, reached by ladder, from which the guard could survey the road in the valley below. The towers are so positioned that it was possible to signal to neighbouring towers so that messages could be transmitted very rapidly to patrolling military forces or to a garrison to warn them of trouble or to appeal for aid. One presumes that the guard stationed up would transmit signals and the guard down would monitor the traffic along the road.[92]

The names of the guards are predominantly Egyptian, though some duties were performed by soldiers. Herennius Antoninus, probably a decurion, wrote to Amatius about the son of Balaneos who was guarding a watchtower though still a child. Amatius was to ensure that the *dekanos* sent a replacement.[93] A separate letter had already been sent to the *dekanos*. These *dekanoi* have been identified with numerous lists of, on average, nine men preserved in the Thebaid. Each *dekanos* was given a number, the highest known being eighty-nine, but not all numbers turn up with equal frequency and numbers below forty appear most often. Bagnall suggests that the *dekanoi* were numbered separately in possibly as many as fifteen different areas and, in most areas, there were not more than forty groups. This would represent a system which could mobilise several thousand Egyptians.[94] The *dekanoi* were controlled by officials of centurial rank but there was also a further group of officers known as *curatores* who, in our archives, acted as intermediaries between the *dekanoi* and the centurion-rank officers. These *curatores* were soldiers who had been given authority over specific areas or specific forts.

There is a great deal of archaeological and epigraphic material of a military nature from the roads across the Eastern Desert. At Bir Hammamat, for instance, where there was a fort and a temple to Pan, soldiers appear in inscriptions from AD 18, 20, 64/5, 79, under Domitian, and 91.[95] A *dekanos* and watchtower guards also appear.[96] There were fortifications in the Eastern Desert from the first century but not all the water points along the roads were fortified and the remains extant in the desert come from different periods. Even on the most heavily fortified road, Koptos to Quseir, there was a civilian settlement with water supplies which was apparently unfortified at Wadi Fawakhir. As this was the find-spot of the Guéraud ostraka, it is likely that soldiers were stationed there. The Roman supervision of the desert probably encompassed many of the water points at which there are no extant remains, though it is perhaps unlikely that a permanent presence was maintained at these sites. It must be remembered that soldiers needed water but they did not necessarily need forts. Even with the fairly heavy fortification of the desert, the security system probably extended far beyond the areas and routes for which we have surviving archaeological evidence.

No watchtowers have been found in the valley of the Nile but the towers were comparatively small, not very distinctive, and would not have attracted archaeological interest, even if any remains had survived. Given the intensive agricultural exploitation of the valley, it is likely that even an extensive system of watchtowers would have been destroyed. The papyrological evidence does attest watchtowers. The people of Taurinus, near Euhemeria, in the Fayum were warned to keep the watchtower manned by the centurion Domitius Annianus.[97] In the second century, two Arsinoites submitted a petition to the *strategos* following an assault on them and the tower-guard near Theadelphia in the Fayum. The guard may well have approached in order to aid the two who were under attack from thieves.[98] A tax for the guards of the watchtowers is also frequently attested.[99] *Dekanoi* collected customs duties at Soknopaiou Nesos in AD 49, and it is likely that the *dekanoi* were used to mobilise large numbers of men to man what appears to have been a fairly extensive security system.[100]

This organisational effort was designed to limit banditry. Egypt was renowned for banditry and several novelists chose Egypt, especially the area of the Boukolia, as the setting for stories of gruesome bandit activities.[101] Xenophon of Ephesus even made his bandit-chief journey around the Eastern Mediterranean before finally settling in Egypt to live off the trade from India.[102] Philo also contrasts the law-abiding Jewish community with the rebellious Egyptians.[103] More telling is the story Eusebius transmits of Dionysios, Bishop of Alexandria, since this claims to give his impressions as to the prevalence of banditry in Egypt; it also has a certain comic irony. The bishop survived the Decian persecution and was forced to account for this embarrassing fact. Once the persecution was announced, Dionysios went home to await arrest. The soldiers, naturally supposing that Dionysios would seek to avoid arrest, sought him across the province but not in his house. Having finally succeeded in finding some soldiers to arrest him, he was imprisoned by them at Taposiris. One of his party eluded capture and retired to a local wedding party, informing the peasants of events. The peasants were so enraged that they set out to rescue the unfortunate bishop. Bursting in on him and his captors, they chased the soldiers away and Dionysios was left imagining them to be bandits, pleading with them to allow him to be taken to his martyrdom or to be killed in the manner of a martyr. The story also details the involvement of the military in pesecutions of Christians, an involvement frequently mentioned by Eusebius.[104] The literary evidence suggests the prevalence of banditry throughout the first three centuries of Roman rule.

The documentary evidence of banditry is decidedly less colourful. The best information concerning the social context of banditry and the problems which banditry caused is *P. Thmouis*, an account of taxes owed and some of the problems in collecting that taxation in the Mendesian nome in the Delta. The entries for individual villages demonstrate a catastrophic demographic decline in the AD 160s which led to several villages being deserted. Populations fell from several hundred in 131/2 to as few as two. There were clearly severe economic problems in the region, problems with which the Roman taxation system struggled to cope. The underlying causes of the fall in population are largely unknown but they were exacerbated by plague, banditry and the reaction of the authorities. The village of Petetei had been in some way 'involved in the recent troubles' and was attacked by a detachment of soldiers who killed all the men there and villagers of Psenharpokrates and Psenbienchou who were staying in the village.[105] The *komogrammateus* reported that the majority of the inhabitants of the village of Kerkenouphis had been killed by the 'impious Nikochites' who had attacked the village and burnt it.[106] Zmoumis was also attacked by the 'impious Nikochites' about whom a report was written by Horion the *strategos* and Quadratus the centurion.[107] The novelists identify the Nikochites as the Boukoloi. These events provide the immediate background for the revolt of the Boukoloi which was to sweep away the Roman forces stationed in the area and threaten the city of Alexandria itself. *P. Thmouis* illustrates a process of demographic and economic decline which resulted in growing social unrest and violence. The banditry was reported to the prefect by a centurion and the *strategos* and a troop of soldiers was sent to root out rebel sympathisers. The population was caught between the bandits and the authorities whose policy is reminiscent of more modern policies of violent repression by foreign powers and must have exacerbated an already difficult situation. Yet these difficulties were recognised by the Roman authorities who reduced the tax burden on these communities. In 172/3, however, the prefect Statianus started to demand payment of arrears. This seems to be extraordinary in the circumstances but Statianus may have felt that the situation required a firm hand. Disappearances were a regular part of Egyptian village life and a recognised form of tax evasion. It is possible that the administration felt that the social problems were not as great as was suggested by the returns of officials or that the military intervention had restored the situation and people would return home. It is probable that this policy resulted in revolt.

Prefects issued several pronouncements designed to suppress or to encourage others to suppress bandit activities. M. Sempronius Liberalis decreed a three-month amnesty for those who had left their homes in recent disturbances. He had sympathy for those who had left because of liturgical commitments they could not fulfil or because of economic difficulties, but those who had fled voluntarily to live by banditry were to be hunted down by the *epistrategoi, strategoi* and soldiers. All those absent from home would be treated as bandits at the end of the amnesty.[108] In 206, Baebius Iuncinus wrote to the *strategoi* to direct their efforts against the bandits. Iuncinus wished the war to be taken to the supporters who would then give the bandits up: a policy which has been followed by authoritarian bandit-hunters from all ages.[109] A complaint of 209, addressed to the prefect, started with brief quotations from imperial decrees and a letter of the prefect Subatianus Aquila. The edicts insisted on the return of those who were living away from their homes and dire penalties were threatened for those who failed to return. A fine of HS 50,000 for each person sheltered was to be imposed by the *epistrategoi*.[110]

We must, I think, presume that these measures were directed against real outbreaks of lawlessness and a certain number of the cases reported to centurions, to which we shall turn in the next section, suggest bandit activities. In addition, there is a report from third-century Soknopaiou Nesos of a night-attack on the village by bandits and there is a small, rather dramatic, excerpt from an interrogation at Antinoopolis in the third century during which a man attempted to withdraw a confession, extracted under torture, which implicated a certain village in an act of brigandage.[111] We need have no doubt as to the fate threatening the village.

Although one can hardly escape the conclusion that there was some banditry in Egypt, the scale and prevalence of the activity are difficult to determine. Many of the literary sources had an interest in portraying Egypt as a violent place (Philo, for instance) and even some official decrees may well have been directed at minor, short-term difficulties or have been enacted by prefects assuring the Egyptian population of their commitment to maintain strict security. The Boukoloi became a myth-ical people of violence and their inclusion in novels does not necessarily suggest that this violence had current social reality. There is little evidence to suggest that Egypt was tottering on the brink of chaos and anarchy throughout this period and the worst outbreak of violence was clearly caused by social and economic difficulties that were of a temporary nature. Undoubtedly, there was a problem with criminal elements of the popu-lation but we should not over-emphasise the difficulties faced by the forces of law and order. Society was able to function, in most periods, tolerably well in spite of the occasional outbreak of banditry and other criminal activity. *P. Thmouis* does, however, show that such outbreaks could, ultimately, threaten Roman control. It is possible that the Boukoloi were traditional bandits whose relationship with neighbouring commu-nities was at best uneasy. The social and economic problems of the 160s, however, probably led directly to an increase in bandit activity as people were forced from the land and sought other means of support, but the violence they offered to those who remained on the land further exacerbated the situation, and the failure of the Roman authorities to deal effectively with the problem (indeed they merely worsened the underlying economic and demographic difficulties) eventually pushed the entire region into revolt. Banditry was an important destabilising factor in the governance of an area which could eventually have led to a complete loss of control.

The fulminations of the prefects against bandit activities have a certain familiarity and the regular nature of the decrees suggests that banditry was never completely suppressed. The policy of the Romans, however, is likely to have had some success. The use of watchtowers to give advance warn-ing and information about the approach of bandits and their place of retreat, the creation of local militias to guard strategic routes against bandit attacks and the employment of the resources of the civilian and military administration in anti-bandit activities, including what appear to have been extensive sweeps of the countryside, arresting all those who had strayed from their registered residence, appears a fairly powerful combination of measures to resist banditry. The authorities seem to have had some understanding of the power and resources of bandits and concentrated on the traditionally perceived weak areas in the defences of the bandits. Bandits need some kind of local support base in order to provide them with food and a place to hide and the authorities sought to attack that base, be it a group of villagers or a comparatively wealthy landowner. The authorities took a very strict line with communities which extended succour to bandits as the villagers of Petetei discovered. The Roman authorities appear to have been confident that when they extended themselves and organised a security sweep they would deal with the local bandits. The security sweep itself must have caused substantial disruption and ill-feeling and the authorities show an understandable reluctance to act. The evidence shows a massive concentration of military resources on the problem of banditry and as a result the Roman authorities probably exercised some control over bandit activities in normal times. The period of the revolt of the Boukolia was, of course, an abnormal time.

THE DISTRICT CENTURIONS

In August of AD 198, Gemellus Horion wrote to the *epistrategos:*

> To the excellent Calpurnius Concessus, *epistrategos,* from Gemellus, also known as Horion, son of C. Apollinarius, Antinoite. I enclose a copy of a petition which I sent to the most illustrious prefect Aemelius Saturninus, and the sacred subscript which I obtained from him. I request, if it is fitting to your fortune, that you write to the empowered centurion in the Arsinoite to send the accused before your court and that you hear my charge against him so that I may obtain justice.

The substance of the petition is a complaint about a minor tax collector, Kastor, who had abused the nearly blind Gemellus Horion and then attacked his house, knocking down his doors with an axe and assaulting his mother. This violence led to Gemellus Horion petitioning the prefect who referred the matter back to the *epistrategos,* who in turn referred the matter to the centurion.[112]

Gemellus Horion, in dispute with a tax collector, petitioned the prefect and the *epistrategos* and secured the intervention of a centurion. Although Gemellus made claims to special status through his Antinoopolite citizenship, a fairly ordinary Egyptian was able to secure the attention and intervention of a fairly senior Roman military official in a dispute with a local tax collector. Gemellus Horion ensured protection and made the first moves towards obtaining a favourable resolution of his problem. The intervention of the centurion to deal with such a minor local difficulty comes as something of a surprise. There was no apparent military interest at stake nor any apparent prior military involvement. We would have expected the matter to have been referred to civilian administrators, the *strategos* or perhaps the *epistrategos*, but not a centurion. The involvement of a centurion at this level of Egyptian society suggests an intimate involvement of the Roman military in the everyday administration and life of the province and points to Roman military power being a very real presence in the villages of the *chora*. If Gemellus Horion could secure a successful resolution of his problems through the intervention of the centurion, the importance of the army was enhanced. Far from being a remote and specialist military, the Roman army would have a real influence on village life, not merely as a vague threat of overwhelming violence which could destroy any challenge to the established order, but as a real and active presence in the local administrative and power structures. It would, therefore, be very important for locals to establish and maintain good relations with military officials and, also, the Roman military would have a means by which the situation in the *chora* could be monitored and controlled. Potentially, the centurions were in a crucial position within the governmental system in Roman Egypt and were a vital means of interaction between the people and the state.

We are not, however, merely reliant upon this one petition. There are a large number of documents which detail the role of these centurions and other officers in similar positions. These documents form a series of anecdotal accounts of village conflicts which illustrate the range of issues which were submitted to centurions in the first three centuries of Roman rule. It is worth providing a brief summary of this material, both for the insight that it gives into conflicts within the communities of the *chora* and to give an impression of the range and type of activities with which a centurion was thought to be concerned. It must be remembered that, normally, we have only copies of petitions submitted to centurions and we cannot know whether the centurions acted on these petitions or how they acted. We must, however, presume that they did act in many cases since, if they had not, the villagers would not have wasted their time in submitting petitions. I shall, therefore, detail the nature of these petitions in the following pages before analysing the role the centurions played in governing the *chora* of Roman Egypt.

In addition to the petitions detailed in Table 5.1 there are several other texts which show the involvement of the local centurions in policing.

(i) At the end of the second or the beginning of the third century, the centurion Domitius Annianus wrote to the people of Taurinus, near Euhemeria in the Fayum, instructing them to ensure that their watch-tower was fully manned.[113]

Table 5.1 Petitions to centurions

Document	Date	Provenance	Officer	Complaint/petition
P.Oslo II 30	20 BC	Sendrypae, Arsinoite	Centurion	Person stands surety for appearance of a woman before the centurion.
SB X 10308	AD 11	Soknopaiou Nesos	Centurion	Dispute over land tenure.
SB I 5238	12	Soknopaiou Nesos	Centurion	Request for protection against person defeated in lawsuit.
P.Oxy. XIX 2234	31	Teis, Oxyrhynchite	Centurion	Against a soldier and others who were stealing fish from a pond.
P.Ryl. II 141 = Doc. Eser. Rom. 76	37	Euhemeria, Arsinoite	Centurion	Assault on a public farmer by shepherds.
P.Corn. inv. 90[114]	49/50	Philadelphia	Centurion	Centurion hears oath given to tax collector.
P.Mich. X 582	49/50	Philadelphia	Centurion	Tax collector demands that a colleague be compelled to do his duty.
P.Oslo II 21	71	Karanis	Centurion	Assault on the assistant of an estate manager.
BGU I 36 = 436 = Doc. Eser. Rom. 82	101–3	Soknopaiou Nesos	Centurion	Assault on a priest who was attempting to collect a debt.
BGU III 908	101–3	Bakchias	Centurion	Request to remove village policeman.
P.Ryl. II 81	104	–	Centurion	From the shore-guard.
P.Amh. II 77	139	Soknopaiou Nesos	Beneficiarius ἐπὶ τῶν τόπων	Arab-archer stumbles across a fraud at a customs post and is beaten up.
P.Grenf. I 47	148	Soknopaiou Nesos	Centurion	Disappearance, in suspicious circumstances, of person to whom land was rented.
BGU II 522	c.167	Soknopaiou Nesos	Centurion ἐπὶ τῶν τόπων	Priestess and defenceless widow makes appeal.
Stud.Pal.Pap. XXII 55	167	Soknopaiou Nesos	Beneficiarius ἐπὶ τῶν τόπων	As previous.
P.Hamb. I 10	167–8?	Theadelphia	Decurion	Assault and robbery of an entire household.
P.Tebt. II 304	167–8	Tebtunis	Decurion	Attempted murder by gang.
P.Thmouis I 116	167–8	Mendesian nome	Centurion	Centurion investigates an attack on a village by Nikochites.
P.Gen. I 3	175–80	Soknopaiou Nesos	Centurion	Dispute over an inheritance has resulted in violence.

Table 5.1 cont.

Document	Date	Provenance	Officer	Complaint/petition
BGU I 4 = XV 2458	177	–	Centurion	Property deposited by a veteran with a soldier who subsequently left the area.
SB XIV 11904	*c.*184	Tebtunis	Centurion	The village elders were extorting grain.
P.Ryl. II 78 and	184	Soknopaiou Nesos	Centurion	A woman was assaulted threatened with death by a man she lived with and owned property with.
P.Petaus 123	184	Aphrodisias	Decurion	
P.Lond. II, p.173, 342	185	–	Beneficiarius ἐπὶ τῶν τόπων	Village elder acting violently.
BGU I 81	188–9	–	Decurion	Collection of grain taxes.
BGU II 651	192	Karanis	Centurion	Vandalism at a threshing floor.
BGU II 515 = *Doc. Eser. Rom.* 78 = W.*Chr.* 268	193	Arsinoite	Centurion	An assault by tax collectors.
BGU II 454 = *Doc. Eser. Rom.* 79	193	Boubastis	Centurion	Theft of vegetable seed.
P.Mich. III 175 = *Doc. Eser. Rom.* 77	193	Soknopaiou Nesos	Centurion	Violent dispute over inheritance.
P.Mich. VI 425	198	Karanis	Centurion	Dispute with a violent tax collector.
P.Mil.Vogl. II 73	II	Tebtunis	Decurion of the Arsinoite	Dispute over a will.
SB VI 9290 = *Doc. Eser. Rom.* 69	II	–	Centurion	Summons issued by the centurion.
SB XIV 12179	II	Karanis	Centurion	
BGU VII 1676	II	Philadelphia	Centurion	Dispute which the centurion had referred to arbitration.
BGU I 157	II–III	Karanis	Centurion	Robbery of woman whose brother was in the army.
Stud. Pal. Pap XXII 54	II–III	Soknopaiou Nesos	Decurion	Assault and robbery.
P.Tebt. II 333 = *Sel. Pap.* II 336 = *Doc. Eser. Rom.* 74	II–III	Tebtunis	Centurion	Two hunters had gone missing, presumed murdered.
P.Tebt. II 334	201	Tebtunis	Centurion	From a deserted Antinoopolite woman who wished to reclaim her dowry.

Table 5.1 cont.

Document	Date	Provenance	Officer	Complaint/petition
Stud. Pal. Pap. XXII 49	201	Soknopaiou Nesos	Centurion	Land dispute.
SB X 10619	201	Soknopaiou Nesos	Decurion	Request for permission to summon entertainers.
P.Gen. I 16	207	Soknopaiou Nesos	Centurion	Land dispute.
P.Gen. I 17 = *Doc. Eser. Rom.* 73	*c.*207	Philadelphia	Centurion and decurion	Tax collector had gone missing: foul play suspected.
BGU I 98	211	Soknopaiou Nesos	Centurion	Accusation of defrauding a ward.
P.Grenf. II 62	*c.*211	Bithynos, Arsinoite	Centurion	Oath before the centurion to produce people for trial.
Stud. Pal. Pap. XXII 87	213	Soknopaiou Nesos	Centurion	Cattle damage of crops.
P.Oslo II 23	214	Karanis	Centurion	A fire destroys a field in crop.
BGU I 275	216	Karanis	Centurion	Burglary and vandalism of a house.
BGU I 322 = *SB* I 6	216	Soknopaiou Nesos	Centurion	Theft by neighbours. A petition also sent to the *strategos* (*BGU* I 321).
SB VI 9203	222–35	Tebtunis	Centurion	Ass of tax collector stolen and killed.
P.Harr. II 200	236	Arsinoite	Centurion and decurion	Theft of sheep. *Strategos* also informed.
P.Flor. I 9	255	Theoxenis, Arsinoite	Decurion	Theft of ass.
P.Stras. III 150	III	Philadelphia	Centurion	Dispute over a will.
SB V 8004	III	–	Decurion	Theft.
PSI III 222 = *Doc. Eser. Rom.* 81	III	Hermopolis Magna	Decurion	Violence offered to a tax collector.
P.Mil.Vogl. IV 233	III	Tebtunis	Centurion ἐπὶ τῶν τόπων	Land embezzled from the city.
P.Mil.Vogl. IV 234	III	Tebtunis	Beneficiarius	Assault

(ii) In Edfu, in 223, the decurion was addressed as 'Isidorianus, decurion in charge of the peace'.[115]

(iii) Magnus Felix Crescentillianus, prefect (AD 253–6), wrote to the *strategoi* of the nomes asking them to hand over their taxes and to remind the centurions, if they delayed in their areas, to return to Alexandria with all speed to celebrate the imperial birthday.[116]

(iv) At Oxyrhynchus, in 257–9, a centurion of the prefect's office was appointed to sit on a land tribunal.[117]

(v) Eusebius tells the story of Nemesion, an Egyptian, who was tried, probably in front of a centurion, for banditry but acquitted. The unfortunate Nemesion was, however, immediately accused of being a Christian and suffered a painful martyrdom. The date of his martyrdom is unclear but it is likely to have been in the Decian persecution or later and, therefore, in the latter half of the third century.[118]

(vi) Harpokras was released by the decurion as a favour to Chromation. When the inevitable questions started, no one was to know where he had gone.[119]

(vii) From third-century Oxyrhynchus comes an invitation from the decurion to his dining hall. The decurion does not give his name.[120]

(viii) Two orders to arrest were issued by the decurion and by the *beneficiarius* on duty, both from the Oxyrhynchite.[121]

(ix) Two documents of 292 refer to the decurion Aurelius Didymus who was in charge of the peace in the Herakleopolite nome.[122]

(x) A complaint addressed to the prefect M. Sempronius Liberalis (prefect 154–9) describes how the complainant was thrown into prison by soldiers for, as far as he claims to be aware, no reason at all.[123]

(xi) In 158, a man was imprisoned in a camp by the horseman Turbo, again with no known motivation.[124]

(xii) An inscription set up to the secretary to the centurions of the Arsinoite proclaimed his virtue.[125]

It is possible to group the cases very generally. Almost half the cases in which some cause can be found involved assault. Another concern was military or administrative misdemeanours which comprised about 25 per cent of cases. Violence against property makes up about a third of cases, including theft which led to about 15 per cent of all cases. Only a small proportion of cases involved people who were accused of evading their social responsibilities, such as defrauding their wards or deserting their wives whilst retaining their dowries. Petitioners often made claims to special status. Tax collectors comprised about 13 per cent of petitioners and higher legal status groups about 22 per cent. Approximately 11 per cent of petitioners were priests and 7 per cent were public farmers. Fifty-five per cent of petitioners made some claim of special status. A few people appealed to the chivalrous instincts of the centurions by suggesting that they had no one else to safeguard their interests.

It is a general rule that all petitioners, not just those who petitioned centurions, attempted to enhance their status, emphasising citizenship status or any other claim to importance they might have, since this might encourage more favourable and rapid treatment of their petitions. In itself, this is rather interesting since it shows a link between the perceived gravity of a case and the social status of the person involved, a rather undemocratic principle, and perhaps crimes against higher status groups could be seen as somehow political, threatening the order of society. Certainly, the centurions appear to have been particularly interested in crimes which could be related to the maintenance of order in society and several of the crimes appear 'political', such as the disappearance of a tax collector and the killing of the tax collector's ass. Centurions were also involved in the investigation of crimes which could be related to large-scale crime or banditry, the disappearance of or assault upon persons in the countryside and the night-time attacks on property. Centurions were also interested in the criminal activities of administrative officials which could be regarded as a perversion of the authority granted to them and may also, by associating the Roman authorities with criminal activity, have caused political discontent. The centurions do not appear, however, to have been particularly interested in disputes over land ownership or over evasion of social duties, unless conflict had boiled over into violence. Yet, although there may have been a widening of the interests of centurions over time, the petitions submitted to the centurions were not restricted to particular areas of administration or law and the centurions were expected to show an interest in many aspects of village life and conflict. Access to the centurions was not limited to persons of higher status and ordinary Egyptians with no claims to special treatment or high status submitted petitions. The range of persons submitting petitions and of the subjects about which the petitions were submitted is impressive.

There are some double petitions: one to the *strategos* and one to the centurion, and other petitions make mention of information passed to the *strategos*. The *strategos* recorded events in official registers. The centurion may be asked to bring individuals to justice, extend searches over large areas, or offer concrete protection. The comparative passivity of the *strategos* was not, however, characteristic of the office. Documents preserved in the office (or house?) of an *archephodos* of Euhemeria, published as *P. Ryl.* II 24–152, frequently mention the *strategos* as the official ordering arrests. They also mention an *epistates phylakeiton*, commander of the guard, an office which could be held jointly with that of *strategos* but which does not appear to have been used after the middle of the first century. The *archephodoi* were the primary police force of the villages and their efforts were assisted by sword-bearers, normally associated with local estates, and numerous guards of various types.[126] The policing of the villages was not the responsibility of the centurions but was under the firm control of the *strategoi* who used the police forces to summon persons to court and administer law and order.

There was clearly a close relationship between the *strategoi* and centurions. Crescentillianus, the prefect, wrote to the *strategoi* instructing them to send the centurions to Alexandria. In the early second century, someone, possibly the prefect, wrote to Teres, decurion, informing him that the *strategos* of the Koptite nome had written to him requesting thirty days' leave for the decurion to sort out private business in the Arsinoite. The unnamed official wrote not only to the *strategos* of the nome to inform him of the success of his request but also to a centurion, Petronius Fidus.[127] The secretary to the centurions was a civilian who stayed in the office when the centurion or decurion moved on. He was not a soldier; not part of a military bureaucracy. The *strategoi* could and did perform many of the administrative tasks submitted to the centurions. The relationship between the centurions and the *strategoi* is far from well defined and in any tree of management responsibilities, there would have been a clash between the two offices, the *strategoi* seemingly having the more important administrative role. The centurions did not supervise the nome administration. They did not give orders to the *strategoi* nor did the *strategoi* give orders to the centurions. There are two occasions when centurions seem to be being given instructions. On only one of these is the instructor known, the *epistrategos*. Senior military officers, prefects or the tribunes of military units of the centurions never appear in this type of evidence. Although both sets of officials worked together and dealt with similar types of issues, neither set had authority over the other. Strictly speaking, the centurions appear to have been administratively superfluous, having no clearly defined role.

There does not appear to have been any close link between the competence of the centurions and the administrative boundaries of the nomes. The geographical competence of the centurions in most documents was vague. The phrase ἐπὶ τῶν τόπων (probably a Greek rendering of the title *centurio regionarius* frequently attested in the western half of the empire) was commonly employed. Later documents were a little more specific, referring to the officer 'in charge of the peace of the Herakleopolite' and there are references to the centurion of the Arsinoite. The relative geographical precision is probably not significant. To write of the decurion or centurion of the Arsinoite may not refer to anything more than a general involvement with the area. Gemellus Horion did not want the *epistrategos* sending his letter to a centurion who was miles from the Arsinoite but one in a position to help. 'Arsinoite' had the force of 'local'.

At the end of the second century, the references from the Arsinoite are close enough together to allow us to assess the length of service. From 201 to 202, there are three separate centurion figures: Gallus, Iulius Claudianus, and Aurelius Antiochianus. In 207, the decurion Iulius Conon appears in the same document as the centurion Iulius Iulianus. Quintillianus appeared in 211 and, in successive years from 213 to 216, the centurions were Aurelius Valerianus, Aurelius Septimius Iulianus, and Aurelius Calvisius Maximus. Most of the centurions are known from one reference only but nearly all references are to the centurions by name and not solely by rank. The centurions were in the areas for a comparatively short period but long enough to become known in the villages. Iulius Iulianus and Iulius Conon were stationed in an area at the same time and it is unlikely that they overlapped by chance or that there was a transitional period when old officials introduced the new to the complexities of the job. Centurions performed duties jointly.

Although we know the names of quite a lot of these local centurions, only one of these men may be attested elsewhere.[128] We do not know what units these men belonged to and so we do not know whether centurions from a particular military unit were stationed in a particular area.[129] The variety of centurion-rank officers, the lack of geographical precision in their stationing, and the overlapping but short terms of service suggest a rather irregular system of stationing these officers in the nomes.

To sum up, the officers were stationed in the localities for comparatively short periods of time; their geographical competence was ill defined; their relationship to the civilian administration was unclear but they received a large number of petitions on various issues submitted by villagers. The role and position of the centurions remain somewhat obscure.

The petitions illustrate only one side of the role of the centurions. Nearly all our information involves communication between villagers and centurions, requests from villagers for centurions to act on their behalf. It represents what villagers thought the centurions could do for them not what the centurions were supposed to be doing in the localities. This role was not necessarily their primary function nor the role that the central authorities envisaged for the centurions. We have little information about the relationship of the centurions with the authorities in Alexandria. We do, however, have the letter to the *strategoi* from Crescentillianus summoning the centurions to Alexandria to celebrate the imperial birthday. This was an act of symbolic importance. The birthday celebrations were a display of loyalty to the ruling house, a reaffirmation of the control of Rome over the prefect and the province. The prefect summoned his military officials to this ceremony and they were all bound in loyalty to the emperor once more. The links between the emperor, the prefect and the military officers were reaffirmed and the centurions would return to the *chora* from a ceremony confirming their place in the political order. The centurions were links between the prefect and the villages. They were powerful men. We cannot know the social status of the centurions but the centurionate was open to men of equestrian status, a Roman aristocratic rank. It is likely that the centurions would have a social status at least as high, and possibly higher than the *strategoi*. Also, they had access to and were representatives of military power and, as we have seen, that military power could sometimes be employed to devastating effect. As representatives of overwhelming power, they could exercise power even though they might be only able to call upon a very few soldiers to support them. If the centurion thought that there was a potentially dangerous situation or the authority of the centurion was flouted, he could call upon the powers of the central authorities, be that through military force or through judicial channels. Normally, of course, he would not need to do so since everyone would be aware of his potential power and hence obey his order. If the prefect wished something to happen, or two parties to cease quarrelling, the local centurion could intervene. The centurion of the *pax Romana* was the equivalent of the gunboat of the *pax Britannica*. The centurion sent to the Boukolia to supervise the collection of taxes who was then killed by the rebels, should have been the guarantor of the safety of the poor tax man who was the main target of their wrath. The death of the centurion ensured a full-scale revolt and the intervention of Roman forces on a very large scale.

The deployment of centurions in the localities was a very powerful governmental mechanism. The centurions brought the power of the central administration to the level of the villages. They formed an economical means of communicating the power and authority of the prefect and the Roman army to ordinary villages when, given the comparatively small numbers of troops stationed in the province, it would otherwise have been rather difficult to impose military authority on the villagers. As such, the centurions could be very useful to the local administration, providing it with access to military authority and coercive power and a further means of communication with the central authorities. For the villagers, these Romans with high social status and a good deal of political power provided an alternative means of redress to the local administrative network, especially useful for villagers who were, for some reason, unable to mobilise that network. The centurions were people of power who could get things done and this alone accounts for the large number and the disparate nature of the petitions submitted to the centurions. For the central authorities, the centurions were an invaluable source of information and means of communication not just to enforce the wishes of the central authorities on the villagers but also between the villagers and the central authorities. The centurions were in an ideal position to assess the effect of a poor harvest in an area or to observe an increase in crime and banditry and advise as to the appropriate action. Any prefect, worried about the state of his province, had an invaluable source of information as well as an important means of enforcing his will. The centurions were, therefore, the linchpin of the Roman government of Egypt, key figures in Rome's largely successful attempts to maintain order in the province.

The centurionate was a possible avenue of progress towards high administrative office, including governorships, but some historians have thought that they, as soldiers, would not be qualified for administrative roles.[130] The Egyptian evidence suggests a completely different assessment of the necessary qualities of a centurion. Centurions needed considerable administrative and legal skills. They supported the activities of the *strategoi* in the administration of the nomes and provided them with access to military power. The centurions were the representatives of Roman authority. They brought the power of the prefect to the villages and, as representatives of the prefect, performed many of the tasks that a prefect was expected to perform. Rome was not a remote power. For the villagers of Egypt, the Roman army was not represented by veterans but by the power and authority of centurions. Their contact with the Roman state was not through the prefect, remote in Alexandria, but through the centurions, the primary and powerful representatives of Roman authority in the province.

EVERYDAY LIFE

The evidence outlined in the preceding sections of this chapter provides a list of activities performed by the Roman troops but such a list does not tell us how the Roman soldier spent his time. Building a bridge or forts along a road may have been an occasional activity which a soldier might perform once in his career and even such tasks that we normally identify as military, such as fighting in wars, may well have been a very occasional activity in the careers of soldiers; it is perfectly possible that some soldiers could have served for twenty-five years without fighting a set-piece campaign or meeting an enemy army. Of course, the activities which occupied the majority of the soldiers' time were not necessarily the most important activities as we can see by analogy with modern armies. In the last forty years the soldiers of most of the armies of Western Europe have seen little major military action but the primary purpose of those armies was to take part in such conflicts. Our sources from Egypt, however, allow us to reconstruct the daily life of a Roman soldier. In so doing, we escape from the view-point of the strategists and the generals to the level of the individual and the interaction of the soldier going about his normal duties with the society in which he operated.

The most detailed account we have of the activities of a group of soldiers is *P.Gen.Lat.* 1 which lists the duties of a century of a legion during ten days in the late first century.[131] Unfortunately the document is only partially preserved but we know the duties of forty of the legionaries. Nine of the men were on extended duty away from the century. There was a *custos armorum*, a guard of the armoury or even, possibly, the armourer; *conductor porcius*, which might be the name of the *conductor* or what he was supplying; *carrarius* Plotinus, which could be seen as service with the cart-driver Plotinus or the soldier might be Plotinus; *secutor* of

the tribune Iulius Severus, a bodyguard; a guard of the house of an officer who was probably a tribune; two soldiers either being *librarii* and *clerici*
or sent to these clerks; a supernumerary; and someone who has to stand
guard at a *statio*, a wayside fort. The remaining thirty-one were each
assigned duties for each of the ten days. It seems that while in camp, the
soldiers had little to do. More than 10 per cent of the entries are blank
suggesting that the soldiers had no duties on those days. Others were given
guard duties around the camp. Several were sent out of the camp in
extended duties during the ten days. Several were sent '*ballio*', the meaning of which is unclear.[132] One soldier went to the arena.[133] Another may
have gone to a local temple. Others were sent out as aides to various
officers.[134] Some were retained in the century, presumably to be employed
at the discretion of the centurion. Quite clearly, the soldiers were not
busy but the list only contains between a half and a third of the century's
troops. The rest were working away from the main camp.

Another section of the same papyrus contains a document listing the
duties of four legionaries over a period of several years. Their duties took
these troops away from the camp. One of the main destinations of the
soldiers was to the state granaries, either to guard the grain tax or to
supervise the administration of that tax. Other duties sent the soldiers
to the mint, to the construction of a harbour, to make paper and off
with an imperial freedman as an aide. The soldiers spent much of their
time away from the camp, a pattern that is confirmed by *P. Hamb.* I
39 = *RMR* 76, a list of hay and money receipts issued by the decurion
L. Iulius Serenus to the horsemen of the *ala veterana Gallica*. The receipts
are dated to the first three months of 179. There are nineteen known
decurions attested for the unit to whose troops Serenus gave the
allowance. The soldiers were dispersed across the Delta in small numbers
and the troops sent to a particular station did not belong to one particular *turma* of the unit. The troops were not dispatched at the same time
to the same place and there is no discernible pattern to the receipts.

The mundane nature of life in garrisons is illuminated by the Guéraud
ostraka from the Wadi Fawakhir in the Eastern Desert, an archive of
letters and other documents many of which concern the soldier Rustius
Barbarus.[135] Barbarus wrote to Pompeius concerning the delivery of
bread.[136] A second communication between the two also concerns food
which was being sent via the horseman Arrianus.[137] Another text
concerns the financial dealings of Iulius who intended to sell grain. The
price of the grain would be brought to Iulius by Albinus, the cavalryman.[138] Lupercus wrote to Licinius about a wagoner called Psentphous
with whom he had unfinished business. Greetings were sent to Domitius
and his fellow soldiers, placing the letter firmly in a military context.[139]
Rufus sent greetings and olives to Silvanus, instructing him to write back
if he needed anything else since he knew that someone was setting

out from Koptos.[140] Saturninus wrote to the officer Norbanus about a transaction involving Didymus and sent the companions of Norbanus greetings.[141] A letter was sent to the soldiers Terentius and Atticus thanking them for gifts and wishing their children health.[142] Antonius Proclus wrote to Valerianus in a document which might be dated to the reign of Gaius Caligula and, therefore, dates the whole archive. Proclus had been hunting wild beasts on the order of the prefect.[143] A soldier asked his brother to send him some paper.[144] The news that a soldier was unwell and might die is transmitted to a person who had to arrange a replacement.[145] Thermonthis wrote to Horion to ask for grain.[146] Longina wrote to her brother (husband?) with a long list of things he was to buy for her.[147] Castor wrote that the soldier Papirius was to be given wine when he delivered a letter to Chresthotes.[148] Parabolos wrote to Zosimus so that he would be sent grain.[149] Food is the theme of several other letters.[150] Religion also figures, with prayers offered to Serapis and Athena and fervent wishes that a family avoid the attention of the evil eye.[151]

Letters from the Florida collection, emanating from the Eastern Desert, attest similar concerns though there is a slightly greater variety. One letter communicates the worries of village elders about a food shortage and famine.[152] Maximus wrote to his sister (wife?), Tinarsiegis, who was pregnant. Maximus tells her to write to him when the child is due as he will attend the birth. He also gives her instructions concerning legal matters and asks that she send him material to weave a basket.[153] The garrison of Aphis received thirty jars (of wine?).[154] Ostraka from Pselchis in Nubia also concern food. They are receipts for food supplied by the *cibarator* or by the *optio* of the unit or units involved.[155]

One of the primary concerns of the soldiers appears to have been the supply of food and communications between officials and between soldiers and friends and family were dominated by the issue of basic supplies. There is a certain air of domesticity about the letters which concern themselves with the small business transactions of the soldiers and the families of the soldiers. The soldiers maintained a range of connections with non-military personnel, be they traders or suppliers or simply members of their family and although they corresponded with soldiers as well, connections with civilians were clearly important. Stuck in a remote and probably rather unpleasant outpost in the Eastern Desert, it is unsurprising that thoughts turned towards home and family.

CONCLUSIONS

The army in Egypt became involved in most of the major conflicts in the East in the first three centuries of Roman rule. Generals gathering forces for campaigns in Parthia or Judaea frequently summoned troops from Egypt and, in the first century, the Egyptian forces were a major element, numerically and strategically, in the army of the East. The two legions, together with the auxiliary units, provided a significant resource of manpower. The army in Egypt was smaller than the major concentration of forces in the East in Syria but the force was far from negligible and provided a strategic counter-weight to the Syrian legions. No governor of Syria could possibly have revolted without being sure of the attitude of the legions in Egypt which would have secured his southern flank and have controlled the important grain supply. Strategically, Alexandria and Antioch controlled the Eastern Mediterranean and the forces based in Syria and Egypt were expected to exert their influence over the entire region. Our sources for the second and third centuries are not as full as those for the first and, of course, the significance of Egypt as a military garrison had been considerably diminished by the reduction of the legionary forces to a single legion. Yet, still, the army in Egypt is known to have contributed forces to several important campaigns in the second and third centuries. The army was expected to fight in major conflicts and although it is possible that some soldiers never ventured beyond the borders of the province, many must have taken part in campaigns in the East and it is perfectly possible that the *legio* II *Traiana* and other units in Egypt sent troops to units across the empire to stiffen forces in a crisis. A soldier could certainly not have been guaranteed a career without major military campaigning.

In Egypt itself, there were few major incidents. The army was sent into Alexandria to quell rioters on several occasions and there were two major revolts in the *chora* in the second century. The first prefect had to deal with a revolt of some kind in the immediate aftermath of Roman conquest but any sense of the size and scale of the revolt is lost in the bombastic, self-congratulatory inscription erected to celebrate the victory. The normal activities of the soldiers appear to have been related to small scale disturbances and the suppression of bandits or similar groups. The frequency of these activities is unclear but although the literary sources emphasise the unruly nature of Egypt, it is possible that the security system maintained by the Roman authorities normally kept the situation firmly under control. The troops were dispersed across the province, probably in small or very small groups, and the hope must have been that this dispersal would be such as to prevent outbreaks of bandit activity becoming serious enough to threaten Roman authority. When the authorities lost control during the revolt of the Boukoloi and the Jewish revolt, the army had very considerable difficulties in suppressing the rebels and suffered significant defeats at their hands. The forces stationed in Egypt were not large when compared with the population and a full-scale revolt could threaten to overwhelm them. Since the soldiers would, unlike modern armies, have had no great technological advantage over rebels armed with whatever came to hand, a large revolt of the Egyptian population would always threaten to sweep away the Roman forces. Dispersal to suppress revolt before it became a major crisis was, then, the sensible policy though it did carry certain tactical disadvantages: faced with a sudden revolt, the forces would have to be concentrated to meet the threat which would mean that some soldiers would have to travel substantial distances across potentially hostile territory. The Romans were, therefore, always in a slightly precarious position unless they could enlist the support of a substantial proportion of the native population and although they could be confident of eventual victory by calling on the support of forces based elsewhere, revolts could inflict very great damage on the Roman forces.

Although the Roman troops were given various tasks such as administering the quarries, the protection of tax collection and supervising the state's economic assets, it seems that the most important role and the one that took up most of the soldiers' time was the supervision of the security system which protected towns and villages from bandits and criminals and monitored the movement of the population. The army acted as a policing agency but the army was not the only nor even the primary police agency in the *chora*. Much of the policing was conducted through civilians, either through the *dekanos* system or through the *strategoi*. Conscripted civilians were the backbone of the security system. Soldiers supervised various elements of the system. In the Eastern Desert, soldiers, either *curatores* or centurion-rank officers, supervised the manning of the watchtowers and in the valley itself, the evidence points to a similar involvement on the part of the military. When the prefects threatened to take action against the bandits, it was not just the army which was to be sent against them, but a combination of forces under the *epistrategos* and the *strategos*. During the Jewish revolt, it was not just soldiers who were sent against the rebels but also hastily raised levies of local peasants, probably under the command of the *strategoi*. Apollonios, whose archive tells us so much about the revolt, took an active part in the fight against the insurgents. The soldiers were one element of the security system and the security of the province was achieved by a mixture of civilian and military action.

The interrelationship between civilians and soldiers was complex. It is to be presumed that the involvement of soldiers in the collection of taxes did not enhance their popularity. Control of prisons may also have increased hostility and it is probable that there was some, perhaps considerable, corruption and abuse of power. Yet, this is not the dominant impression of our survey of the Egyptian evidence. The soldiers tended not to serve in camps remote from civilian life. They were not physically separated from civilian society. They spent much of their time serving in the *chora* in small groups and must have been in continual contact with Egyptians, not just as administrators of Roman order, oppressing the population, but also as colleagues, working with, though probably in a superior position to, Egyptians. The soldiers were reliant upon civilian transportation to bring them their basic necessities, to trade with and to carry letters to their homes in the valley. As soon as one examines the private business of the soldiers, whether they be the soldiers attested in the ostraka or those of Karanis, we become aware of the host of trans- actions through which Egyptians and soldiers communicated. Many of the soldiers must, after all, have been of Egyptian origin themselves and many more will have been married to Egyptian women. The soldiers would, when asked, destroy a village such as Petetei. The Roman army was probably as brutal as any other army when it put down rebellions or revolts, but it is impossible to believe that the transactions attested in our evidence were conducted in an atmosphere of mutual distrust and hatred. The deep involvement of the soldiery in civilian society and the level of integration demonstrated by the soldiery demand an absence of real hostility between the groups. The boundaries between soldier and civilian were too slight and crossed at too many levels to allow a radical division between the groups.

Many of the letters of soldiers were concerned with securing supplies. The army must have provided them with essentials but many of the letters request wine or olives from home and other non-essentials such as paper. The soldiers may have been looking merely to supplement a perfectly adequate diet or have been using food as a form of gift-exchange, a token of the continued connection with their friends and family, much as people take food to the sick or chocolates to dinner parties, when the giving of the gift matters more than the gift itself. The desire of soldiers for basic goods suggests, however, that the soldiers could not purchase these where they were stationed. This may indeed have been the case in the Eastern Desert, but is more difficult to explain in the Nile Valley. Soldiers provided a market for goods and services of all kinds and it is often presumed that they had a certain amount of money. In the next chapter, we look more closely at the economic impact of the army on the individuals who joined it and on the economy of Egypt as a whole.

6

THE ARMY AND THE ECONOMY

INTRODUCTION

Ancient historians have, from time to time, turned their attention to the economic impact of the army on the provinces in which it was stationed and have also considered the economic status of the recruits, veterans and soldiers of the army. By far the greatest attention has been paid to the institutional aspects of these questions, specifically the issue of the pay of the soldiers. This chapter will not, however, concentrate on pay but will deal with a whole range of broadly economic issues. The significant advantage of the Egyptian material is that it allows the evidence to be set within a specific economic context so that we can assess the income and economic status of soldiers and veterans in relation to the probable income of their Graeco-Egyptian neighbours, though I also make some attempt to relate the pay of soldiers to the Italian economy of the first century AD. Moreover, the army is frequently seen as an economically important organisation. The impact of the army was, supposedly, important in two ways. First, the army was probably the major item of expenditure in the imperial budget and much of the tax revenue was consumed in supporting the army. This had the effect of taking money from all the provinces of the empire and distributing it to those areas in which the army was based, mainly the frontier regions. The army then formed a significant market and source of coinage, necessary for paying taxes, which encouraged the establishment of trade routes directed towards the supply of the army and provided a significant boost to the economies of frontier regions, thereby encouraging the Romanisation of those areas. In the West, the army is seen as transforming local economies and the cause of major shifts in the pattern of settlement.[1] Second, in marked contrast, the army is seen as having a debilitating effect on local economies. The taxation necessary to support the ever-increasing expenses of the military drained the treasury, causing fiscal problems which generated the twin evils of debasement of the currency, leading to inflation, and an increase in taxation, leading to a gradual decline in the economy of the empire. In the later Roman empire

102

especially, the demands of the troops for money and supplies are seen as placing insupportable burdens on a fairly fragile economy and being in part responsible for the decline of the Roman empire.[2] These problems cannot be completely resolved by a study of the Egyptian evidence but a study of the impact of the army on a particular Eastern province will place the various theories in a concrete context which will allow a more balanced assessment of their merits. We will start, however, at the level of the individual soldier and the issue of military pay.

PAY

Military historians have proposed a number of different schemes to explain the evidence concerning military pay and have produced numerous tables showing the pay of the troops of various units. In my opinion, none of these tables is convincing and I offer a fresh exploration of the issue. I will not produce here a detailed refutation of all previously proposed explanations of Roman military pay rates since I have already published an article in the *Journal of Roman Studies*, 1994, which analyses these theories in detail. I merely summarise my views in this section.[3]

Our first source to deal with Roman military pay is Polybius (VI 39.12) whose daily rates of pay would suggest annual rates of about 120 *denarii* per year for infantry and 360 for cavalry. Caesar apparently doubled pay,[4] but Tacitus *Ann*. I 17, an account of a mutiny over, among many other matters, pay, gives a daily rate which translates into an annual rate of 225 *denarii* per infantryman. The next increase came under Domitian who in 83 raised pay 75 *denarii* to 300 *denarii*.[5] Pay rates remained stable for the next century. In 197 pay was increased but neither Herodian (III 8.4) nor the *Historia Augusta* (*Severus*, 12.2) quantify the increase. Herodian, IV 4.7 attests a 50 per cent increase in pay under Caracalla in 212. The final known increase in pay in our period was in 234 when Maximinus Thrax doubled the pay of the troops.[6]

To calculate third-century pay rates we first need to establish the size of the increase under Severus. Unfortunately, although historians have made guesses at the figure, we simply do not have sufficient evidence to reconstruct the level of the increase. Certain observations concerning pay rates in earlier periods do, however, provide some guidelines for estimates. From the time of Caesar, it is likely that although pay was calculated on a daily rate, that rate was manipulated to produce an annual rate payable in *aureii* (gold coins worth 25 *denarii*). Caesar is also probably responsible for the introduction of a regular system of payment on three specified days during the year. So, under Caesar and the early emperors the troops received three payments of three *aureii* (3 × 75 *denarii*) and Domitian increased pay to three payments of four *aureii* (3 × 100 *denarii*). It seems possible that Severus' increase in pay conformed to the

103

same system: three payments in *aureii*. The only other figure that we have for military pay is Dio's statement (LXXVIII 36.3) that the increase in military pay under Caracalla cost 70,000,000 *denarii*. Given the numbers of troops (there were probably about 165,000 legionaries, at least as many auxiliaries, plus soldiers on higher rates of pay, and troops based in the city of Rome) this figure seems quite modest and rules out any estimate for the increase under Severus, which is a significant element of the cost of the rise under Caracalla, of over 50 per cent. In any case, the rates of pay after 197 cannot safely be estimated from the currently available evidence.

The main historical argument has centred on rates of pay for auxiliaries. Documents from Egypt, *P. Gen. Lat.* 1 = *Doc. Eser. Rom.* 10 = *CPL* 106 = *ChLA* I 7 = *RMR* 68 and *P. Gen. Lat.* 4 = *RMR* 69 have been central to the argument. Recently, a text from Masada, *P. Yadin* 722, has clarified many of the difficulties. These three texts conform, broadly, to the same pattern. They are accounts of individual soldiers. A certain amount of money is paid into the account and then deductions for camp expenses are made at fixed rates. Several historians have wished to believe that the money paid into the accounts, an amount which in none of the cases corresponds exactly to the attested levels of legionary pay for the date of the document, was the actual and (nearly) full pay of the soldier and that the soldiers attested in *P. Gen. Lat.* 1 were, in fact, auxiliaries. The amounts paid into the accounts were, therefore, good evidence for the rate of auxiliary pay. It seems very likely, however, that the soldiers mentioned in these accounts were legionaries and that the money paid into the accounts was an amount set aside from pay to meet the expenses of the camp. The money paid into the accounts, though obviously reflecting the absolute rates of pay of the soldiers, cannot be related to the level of pay by application of a simple formula. There is, in fact, no direct, good evidence for the rates of pay of auxiliaries.

The documents can, however, be used to estimate the likely level of pay of auxiliaries. Roman legionaries had to meet camp expenses, including such items as food, clothing and equipment, from their pay. It seems very likely that auxiliaries also had to meet these expenses and since the administrative difficulties of imposing differentiated charges on auxiliaries and legionaries would have been enormous, the standard expenses attested in these documents provide us with a minimum level above which the auxiliaries had to be paid. One must also presume that auxiliaries enjoyed a small surplus. The two soldiers whose accounts form part of *P.Gen. Lat.* 1 = *RMR* 68 incurred expenses of 133.875 *denarii* and 143.875 *denarii*, while the soldier of *P. Yadin* 722 spent 50 *denarii* in a third of the year, suggesting annual expenses of 150 *denarii*. Legionary pay in this period was 225 *denarii*. None of the soldiers bought any particularly expensive equipment in the period of the accounts and so a subsistence level of pay would have had to have been a little higher than this figure. If one also makes allowance for auxiliaries profiting from service, it becomes difficult to believe that the auxiliaries received less than 200 *denarii* per year in this period. Since the legionaries were receiving a mere 25 *denarii* more, the neatest and most obvious solution to the problem would be to assume that all infantry received the same level of payment.

The cavalry would need more pay since they had the additional expense of maintaining a horse. In fact, there were at least two basic rates of pay for the cavalry, one for the cavalrymen of the *cohortes equitatae* and another for those in the *alae*. There is very little evidence for cavalry pay and one can only make very limited progress by estimating the annual cost of feeding a horse, probably slightly less than 50 *denarii* per year. A minimum figure for cavalry pay would be about 300 *denarii* per year in the early first century AD, but it is likely that they received considerably more money, especially since Polybius' figure for legionary cavalry pay in the second century BC would suggest an annual rate of pay of 360 *denarii*.

ECONOMIC STATUS

A very large proportion of the pay of legionaries in the first century AD was spent on essentials such as food and clothing. Their disposable income, which is important for assessing the economic status of soldiers, was much less than their pay. In *RMR* 68, one of the soldiers deposited 206 *drachmae* and the other 166 in the course of the year and, if they saved at the same rate throughout their careers, they would have retired with accumulated savings of 4,000–5,000 *drachmae*. In *RMR* 70, a late second-century military account, most soldiers withdrew amounts of 79 *denarii* (316 *drachmae*) from one payment of their salary. There were, however, no deductions for essentials from this account either because deductions were not made at this date or because of a change in accounting procedures. Soldiers had other expenses to meet so we cannot confidently estimate the career savings of the soldiers from these texts. We can, however, use a second-century text, *RMR* 73, which lists the deposits of members of an auxiliary unit. A cavalryman had the very large sum of 1,459 *denarii* (5,836 *drachmae*) on deposit. Other deposits are smaller. In column iii, readable deposits average about 390 *denarii* (1,560 *drachmae*), though the average deposit for all the soldiers in the column may be as much as 622 *denarii* (2,488 *drachmae*). These were substantial amounts of money, about two years' pay for an ordinary legionary, and it is likely that older soldiers will have had substantially more than average on deposit.

There is little evidence for the rewards to soldiers upon retirement, the *praemia militaria*. In AD 5, Augustus fixed the levels at 5,000 *denarii* for praetorians and 3,000 for others.[7] This bonus is about five times the accumulated deposits in the cases above and thirteen times the contemporary salary, though only ten times the post-83 salary. There is no evidence of the payment of this bonus after the Julio-Claudian period and no evidence of the payment of the bonus to auxiliaries, though this is not proof of non-payment.[8]

These figures mean little, however, unless we can provide a context for the income of soldiers. The *Digest* gives three subsistence levels for adults: 21.75 *denarii*, 10.5 *denarii* and 10 *denarii* per month.[9] Martial states that clients eked out a meagre existence in Rome on just over 1.5 *denarii* per day in gifts from a patron. It is probable that the client would not be able to secure the gift every day but the source must be treated with a certain caution.[10] For subsistence, the minimum amount of food was about five *modii* of grain per month. Grain prices varied considerably according to season and the size of harvest but an average Italian rate of one *denarius* per *modius* is reasonable.[11] This would make an income of 5 *denarii* per month the minimum for life. The *Digest* rates are, therefore, extremely low.

Man cannot live on bread alone and substantially more money would be needed to support a reasonable standard of living. Pliny left 1,866,666⅔ *sesterces* (four *sesterces* to the *denarius*) in trust to support 100 freedmen. This is not the kind of sum that is chosen at random and must have been intended to produce a precisely chosen income. The standard return on invested property was 6 per cent.[12] On 6 per cent, the income per year per freedman was HS 1,120 (280 *denarii*). Pliny's estates were probably worth about 5,000,000 *denarii*.[13] If we convert these figures into annual income, we get the figures in Table 6.1.

Table 6.1 Annual rates of income in *denarii*
(late first century – second century AD)

Source	Figures	Annual income
Subsistence (grain price)	5/month	60
Subsistence (*Digest*)	10/month	120
Subsistence (*Digest*)	10.5/month	126
Veterans (retirement bonus)	3,000 capital	180[1]
Subsistence (*Digest*)	20.75/month	249
Freedmen (Pliny's will)	4,666.66 capital	280
Soldiers (pay)	300/year	300
Subsistence (Martial)	1.5/day	450[2]
Pliny (estates)	5,000,000 capital	300,000[3]

1   Assuming a return of 6%.
2   Calculated on the assumption of the client securing the gift on 300 days a year.
3   Assuming a return of 6%.

All the data for Table 6.1 come from Italy and there is a general convergence of the figures for annual income which would suggest that an annual income of about 300 *denarii* was considered a 'living wage' in late first- and early second-century Italy. Italy, as a highly monetarised and developed economy, benefiting from the influx of wealth from the empire, may have had higher prices than elsewhere.

It is probable that the income necessary to reach subsistence levels was lower in Egypt than in Italy. Duncan-Jones suggests that the minimum expenditure on grain to support life at Egyptian prices would be around 13 *drachmae* per month (39 *denarii* per year).[14] Given the mathematical relationship of the costs of living in Italy and Egypt, we might assume that a level for Egypt comparable to the 300 *denarii* level in Italy would be 780 *drachmae* per year. This figure is remarkably similar to Drexhage's estimate of the income needed to support a six-person household in the first century, 753 *drachmae*. Drexhage estimates that, in the second century, the equivalent necessary income would be 1,090 *drachmae*, rising to 1,654 *drachmae* in the third century.[15] Further evidence for average economic status comes from Lewis' collection of evidence concerning compulsory public services, several of which had a minimum *poros*. This was property that could be used as security in case of neglect of duties or would ensure that the liturgist had sufficient income to be able to perform the duties. Some of the *poroi* are very low indeed, 200 *drachmae* being the lowest. Twelve *poroi* were set at 600 *drachmae* or under, seventeen below 1,000 *drachmae*, twenty-four below 3,000 *drachmae* and only six above 3,000 *drachmae*.[16]

Drexhage has collected a series of land prices from the first to the third centuries AD.[17] Prices per *aroura* ranged from 12 *drachmae* to over 1,000 showing that we cannot use a simple average of all prices since we are dealing with essentially different commodities. I have, therefore, grouped the prices into three broad price bands, though these are fairly artificial creations since there was some continuity from the lowest quality to the best quality land. The lowest band includes all prices up to 80 *drachmae* per *aroura*. The middle band includes all prices between 80 and 599 *drachmae*. The third band, mainly encompassing sales of olive, grape or date producing land, includes all prices above 600 *drachmae*. The samples are small but analysis of the median prices in each category suggests that the mean prices given in Table 6.2 are quite accurate.

Several liturgies demand *poroi* of about 600 *drachmae*. P. Petaus 65, of AD 185, is a list of nominees for the office of *praktor argurikon* which has a *poros* of 600 *drachmae*. As the *praktor argurikon* was a tax collector, we would expect that the *poros* would be set at a level to exclude the poorest of the village. A *poros* of 600 *drachmae* represented under three *arourai* of grain land and it is probable that the liturgist would not be able to live off this property alone.[18] Villagers would supplement their

Table 6.2 Average land prices in *drachmae* per *aroura*

Century	Low quality land		Average land		High quality land	
	No. of prices	Average price	No. of prices	Average price	No. of prices	Average price
I	6	19	8	291	4	644
II	11	48	21	254	10	725
III	3	55	9	301	3	1379

income by working on estate land or by renting land but the *praktores argurikon* represent the lowest level of the property-owning class and, in the eyes of the state, respectability.

In the second century, a retirement gratuity of 12,000 *drachmae* would purchase about forty-seven *arourai* of grain land or about seventeen *arourai* of the higher quality land. Even if we assume that the veterans had to spend 2,000–3,000 *drachmae* on other expenses, such as a house, before purchasing land, veterans would have been able to buy about thirty-six *arourai* of grain land. This was a substantial estate in village terms. It would have made the veterans the largest private landowners in the villages of the Fayum without the addition of any property that they had inherited or income saved from pay. The veterans of Karanis did not approach this level of wealth. The prosperous family of Iulii Sabinus and Apollinarius, which was of metropolite origin and which probably had substantial assets before either man served in the army, can only be shown to have had assets of 7¾ *arourai* of which five *arourai* were of olives, and although it will have provided a reasonable income, the capital value of the land was less than half the retirement gratuity. There appears to be only one obvious solution: the retirement gratuity was not paid in th:s period.[19] The relative material prosperity of veterans in the second century resulted either from property which they had inherited or from the profits and savings accumulated during their service. The accumulated deposits in *RMR* 73 would allow a soldier to purchase a substantial area of land on a village scale and this, together with their inherited property, accounts for the comparative material prosperity of veterans.

These figures put the pay of the soldiers into context. Although much of the pay of the soldiers was deducted before the soldiers received their money, an annual income of 1,200 *drachmae* (300 *denarii*), assuming 10 per cent return on invested income, could be derived from investments totalling 12,000 *drachmae*, enough to buy a substantial estate and more than the highest *poroi* needed to perform liturgies.[20] In this context, we can understand why some soldiers had difficulty in securing a place in the legions or other military units and why military service appealed to members of privileged groups in Egyptian society.

CHANGES IN ECONOMIC STATUS

The very gradual inflation of the first three centuries of Roman rule in Egypt provided perhaps the most substantial threat to the economic status of soldiers. Using Drexhage's composite figures for the cost of living in the first three centuries and taking the legionary level of pay after 83 as the first-century level, pay would have had to be increased to about 660 *denarii* by the mid-third century to account for inflation.[21] There would, therefore, probably have been some considerable erosion in status before the Severan pay increase and even Caracalla's increase in pay may not have restored the troops to first-century levels of prosperity. It is only with the supposed doubling of pay under Maximinus Thrax, and we must wonder whether he could have afforded such extravagance, that the soldiers saw a significant increase in their relative incomes, an increase which was eroded by the rapid inflation at the end of the third century.

It is, however, far from clear that the pay of the soldiers in the first century is strictly comparable to pay in the third century. In the first century, there were substantial deductions from the pay of the soldiers to cover the cost of basic supplies. If the state were to provide those supplies without charge or not to increase the cost of those supplies to the soldiers, then the soldiers would, in effect, receive a further increase in pay.

After the first-century texts mentioned above, there is very little evidence for deductions from pay to meet camp expenses. There is, however, equally little evidence to suggest that these goods were being provided without charge. The best evidence for the soldiers receiving their food without charge comes in two passages from Dio, LXXVIII 28 and 34, both dated to 218. Macrinus, in an effort to save money, withdrew certain privileges from the soldiers but was almost immediately forced to restore those privileges, one of which was sustenance, τροφή. This would suggest that by 218 the soldiers were in receipt of free food. By AD 300, the supply of food and other goods to the soldiers without charge on their pay had become so established that although some payments were still made in oil and salt, the *annona*, the equivalent of τροφή, had been converted into a monetary payment.[22] The origins of the *annona militaris* are difficult to ascertain, in part because of a conceptual and terminological difficulty to which we shall turn below. There is no firm date for the establishment of the *annona* system and although there have been various attempts to connect the introduction of the *annona militaris* with Septimius Severus, it is perhaps more likely that the *annona militaris* evolved over the second and third centuries.[23]

A third source of income became increasingly important in the third century, the *donativa*. These were payments made to soldiers to celebrate significant events, such as the accession of a new emperor or the victory of an emperor on campaign. As occasional payments, they performed the very useful functions of establishing links between a new, possibly insecure, emperor and the army and rewarding the army for its loyalty during a difficult period. The payments may well have been flexible, the size of the donative being dependent on the insecurity of the emperor and the state of the treasury. In the first and second centuries, the donatives, although significant as single payments, probably did not form a large part of the soldier's income over his career. In the third century, however, when the political insecurities were such that emperors had regularly to ensure the good will of the soldiers, the donatives were paid annually or even more regularly and were an important part of a soldier's annual income by AD 300.

If our sources are correct in attributing a doubling of military pay to Maximinus, then it was only after this date that pay was restored to and significantly increased above first-century levels. In the second and third centuries, however, the soldiers benefited from certain changes in the way they were rewarded for service. On the one hand, there was an increase in the significance of donatives as part of income. On the other, the move towards providing food and clothing without charge reduced the expenditure of soldiers and increased their disposable income. These changes cannot be dated with confidence but we can perhaps conclude that the early third century was a time of increased prosperity for the ordinary soldier. The rapid inflation of the mid- and late third century eroded the income of the soldiers and it is not clear that the soldiers of Diocletian's army were substantially wealthier than those of the Augustan army three centuries earlier.

SUPPLY SYSTEM

Whether the soldiers paid for the goods or not, the basic needs of the Roman troops were met by the supply services of the army and the demand for supplies for the army placed an additional burden on the Egyptian population. There are a number of texts which are concerned with the supplying of the Roman army but the organisation of the supply services is far from clear. There is no sign of a central office to administer the collection and distribution of supplies to the troops. Supplies appear to have been organised by unit with an officer from the unit approaching local officials to obtain the necessary goods.[24] In many cases, it does not appear that the officers would pay for basic items, such as grain, but the items were not simply requisitioned. The representatives of the community from which the items were obtained were given receipts and, as grain and other comestibles could hardly be returned, we must presume that the receipts could be used either to obtain recompense from another source or, more likely, to reduce the tax the village still had to pay. Obtaining grain direct from neighbouring villages, therefore, avoided the grain being passed to a state granary before being distributed to the troops and was an efficient way of ensuring supply. Almost contemporary with the receipts for grain in which no payment was apparently made, is a receipt from Soknopaiou Nesos in which grain was purchased at the customary, but unstated, price and, in 232, grain was purchased for the soldiers at Alexandria from the village of Alexandru Nesos in the Fayum.[25]

Although military officers were involved in the supply services, other persons of uncertain status and civilians were also involved. *Cibariatores* and *conductores* are the most prominently attested officials who dealt with supply. It is, however, unclear whether these men were soldiers or civilians. A small archive of texts from Mons Claudianus, *O. Claud.* 3–8, relates to the activities of a servant of the *cibariator* Magios. The servant received bread from various men, all of whom had Graeco-Egyptian names. The *cibariatores* in the Pselchis ostraka mainly had Graeco-Egyptian names, though one was called Petronius.[26]

It is certain, however, that the people responsible for transporting supplies to the desert garrisons were Egyptian. Transport was one area in which there was no reluctance to use civilians. Ostraka from Thebes record the arrival of several loads of chaff but there is no mention of payment or of the weight of the chaff and unless we presume that the chaff was bought in loads rather than by more precise measures, the receipt was concerned solely with transportation.[27] Indeed, although the army was quite prepared to buy camels for the use of military units, camels were also requisitioned for temporary transportation duties which, in one case, took the camels as far as Syria, much to the distress of the camels' owner.[28]

There is a similarly varied pattern in the securing of items such as clothing and weapons. In 215, a receipt was given to a *praktor* for the supply of leather for weapons for which a small payment was made.[29] Yet, the shafts of spears obtained from Soknopaiou Nesos in the third century, presumably items of some value, do not appear to have been paid for.[30] Even as late as the early fourth century, however, payments were made for tunics and cloaks purchased from Karanis, though wood was provided free of charge.[31] It was not just the army of Egypt which commissioned the production of goods in the province. In AD 128, the army of Judaea placed an order for cloth in Soknopaiou Nesos.[32] Ten years later, the weavers of Philadelphia had to provide cloaks for the army in Cappadocia.[33] The placing of these orders in other provinces must be a result of problems in the provinces in which the armies were stationed.[34] Orders placed with villages appear to have been quite small and a text from Oxyrhynchus, *P.Oxy.* XII 1448 of AD 318, shows that the order was placed with the nome authorities and subsequently divided amongst the various communities of the nome.

Prices were sometimes paid for goods obtained but the prices were set by the purchaser and may have borne little relation to the market price. At Dura-Europos in Syria, in AD 208 and 251, horses attached to the auxiliary unit were valued at the surprisingly low and uniform price of 125 *denarii* irrespective of the standard, health or age of the horse and a third-century text from Oxyrhynchus records the complaints of weavers who were required to produce goods for the army at an extremely low price, even though the city council had more than doubled the remuneration from city funds.[35] It would appear that the supply services of the army made no allowance for inflation and so any compensation paid to the provincials would, by the third century, not have reflected the market price of those goods, even if prices had done so in the first century. Material, though formally purchased, was actually requisitioned.

It is remarkably difficult to distinguish any trends in the supply of the army. There was no general shift from acquiring supplies by compulsory purchase to one in which supplies were merely requisitioned or obtained through taxation. Several different procedures appear to have operated concurrently and several different officials were involved in securing supplies. It may be that the army also contracted the supply of some goods to Egyptians and civilians were used to transport goods, either of their own free will or under some compulsion. There appears to be an increase in services and goods demanded from the population without recompense in the third century but since the compensation for these goods may well have been at first-century rates, the major problem was not whether the army in the third century paid for the goods but whether the demands on the people were equitably distributed and there is reason to believe that this was the case.

ECONOMIC IMPACT OF THE ARMY

Although it is traditional to estimate the Egyptian population at 8,000,000–10,000,000 in the Roman period, Rathbone has shown that this estimate is far too high and suggests a maximum population of about 5,000,000.[36] Proportionately, the Roman army was tiny. Although troops were paid well and it is possible that average incomes in Egypt were very low, the soldiers did not possess the same levels of wealth as the aristocrats of the Mediterranean. Pliny's income was probably a thousand times greater than the income of a soldier. In terms of the whole province, the soldiers were neither numerous enough nor wealthy enough to have any considerable impact on its economic structure.

It is also unlikely that the province would have been bankrupted by supporting the needs of the army. The total annual tax revenues for the province have been estimated by Carrié at 1,220,000,000 *drachmae* in the first century AD and it seems unlikely that the total cost in wages for the army of that period could have surpassed 25,200,000 *drachmae* per year, about 2 per cent of total tax revenues.[37] The introduction of the *annona militaris* cannot have changed the situation greatly. There has been considerable dispute as to the nature of the *annona militaris* and the date and significance of its introduction. Cerati's very long analysis of the tax pointed out the extreme difficulties of distinguishing between the collection of taxes for the troops and for the supply of cities, prompting van Berchem to reply asserting the existence of the *annona*.[38] By the fourth century, we see the emergence of two distinct military taxes, the *vestris militaris* and the *aurum tirocinum*. One would assume that these taxes were originally meant to supply the army with its clothing and to provide allowances for new recruits but it is far from clear, in the case of the latter tax, that the money went to recruits. There does appear to have been a gradual shift in the fourth century to taxation in kind and it is likely that many goods were intended for immediate use by the army. It is not, however, apparent that there was a considerable increase in the burden of taxation as a direct result of the demands of the army.[39]

The size of the army in comparison with the size of the province was such that it seems very unlikely that the support of the army could have posed significant economic problems for the Egyptian population, provided that the demands of the army were evenly distributed. There remains, however, some doubt about this. If the army requisitioned material which was later accounted for as part of the tax due on the community, then there should have been no problem for the community. It is, however, apparent that this was not always the case and that the army simply requisitioned goods and men, or at least their labour, when there was a need. The army had considerable powers to requisition, partly by the force of law, but partly because armies sometimes have needs that would override legal niceties. Such emergency demands may not have been evenly distributed. Indeed, it is rather difficult to see how an army perhaps going on campaign or passing through an area could have distributed the burden equitably. It is also likely that these irregular demands were resented by the populations forced to provide goods and services. We must, however, return to the main issue: would this have had a deleterious effect on the economy of those areas which suffered these demands? Abuses of powers of requisition by officials were no doubt commonplace but it is very difficult to believe that these abuses would be on such a scale as to cause economic problems for whole communities, unless the community was particularly prone to visits from important officials, and the administration appears to have made some effort to spread the burden of supplying the army in an equitable manner.[40] There will have been individual complaints, no doubt justified, but one is forced to conclude that the supply of the army was not an economically damaging burden in the first three centuries of Roman rule. By the fourth century, the bureaucratic organisation of the supply of the army was such that the burden would have been spread across the majority of the population.

Similar questions must be asked about the economic benefits brought by the army. Potentially, the soldiers provided a significant concentration of wealth which could be exploited by traders and the stationing of a military unit in an area may well have provided a stimulus to the local market. We have, however, seen that the army was not concentrated in camps but dispersed so that only a relatively small proportion of the troops was in camp at any one time. During the first century, the soldiers received only a small proportion of their pay, the rest being deposited to cover the expenses of the soldiers. We have also seen that the troops frequently wrote home for fairly basic goods, such as paper and food stuffs, not provided by the army's supply services. This, of course, may in part be a result of the number of ostraka which have been found in the Eastern Desert where, we would presume, the soldiers were fairly thinly spread and there were few centres of population to provide additional means of support for the traders. Letters from places other than the Desert requesting or acknowledging receipt of goods from home may partly be a result of temporary penury or an emotional need to maintain connections with an original community. In spite of these considerations, it seems that the soldiers were frequently unable to purchase fairly basic goods or found it more convenient to obtain those goods from their home communities rather than purchase them where they were stationed. The army did not significantly alter local trade patterns to attract traders to the immediate environs of the camp. Egypt was relatively highly urbanised for an ancient state and the economy was highly monetarised. The economy was already sophisticated and there were established markets in the towns. Also, the largest single concentration of troops was just outside the largest urban community in the province, Alexandria. It is highly unlikely that the presence of perhaps 5,000 well-paid troops would have altered the market centres of an established settlement of perhaps 300,000 people.

Study of the economic impact of the army on the province as a whole has produced a whole string of negative conclusions. This does not mean, however, that our investigation has produced no significant results. The army in the West has been portrayed by scholars as the economic driving force in many of the clear and impressive changes in the economy of those provinces. From the monetarisation of the economy to the urbanisation of the West, the army is seen as having a crucial role. Our investigation has shown that this was not the case in Egypt. The army was undoubtedly a major item of government expenditure but the costs of the army were insignificant in comparison with the profits made from the province in taxation. If we accept Carrié's estimate of the taxation exacted from Egypt, then Egypt alone will have provided enough revenue to pay for the whole of the imperial army. Even when there were two legions in Egypt, expenditure on the army or by the army could only have had a marginal effect on the economy of the province. We must disagree, therefore, with both the optimists who would portray the army as a centre of expenditure, encouraging growth in local economies, and the pessimists who view the army as a predatory presence, draining the economies of the provinces. In the comparatively developed economies of the East, it would be very difficult to attribute any economic change in this period to the military. The army could not have transformed the economic structure of the province.

CONCLUSIONS

I have not been able to establish rates of pay for all units at all periods but I have suggested that the auxiliaries cannot have been paid a great deal less than the legionaries and there is a possibility that auxiliary and legionary pay rates were the same. In addition, we have been able to escape from the rather academic arguments as to the precise rates of pay by setting the known figures in context. This has provided us with two rather startling discoveries. First, the retirement bonus created by Augustus does not appear to have been paid in the second century AD.[41] The failure of our sources to note such a seemingly important change in the rewards of military service is remarkable, perhaps even improbable. One would have to envisage such a change taking place either at a time of tremendous strain on the treasury or under an emperor unpopular with our sources. If Domitian, for instance, had stopped payment of the retirement gratuity to provide the treasury with some compensation for the increased expenditure due to the rise in pay, our sources may have ignored this sensible measure in order not to deflect attention from a condemnation of the financial excesses and dangerous generosity towards the soldiers of the profligate and anti-senatorial emperor. One can, however, only speculate as to the occasion for the abandonment of the retirement gratuity.

The second and more important conclusion is that the soldiers were well paid for their military service. Comparable Italian figures for annual income suggest that the soldiers would have enjoyed a reasonable standard of living, neither luxurious nor penurious, in Italy. Prices appear to have been considerably lower in Egypt and soldiers stationed in Egypt enjoyed a high level of remuneration. For most of the period, there can be no doubt that service in the army was economically attractive, offering a comparatively high standard of living even for the ordinary soldier. Soldiers were able to accumulate large sums of money as savings and, on retirement, these sums were sufficient to assure the veterans a certain measure of prosperity, explaining the relatively high economic status of veterans and their families in the Fayum villages. The higher remuneration granted to officers may well have made military service appealing to recruits from higher social status groups and if a soldier were to progress to centurial or similar office, then the rewards would have made him wealthy, since a centurion received perhaps as much as five times legionary salary.[42] The prosperity of the soldiers was only comparative. In comparison with the imperial elite, the soldiers were poor. In village terms, however, the financial rewards of service enabled the army to pick its own recruits and ensured that there was no necessity for conscription.

The wealth of the veterans remained, however, on a village scale. There were equally rich villagers from non-veteran families and their economic status was not sufficient to differentiate the veterans economically from other groups within the village. The veterans could afford more luxuries than average but their wealth was not such that it enabled them to introduce new cultural and economic values into the villages. They were dependent on the same sources of local supply for their basic goods. As we shall see in the next chapter, even in a relatively small community such as Karanis, the veterans did not bring with them enough wealth to transform the village and thus impose new cultural values on the population. To a large extent, veterans, as all our other evidence has shown, though they might retain certain elements of any different life-style they had enjoyed while in the army, would be forced, on retirement, to integrate with the economically and numerically dominant element of the population.

7

KARANIS
A village in Egypt

INTRODUCTION

A modern traveller, journeying from Cairo to the Fayum is treated to
remarkable contrasts. The bus leaves the metropolis of Cairo and, heading
out through Giza, enters the desert. The grey concrete of the city is
replaced by the brown sand of the desert. Then, after many miles of
desolation, broken by ridges of hills and the occasional police outpost,
the bus turns a corner, descends what only seems a few feet, and enters
the Fayum. The brown of the desert is replaced by the green of intensive agricultural exploitation. The change dramatically illustrates the
fertility of the waters of the Nile since, within a few paces, one moves
from desert to marginal land to intensively farmed, irrigated agricultural
land, a journey accomplished by bus in a matter of seconds. The Fayum
is the garden of Egypt, a predominantly rural landscape and, after the
bustle and dust of Cairo, the main town, Medinet el Fayum, has a relaxed
air. This is not a place which attracts many tourists and it has few sites
to rival those of Upper Egypt but, as the bus turns to descend into the
Fayum, at the very moment of transformation, it passes the site of Kom
Aushim, the ancient town of Karanis.

The site was visited by Grenfell and Hogarth in 1895–6 in their search
for papyrus but, after preliminary investigations, they decided that native
diggers had excavated all that was useful.[1] In 1928, a team from the
University of Michigan started work on the site. They were rewarded
by the discovery of very large numbers of papyri relating to the Roman
town. Karanis is one of the few Egyptian sites which has both produced
substantial papyrological remains and been subject to scientific archaeological excavation. The resulting publications allow us to reconstruct the
workings of the Roman town in some detail.[2] The papyrological evidence
attests large numbers of Roman veterans settled at Karanis and we are
able, therefore, to examine the lives of veterans in the context of a village
which is uniquely well documented.

There are various possible models for the interaction of representatives
of an imperial power and the conquered peoples. The veterans could

117

have formed an elite, controlling the politics and economic life of Karanis. They might have formed a closed group, a caste within the village, separate from mainstream village life, refusing to integrate and perhaps even hostile to the rest of the community. In such a case, they could either have been more prosperous than their neighbours without actually forming an elite, or have enjoyed similar levels of prosperity. Or, the veterans could have integrated with their neighbours, becoming culturally and economically similar. These models, applied on an empire-wide scale, obviously present very different views of Roman imperialism. Did the Romans impose an elite on the natives, did they form a distinct ethnic group or did they merge with the native population with all that that implies for the political outlook of the various groups? Before, however, we can attempt to formulate answers to these questions, we must examine the material from Karanis in some detail to establish an understanding of the community into which these veterans came and, in the next few pages, we shall reconstruct, as far as is possible, the economy, the culture and the population of this village. Only when this context is established can we attempt to understand the role of the veteran community within the village.

THE VILLAGE

Karanis was situated on the north-eastern border of the Fayum, near the edge of the cultivated zone. This was more extensive than it is today, but during the gradual retraction of the damp, fertile area, the village and the fields on which the village was dependent were desiccated, causing the desertion of the site and allowing the preservation of papyri. Similar desiccation occurred at the nearby villages of Soknopaiou Nesos, Bakchias and Philadelphia. The former, the most northerly of the towns and geographically separated from the rest of the Fayum by Lake Moeris, was the first to dry out. Although Soknopaiou Nesos was on the north shore of the lake, the waters for irrigation came from the north-east of the village in a long canal, which also supplied many of the villages of the northern Fayum, making Soknopaiou Nesos the most vulnerable of the villages to problems in the canal system.[3] The village was in terminal decline by the early third century and a similar fate befell Karanis, Bakchias, and Philadelphia in subsequent centuries.

Karanis remained untouched until the late nineteenth century when illicit excavation began to produce large numbers of papyri which arrived on the Cairo antiquities' market. By the time the University of Michigan commenced excavations on the site, the site was being exploited by an Italian company which dug up and sold the ancient rubbish, known as *sebakh*, as fertiliser. The Egyptian government had to balance the commercial needs of agriculture and those of the archaeologists with the result

118

that the archaeologists were required to provide the fertiliser company with enough *sebakh* to keep the railway, which had been built to remove the *sebakh* from the site, running. The remains of the site were dug extensively between 1928 and 1935 in an early example of rescue archaeology. It is not surprising, therefore, that at times the excavation fell below modern scientific excavation standards but, given the problems of the site, the achievement of the excavators was notable.

According to the archaeological reports, the village spread over a distance of approximately 1,050 m × 750 m. The first traces at the South Temple point to a first-century BC origin. The village spread from the south during the late Ptolemaic period but remained small until the Roman period when the North Temple was erected and the South rebuilt.[4] The golden age of expansion seems to have been from the mid-first until the mid-second century AD. By the end of this period, corresponding to period C in the archaeological reports, the village had reached its full extent. Towards the end of the period, the archaeologists detected signs of extensive disturbance. The rebuilding that had been going on in late C appeared slowly to cease. There was a distinct recession *c.* AD 160. The town appeared to revive in the first half of the third century but, in the second half, it went into terminal decline. By the end of the century, many houses had fallen down and by the fourth century, even the two great temples may have disappeared from view.[5]

There are, however, problems with this relatively clear picture of the history of the site. According to the archaeological reports, the major period of occupation was between the first century BC and the end of the third century AD. There are, however, substantial problems in accepting this chronological framework and the attributions of buildings and objects to the archaeological periods proposed in the reports. The stratigraphy of the site is extremely complicated. The depredations of the *sebakhin* confused the stratigraphy but the practice of building houses on the ruins of other houses and perhaps using the remains of the older housing as basements means that even in undisturbed areas items could have slipped into older layers of the site.[6] Grande has pointed out that the date the lamps found on the site would be given on stylistic grounds differs greatly from the date established from the stratigraphy.[7] In addition, the coins from the site range in date from the third century BC to the seventh century AD and there are large numbers of coins from the fourth and fifth centuries AD.[8] Nearly all the glass found on the site is from the third century or later.[9] The first papyrological mention of a community at Karanis is an unpublished complaint from a *basilikos georgos* (royal farmer) of the village dated to 250–230 BC.[10] Instead of a main period of occupation from *c.* 100 BC to *c.* AD 300, we must suppose substantial occupation from *c.* 270 BC to *c.* AD 500. The chronological framework of the reports is too narrow. We must, therefore, consider the

119

village broadly within its material culture and not date specific remains too rigidly.

The centre of the site suffered most from the damage caused by the search for fertiliser and this is where we would expect to find any public buildings, though there were few attested in the papyrological record. The only public buildings identified in the archaeological record are the two temples that today still stand out dramatically above the sand. The South Temple was the first to be built. The excavators recognised traces of a mud brick building of no great size of the first century BC on the site of the later Roman temple.[11] This temple was rebuilt in stone in the early Roman period. Excluding the *temenos* wall the complex was 60 m × 16 m and the wall enclosed an area of around 5,340 m^2. The plan and the arrangement of the temple were Egyptian with its gateway, smaller pylon, and court-yard before reaching the main temple. The central pylon was probably 4.5 m high. There is evidence for the repair and improvement of the temple in 155/4 BC, 95 BC, AD 61, 73, and 190.[12] The history of the temple mirrors that of the site as a whole and, according to the archaeological reports, decay had set in by the late third century.[13] The temple was dedicated to Pnepheros and Petesouchos, the local crocodile gods.

The North Temple was much smaller than the South being only 32.7 m × 10.5 m, about a third of the size of the larger complex. The pylon was 0.5 m smaller than the South Temple and it had nothing like the same intricacy of approach as the larger complex. The ground plan of the North Temple struck the excavators as being typically Egyptian but the evidence for the god, or gods, worshipped in the complex is nowhere near as clear as for the South.[14] An altar to Zeus Ammon Serapis Helios was found on the site together with some physical remains which suggest crocodile worship and the report concludes 'it is . . . quite possible that this temple was devoted to the cult of Souchos in the form Soknopaios combined with that of Zeus Ammon Serapis Helios and possibly that of Isis.'[15] The temple was erected at about the time the South Temple was rebuilt in stone, at the beginning of the first century AD, and continued in use until the mid- to late third century.

There are no other buildings which were certainly public. House C178 may have been a Mithraeum and, more spectacularly, recent excavations by the French Institute have uncovered a bath complex towards the south of the town, in an area untouched by the Michigan excavations. It is impossible to say whether the baths were private or not and the exca-vators have not dated the complex. In any event, the baths, though intri-cate, were quite small.[16] There were other buildings which have yet to be identified, such as a record office (*grapheion*). There may have been other offices which were used by the officials of the village but since the administration of the village was amateur, officials may have used their own homes, open areas, or the *grapheion* to conduct their business.[17]

The expansion of the village seems to have been unplanned. There was little regularity in the topography.

> Topographically, Karanis consisted of a series of *insulae*, or blocks, of houses along and between several main thoroughfares that ran from north to south. . . . There were no through streets from east to west in Karanis. In order to traverse the town from east to west it was necessary to follow a zig-zag course along several inter-connected short streets.[18]

This is in marked contrast to the village of Philadelphia which had a regular town plan, showing the influence of Ptolemaic town planning.[19]

The population of the village can be estimated from the tax rolls published in *P.Mich.* IV, dating to 171–4, and a summary of poll tax receipts for the village, *P.Ryl.* IV 594, dating to 145–6. There are disputes as to the correct method of calculating the overall population from the figures given in these accounts but I estimate that the population in 145–6 was about 3,316 and in 171–4 the population was about 1,907 to 2,135. About 14 per cent of this population were Roman.[20]

The houses of the village vary considerably in architectural style and in size. Even the largest houses, however, were small. The mean area of the ground plan of 125 houses at Karanis is less than 70 m^2 and over 70 per cent of houses had areas of less than 100 m^2. The smallness of the ground plans is slightly misleading since many of the houses were multi-storey and most had access to the roof which, for climatic reasons, was often used as a sleeping area. All but the smallest houses had internal divisions but it is not possible to attribute different functions to the different rooms. The houses do not appear to have had a main communal room, such as an *atrium* or similar structure, and there is no sign of any room suitable for a large gathering of people. The chief communal area was probably outside the house proper in the *aule*. All houses had an *aule* or courtyard and it was here that many of the main activities of the house took place. There were stoves and bread ovens and there is evidence of troughs and pens. Many courtyards had mud floors. The *aule* was a work area within the house-complex. Courtyards were extensions of houses and were privately owned. Apart from whether an *aule* was included and the number of floors, few details are given in house sale documents. Houses are not identified by architectural features but by the owners of neighbouring plots. In spite of the variations in size and in design, the dominant impression is one of uniformity. In plan, the houses show variety, but the plans do not suggest that the houses were built for a community with wide cultural or social divisions.[21]

The archaeological and papyrological data for housing in the village leaves the distinct impression that Karanis was a poor community and although some villagers were more wealthy than others, as can be seen in internal decoration and as might have been expressed in greater living area per person, there was only limited social differentiation between villagers.

Economically, the village seems to have been almost entirely agricultural. There is no evidence of large scale industry or of a large number of specialist traders in the village. Indeed, the archaeological evidence suggests that trade was limited to the immediate region.[22] The texts from the site abound with references to olive production and two olive presses have been found, but the number of granaries discovered suggests that the main crop produced in the fields of the village was grain.[23] The bone report shows the presence of pig, mule or ass, antelope, cow, dog, crocodile, and horse, with pig being the most commonly attested. It is unlikely that antelope was eaten in large numbers since the volume of remains is small and it is probable that hunting did not play a large part in the daily life or diet of the Karanis peasant. Dovecotes may have provided some additional meat as well as fertiliser. There is no mention of fish in the documentary evidence. Fundamentally, the economy was agrarian and not pastoral and the general diet of grain was occasionally supplemented by meat, mostly pork.[24]

When looking at the ownership of land, it is striking that the vast majority of transactions for the late first and second centuries concerned very small parcels of land. *BGU* I 227 records the rental of one *aroura* (1 *aroura* = 0.27 hectares) of grain land by the veteran C. Valerius. Longina Sempronia rented out five *arourai* of grain land to Pnepheros, son of Petais.[25] *BGU* XIII 2345 records the rental of four *arourai* of grain land belonging to the children of Sextus Priscus. In addition to these small holdings, there were several *ousiai*, or large estates, some of which appear in a late second-century land register, *P. Mich.* VI 372, showing that six estates mentioned controlled 1,847 *arourai* of land. To these six estates of Maecenas, Anthus, Pallas, Gallia Pollia, Germanicus and Kamelius could be added the estates of Antonia (*BGU* XV 2554), Doryphorus (*P. Oslo.* II 21) and Livia (*P. Mich.* IX 560). Bagnall estimates that there were twelve estates around Karanis, probably occupying around 3,700 *arourai* of land. He calculates from the total amount of grain collected on other types of land in *P. Mich.* VI 372 the amount of land in other categories, both public and private land, to be 7,855 *arourai* giving a total of about 11,600 *arourai* of which the villagers owned probably between 3,000 and 4,500 *arourai*.[26] The villagers, therefore, owned only about one-third of the land of the village and the average holding per poll tax payer was probably 3 to 4.5 *arourai* before the fall in population and 5–8 *arourai* after the fall.[27] This was a very small amount of land. The land owned by external agents had, however, to be farmed and, since there was no labour force of slaves, the land was leased to villagers. To farm this land, the villagers organised themselves, or were organised, into numbered associations called klerouchies, the highest number known being 94.[28]

Although a much larger percentage of the produce of this land was consumed outside the village in taxes or rents, this land made a major contribution to the village's food supply. Two summaries of land registers of the early fourth century are preserved amongst the papers of Aurelius Isidorus. The grain land under cultivation at Karanis had declined by this period to about 4,200 *arourai* of which about 2,210 *arourai* was private land, the rest being state owned.[29]

Geremek listed the larger owners of private land within the village. Her figures show that in the second century few land holders had more than 10 *arourai* and the largest attested holding was 15 *arourai*.[30] Compared with the neighbouring village of Philadelphia in AD 216, these estates seem very small since there the average holding, based on those who actually held land, not on total population, was 13–14.5 *arourai* of grain land.[31] We also have series of figures for land holding in Karanis in the early fourth century which show that there was a far higher level of concentration of land holdings with villagers controlling estates of over 100 *arourai*, though the quality of that land is extremely suspect.[32] There was clearly a trend towards the concentration of land but, in the second century, land was fairly evenly distributed amongst a large proportion of the villagers.

We can, therefore, establish a context for our study of the veteran community of the village. Economically, the village was fairly poor and mainly dependent upon the grain harvest, though some olives were grown. There is little sign of evidence of any great social or economic stratification. Culturally, the village seems to have been more closely associated with the Delta than with Upper Egypt. The material remains suggest a Hellenised Egyptian village. Nothing suggests that the village was exceptional or different from others in the Fayum.

VETERANS

Approximately 14 per cent of the population of Karanis in the tax lists of 171–4 had Roman names but not all were Roman veterans. The children of veterans generally enjoyed Roman citizenship and it is possible that citizenship could be passed down to following generations if the children of veterans married other Romans. Thus, only a relatively small proportion of those with Roman names may have been veterans. It is, however, likely that all or nearly all the Roman citizens in Karanis owed their original grant of citizenship or their presence in Egypt to military service.

The actual veteran element of the population is impossible to quantify. The tax lists which allow the Roman element to be quantified do not reliably mention veteran status and the use of the designation 'veteran' by the men themselves was decidedly irregular. It is evident, however, that the veterans were a significant minority of the population and Table 7.1

Table 7.1 Military personnel of Karanis

Name	Unit or Status	Date	Reference
Amatius Priscus	Veteran	c.150	P. Kar. Goodsp. 29.
M. Anthestius Gemellus	III Itur.	90	P. Mich. IX 568–9.
M. Anthestius Gemellus	Veteran	172/3	SB V 7558.
Antonius Tiberianus	Veteran	168	P. Lond. II, p. 212, 470 & P. Kar. Goodsp. 29.
Ammonianus	Veteran	277	O. Mich. 989.
Apollonius	Veteran	300–5	P. Cair. Isid. 6.
Apollonius, son of Apollonius	Ulp. Afrorum	II?	BGU I 241
Asklepiades	Veteran	276	P. Cair. Isid. 31.
Aurelius Ammonianus, son of Theoninus	Veteran	302	P. Mich. XII 636.
Aurelius Aphrodisius	Soldier	280/1	P. Cair. Isid. 110.
M. Aurelius Iulius Ptolemaios	vet. Gall.	247	BGU II 614
Aurelius Nilos	Veteran	309	P. Cair. Isid. 91.
Cassianus Gemellus	Veteran	II	P. Wisc. II 71
Castor	Cavalryman	172/3	P. Mich. IV 224, 4832.
Chairemon	Veteran	297	O. Mich. 904.
Claudius Terentianus	Vet. III Cyr.	II	See pp. 135–7.
Claudius Tiberianus	Legionary	I/II	See pp. 135–7.
Deios	Veteran	III/IV	P. Mich. VI 376.
Dioskoros	Veteran	III/IV	O. Mich. 939.
C. Domitius Clemens	Veteran	131	CPL 220.
C. Fabullius Macer	Vet. of fleet	166	P. Lond. II 229 & BGU I 372.
Herakleidion	Veteran	295	O. Mich. 895.
Herakles	Veteran	311	P. Cair. Isid. 10.
Horis son of Horion	Veteran	173/4	P. Mich. IV 225, 2091.
Isidoros	Veteran	173/4	P. Mich. IV 224, 4046.
Ision	Veteran	173/4	P. Mich. IV 224, 6252.
Iulius Agrippianus	Apriana	c. 120	BGU I 69
C. Iulius Agrippianus	Leg. II Tr.	147–8	BGU XI 2012–13
C. Iulius Apollinarius	Leg.	II	See pp. 134–5.
C. Iulius Apollinarius	I Apamenor	144	BGU III 729; 888
Iulius Apollinarius	Veteran	II/III	BGU I 168.
Iulius Clemens	Cent. Leg. XXII	117–38	P. Mich. VIII 483–4.
C. Iulius Gemellus	Veteran	134	P. Mich. VI 427.
Iulius Gemellus	Veteran	189–94	BGU I 326.
C. Iulius Nepotianus	Veteran	176–9	P. Mich. IX 535.
C. Iulius Niger	Vet. vet. Gall.	154	See pp. 129–32.
C. Iulius Sabinus	Leg. III Cyr.	I/II	See pp. 134–5.
C. Iulius Saturninus	Veteran	148	BGU I 300.
C. Iulius Serenus	Vet. vet. Gall.	214/15	P. Hamb. I 39f.
Iulius Terentianus	Soldier	99	P. Mich. VIII 464.
Longinus	Soldier	169–77	P. Lond. II, p. 172, 198
C. Longinus Apollinarius	Veteran	176	BGU I 327.

Name	Unit or Status	Date	Reference
C. Longinus Apollinarius	Veteran	189	*P. Mich.* VI 370.
C. Longinus Aquila	Veteran	189	*BGU* I 71.
C. Longinus Castor	Vet. of fleet	176	*BGU* I 326.
Longinus Clemens	Veteran	II	*P. Mich.* VIII 489
C. Longinus Priscus	Veteran	133	*BGU* II 581.
L. Octavius Longus	Veteran	133	*BGU* II 581.
P. Olius Maximus	Veteran	151	*P. Oxf.* 9.
C. Petronius	Legionary?	29	*P. Oslo.* I 33.
Sarapion, son of Sempronius	Veteran	III	*O. Mich.* 832.
M. Sempronius Clemens	Veteran	148	*BGU* I 300.
M. Sempronius Gemellus	Leg. III *Cyr.*	95	*P. Lond.* II, p. 203, 142.
Sempronius Hermeinus	*Thrac. Maur.*	175	*BGU* II 447.
C. Sempronius Priscus	Legionary	81–96	*P. Mich.* IX 554.
M. Sempronius Sabinus	Vet. *Apriana*	139–57	*BGU* II 645.
M. Sempronius Serenus	Veteran	152/3	*BGU* II 448/I 69.
Serenus	Veteran	296	*O. Mich.* 1029.
Timotheus	Veteran	300–5	*P. Cair. Isid.* 6.
Tius	Veteran	171/2	*P. Mich.* IV 223, 1542.
Valerius Aphrodisus	Coh. eq.	175	*BGU* II 447.
Valerius Apollinarius	Veteran	119	*BGU* XI 2070, I 69/II 448.
M. Valerius Chairemonianus	Veteran	148	*BGU* I 300.
Valerius Clemens	II. *Itur.*	177–88	*SB* IV 7362.
C. Valerius Gemellus	Fleet	II	*P. Mich.* VII 442.
Valerius Gemellus	Soldier	II	*P. Mich.* VIII 502.
C. Valerius Longus	Legionary	103	*P. Mich.* IX 551.
Valerius Paulinus	Veteran	136	*SB* VI 9636.
L. Valerius Serenus	Leg. II *Tr.*	III	*SB* III 6272/3.
L. Vespasianus Gemellus	Veteran	150	*P. Athen.* 27
L. Vibius Crispus	Legionary	81–96	*P. Mich.* IX 554

lists all veterans or soldiers attested in a civilian capacity at Karanis. It is evident that a considerable number of Roman men attested in the village might have been veterans, but only cases about which there can be no reasonable doubt are included here. The table is not intended as a prosopography and so a minimum number of references is cited.

Although these men identified themselves, or were identified, as soldiers or veterans, they did not, in the majority of cases, identify the units to which they had belonged. The units whose veterans and soldiers are attested are the legions II *Traiana*, III *Cyrenaica* and XXII *Deiotariana*, the *alae Thracum Mauretana, veterana Gallica* and *Apriana*, the cohorts II and III *Ituraeorum, Apamenorum* and *Ulpia Afrorum*, and the fleet. Eleven different units are attested in nineteen attestations of units. These statistics lead one to believe that if we had more attestations of units, we

125

would find that the veterans of Karanis had served in most of the military units stationed in Egypt.

The soldiers and veterans first appear in numbers towards the end of the first century AD, at exactly the same period as the papyrological record for the village suddenly improves. There are, however, substantial numbers of ostraka from the early first century AD and these do not attest a significant veteran presence in the village. Similarly, there are comparatively few veterans attested after the early third century. There are a number of veterans attested on ostraka and papyri when the evidence dramatically improves in the very late third and early fourth centuries, but these men formed only a small proportion of the total population. The golden age of Karanis as a site for veteran settlement was the period from the late first to early third century AD. The military connection with Karanis was maintained for about 120 years or four to five generations of soldiers.

VETERANS' FAMILIES: CASE STUDIES

The papyri have not, in general, been preserved in archives and the vast majority of people mentioned in the records are only mentioned once. As we have already noted, however, the papyrological record tends to chronicle the lives of the more economically prosperous and officially active and so certain names recur in the record allowing the researcher to hypothesise a connection between persons with the same name. By collecting the documents in which this character appears, we can begin to reconstruct certain elements of his or her life. By adding to the dossier, we not only gain the information from each document but we add to the sum of our understanding by relating the information from one document to another.

There are, however, certain difficulties with this dossier-building. There were probably at no time during the second century more than 525 Romans in Karanis, of whom about half were women. If we come across a Iulius Saturninus at the beginning of the second century, another Iulius Saturninus in the middle of the century and a third towards the end, it might be assumed that all three were related. The two elements of the name are, however, amongst the most popular in Roman Egypt and although it would certainly not be surprising if the Iulii Saturnini were connected, such a connection cannot be demonstrated.

Minucii

I have found twenty-three references to Minucii, with ten different spellings, from the whole of Egypt. Three documents which can be related to a single family at Karanis are discussed below but there were also other Minucii active in the region. In 130, Minucius Valerianus was in Karanis and a Minucius farmed private land at Karanis in the late second or early third centuries.[33] L. Minucius Pudens was active at Soknopaiou Nesos between 125 and 129 and a Minucius appears on a tax list from Philadelphia in the second century.[34] We cannot, however, simply assume that these Minucii were related to our veteran family. Two prefects of Egypt were called Minucius, Sanctus (AD 177–80) and Italus (AD 101–3). The brother of Italus was prefect of the *cohors* III *Ituraeorum* in 103, Minucius Corellianus was *epistrategos* in the Hermopolite nome in 145–6, and, in the first century, Minucius Celer was *nomarch* of the Arsinoite.[35] Minucius was a name which would be familiar to ordinary Egyptians in the second century and it is perfectly possible that an Egyptian, searching for a new name, would have lighted on Minucius. The number of Minucii in the Fayum may not, then, be a result of the grant of citizenship to, or the settlement of, a single forebear but of several different settlements or grants of citizenship. The stock of names was not great and repetition must have been common. In the third century, most Romano-Egyptians had the *gentilicium* Aurelius and although there was a fairly large number of Egyptian names in popular usage in the Graeco-Roman period, certain communities, such as Soknopaiou Nesos, limited themselves to a very small number of theo-phoric names so that many members of the community must have carried the same name. We must be aware, therefore, that it was common for the same name to recur even in a comparatively small community without there necessarily being any relationship between the persons bearing that name. The situation is further complicated by families which do not seem to follow normal Roman practice such as the family of Iulius Niger where the *gentilicium*, Iulius, was not preserved through the gener-ations. We must, therefore, exercise a certain amount of caution in our investigations.

The friends of C. Longinus Castor

Tracing connections from a single text can produce interesting, if some-times bewildering patterns. Let us take the text of the will of C. Longinus Castor, veteran of the fleet of Misenum. Although the document is not completely preserved, the main terms of the will may be deduced. Most of his property was left to Marcella and Cleopatra, two freedwomen. There were also substantial legacies left to Serapia, daughter of his freed-woman and to his relative Iulius Serenus. It is not possible to reconstruct the size of the estate but as the legacy in favour of Serapia consisted of five *arourai* of arable land, which might suggest that the estate left to the two freedwomen was larger than this, we may confidently place Castor among the richer people of the village. The will was written in 189.[36]

The only other document in which Castor appears is a complaint of 176 against C. Fabullius Macer, veteran of the fleet, who had failed to pay a legacy due to Castor from the will of Aetius Fronto.[37] The scribe of this document was C. Longinus Apollinarius, veteran. Apollinarius appears in the Karanis tax registers and was married to Longina Thermutharion, daughter of C. Lucius Priscus.[38] Several Romans appear in the will either as witnesses or as legal advisers: Iulius Petronianus, C. Iulius Saturninus, M. Sempronius Heraclianus, C. Iulius Aquila (Akulas in the text), Iulius Volusius, M. Anthestius Petronianus, Longinus Aquila, Iulius Gemellus (veteran), Iulius Philoxenus, C. Lucretius Saturninus and C. Lucius Geminianus. The names of various of these Romans reappear in other documents. In 170, C. Lucius Geminianus was a witness to the will of Lucretia Diodora who left her property in Philadelphia to her grand-daughter, Valeria Serapia.[39] Three witnesses were also active in Philadelphia, T. Flavius Iulianus, C. Iulius Antoninus and L. Valerius Lucretianus.[40] Iulius Gemellus, the only witness who claimed veteran status, appears in the Karanis tax registers in which his alias, Longinus, is also given.[41] In 185, he witnessed the *epikrisis* of Valerius Clemens who settled at Karanis.[42] Other Iulii Gemelli are known from the area but are not of the right date to allow a connection with this man. C. Longinus Aquila appears in a document of 189 in which he and his brother C. Longinus Valerianus came to an agreement over property with Gaia, daughter of Longinus, almost certainly their sister. Their mother had a Graeco-Egyptian name, Thaesis. In this document, Aquila iden-tifies himself as a veteran.[43] Aquila paid taxes on his land at Karanis in the early 170s and appears three times on the tax rolls. In *P. Mich.* IV 224, 4345f and 225, 3406f the amounts he pays are slight but in 223, 2197f he pays a large amount of tax on garden land, the most heavily taxed but most profitable type of land.[44] The only other name for which connections could be made is C. Iulius Saturninus. The documents attached to this name have formed the basis of two articles, one by Sanders and the other by Gilliam.[45] These articles discuss the connec-tions between Saturninus and the family of Sempronia Gemella who had two illegitimate children, M.M. Sempronii Sarapion and Socrates. But the names Sempronius and Saturninus were very popular in Egypt and appear frequently within the papyrological record, often connected.[46]

Such investigations have clear limitations but we can see that the inter-ests of the community stretched beyond the borders of the village to the neighbouring community of Philadelphia which also had a significant veteran community. A large number of those involved in the will, however, reappear at Karanis and several witnesses were resident at Karanis. Castor's social group was not cosmopolitan. The persons mentioned in the various documents were exclusively Roman but this need not be significant. The majority of texts dealt with legal matters for which it was necessary to have fellow Romans as witnesses or advisers, or family matters and normally, therefore, the main participants were also Romans.

C. Iulius Niger and family[47]

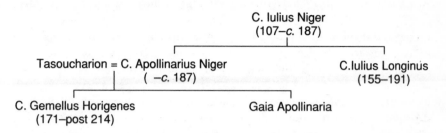

The majority of the archive is made up of the documents of C. Gemellus Horigenes, who also appears as Horion (also known as Gemellus), and Horion, son of Apollinarius, and Gemellus Horion. He has a Roman name (C. Gemellus Horigenes), an Egyptian name (Horion) and a name which combines the two (Gemellus Horion), a combination which, since names are related to status, not only leads to confusion for the modern reader but also suggests a certain confusion of legal and cultural identity on the part of Gemellus Horion, as I shall call him. He details his descent in a certificate of 214 in which he registered property inherited from his father and derived ultimately from the estate of his grandfather, C. Iulius Niger. In a complaint to the prefect in 197, he describes property that had passed to him and his sister from C. Apollinarius, Antinoopolite. Gemellus Horion's uncle, C. Iulius Longinus, died in 191 and his property also passed to Gemellus. His sister and mother appear in a census declaration of 189. From *P. Mich.* VI 428 of 154, we know that Iulius Niger was born in 107. He was still alive in 186 but his death must have occurred soon after this for property bought by him in 154 was registered as belonging to Gemellus Horion and Gaia Apollinaria in 189. Iulius Longinus was born in 155 and, in *P. Mich.* VI 422 of 197, his death is dated to 189. The date of birth of Apollinarius Niger is unknown but he was still alive in 183. *P. Mich.* VI 422 of 197 states that he had been dead for some time which would suggest longer than the eight years of his brother. In *P. Mich.* VI 423–4 of 197 Gemellus Horion states that he was born *c.* 171. The last document of the archive comes from 214.

The first appearance of Iulius Niger is in 154. Niger, described as a discharged cavalryman of the *ala veterana Gallica*, being around 47 years of age, paid 800 *drachmae* in full and in one instalment to Valeria Diodora, who will appear below in the discussion of the Minucius family, for a house in Karanis. The new house was followed in the next year by the birth of a son, [Iu]lius Long[in]us. Niger appears as an Antinoopolite of the Osirantis tribe and the birth certificate of his son is witnessed by three other Antinoopolites.[48] In 172–3, Niger petitioned the *epistrategos* Iulius Lucullus. He identified himself as an Antinoopolite and requested that he be exempted from the guardianship of the daughter of M. Anthestius Gemellus, Valeria Tertia. Niger had been assigned as guardian with Valerius Komon but was able to escape his burden. Iulius Niger's involvement with the family of M. Anthestius Gemellus will be discussed in relation to that family. Valeria Tertia and her father were both of Antinoopolite status, a high status group, and it was necessary to recruit an Antinoopolite to act as guardian for Valeria. Niger escaped this task by using a legal loophole. As part of the privileges of citizenship, Antinoopolites could not be forced to act as guardians for people outside their city and as the property of Valeria Tertia lay in Karanis, Niger escaped. It is not clear why he should want to do so. It could not have been inconvenient for him to take a hand in the administration of her estates and it may have provided him with an opportunity for some financial gain.

As a veteran of a Roman auxiliary unit, Iulius Niger would have been granted Roman citizenship on discharge. This was probably not long before the house was bought from Valeria Diodora. Both his sons probably had Roman citizenship and as Niger had Antinoopolite citizenship, they would have taken that as well. Iulius Niger's wife is unknown. Apollinarius Niger's wife was Tasoucharion, daughter of Serapia, Antinoopolite. Serapia used a metronymic rather than a patronymic because her father's identity was unknown or because the relationship between her mother and father did not constitute a legal marriage. As both Gemellus Horion's parents were Antinoopolites, there could be no question as to the status of the children. Tasoucharion was not a Roman citizen and since the children of a marriage between a Roman citizen and a person of different status normally adopted the lower status, her children could not be Roman citizens. Indeed the litigious Gemellus Horion, although vociferously proclaiming on all possible occasions his Antinoopolite status with a righteous indignation which he must have learnt from his grandfather, judging by the undated complaint *SB* XII 11114, only once claims Roman citizenship. In 214, he was, for the first and only time in the archive, C. Gemellus Horigenes, Roman and Antinoopolite. It is difficult to see how Gemellus Horion could have suddenly developed Roman citizenship. He had not served in the army and did nothing worthy of a special grant of privilege. He was not entitled to citizenship by birth, unless his father and mother had enjoyed the special right of *conubium* which allowed Roman citizens to marry non-citizens and for their children to be Roman. If this was the case, and we have no reason to believe that it was, Gemellus Horion would surely have mentioned it before 214. Another possible source for citizenship was Caracalla's grant of universal citizenship, conventionally dated to 212. In this case, it would plainly be perverse to start crowing about a privilege which everyone else enjoyed and Gemellus Horion did not adopt the *gentilicium* Aurelius as other beneficiaries of the *Constitutio Antoniniana* did. We must conclude that Gemellus was trying to inflate his importance by falsely claiming Roman citizenship by association with his grandfather. It is to be noted that this is in a note to the village scribe and not to a Roman official.

We have several petitions from Gemellus Horion. He entered into dispute with Sotas and Iulius, sons of Eudas, over ownership of land. Gemellus was, by 197, losing his sight and the two brothers allegedly took advantage of this to attempt the theft of land claimed by Gemellus. He wrote to the *strategos*, to the prefect, and to the *epistrategos* about the incident. In 198, he was again writing to the *epistrategos*, demanding his intervention in a case of alleged intimidation and assault by the tax collector, Kastor. Gemellus was told to refer his case to the local centurion. In 199/200, he once more wrote to the *epistrategos* about the imposition of a liturgy from which he was exempted because of blindness and Antinoopolite citizenship. The final petition of the series is from 211/12 and in this he, together with Gellius Serenus, headed a petition claiming to come from all the farmers of Kerkesoucha, a small satellite community of Karanis, about the water available for irrigation.

These documents reveal much about Gemellus Horion's status within the community. His early petitions portray him as a weak and defenceless man of high legal status, oppressed because of his illness. Yet the petitions show him attempting to gain access to official protection and although we cannot know whether he was successful or not, it is clear that officials wrote back. His emphasis on his status and disability were tactics to ensure that officials would take up his case and this may have led to his high social status amongst the farmers of Kerkesoucha. Gemellus Horion may have been going blind but he was certainly capable of looking after his own interests. His false claim of Roman citizenship in 214 was part of his campaign to enhance his status and manipulate the authorities.

Many of Iulius Niger's documents concern land and the payment of taxes. We do not have a cumulative total for the amount of land involved but none of the transactions concerns a parcel of land of any considerable size. Gemellus Horion states that he inherited, in three parcels, land totalling 3½ *arourai* around Psenarsenesis, which he registered with the village scribe of Karanis in 214. The registers of taxes paid for Niger by his sons in the 180s all involve very small amounts of produce. The most complete register, *P. Mich.* VI 385, suggests that the maximum amount of land in the possession of the family was around three *arourai*. The housing property owned by Horion and his sister was quite extensive. The census declaration of 189 lists the property of Tasoucharion and her two children which probably consisted of the entire wealth of the family since Niger and the two sons of Niger were dead. The property includes a house and a courtyard, a third share in a house, a house and two court-yards formerly owned by Valeria Diodora, a third share of two houses and two courtyards, a third share of house and courtyard and another courtyard, a house and courtyard formerly belonging to C. Longinus Apollinarius, two courtyards, a courtyard and a house formerly belonging to Ptolemaios, and a third share of a house and courtyard. Assuming that the property of their mother would pass eventually to the children, they would possess 5⅔ houses and 9⅔ courtyards, a sizeable amount of prop-erty even in the depressed conditions of the late second century.

The family of Minucia Thermutharion[49]

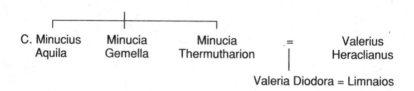

Nowhere in the documents relating to this family is there an explicit reference to the military service of any member of the family. It is, however, extremely probable that the father of the three Minucii was a Roman soldier. Not only was the son of the family named Aquila, a name which has distinct military connotations, but also the guardians of the daughters were both legionary veterans, C. Sempronius Priscus and L. Vibius Crispus. The three texts hardly constitute an archive. *P. Mich.* VI 428, and probably also *P. Mich.* IX 554 were preserved in the archive of Iulius Niger. *BGU* II 472, however, must have had a separate history.

The most interesting and earliest document is a Domitianic division of property. Aquila and his sisters, both acting through their guardians, agreed to divide the property of their parents. Aquila received 6 *arourai* at Kerkesoucha, 1 *aroura* of newly planted olive grove, a house at Karanis, a granary and a dovecote. The sisters received in common 2¼ *arourai* of land at Karanis, 1¼ *aroura* of land imposed by the village at Karanis, 3 *arourai* of land at Kerkesoucha, and 1½ houses at Karanis. In 154, the house and two courtyards bought by Iulius Niger were in the possession of Valeria Diodora since they had been bequeathed to her by her mother, Minucia Thermutharion. In this transaction, Valeria Diodora was supported by her husband and guardian Limnaios, son of Pentheus, son of Atreus. In 139, Valeria Diodora sold another piece of her inheritance but does not tell us the previous owner. This property was sold for 408 *drachmae*.

The information given in these three documents allows us to trace the changes in ownership of the Minucius estate. The property passed to the Minucii children from both father and mother. Father brought the majority of the property: 6 *arourai* at Kerkesoucha, the olive grove, the 2¼ *arourai* of katoikic land at Karanis, the village imposition and two houses, a dovecote and granary at Karanis. The mother's estate provided only 3 *arourai* at Kerkesoucha and half a house at Karanis. In village terms, the estate was quite large, being 12¾ *arourai* of grain land and one *aroura* of olives. The majority of this property passed into the hands of the son but the property that remained in the hands of the daughters individually was in excess of the property owned by their mother, if only slightly. The topographical details given in this division of the estate suggest that the whole estate was in Valeria Diodora's hands when she sold a house to Iulius Niger.[50] The property had once more been concentrated, either in the hands of Valeria Diodora or her mother Minucia Thermutharion, passing eventually to Diodora.

Of the offspring of the father Minucius, only Minucia Thermutharion produced a child that survived to adulthood. She had married Valerius Heraclianus and their child, Valeria Diodora, had been born about AD 94. Valeria Diodora married Limnaios, son of Pentheus, son of Atreus and, after the death of her mother, uncle and aunt, the Minucius estate concentrated in her hands.

The Minucii children were all Roman citizens and Minucia Thermutharion married someone with a Roman name. It seems likely that he was a Roman citizen. Their daughter carried a Roman name but married a Graeco-Egyptian. The children of this marriage, of whom there is no evidence, would have been Graeco-Egyptian.

The Anthestii[51]

The documents concerning the Anthestii of Karanis, like those of the Minucii, do not constitute an archive. Only two of the Anthestii can be firmly linked, though since Anthestius was a fairly unusual name, there is a reasonable chance that there was some connection between the various Anthestii. In 172, M. Anthestius Gemellus left Valerius Komon (a probable relative of Valeria Sempronilla, his wife) and Iulius Niger as guardians to his daughter, Valeria Tertia. Niger subsequently evaded his responsibilities. In the same year, Apollinarius Niger, son of Iulius Niger, and the aforementioned Valerius Komon paid taxes on behalf of Anthestius Tertianus.

133

An M. Anthestius Gemellus is attested in the village in AD 90, probably in 117–18, 122, 166–9 and 172–3. Since the Gemellus of AD 90 was born in AD 55, it is extremely improbable that he was still active in 172–3 at the age of 118. The Gemellus of 90, when he represented his mother in a rescheduling of a loan of 440 *drachmae* to an Egyptian woman, was serving with the *cohors* III *Ituraeorum*. In 122, Gemellus rented out property at Bakchias amounting to five *arourai* of grain land. Gemellus may have served in a liturgic office at Tebtunis in 117–18. The evidence suggests some wealth but it is impossible to quantify. The later Gemellus was a Roman and Antinoopolite but there is no evidence of his economic status. Tertianus paid taxes on between eight and nine *arourai* of land in 172 which again would suggest some prosperity.

There is no evidence of a connection between these two men or between these men and the other Anthestii active in the village, notably Anthestius Capitolinus. It is, however, probable that the veteran Gemellus active in the 120s in Karanis was the forebear of the Gemellus making arrangements for his estate in the 170s and possibly of other Anthestii in the village as well.

Iulius Sabinus and Iulius Apollinarius[52]

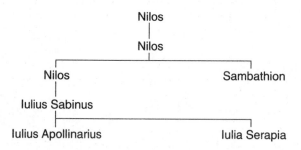

The next two archives contain a number of Latin documents and are comprised mainly of letters.

C. Iulius Sabinus was a soldier of *legio* III *Cyrenaica* in AD 96. The writer of *P. Mich.* VIII 485 addressed him as *signifer*. C. Iulius Apollinarius was a soldier of the same legion in 107. His two letters of that year celebrate his promotion through the direct influence of the commander of the forces, Claudius Severus. Apollinarius was based in the new province of Arabia. By 119, Apollinarius' rise had brought him to the position of *frumentarius* of Rome (a type of messenger) while attached to the same legion.[53]

The letters of the archive, like all personal communications, rely upon the common knowledge of the author and recipient but there is sufficient material preserved to allow us to reconstruct in part the family and the social circle of these two men. The 'grandmother' of Apollinarius was Sambathion, mentioned in *P. Mich.* VIII 465, whose will was dated to 117–8. Sambathion was the daughter of Nilos, son of Nilos, from the *metropolis* (the nome capital) and wrote her will with the help of Sokrates, son of Sarapion. Sambathion left the slave Abaskantos to Iulius Sabinus, the son of her brother Nilos, who served with the legion and also left something to Iulius Apollinarius, son of Sabinus.[54] *P. Mich.* VIII 465 also mentions Apollinarius' sister, Iulia Serapia, who appears in an unpublished census declaration in which Sokrates, son of Sarapion, acted for both Serapia and Apollinarius. The rest of the archive is littered with names, many of which are Roman, as we would expect in correspondence between soldiers. The letters home tell a different story. Greetings are sent to Ptolemaios, Ammonios, Thermouthis, and Aphrodisia.

There is a little information about the financial state of the family. In 119, Apollinarius rented to Sabinus, son of Sokrates, two *arourai* around Bakchias, three-quarters of an *aroura* around Karanis, two *arourai* of olives around Onkos, near Alkias, another *aroura* of olives, and another two *arourai* of olives around Hiera. The recurrence of the names Sabinus and Sokrates suggests that this was not a purely economic transaction. Apollinarius was a legionary *frumentarius* in 119 and it is possible that he was renting out his entire estate since he was unable to give it due attention himself, a hypothesis supported by the dispersal and number of the plots. The olive groves were quite large and suggest relative wealth.

The family was of Egyptian origin, though they were of the privileged metropolite group. Although many of the names mentioned in the archive were Roman, a number of their associates had Greek or Egyptian names. Away from the immediate context of the army, both Sabinus and Apollinarius associated both with Graeco-Egyptians and other Romans.

Apollinarius used his connections to rise within the ranks of the Roman legion and the letters show him using that influence for others. It is not surprising to discover that they were a family of some means within village society.

Claudius Terentianus and Claudius Tiberianus[55]

The relationship between Claudii Terentianus and Tiberianus was not simple. Terentianus always referred to Tiberianus as his father yet Tiberianus was removed from the centre of Terentianus' family life. *P. Mich.* VIII 471, an account of a quarrel, includes the news that Terentianus' mother was with child. Later in the story, she gave birth, after which she was able to accompany Terentianus to Alexandria. The man at the centre of the story was Ptolemaios, also described as the father of Terentianus. The relationship between the two Romans could be dismissed as one between an older and younger man who addressed each other using familial designations, if the actual nomenclature of the two was not suggestive of a blood tie. Also, Terentianus requested Tiberianus' permission to buy a concubine slave, suggesting that Tiberianus had some moral or legal authority over him. Terentianus did not have any problems with his paternity, relating to both men as if they were his father, and I suspect that the biological paternity of Terentianus was unimportant. One father had an Egyptian name and the other had a Roman name and this places both Tiberianus and Terentianus firmly within a Graeco-Egyptian setting.[56]

The first notice of Terentianus' military career comes in a letter to Tiberianus, written to inform him that Terentianus was going to Syria with a vexillation. Terentianus had joined the fleet together with two friends, both of whom had Graeco-Egyptian names. Indeed, these friends appear to have been instrumental in obtaining a post for Terentianus. Terentianus himself was far from happy with his post, however, preferring it only to a life of wandering, perhaps as a bandit, though more likely Terentianus, whose expression is often a little sentimental, had a more prosaic career in mind. Terentianus asked Tiberianus to send equipment for his new career: a sword, a grappling-iron, lances, a pick-axe, a tunic, trousers, and a cloak. The letter ends with greetings from Ptolemaios (the other father) and his brothers. Interestingly, Terentianus had failed to join the legion in spite of the fact that Tiberianus was a *speculator*, an officer entrusted with scouting and security roles, and someone who presumably had regular contact with quite senior officers. Another letter (VIII 468) seems almost to be an appeal to Tiberianus to use this influence. Terentianus had been ill while on board ship and some of his equipment was stolen by the *optio*, a junior officer. Terentianus was attempting to transfer from the fleet to a legion. He complains, however, that nothing could be accomplished without money, presumably to oil the wheels of bureaucracy, and letters of commendation. He notes that a certain Dius had joined the legion, having had greater good fortune than Terentianus. Again members of the circles of friends and family, one of whom is a centurion, are listed in the exchange of greetings. Whether Tiberianus exerted his influence or not, Terentianus accomplished his transfer to the land forces. He was involved in the suppression of rioting in Alexandria and, perhaps as a result of the civil disturbances, was wounded. Perhaps the most interesting of the remaining letters is from Tabatheus who claims to be Terentianus' sister. Tabatheus prays for Terentianus before Souchos, placing the letter and the family in the context of the Fayum. The substance of the letter is not entirely clear but appears to involve the payment of money possibly to compensate a family after a murder.

Much of the action in these letters takes place in Alexandria but the relationship of the family to the Fayum is also clear. The military context of many of the letters means that the archive is littered with Roman names, but the domestic context, the friends of the family and possibly most members of the family itself, had Graeco-Egyptian names. The family was clearly integrated into Graeco-Egyptian society. Although several of the letters are in Latin, perhaps suggesting an Italian origin for certain members of the family, the family was Egyptianised.

CONCLUSIONS

These investigations into the society of Roman Karanis and, more particularly, of the veterans and their families allow us to piece together some of the connections and relationships which made up the community. Veterans formed links with other veterans and their families formed links with other families and thus the community was bound together almost as if by the threads of a spider's web. The threads of the community spread outside the village and its satellite communities to the neighbouring village of Philadelphia, a village which itself had a substantial Roman and veteran population. The ties between Philadelphia and Karanis were not, however, very close. The communities were connected but separate. The community was based on the village rather than on the region: we must talk of the veteran communities of Karanis and Philadelphia and not the veteran community of the North Fayum.

Other threads connect the village to military life in Alexandria and elsewhere. The archives of the Iulii Sabinus and Apollinarius and the Claudii Terentianus and Tiberianus demonstrate the importance of these military connections but we can also perceive a hint of these connections with the Minucii, the guardians of the daughters being two legionary veterans. Both Iulius Apollinarius and Claudius Terentianus sought to benefit from connections, using letters of recommendation and personal contacts to obtain promotion in one case and a posting in a legion in the other. Apollinarius, in turn, used his status to benefit others. The careers of these soldiers were determined by this web of personal connections. It is this personal element which comes to the fore in the letters. Fundamentally, this system was conservative. Connections made careers and assured social status. Social status could be used to gain access to authority, to create new connections. It is possible that success could have been achieved on merit but the path to success was considerably eased by letters of recommendation and social connections. Even access to military units was partially dependent upon social connections. A soldier who developed connections with important fellow soldiers could use his influence to further the career of a relative or neighbour and his association with the successful relative or neighbour would further increase his social standing. Connections were a commodity which gave status and power and, therefore, they had to be fostered. It is no coincidence that the most successful family attested, the Iulii Sabinus and Apollinarius, being metropolites and not villagers, had also the most elevated social origins.

Although legal practice encouraged Romans to form connections with other Romans, their social circles also included Egyptians. This can be seen relatively clearly in the marriages made by the children of veterans. The community of Karanis was sufficiently large to allow Romans to search for other Romans as marriage partners and, of course, the Romans could also have turned to Philadelphia, but our evidence suggests that there was little attempt to limit marriage to within the Roman element of the community even though this was the only means at their disposal to preserve citizenship for future generations. The letters of soldiers to their families demonstrate the closeness of non-Romans to veteran households. Many of the families had started as Egyptians and many of the families maintained close links with Egyptians.

The maintenance of links leads us to consider in what sense the troops were Roman. Legally defined, the soldiers and veterans were Roman but what about their culture? The vast majority of documents concerning or written by veterans from Karanis are in Greek, though two of our archives contain texts in Latin. Latin was the official language of the army in which most records were written, though Greek was also sometimes used. Army officers needed some knowledge of Latin but it is not necessarily the case that orders were transmitted to the troops in Latin or that the army in Egypt was a predominantly Latin-speaking institution. Apart from these few letters in Latin, there is very little other evidence which connects the village with any aspect of specifically Roman culture. By the second century AD, however, the Romans had absorbed much of Greek culture and in the Eastern empire, Greek culture was the culture of the ruling elite. The settlement of a large number of troops in an Egyptian village community may have led, therefore, not to Romanisation but to Hellenisation of the local culture.

There was a strong Egyptian element in village religion which appears to have been dominated by the local crocodile deity. One of the few foreign importations attested in the archaeological remains is the god Heron who appears on a wall painting depicted as a horseman.[57] The divinity also appears on a wall at Soknopaiou Nesos. There is a faint possibility that Heron should be connected with the Egyptian god Atum whose city was known as Heroonopolis but Atum was a creator god depicted in human form and not associated with the horse. Heron is, however, normally understood to be a Thracian deity.[58] There is a temptation, therefore, to associate worship of the god with Roman troops of Northern Greek origin such as the horsemen of the *ala Thracum Mauretana*, but the spread of depictions of Heron throughout the Fayum and in areas which had no particular military connections suggests that

Heron was a Ptolemaic importation. There are clear signs of the Hellenisation of local religion, however, and Greek deities are mentioned in the papyri at least as frequently as Egyptian ones. There are indications that there was Hellenisation of material culture in the decoration of the bath house and in the small finds, but this was a general process, affecting all areas of Egypt. The Fayum, which had been the scene of quite large-scale Greek immigration and settlement during the Ptolemaic period, was, to a certain extent, Hellenised before the arrival of the Romans. The lamps and pottery of the village show connections with Lower Egypt but not with any more distant land until the mid-third century at the earliest, a time when African pottery was becoming more common throughout Egypt and the rest of the empire. The soldiers did not bring with them a more cosmopolitan set of artefacts. In fact, the cultural impact of the soldiers on the town is not archaeologically detectable and the papyri do not suggest that the soldiers differed in cultural terms from their Graeco-Egyptian neighbours.

The Romans we have studied appear to have been towards the wealthier end of the spectrum of village society. None of the veterans studied had vast amounts of land or property. According to Geremek, both Romans and Egyptians appear in every economic group from the richest of the village to the poorest, though Romans, at only 14 per cent of the population, appear disproportionately amongst the upper levels.[59] It is possible that this comparative wealth was due to the rewards of military service, but there are also other possible explanations. One of the major means of enhancing one's economic position in the ancient world was through inheritance. We see this in the case of Valeria Diodora whose maternal estate was small but who also inherited the property of her uncle and aunt. Gemellus Horion not only inherited the property of his father and his father's portion of his grandfather's estate, but also the property of his uncle and of his mother. In theory, the distribution of wealth was, therefore, cyclical, with the young having little property but gradually accumulating more through inheritance from other branches of the family before, on their death, their property was divided amongst their heirs. To accumulate wealth, a father had to outlive his relatives and for his children to be wealthy, he had to ensure the minimum number of heirs. Since there was a low life expectancy at birth, a veteran who had served twenty-five years and was probably aged about 45 at the time of discharge had already outlived most of his contemporaries.[60]

In a farming community, children could be used for economically productive tasks from a very early age.[61] They increased the available workforce and might have enabled the farmer to work his land more effectively so that there were some economic benefits for a farmer in marrying. These benefits did not apply to the soldier. Given other peculiarities of the military career which might have discouraged soldiers from marrying, it is probable that many soldiers did not marry or only married on discharge from the legion. Two of our soldiers do not appear to have married: Iulius Apollinarius and Claudius Terentianus. Terentianus asked permission to purchase a concubine-wife but we do not have the reply and the archive does not mention any children. Tiberianus, himself, may not have had children if Terentianus was the son of Ptolemaios. The children of Iulius Niger were probably born to him comparatively late in life. Veterans, therefore, having outlived their contemporaries and accumulated property by inheritance, might have limited the size of their family by marrying late and thus the demographics of military service may well have led to veterans and their families enjoying slightly greater prosperity than their non-military neighbours.

In any case, many of the veterans of the second century were natives of the village who returned there after service. Veterans did not, therefore, start in village life with a *tabula rasa* but had inherited property. The comparative wealth of veterans may be due to recruitment of troops from the wealthier group within the village rather than from any economic benefit accruing from service. The wealth of the Roman element of the population is, however, only comparative. Veterans were only marginally wealthier, on average, than their neighbours, a position illustrated by an unpublished land register from Philadelphia.[62] Veterans did not form a separate economic class nor were they involved in economic activities different from those of the non-veteran population. Economically, the veterans differed little from their non-veteran neighbours.

Karanis, with its large number of Romans and veterans, provides the historian with data to test hypotheses about the relationship between the ordinary Egyptian population and their conquerors as represented by the army. We started the chapter with three main models of interaction portraying the veterans and Romans as an elite, or the veterans and Romans as an entirely separate group, or the veterans and Romans as an integrated part of the wider community. Clearly, the veterans do not conform to the first of these models. None of the architectural, archaeological or papyrological data from the village in the years when there was a substantial veteran presence there suggest that there was a clearly defined elite within the village. The Romans were, in general, wealthier than the Egyptians, but the difference was not substantial and there is little sign of Egyptians deferring to Romans, acting as clients, or otherwise being dependent upon the Roman community. The Romans did not control the village administration, nor was access to judicial authority, higher administration or economic resources controlled by the Romans of the village. The veterans were not in control of the political and economic life of the village. The veterans were not a caste. Many of the dealings of the Romans studied in this chapter were with other Romans. For certain legal matters, Romans required other Romans as witnesses. Our texts, biased towards legal matters, probably over-emphasise the Romanity of the social life of the veterans. Karanis was a small community. Once we trace connections, even with our far from perfect data, the threads between the different archives are suggestive of a sense of community and the interaction and interconnection of large numbers of Romans. It is easy to believe that the community was close-knit and that everybody knew everybody else. Yet, this community was far from exclusively Roman. The web included large numbers of Egyptians. If we escape from the legal documents to the letters and other texts which provide an insight into more domestic circles, the veterans appear part of a wider community, a community which was Graeco-Egyptian and not exclusively, nor even mainly, Roman.

It is, however, true that the Romans remained in some respects separated and attempted to assert a higher status than their Egyptian neighbours as can be seen in the case of Gemellus Horion. Much of Horion's petitioning is concerned with the issue of status. He affirms his Antinoopolite status on several occasions and uses that status not only as a legal argument against his oppressors but also as a means of gaining access to the authorities and a way of impressing on those authorities his importance. His fascinating claim of Roman citizenship was a similar attempt to impress his status on a village official and he related that status not to his own father but to his grandfather, the veteran. Gemellus Horion cried out to the authorities and to anyone else that he was a person of importance and high status so that attacks on him threatened the order of Roman society. Gemellus Horion fights a continuing battle with the authorities and villagers to assert a superior status but also acts within his community when representing the villagers of Kerkesoucha in a petition. We may, as outsiders, view the Roman community as econom-ically and socially integrated but the Romans themselves may have placed far more emphasis on the differences between them and the ordinary villagers. In spite of this, there is no real sense of ethnic division or conflict between Romans and non-Romans in the village. The Roman community was united for legal matters and the veterans may have felt some mutual loyalty due to military service, but Karanis was not a divided village.

Historians of the Roman empire have devoted much scholarly effort to the study of cultural change in the empire, more specifically the trans-formation of many diverse local cultures into a single imperial culture, and have spent much time arguing about the relative extent of that cultural change and the possible causes of cultural change. Karanis presents us with an example of a seemingly ordinary village which received a considerable number of Roman veterans. The army has traditionally been seen as one of the main ways in which the imperial culture was disseminated among the provincials and so we might have expected to see considerable evidence of cultural change in Karanis resultant upon the arrival of all these Romans. The evidence, however, does not suggest that the Romans had any major impact on the culture of the village. The Romans of the village lived very much like the rest of the community. There was cultural change at Karanis, as there was cultural change in every settlement in Egypt, but that cultural change was not related to the numbers of veterans resident in the community. The veterans of Karanis were not at the forefront of the process of Romanisation. In spite of the presence of a significant minority of Romans, Karanis remained a typical, if somewhat large, Egyptian village.

8

DIOCLETIAN AND AFTER

The terminal date for this study is AD 284, the accession of Diocletian, an artificial but traditional point of division between what French historians call the High and Low Empires. There are other dates which one could choose. There would be some logic in ending with the Severan period which not only ushered in an end to a century of relative civil concord but also brought many administrative changes to Egypt, including the universal grant of Roman citizenship in AD 212 which made superfluous one of the principal privileges of military service and, incidentally, made the identification of veterans and their families considerably more difficult. We could also look for a later date, continuing beyond the military and other reforms of Diocletian and Constantine to the final collapse of Roman or rather, by this time, Byzantine rule in Egypt with the invasion of Egypt by the Arabs in 639–41. There was still a Byzantine army to resist the Arab invasion and although the initial invasion force was tiny, about 4,000 men, the Arab army that besieged and captured the main military bases of Babylon and Alexandria was probably at least 15,000 strong.[1] There were continuities between the earlier and later periods but, though I have occasionally strayed beyond 284 in collecting evidence, there are advantages in using 284 as a terminal date. The conventional date not only provides us with a convenient period of study of three centuries but also has some real historical value as a point of change between two different systems of government and military organisation: the army that defended Egypt against the Arabs was not the same army that supervised the conquest and pacification of Egypt in the first century BC. The changes were probably more evolutionary than revolutionary but 284 is a convenient point from which to assess the nature of the army of the later Roman empire.[2]

There were substantial differences between the armies of the early and later Roman empire. In strategic terms, the most important change was a shift from a reliance upon legions dispersed along the frontiers. These legions, concentrated in a relatively small number of military provinces under the direct control of the emperor, had responded to any local threats on a regional basis and only if that threat had escalated had troops been summoned from further afield. In the later empire, the political situation necessitated a change. Emperors were made by armies and the emperors could not afford to concentrate large military forces under generals whose loyalty was open to question. The insecurities were such that emperors had to remain close to their armies at all times and, gradually, during the third century, we see the emergence of a central force, stationed with the emperor, which would form the nucleus of any major expeditionary force. Although securing the position of the emperor, the use of a central reserve was strategically inflexible since threats on more than one frontier could not easily be dealt with. The creation of a central reserve of elite troops led, of necessity, to a comparative devaluation of the status of the troops stationed in the provinces. We should not, however, exaggerate the speed of these alterations. There had always been a substantial number of troops stationed close to the emperor and these were used from the first century onwards to supplement ordinary forces in imperial expeditions. The army in the provinces in the fourth century remained a significant military force and it would be a mistake to see the provincial armies as merely border guards or as a kind of frontier militia.

The change was, however, politically significant. Diocletian's solution to the political and military problems which had destabilised so many of his immediate predecessors was to create a collegiate imperial position: the tetrarchy. Four colleagues with four field armies were able to use those armies in four different theatres of war and deal simultaneously with threats to the empire on several different fronts. The emperors became primarily generals of the field armies and were more closely associated with the troops than at virtually any time during the Principate. There was no longer any pretence that the emperors were simply senators or members of the Roman elite. They were openly reliant upon military force and court ceremonial emphasised not only these military aspects of the emperors but also the division between the imperial figure and the ordinary senator. Diocletian introduced elaborate ceremonials at court and the identification between the emperor and the divine became more obvious. The relatively short-lived experiment of the tetrarchy worked as long as Diocletian was able to exercise some authority over his colleagues but after Diocletian's retirement, the cohesion of the tetrarchs broke down and there was civil war. The twin problems of ensuring the stability of the political system and effective defence of the frontiers against major threats on more than one frontier continued to plague the later Roman empire. The unity of empire, re-established by Constantine, could not survive his successors and gradually a *de facto* division emerged. The problems were not solved in the fourth century and the West came under increasing pressure, leading to the fall of the empire in the West in the fifth century. In the East, the empire survived and even flourished, overcoming the military difficulties posed by invasions from the north and the Persians in the east. The army also did not change so drastically. Eastern emperors were not so reliant upon semi-independent allies for their armies, a reliance which many have seen as the ultimate military cause for the collapse of the West. Large central armies reduced the reliance of the emperors on the armies of the frontiers and gave them more independence both from the governors of these provinces and from the provinces themselves.

It is not, however, changes in the military which are commonly used to mark the transition from the early to the late empire. The period sees the culmination of a whole series of political and administrative changes and some entirely fresh departures. Diocletian is normally credited with extensive administrative reforms, reforms which changed the nature of the empire. The rampant inflation and the devaluation of the currency in the third century had seriously disrupted the taxation system, though it had perhaps caused few serious economic difficulties. Regular censuses formed the basis of a new taxation system. The coinage was re-established on a new standard though problems with inflation were not solved. The period also sees the end of the administrative unity of Egypt itself. The province was divided into several smaller administrative units, the main divisions in the valley being Iovia, Herculea and the Thebaid.[3] In the fourth century, this administrative division was reflected in a military division between the *Dux Thebaidos* in Upper Egypt and the *Comes limitis Aegypti* in Lower Egypt.

The most obvious change between the early and later empire was in religion. The adoption of Christianity as the religion of the empire in the fourth century and the success of Christianity in securing official support for most of the succeeding centuries has traditionally been seen as a watershed in the history of the Roman empire. Again, the importance of the change has probably been overly stressed. The dominant culture of the empire remained firmly rooted in the traditions of classical antiquity and modern scholarship places great emphasis on the continuity in cultural expression from early to late antiquity.[4] In some ways, the transformation of the empire was a change in rhetoric rather than a real structural change in the nature of the ancient world.

The Christianisation of the empire is, however, very important for the history of Egypt since a distinctive form of Christianity emerged in Egypt, a form which has survived until the present day. Coptic Christianity did not have radically different intellectual roots from the Christianity of the rest of the empire and many ideas were shared and communicated. Egyptian Christianity was instrumental in the development of the monastic tradition and Egypt became an important centre of monastic activity. The very vitality of Egyptian Christianity was perhaps in part responsible for the problems which faced Coptic Christians in various periods when they found themselves theologically opposed to the dominant ideologies of the Church and, therefore, in the rather unfortunate position of officially being heretics. Christianity complicated the relationship between Mediterranean ideologies and power structures and the Egyptian population so that theological debate gave a forum in which wider political differences could be expressed.

A similarly important but gradual transformation occurred in Egyptian economic life. The third and fourth centuries saw the emergence of land owners whose control of large estates enabled them to dominate entire communities. This transformation has recently been illustrated by Bagnall who shows that there was an increasing level of inequality in Egyptian society from the second to the fourth century.[5] We should, however, exercise some caution. As Bagnall shows, the free peasantry did not disappear and still held a large proportion of the land in the mid-fourth century. There were important land owners in Egypt in most periods, but the great estates do not figure greatly in the economic and social history of the first two centuries of Roman rule, though they were of great importance in the last three or four centuries of Roman dominion.

AD 284 is an artificial moment at which to date the change but the society, culture, strategy and politics of the fourth century are sufficiently different from those of the preceding centuries to give good grounds for not extending my analysis of the Roman army beyond this point. This chapter is, therefore, an epilogue, in which I propose to analyse the processes that transformed the army of the first three centuries of Roman rule into the rather different organisation that was the Roman army of the fourth century.

We have, in a previous chapter, already discussed the events of the mid-third century which disrupted the garrison of the province. The invasion of Egypt from Palmyra and the subsequent recapture of the province by Roman forces coincided with a period of increased activity on the part of the tribes to the south of Egypt. These tribes remained an intermittent problem throughout the following centuries. Diocletian made an attempt to solve the problems of the frontier, though simply restoring order to Egypt and to the empire in general was possibly of greater importance in stabilising the frontier than any specific measures instituted to deal with the problem. The 290s saw a series of military crises in Egypt which culminated in the revolt of Domitius Domitianus and the invasion of Egypt by Diocletian. After a long siege of Alexandria, probably brought to an end in 298, Diocletian subjugated the province and may well have subsequently reorganised the defences and administration of the country.[6] In any case, the numerous military events of the late third century provided ample opportunity for reforming the garrison and the organisation of military forces within Egypt. The shape of the new army which controlled Egypt can be seen from a list of military units of the province, probably dating to the early or mid-fourth century, the *Notitia Dignitatum*.

The most striking difference between the army outlined in the *Notitia* and the army of the preceding centuries is the proliferation of military units stationed in the province. Some of the units in the *Notitia* were in Egypt during the first three centuries: the *legio* II *Traiana, ala veterana Gallica, ala Apriana,* the *cohortes* II *Ituraeorum,* I *Lusitanorum, scutata civium Romanorum,* and I *Apamenorum* are all familiar. The rest are not. Together with this expansion in the number of units, there is also an apparent shift in the ratio of cavalry to infantry. In the first centuries, the infantry had always far outnumbered the cavalry but, in the *Notitia*, at least forty-one of the seventy units were cavalry and there are likely to have been cavalry serving with other units as well. The absolute number of troops in each branch of the army cannot be ascertained since there is no reasonable basis for calculating the number of troops in each unit.[7] Assuming Principate manning levels, these units would form a massive army comfortably in excess of 180,000 men. It is likely, however, that there had been a considerable reduction in the number of men per unit and the establishment of the army must have been much less than this. Although the names of the types of units had not changed, it appears that the organisational structure of the army had.

These units occupied a large number of military bases. In addition, the small desert forts, the outposts along the roads to the quarries and the Red Sea ports were not the main bases of units and were not, therefore, entered in the *Notitia*. The level of dispersal of this new army is impressive and may be the cause of the sudden increase in archaeological evidence for the army in this period. There is very little archaeological data from the first, second or early third centuries, except for the forts in the Eastern Desert. In the late third and early fourth century, there is a sudden increase in available evidence. The dating of forts is often not precise, especially when the dating is from architectural features rather than from dated papyrological, epigraphic or numismatic evidence, but there are certain coincidences and peculiarities of architectural style between firmly dated and undated forts which allow us to estimate the dates of the latter with a reasonable degree of confidence. We have epigraphic evidence for the construction of forts at Qantara and at Hierakonpolis in AD 288.[8] The fort at Luxor was constructed about AD 301. The fort at Abu Sha'r, on the Red Sea coast, was constructed between AD 306 and 337. The excavated fort at Kysis (Qasr Dush) in the Western Desert dates from about AD 300 and the fort at Dionysias was built in either the very late third century or the first years of the fourth. These forts are accurately dated and they also bear a marked resemblance to other Egyptian forts. Dionysias appears similar in design to forts at Mehendi and Tell el Herr. Given the general paucity of archaeological information for the Roman army from the Nile valley, the number of forts which can be dated in the late third and early fourth centuries shows that there was an extensive programme of fort construction in these years.[9]

The increase in the number of forts in the later empire does appear to be a rather fundamental change since there is little evidence for an extensive system of military fortifications in the earlier period. The forts were impressive structures. The fort at Luxor was built within the remains of the great temple of the town, possibly the most prominent site in the city. The stylistic peculiarity of many of these forts is a long colonnaded street, running the length of the fort, from the main gate to the principal building, with the attention of a visitor perhaps focused on some kind of religious or military symbol at the heart of that building. Although there were sound military reasons for constructing these forts with towers and bastions, the towers added to the imposing quality of the fortification, impressing passers-by with the authority of the soldiers within far more than a simple wall would have done. The design was not simply functional: it was meant to impress. These forts were not just containers of soldiers but were assertions of the power and importance of the military.

The increase in the number of forts does not, however, necessarily signify a real change in the role of the army. In the first three centuries, the army was represented by centurions and others who did not necessarily need a fort through which to conduct their business. These officers almost certainly lived in houses in the villages and towns where they were stationed and their presence in these settlements is archaeologically undetectable. The forts made the army more visible but it is not evident that the forts are manifestations of an increase in military power in the later Roman empire. The later empire is commonly seen as a period of increasing militarisation and one in which the emperors were more willing to reward their troops and more reliant upon the power of their soldiers. There is some evidence to support the proposition. In a speech dated to after 388, Libanius complained about the decline in the power and status of the aristocracy of Antioch who were no longer able to exercise control over and collect revenues from client villages since these villages received the protection of military officials against whom the aristocrats were powerless.[10] Carrié has suggested that similar processes were at work in Egypt and that the urban aristocracy was in competition with the military aristocracy, but Bagnall has shown, using land registers from mid-fourth-century Hermopolis, that officers and former soldiers did not own significant areas of land.[11] Army officers were not drawn from the poorest groups in Egyptian society but the evidence does not suggest that military officers formed a new elite in the fourth century.

We possess a valuable insight into the activities of a garrison commander in the period AD 342–4 because of the preservation of the papers of Abinnaeus. Abinnaeus had served as a junior officer in Egypt until he accompanied an embassy to the imperial court. He was noticed and advanced to the command of the *ala* stationed at Dionysias in the Fayum. After some difficulties in getting his commission accepted, Abinnaeus commanded the unit for two years. Much of his correspondence is concerned with the collection of taxation and ensuring the supply of his unit. He was also asked to intervene in village disputes and to secure order.[12] Abinnaeus' control of the troops appears to have been less than perfect and he was the recipient of three angry letters denouncing the excesses of soldiers and threatening to take the matter further.[13] It may well have been known that Abinnaeus was not the favoured candidate of the local senior military official for command at Dionysias and that his position was, therefore, insecure. The archive shows that the concerns of the military had changed little from those of the earlier period and that many petitions were submitted to Abinnaeus of a similar type to those which had been submitted to the centurions in the first three centuries of Roman rule. Abinnaeus does not appear to have wielded any more power than the centurions, nor any less. The only possible difference in the nature of the material is that there appears to have been considerably more friction between ordinary soldiers and civilians.

The soldiers in the unit at Dionysias appear to have been conscripted. *P.Abinn.* 19 is a letter to Abinnaeus from a priest who sought to use his influence on Abinnaeus to persuade him to free a recruit from military duties. Another text suggests that recruits were conscripted to the army.[14] The army conscripted troops from at least the time of Diocletian in whose reign the *passio Maximiliani* is set. Maximilian was a conscientious objector who could not reconcile military service with his Christian beliefs and, though it was admitted that many Christians were serving in the army at the time, could not be persuaded to renounce his principles. The recruiting officer would not free Maximilian from conscription since he fulfilled the physical requirements and so Maximilian was martyred.[15] By the late fourth century, the status of soldiers had declined to the extent that extreme measures had to be taken to detect soldiers who deserted and soldiers were tattooed on enlistment.[16] Service in the army had become compulsory for sons of soldiers but, far from forming a military elite, the soldiers had a very low status.

In part, this low status must be related to the material benefits of service. The citizenship was no longer relevant for most recruits and the inflation of the late third and fourth centuries had significantly reduced the value of military pay. The taxation system provided for the soldiers' needs but it is possible that the soldiers did not have much or any supplementary income. Legally enforceable hereditary entry, conscription and the physical marking of recruits establish beyond reasonable doubt the decline in the status of the ordinary soldiers in the late third and fourth centuries. In the same oration in which Libanius complained of the encroachment of military officials on the power of the urban aristocracy, he also portrays the ordinary soldiers in a state of extreme deprivation, bordering on starvation.[17] At exactly the time when the Roman army was supposedly politically dominant, the standing of the ordinary soldier was in decline. We may wonder whether the changes in the material well-being and the social status of the soldiers were responsible for the increased hostility between civilians and soldiers observable in the Abinnaeus archive.

The military effectiveness of the late Roman army has often been doubted and it seems unlikely that those unquantifiable measures of military effectiveness, morale, willingness to fight and unit cohesion, were as high as in the Principate. On more concrete grounds, the strategic effectiveness of the army was supposedly reduced because of the difficulty in moving units from one area to another, a difficulty seen most clearly in the supposed reluctance of troops from the West under the command of Julian to transfer East. The *Notitia* shows an increase in the number of units stationed in the province from the third century and many of the new units may well have been fairly recently recruited from peoples on the borders of the empire and transferred to Egypt. A papyrus from Edfu from the fifth century gives a number of names of soldiers serving in the Hermopolite. The nomenclature was not Egyptian and strongly suggests that the troops were recruited from communities outside Egypt.[18] There is also a rather intriguing series of stories from the Rhine frontier about a legion of Egyptians serving in the region in the early fourth century. These troops were recruited from the Thebaid and were Christians. When required to round up the local Christians, the legionaries refused and were decimated. They refused again and were once more decimated. The story of these military martyrs only emerged into our written records *c.* 420 and later received further embroidering. The historical reality behind the tale cannot be established but there is at least a suggestion that large numbers of Egyptians served in the West in the late third or early fourth centuries.[19] Some flexibility in deployment and transfer of units was preserved into the fourth and fifth centuries. We have little evidence on which to judge the military effectiveness of units in either the Principate or the later Empire but the army was able to maintain Byzantine control of Egypt for another three centuries after the reforms of Diocletian and Constantine. The army of the seventh century may not have been able to deal with the initial small Arab expeditionary force but it was a far larger Arab army which conquered Egypt and that conquest was hard fought. Judging the army in Egypt by results, it remained effective and powerful to the very end of Roman rule.[20]

Price argues that the deployment of forces in Lower Egypt observable in the *Notitia* was motivated primarily by the strategic concerns of defence against possible attack from the East. Pointing to the control exercised over the major routes of communication and the routes of access to and from Egypt, Price suggests that the primary concern of the programme of fortification and the deployment of the troops was defensive. In Upper Egypt, the large numbers of units (and troops?) were designed to meet the threat of desert raids and combat the problems posed by the Blemmyes.[21] We have already noted that the main routes into and out of Egypt were guarded during the Principate and the continuity of concern into the later empire comes as no surprise. We have also seen, however, that merely being concerned to control these routes did not mean that the deployment of the army was solely for the defence of the province against external attack. In the first three centuries of Roman rule, the political structure of the province was more important than its physical geography in determining the location of the different units. Controlling the major routes of communication within Egypt and access to and from Egypt is one of the more effective ways of maintaining military control of the Egyptian population and the deployment of units and forts along the roads to the frontier does not mean that the army was mainly or solely concerned with external threats. The very number of forts and stations occupied by these units suggests a dispersal of the army to control the Egyptian population. If the army had been principally concerned with the threat of invasion from the East, the natural strategic response would have been to concentrate a substantial fighting force in a position to deal with the threat and perhaps the most obvious position for a concentration of force to deal with a threat from Persia, surely the only major threat on the frontier before the rise of the Arabs in the seventh century, was in Syria. The deployment of troops attested in the *Notitia* suggests that there had been no real change in the essential purpose of the army in Egypt which was to control the Egyptian population. The army was, of course, also concerned to deal with threats from outside the province but, on the whole, the threat was not large-scale invasion but the small-scale raid and the army was best able to deal with this threat by dispersing the troops to a large number of local bases. There was little difference in the strategic organisation of the army in Egypt in the fourth century.

The major alteration in the position of the army appears to be an increased formality in the manner of the army's dispersal. During the first three centuries, the army was dispersed from its bases over very large areas. Camps were shared by several units and similarly supervision of regions would be shared between the soldiers and officers of different units. There was a lack of geographical exactness in the deployment and dispersal of the unit so although soldiers would be associated with a specific camp, it would be impossible to speak of a single unit controlling the North Fayum or another specific region. In the fourth century, although there were still some multi-unit camps, units were given forts in specific areas and exercised control of those areas. In the Abinnaeus archive the names of units are not used. Units were identified by the fortresses they occupied so Abinnaeus was commander of the *ala* stationed at Dionysias. There was an identification between a specific area and a military unit. The range of the unit was much reduced and whereas previously there were one or more district centurions to whom problems could be brought, now there was a military commander, stationed in a nearby fort. This more rigid pattern may well have eased the logistical problems of supply with local units surviving mainly or solely from the taxation of the surrounding communities.[22]

Whatever the organisational reason for the change, the identification of particular units with particular areas encouraged integration of units into local communities. During his two years in command of the *ala* at Dionysias, Abinnaeus would have had to deal with local officials, important local land owners and village communities. His troops will have been stationed in the fort for a longer period and many were recruited from neighbouring communities. They must have been open to considerable pressures and to the influence of locals of wealth or power. There is a substantial difference between this situation and that of the first three centuries. The centurions exercised considerable influence in the districts in which they served. They were able to use their influence to interfere in local matters and were in a very powerful position. They were, however, comparatively mobile and their power sprang from their ability to influence the central administration. Although it is possible that some centurions developed strong personal ties in the areas in which they served, the most important connections for the centurions were with the central administration and their senior officers in the army. For the soldiers at Dionysias, ties to the central authorities were not so important. The soldiers gathered most of their supplies from the neighbouring communities, developed links with those communities, assuming that they were not originally from the region, and exercised influence and power on a local basis. Connections between an individual military unit and a particular region were long term and far more intimate than in the first three centuries of Roman rule.

This does not necessarily mean that soldiers were more powerful, either as a body or as individuals. The forts were, in many ways, physical representations of the control exercised by the army. They were built to impress. They were a statement of authority which might lead us to believe that the army, physically asserting its presence in communities, was a far more powerful institution than in previous centuries. We know, however, that the army exercised considerable influence in earlier periods and it is difficult to believe that the power of the army could have substantially increased in the fourth century. The presence of an archaeological artefact attesting an assertion of power does not mean that the power asserted was new or greater than before or even that it was real. Modern dictators make grand declarations of their popularity or build great structures asserting their authority even when that power is waning and revolution is in the air. We may wonder why the army of the fourth century needed to monumentalise its authority when the army of the preceding centuries had exercised considerable influence without such structures.

Roman Egypt was in a state of change. Great land owners with privileged positions controlled vast tracts of land and, one presumes, exercised considerable power and influence. The military at all levels were open to the influence of powerful men and institutions. Neither Abinnaeus nor his soldiers were particularly wealthy. Abinnaeus was a man of some importance but his insecure hold on office was threatened by people more powerful than him who could gain access to his superior officers. The power and influence which the army had exercised in the first three centuries were under threat and the commander of an *ala*, a fairly senior military official, was not necessarily the most powerful man in the neighbourhood. Military rank no longer gave even commanders of units the highest social and political status. Senior military commanders, such as Abinnaeus, would be open to the influence of the more important local magnates and leaders who, of course, exercised even more influence over the ordinary soldiers in his unit, men who might have come from villages completely controlled by the magnates. Although people threaten Abinnaeus with higher authorities, the only person who sought to use his influence on Abinnaeus was a priest. The Church represented another new and influential power group in Egyptian society with the links from the village communities to the high society of Alexandria. The Church exercised religious and institutional power in comparison to which a commander of an *ala* was in a rather weak position. Abinnaeus may have been able to refuse this particular request but a priest was a person of note whom Abinnaeus probably wished to please. The power of the centurions and the army had rested on the connections between the central authorities and the military officials in the districts and on the ability of the centurions to call upon overwhelming force. In the fourth century, with the unit closely related to particular areas, the district commander may not have been able to call upon overwhelming force, not without considerable difficulties anyhow, and the key position which the officers had occupied within the administrative and political structure of the province was threatened by other groups, the great land owners and the Church.

The assertion of power by the building of forts may have been an effort to counteract the first signs of the decline in the power of the army, obviously asserting military control over many of the communities of Egypt. Restoring the dominance of the military over civilian society may have been seen as a means of solving the military and political problems which afflicted Egypt at the end of the third century. The decline in the fortunes and power of the army was, however, caused by wider political, economic and social changes. By making the troops more reliant upon the localities in which they served, integrating them further into the social and political structures of local communities, the reforms actually further weakened central control over the troops. The army had been an invaluable tool by which the central administration had asserted its power in the villages and towns of the *chora* but, in the fourth century, instead of being in control, the army was open to control by local power interests. The integration of the army into the local power structures considerably reduced the effectiveness of the army as an administrative and political tool. Libanius' main complaint about the army in Syria was that it was no longer controlled by the central authorities. It competed with and for local power interests and the aristocracy of Antioch was losing the competition. Although it does not apparently happen in this period, one could see how in this state of weak central control, a military or political crisis could lead to the dissolution of the unity of the army in a way that is simply inconceivable for the army of the Principate. In spite of the number of units and perhaps the greater number of men, the army of the fourth century was not only politically less effective in controlling the *chora* but was also militarily considerably weaker than the army of the preceding centuries.

The army of the fourth century shows some similarities with the army of the previous centuries. The differences are, however, more striking. The proliferation of units and forts is only the most obvious of changes. We cannot accurately assess the strength of the army or of individual units and so we cannot know whether the army was substantially larger than in previous centuries. The army was expected to perform a similar role but the most important changes appear to have been in the status of the army as a whole and in the status of individual soldiers. No longer was a military career a desirable alternative to life in village communities. Potential recruits no longer competed or sought to use influence to join the army. In the fourth century, influence was used to keep potential recruits out of the army. The army was forced to recruit by conscription, with all the associated problems of desertion and unwillingness to serve. In part, this may explain the general decline in the status and importance of the army but the major cause of the gradual decline in the power of the army was the evolution of Egyptian society. Social, economic and political change within Egypt marginalised the role of the army so that, by the fourth century, the army was no longer the linchpin of Roman administration. Viewing the army in the context in which it operated, we see that the army of the fourth century was very different from and less important than that of the preceding period.

9

CONCLUSION

In the introduction to this book, I claimed a general applicability for my study. In concluding the book, I will offer some evidence for that claim and trace the fragments of archaeological, literary and other material from provinces other than Egypt which show that this picture of the army in Egypt is also useful in the interpretation of the role of the army in other provinces.

The argument for the uniqueness of Roman Egypt rests upon rather shaky foundations: Egypt was governed by an equestrian prefect rather than a senatorial legate, even though it had a legionary garrison and was, therefore, a province of some importance; the administrative infrastructure of the province was inherited from the Ptolemies; the Roman authorities did not integrate the Egyptian currency with that of the rest of the empire. The similarities between the government of Egypt and that of other provinces, however, far outweigh these differences: Egypt, like other provinces, was governed by a Roman aristocrat sent out from Rome and under the authority of the emperor; Egypt paid taxes to Rome; Rome was the ultimate centre of judicial and political authority; the administrative system, though largely inherited, was shaped to Roman needs and modified by Roman practices.[1] Even the culture of the province had been subjected to the influence of Greek culture and changed during the Roman period. Egypt differed from other provinces, but so did Arabia, Syria, and Britain. Roman imperialism involved the assimilation of many local structures and so distinctive elements of local cultures were preserved in many Roman provinces. In turn, the army must have responded differently to differing military, geographical and political situations, but there is no reason to believe that the army, as an institution, differed much from province to province. Officers who served in Egypt will also have served in other provinces and military units were transferred from province to province. Egypt may have been a particularly troublesome province and the taxes extracted from the province may have been substantially greater than those from other provinces, but none of our sources suggests that, beyond the exclusion of persons of senatorial rank from the province, there was anything peculiar about the government of the province. We would, therefore, assume, a priori, that evidence from Egypt was applicable to other provinces, especially when it concerns an empire-wide institution such as the army.

One of the major differences between Egypt and the rest of the empire is the source material that historians are able to work with. The papyri provide a unique insight into provincial society and, since the source material is unique, the history we can write is unique. The inevitable result of this is that we cannot hope to create directly comparable studies for other provinces. We are reliant, therefore, on spotting similarities between the Egyptian situation and that in other provinces from rather different sources.

The only area in which there can be detailed comparison with the army outside Egypt is that of policing. The recent discovery and publication of texts from the fort at Vindolanda on Hadrian's Wall offers some comparison with the material from Egypt. In style and content, much of the material is remarkably similar to the ostraka from the Eastern Desert. The impression of similarity is reinforced by a strength report which shows that the unit based at the fort had men dispersed across the province.[2] The evidence from the record office of the *cohors* XX *Palmyrorum* at Dura-Europos in Syria shows that that unit spread its forces over a considerable area.[3] Hunt's *pridianum* from Stobii on the Danube, a text which found its way to Egypt and was preserved amongst the other papyri, also shows that troops were sent out from the camp on many different missions.[4] Literary and epigraphic sources present centurions and soldiers acting as police.[5] There are several tombstones which show ordinary soldiers carrying writing tablets and vine-sticks. The vine-stick was a symbol of a centurion's office but these men were not centurions. Centurions used the stick to chastise soldiers and, if we regard the stick as the symbol of a function rather than an office, we can understand the tombstones as portrayals of the soldiers as men who chastise rather than men who kill. By including both the stick and the writing tablets on their tombstones, the soldiers were making reference to their role as police.[6] An inscription from Bath commemorates the repair of a religious monument which had been vandalised. The repair was carried out by the *centurio reg(ioni)*, the centurion of the region, the equivalent of the Greek επὶ τῶν τόπων.[7] These sources point to the involvement of the armies of other provinces in similar types of policing activity to those which we have abundantly attested in Egypt.

We have little comparable data on the social standing of soldiers. We have to proceed through generalities. Rates of pay were the same throughout the empire but there were differences in the value of that pay from province to province and we must presume that the economic status of the soldiers would also vary. We have seen that even in Italy the income of the soldiers was quite high and would have ensured a reasonable standard of living. Also, since expenses were deducted at fixed rates, the soldiers were probably insulated from the higher cost of living in more expensive provinces. In any case, the economic benefits of military service in Egypt were not sufficient to raise veterans beyond the economic level of the village and one supposes that the veterans who settled in Italy will have settled at a similar, if slightly lower, economic level.

Our study of legal status has shown that it was not the actual legal privileges of the soldiers and veterans which mattered, and these would have been broadly the same in all provinces of the empire, but the ability of the veterans to enforce their legal rights. In Egypt, the veterans appear to have had considerable difficulties in securing their rights, especially from the middle of the second century. This was clearly a political issue and must have varied according to political circumstances. In provinces in which the veterans had little or no political power as a group and individual veterans had little standing, the privileges of veterans were probably widely ignored. In a recently conquered province, however, when a governor may well have felt politically or militarily dependent upon the veteran community in case of military crisis and one in which the veterans had a certain political organisation and unity, then the veterans were probably able to enforce their privileges. In Egypt, we see that the foundation of Antinoopolis provided some veterans with a more effective means of securing status and privileges. In Britain, if Tacitus is to be believed, a major contributory factor in the Boudiccan revolt was the behaviour of the military colonists at Colchester who were not restrained by officials when they seized land from the local tribesmen. The power of the colonists must be related to the political situation in a relatively recently conquered province.[8] This influence is in marked contrast to the impression we gain from the Egyptian material. The decline in the importance of veterans as Roman rule became more established is symbolised by the abolition of one of the principal privileges of military service and the main division between the ordinary provincials and veterans. The grant of universal Roman citizenship effectively abolished citizenship as a marker of high status and veterans were one the principal groups that lost in the change. It is very likely that the historical and political processes which influenced the standing of veterans in Egypt also applied in other provinces and the resulting decline in the standing of veterans in Egypt was probably mirrored in most provinces. The evidence, both general and specific, points to the history of the army in Egypt being a good model for the history of the army elsewhere.

There are considerable benefits in using Egypt as a case study for the history of the army. The evidence from Egypt, even concerning such issues as the organisation of military units, is simply unrivalled by the material from other provinces. The number of attestations of the various military units has enabled me to draw up a fairly complete and detailed picture of the garrison for the first three centuries of Roman rule. We can, with some confidence, assess the numbers of troops in the province, certainly up to about AD 230, though there may have been some changes in the garrison between then and AD 284. The real benefit of the Egyptian material does not, however, lie in the more detailed evidence for the numbers and types of units that formed the garrison but in the illumination of the everyday activities of that garrison and the interaction of the garrison with the Egyptian population. The evidence allows us to investigate these areas without having to rely upon the rhetorical biases of our literary sources and we can understand the relationship between the provincials and the army not from the macro-political level of the Roman emperor or the level of the literary sources but at the level of the village, a social level unattested in other sources. It is in this context that we can see and understand the work and role of the Roman army.

We have been able to trace the personal connections and relations of the veterans settled in the village of Karanis. The documentation illustrates the everyday transactions of the veterans: the payment of taxes, the leasing of land, the legal documents to deal with the major events of life such as birth, death, marriage and divorce. In themselves, these documents illustrate particular events of little historical significance but, by gathering the texts together, we can begin to reconstruct the society of the village and the relationship between veterans and the society in which they lived. Study of Karanis shows the integration of the veterans into Egyptian society. They differed little from their Graeco-Egyptian neighbours in culture or in social and economic status. Veterans and their families were, on average, marginally wealthier than the average villager but the only significant difference between veterans and other villagers was in legal status and even in this area, the veterans were frequently unable to assert their privileges.

Soldiers and veterans were in continual contact with civilian Egyptians. Soldiers worked with Egyptian civilians in manning the extensive security system of the province. They supervised the collection of taxes. They worked with local police in the nomes. They traded with civilians and probably received many supplies from civilian contractors. They married and the resultant children lived in Graeco-Egyptian settlements. There was no great cultural, social or economic division and it is unsurprising, viewed from this level, that the soldiers integrated. Other historians, writing about the relationship between soldiers and civilians from another view-point, have not reached the same conclusions. Veterans and soldiers have been seen as isolated from the local populations, sometimes terrorising them, sometimes simply living in remote frontier districts or within the military confines of the camp. The portrayal of soldiers as men recruited from the immediate neighbourhood of the camp, living and working in the camp and, finally, retiring to the satellite community of the camp, minimises the interaction of soldiers and provincials. Contrary to this, some portray the soldiers and veterans as the leading lights of provincial society, using their privileges and wealth to obtain high social status and, through their dominant position in society, encouraging social and economic change. Neither of these two views can be accepted. At this general level, the integration of the soldiers comes as something of a surprise. In most interpretations, which perhaps take as a model the European experience of colonial empires, separation of the military is assumed.

Many Roman soldiers were not Egyptians. They came from disparate cultural backgrounds and served in a Roman institution. Their eventual integration needs, therefore, explanation. If we escape from broad ethnic or other categorisations and concentrate on individual interactions, then the processes at work become clear. The continual involvement of the troops with civilian society and the forming of professional and non-professional relationships with Egyptian civilians meant that soldiers would spend a large proportion of their years in service mixing with locals. As soldiers were men of some influence, the locals would be interested in gaining their confidence and friendly relations with the local population will have considerably eased the lives of the troops. If we accept an absence of nationalism and an absence of strong barriers between the troops and the provincials, then integration becomes possible.

We have seen that the Roman army could, on occasion, act brutally in the suppression of rebels. It is also clear that the Roman army maintained the unity and loyalty of the troops. The soldiers could be used to suppress rebellion; they did not side with the rebels in a revolutionary fashion. The explanation for the maintenance of loyalty, in spite of the integration of the troops into Egyptian society, lies also in our concentration on the individual. Soldiers gained access to the army through recommendation. They competed for military careers and, once they had gained access to the army, were dependent upon friendships and personal connections for favours and promotion. Ties of obligation, friendship and loyalty would bind members of a unit together and would further bind those men to their commanding officer. These ties of obligation can be traced through the ranks until they reach the ultimate source of all advancement and patronage, the emperor. It was the emperor who paid the troops, who sent them gifts, who made every effort to secure their personal loyalty. Those gifts, ultimately emanating from the emperor, would be administered by the governor and his senior officials and passed through the officers to the men. Modernising conceptions of society as divided into social classes and ethnic groups must be set aside. Ancient society emphasised personal contacts. Patronage and friendship were fundamental social bonds and these created vertical links between rich and poor, the powerful and weak. Mutual bonds of friendship and patronage held military units together, reinforced connections with the centre and allowed the soldiers to act with such brutality in the suppression of rebels to whom they had no cultural, ethnic, or class loyalty.

These vertical links in society were avenues through which favours could be communicated but also allowed the transmission of power. These avenues explain the success of Roman military government in the first three centuries of Roman rule. The centurion, the linchpin of the Roman governmental system, was a direct route of communication between the ordinary people and the central authorities. He was the representative of the considerable power of the central authorities. Each centurion was potentially supported by 10,000 soldiers, but there was, as everyone knew this, no need to deploy those 10,000 soldiers with each centurion. An occasional display of force was sufficient to reinforce the impression of the potential power of the centurions. Thus, with a very small force, the army was able to exert considerable power throughout the province. To make up for the fact that the actual manpower in support of each district centurion was minimal, the Roman authorities recruited substantial numbers of Egyptians into the security system. The centurions and the civilian security system made a powerful combination which, given the technological conditions of ancient states, brought Roman power to a surprisingly low level of society. For the Egyptian villagers, the Roman state was not a remote power to which taxes were sent but which had little other impact on their lives; the Roman state was a real and powerful presence. The military security system assured the successful control of a populous province with a very small garrison for three centuries, a considerable administrative and political achievement. Roman imperialism in Egypt did not depend on a class of soldiers and veterans becoming a bastion of civilisation and loyalty in a hostile land. It did depend on the army. The army policed Egypt under the authority of the centurions. The *strategoi* may have overseen the appointing of the village police but the centurions looked after the security of the nomes. Egypt was administered by the *strategoi* but ruled by the army.

This study provides a new context for writing about the Roman army. We have seen that the traditional models used to explain the evidence for the Roman army are inadequate. We cannot consider the army in isolation from the society in which it was formed or the societies in which it operated. We must be sensitive to the fact that any social group is, in fact, made up of individuals and those individuals will respond to social pressures and situations as individuals. The resulting changes and the relationship between the social group and broader society can be analysed and discussed in terms of the group but any explanation of the position of that group must start from the level at which individuals operated. The army was not a completely separate organisation simply because the soldiers who formed that army could never be separate from the society which surrounded them. The ban on marriage is a clear example of this. Although the ban technically separated soldiers from one of the normal forms of social relationship in ancient society, soldiers continued to form these relationships. They continued to behave like normal members of society. Soldiers, and therefore the army, continued to be influenced by normal society and so we cannot understand either the individual soldiers or the institution without reference to that society. We have also seen how the army exercised military and political control over Egypt. The troops brought Roman power to the *chora*. This was one of the principal functions of the Roman military and any attempt to understand the nature of the Roman army without first understanding its political and administrative role is doomed to failure. The history of the Roman army is more than the history of organisational arrangements and changes. It must be the history of the societies in which the army operated. The changes in the nature of the Roman army at the end of the third century or in the fourth century were related not to any internal difficulties in organisational structure but to political and social changes in the wider society of Egypt and, ultimately, in the empire as a whole. Meaning can only be derived from context. We have studied the Roman army in a specific context and this context has not only provided us with a new meaning for the Roman army but also offered a new interpretation of the Roman empire.

APPENDIX 1
Military units

LEGIONS

There are very large numbers of documents which refer to the legions in Alexandria and it is pointless to try and list all the material. A brief survey of the material collected in *CIL* III from Alexandria shows that there were many legionaries whose tombstones were erected in the immediate environs of the camp which lay about two miles outside the city.[1] There are also a large number of papyrological sources which associate all three legions with the Alexandrian area. There can be no doubt that Alexandria was the main base for the legionary forces in Egypt.[2] There are, however, some other references to legionaries which make it clear that not all the troops were confined to the city. Soldiers of III *Cyrenaica* and XXII *Deiotariana* were at Talmis (Kalabsha), about forty-five miles south of Syene (Aswan), worshipping the god Mandoulis in AD 104/5.[3] There was also a legionary presence at Pselchis (Dakke), about thirty-five miles to the south of Talmis with soldiers of all three legions attested.[4] The legions also appear associated with building works at Koptos in two first-century AD inscriptions and there are two tombstones from Koptos, one for a soldier of III *Cyrenaica* and the other for a *speculator*, an officer below the rank of centurion, of II *Traiana*.[5] Individual soldiers appear in the Oxyrhynchite serving as *epiplooi*, a duty which involved sailing down the Nile as guards on grain boats, and we can assume that soldiers performed this role in many nomes.[6] Centurions from II *Traiana* commanded the *cohors* I *Flavia Cilicia* stationed in Syene in the second century.[7] A number of legionaries, mostly centurions, inscribed their names at the statues of the Memnonia at Thebes.[8] A centurion appeared at Silsilis, to the north of Kom Ombo, erecting an altar and another centurion appears at Ptolemais Hormou.[9] At the station of Aphrodito, on the route to the Red Sea, there was an inscription testifying to the presence of a centurion of the XXII legion.[10] From Akoris (Tehna) come a series of inscriptions of two centurions of XXII *Deiotariana*, one of III *Cyrenaica* and a tombstone of a soldier of III *Cyrenaica*.[11]

There is a certain amount of evidence that suggests that there was another legion based in Egypt, the XV *Apollinaris*. There are, however, only two attestations of this legion, one literary, telling us that Titus collected the legion from Egypt when Vespasian had been entrusted with the campaign against the Jews, and the other epigraphic, attesting the presence of a centurion at the quarry of Mons Claudianus in the Trajanic period.[12] However, after the Jewish war had been brought to a successful conclusion, Titus, having arrived back in Egypt with his prisoners and with two legions, one of which was XV *Apollinaris*, sent the legions back to where they had come from and XV *Apollinaris* returned to Pannonia.[13] It is probable that Nero had stationed the legion in Egypt temporarily as part of his preparations for a major campaign.[14] The presence of the centurion in the Trajanic period is not necessarily significant since the presence of one centurion does not mean that the whole legion was in the province or even that part of the legion was there.[15] Josephus' narrative makes clear that he regarded the garrison of Egypt as being two legions during this period.[16]

There are a considerable number of documents concerning the auxiliary units which were stationed in Egypt during this period. This appendix collects the evidence and briefly discusses each unit. The main conclusions of this discussion form the basis of Tables 2.1 and 2.2. The references below are as brief as possible. Descriptions such as 'prefect' or 'veteran' refer to attestations of the activities of these persons which, of course, tells us very little about the unit itself. All references to Römer refer to the publication of the diploma of 179, C. Römer, 'Diplom für einen Fussoldaten aus Koptos vom 23. März 179', *ZPE*, 1990, vol. 82, pp. 137–53. I discuss the *alae*, then the cohorts, then other units. Units in each section are in alphabetical order, excepting dubious cases which I deal with at the end of each section. Wherever possible I have given the place where the document was written, assuming, unless there is evidence to the contrary, that this was identical to the place where the document was found. Several documents could not be placed and the origins for these documents have been left blank. At the end of the survey (pp. 190–1), Table A1.1 lists the units entered in the *Notitia Dignitatum*.

ALAE

Apriana

Document	Date	Origin	Description
ChLA XI 501	48		Strength report.
P. Mich, III 41–68			Property dispute.
159; *CPL* 212			
PSI VI 729;	77	Cappodocia/	Sale of horse.
CPL 186		Egypt	
CIL XVI 29	83	Koptos	Diploma.
RMD 9	105		Diploma.
BGU IV 1033	98–117		*Epikrisis.*
BGU I 69	120	Arsinoite	Soldiers' loan.
P. Hamb. I 31a	117–38	Arsinoite	*Epikrisis.*
SB IV 7523	153	Philadelphia	Veteran.
CIL III 49;	170	Thebes	Prefect's offering to
I. Memnon 56			Memnon.
Römer (1990)	179	Koptos	Diploma.
P. Oxy. XXXVI	179/80	Oxyrhynchus/	Veteran delivering military
2760		Alexandria	supplies.
P. Köln II 94;	213	Oxyrhynchite	Grain receipt. Unit stationed
SB X 10497			at Small Oasis.
SPP XX 71	268–70	Hermopolis	Sale of slave.
		Magna	
CIL III 6026		Syene	Tombstone.

This unit has a good spread of attestations throughout the period and into the third century. The unit does not appear in the diploma of 156–61. The references immediately before 156 concern veterans but it is likely that the unit was in Egypt at the time of the Hadrianic *epikrisis* and in 170, when the prefect visited the statues of Memnon at Thebes. We must, therefore, restore its name in this diploma.

The *ala Apriana* is first attested in the early first century AD. In 120, the unit was stationed in Koptos where a horseman contracted a loan which was to plague his heir and the heir of the lender, C. Iulius Agrippianus.[17] Sex. Mevius Sex. f. Fab. Domitius of this *ala* died at Syene. Two documents connect the unit with the Oxyrhynchite. *P. Oxy.* XXXVI 2760 concerns a veteran of the unit who had settled in the Oxyrhynchite and *P. Köln* II 94 = *SB* X 10497 shows that the unit was at the Small Oasis (Bahariya Oasis) in 213 but was collecting grain from the Oxyrhynchite. The oasis is connected to the region by a route across the Western Desert which meant that the Oxyrhynchite was an obvious place to look for supplies.

Augusta

Document	Date	Origin	Description
P. Hamb. III 217	Pre–50	Oxyrhynchus	Contract.
P. Hamb. I 1	57		Loan.
CIL XVI 29	83	Koptos	Diploma.
P. Hamb. I 31	103		*Epikrisis.*
RMD 9	105		Diploma.

There are a number of documents mentioning the ala Augusta from outside Egypt:

Document	Date	Origin	Description
CIL III 600	*c.* 163	Macedonia	Unit in Mesopotamia.
CIL VII 340	188	Britain	Prefect.
CIL VII 341	191	Britain	Prefect.
CIL VII 342	*c.* 193	Britain	Prefect.
CIL VII 351	213	Britain	Dedication to emperors.
CIL III 4812	238	Noricum	Dedication.
CIL VII 344	242	Britain	Dedication of altar.
CIL VII 353		Britain	Tombstone.
CIL VII 338		Britain	Prefect.
CIL III 5819		Raetia	Tombstones of *eques.*
CIL III 4834		Noricum	Tombstone of a veteran of a vexillation.
CIL V 6478		Italy	Prefect.
CIL V 7008		Italy	Prefect.

This unit was in Egypt during the first century but later transferred from the province. Its first appearance elsewhere was as part of a force commanded by M. Valerius Lollianus in Mesopotamia. It is clear that there were several *alae Augustae.*

Commagenorum

Document	Date	Origin	Description
ChLA XI 501	48		Strength report.
CIL XVI 29	83	Koptos	Diploma.
O. Tait II 1689	165		Receipt.
SB I 4587		Talmis	Dedication.
SB I 4575		Talmis	Dedication.
Lesquier, No. 43★		Talmis	Dedication.

★ L.J. Lesquier, *L'armée romaine de L'Egypte d'Auguste à Dioclétien*, Cairo, IFAO, 1918, Appendix I.

This unit remains virtually unknown. The reading of *ChLA* XI 501 is uncertain. The name of the unit has been read from the first two letters of Commagenorum and even they are unclear. The *ala* is attested in Noricum in 106 (*CIL XVI* 52) and in 135/138 (*RMD* 93, cf. *CIL* III 5224). The reference of 165 is, however, certain.

Veterana Gallica

Document	Date	Origin	Description
CIL III 55; *I. Memnon* 14	I	Thebes	Dedication by the *Praefectus Gallorum* et Ber [.
P. Lond. II p. 42, 482; *CPL* 114; *RMR* 80; *ChLA* III 203	130		Hay receipt from *procurator faenaris*, Serenus.
P. Wisc. I 14	131	Syene	Legal case where *eques* of *ala* represented soldier of II *Thracum*.
P. Mich, VII 438; *CPL* 188	140	Alexandria	Loan.
P. Grenf. II 51	143	Soknopaiou Nesos	Veteran.
P. Fouad I 45; *CPL* 185	153	Nikopolis	Soldiers' loan.
P. Mich VI 428	154	Bakchias/Karanis	Veteran.
CIL XVI 184	156–61		Diploma.
P. Gen. I 35; *Doc. Eser. Rom.* 56	161		Camels purchased by decurion of *ala*.
P. Hamb. I 139; *RMR* 76	179		Hay receipts.
Römer	179	Koptos	Diploma.
P. Grenf. II 48	191	Soknopaiou Nesos	Grain receipt.
CIL III 6581	199	Nikopolis	List of decurions.
SB X 10619; P. Alex & Giss 3	201–2	Soknopaiou Nesos	Request for entertainers.
BGU II 614	216–17	Arsinoite, Herakleides district	Mention of *ala Antoniniana Gallica*.
P. Mich. VII 455 & 456; *RMR* 53	225–50		Fragment mentions *ala* and legionary.
P. Mich. III 164; *CPL* 143; *RMR* 20	243–4		Promotion to decurion.
P. Mich. VII 455; *CPL* 133	III		Mentioned in report of unknown unit.
SEG XXIV (1969) 1216			Tombstone of prefect's freedman.

Document	Date	Origin	Description
Sources external to Egypt:			
CIL XVI 3	54		Diploma gives an *ala veterana Gallorum et Thracum*.
CIL XVI 35	88	Syria	Diploma.
RMD 5	91	Syria	Diploma.
Smallwood★	post-117	Ephesus	Prefect.
CIL III 320		Asia Minor	Prefect.
CIL IX 5439	III	Italy	Prefect.

The *ala veterana Gallica* is extraordinarily well attested. The first attestation of the unit in Egypt has been dated by Bernand to the late first century on the style of the script and the mention of the prefect of Mons Berenike. This creates a minor problem as the unit is not attested on the diploma of 105 (*RMD* 9), suggesting that the unit had yet to arrive in Egypt. The unit was in Egypt by 130 and the last attestation of the unit in Syria was in 91. This encouraged Bernand to give the inscription a later date than the hand suggested. It is possible, however, that the inscription is either second century or early first century and refers to a different unit. A very early diploma, the diploma of AD 54, suggests that the naming system of auxiliary units had not been fully established by this date.[18]

It is not certain that *P. Grenf.* II 51 involved a soldier of this unit. The identification rests upon the striking similarity of the text to *P. Fouad* I 45 of 153 which involves a man whose name could be read as Heronianus, *eques* of the *ala*, although the first letter of his name is unclear. The earlier text involves Antonius Heronianus, *eques*.

The editor of *P. Alex & Giss.* 3 = *SB* X 10619 has identified the decurion in that document with Antonius Antiochianus of the *ala veterana Gallica* who appears in *CIL* III 6581, a list of decurions of the *ala* for 199. The decurion is not, however, necessarily the same man since the editor could only read two of the letters of 'Antiochianus'.

The *ala veterana Gallica* is one of the best known of the auxiliary units in Egypt. The first appearance of the unit involves a *custos armorum* who attended a court case in Syene as a representative of an absent party. This suggests that the unit was probably stationed in the area. It seems that the unit was stationed in Lower Egypt by the middle of the second century and, for 179, we have a series of hay and money receipts preserved on one roll of papyrus (*P. Hamb.* I 39). These detail not only the hay given to the various members of the unit by L. Iulius Serenus but also

---

★ E.M. Smallwood, *Documents Illustrating the Principles of Nerva, Trajan and Hadrian*, Cambridge, Cambridge University Press, 1966, p. 246.

the stations to which the horsemen were sent. These were Aphrodito, Boukolia, Taposiris, Mareotis, Skenai Mandrai, Skenai, Skenai Mikrai, the Arsinoite, Laura and Klysma. Some of these places are quite easily identified. Klysma was one of the many names of Suez. Laura was near El-Arish on the Mediterranean coast of the Sinai. Aphrodito (Atfih) is about 64 km south of Babylon (Cairo) and Skenai Mandrai was between Babylon and Aphrodito. Mareotis was the name of a town to the west of Alexandria but along the Mediterranean coast. Boukolia is unknown but since one of the mouths of the Nile was the Boukolic, we may guess that it was towards the coast of the Delta. There are various possibilities for the Skenai but as *skenai* can just mean camp, any later evidence of places called Skenai might not refer to the particular camps of this document. The troops sent out over this three-month period were assigned duties which did not correspond to the divisions of the unit into *turmae*. The base camp from which the troops were sent out is not known but may have been Nikopolis from where there is an inscription dated to 199 listing the decurions of the unit and of the *ala* I *Thracum Mauretana* (CIL III 6581). *P. Alex. & Giss.* 3 = SB X 10619 of 201/2 may be addressed to a decurion of the unit who was supervising affairs at Soknopaiou Nesos (Dimai), on the northern bank of Lake Moeris (Birket Qarun). The *Notitia Dignitatum* places the unit at Rhinocolura, the major settlement near Laura (*Or.* xxviii 28).

Heracliana

Document	Date	Origin	Description
P. Amh., 107 CPL 190	185	Hermopolite	Grain receipt. *Ala* at Koptos.
P. Ryl. II 85	185		Grain receipt. *Ala* at Koptos.
BGU II 807	185	Magdola	Grain receipt. *Ala* at Koptos.
P. Amh. 109	185–6	Hermopolite	Receipt for supplies.
P. Amh. 108	186	Hermopolite	Grain receipt. *Ala* at Koptos.
WO 961	188	Thebes	Receipt.
WO 1012	II	Thebes	Receipt.
WO 1013	202	Thebes	Receipt.
P. Brooklyn 24	215		*Ala He*[ ] attested.
P. Alex. 465; *P. Alex & Gliss.* 8 *SB* X 10624		Arsinoite	Business dealings of *eques* through an agent.
Outside Egypt:			
CIL III 600	c.163	Macedonia	Vexillation of *ala*.
IGRR 1536	167–8	Palmyra	Former prefect.
CIL II 4329		Tarraco	Possible prefect.

This *ala* is very well attested for a very short period in the mid-second century. This is largely due to the survival of an achive of Iulius Iustinus (Vestinus in *BGU* II 807, but Iustinus in the Rylands and Amherst papyri) concerning the supply of the unit. The unit was based in Koptos at the time. Ostraka from the Thebaid from the late second century do not give the unit any numeral but establish the probable station of the unit. This relative lack of information leaves open a possible identification with the *ala Thracum Herculiana* attested in Syria in 157 (*CIL* XVI 106). The unit does not appear on any of the diplomas which suggests that it did not arrive in Egypt until the early 180s.

I *Thracum Mauretana*

Document	Date	Origin	Description
CIL XVI 29	83	Koptos	Diploma.
BGU II 696; *CPL* 118	156	Contrapol- lonospolis Magna	Officer served with *ala* but returns to his own cohort.
BGU I 26/II 447	173/4	Karanis	Census return.
Römer	179	Koptos	Diploma.
CIL III 6581	199	Nikopolis	List of decurions.
CPL 221	II	Nikopolis	Military will.
P. Mich. inv. 256★	205	Hermopolite	Loan to priest.
CIL 75	206–11	Syene	Dedication.
CIL III 13578	288	Qantara	Rebuilding of camp.
CPR VI 76	II/III		Will
P. Coll. Youtie I 53			Private letter.
CIL III 14139		Alexandria	Tombstone of veteran.

The first reference to this *ala* is from 156 and suggests that the *ala* should be read in one of the *lacunae* in the diploma of 156–61. Two *alae* are certain in the diploma, *Vocontiorum* and *veterana Gallica*, and there is space for another two, one of which must be the *ala Apriana*. With one available space left, the original editor suggested the inclusion of the *ala Heracliana*, while the more recent reading has been *ala Mauretana*.[19] The *ala Thracum Mauretana* must be restored.

The most interesting document is *P. Coll. Youtie* I 53. The script suggests a second-century date. The letter details troop movements prior to the sending of a detachment from the Egyptian forces to Mauretania. The soldier involved had written to his mother as she had had to appear in

★ N. Priest, 'A loan of money with some notes on the *ala Mauretana*', *ZPE*, 1983, vol. 51, pp. 65–70.

court. He wished her to write to him and to write soon or else he would be out of communication in Mauretania. To encourage her rapid reply, he details the planned manoeuvres. This involved the movement of his cohort to Alexandria prior to being shipped abroad. The African cohort was either replacing them in their current station or was being amalgamated with them in order to strengthen the unit. The Moorish *ala*, which must be this *ala*, would join them at some point. The soldier envisaged his return to Egypt within three years. It is likely that these movements were in response to a crisis which suggests a date of 145–152.[20]

The unit was at Nikopolis in 199 with the *veterana Gallica* (CIL III 6581) and *CPL* 221 was drawn up at the winter quarters of the II *Traiana*.

Vocontiorum

Document	Date	Origin	Description
P. Mich. III 159; *CPL* 212	41–68		Dispute over military will heard by a decurion of *ala*.
P. Wisc. II 53	55	Koptos	Receipt for down-payment on house.
P. Hamb. I 2	59	Babylon	Loan of money to civilians.
RMD 9	105		Diploma.
SB I 4383	116	Mons Porphyrites	Dedication to Trajan and Isis.
AE (1906) No. 22; *CPL* 113	122	Arsinoite	Discharge certificate.
IGRR 1200	122/3	Thebes	Dedication by prefect.
BGU I 114; M. *Chr.* 372	134	Koptos	Legal cases.
SB XVI 12508	149	Arsinoite, Herakleides district	Certificate of exemption from poll tax.
SB I 5218	156	Theadelphia	Private letter.
CIL XVI 184	156–61	Karanis	Diploma.
SB I 4280	165	Koptos	Dedication.
BGU I 4/XV 2458	177		Complaint.
Römer	179	Koptos	Diploma.
ChLA IV 264	II	Oxyrhynchus	Tax receipts.
CIL III 12068 (*cf. CIL* III 12067)		Ptolemais	Inscription for decurion Q. Caesius Valens.
AE 1911 No. 121; *I. Koptos* 19		Hormou Hammamat	Dedication to the emperor at the end of term of service.
Outside Egypt:			
ILS 628		Dmeir, Arabia	Prefect's *strator* (servant).
CIL XIII 8805		Arnheim, Germany	Part of the British army on duty in Germany.
CIL XIII 8865		Germany	Veteran.
CIL VII 1080		Newstead	Decurion of *ala Augusta Vocontiorum*.

Document	Date	Origin	Description
CIL XIII 4030		Belgica	Prefect of *ala*.
CIL XIII 3463		Belgica	Tombstone of *eques*.
CIL XIII 1835		Lyons	Tombstone of decurion's daughter.
CIL XIII 8671		Germania Inferior	Tombstone of *missicus*.

The *ala Vocontiorum* is one of the best attested *alae* from Egypt and one of the earliest attested auxiliary units in Egypt. Prior to 60, the unit is attested twice or three times but does not appear again until 105. It is attested several times before 179. After 179, the unit disappears. A major alteration in the auxiliary garrison would be expected in the early period with the campaigns of Corbulo, the Jewish war and the Flavian march on Rome. It is tempting to date the epigraphic evidence from northern Europe to the Flavian period. The unit seems to have served on the German frontier and in Belgica, areas severely disrupted by the rebellion of the Batavians. This hypothesis cannot be proved because of the difficulties in dating the European inscriptions. The *ala Augusta Vocontiorum* shows that there were at least two *alae* with this tribal origin.

Two of the documents from the first period in which the unit was in Egypt emanate from the Koptite region, *P. Wisc.* II 53 and *AE* (1911) No. 121 = *I. Koptos* 19, the second of which is undated but was set up by a Volquian, a member of the neighbouring tribe to the Voconti. This shows continuing contacts with the homeland of the *ala*. Another early reference comes from Babylon (*P. Hamb.* I 2). When the unit returned to Egypt, the references once more emanate from the Koptite area. In 177, *BGU* I 4 = XV 2458 shows that the *ala* was not at Pelusium since the letter is an appeal from a veteran to a centurion for his help in restoring goods which had been deposited with Petesouchos. Petesouchos had joined the *ala* and left the area.

Xoitana

Document	Date	Origin	Description
P. Mich. III 159; *CPL* 212	41–68		Legal dispute.

This *ala* is known from a single reference to a decurion who heard a case concerning a disputed inheritance involving soldiers of the *alae Apriana* and *Vocontiorum*. This decurion made a third on the panel of judges. It is probable that the unit was serving in Egypt but it is otherwise unknown. The name is derived from the town of Xois, south of Lake Mareotis and east of Alexandria. This suggests that the *ala* was raised in Egypt making it the only *ala* to be raised in Egypt, though there were two cohorts, the I and II *Thebaeorum*. Alternatively, the name may be derived from the station of the unit.

Paullini

Document	Date	Origin	Description
SB XVI 12609	27	Alexandria	Loan

This is another unit known only from a single reference. This text also provides the single attestation of the *cohors Ae[lii] Habeti*. These units were probably named after their commanders by a process similar to that by which the centuries and *turmae* were named after their commanding officers.

COHORTS

I *Ulpia Afrorum equitata*

Document	Date	Origin	Description
CIL XVI 184	156–61	Karanis	Diploma.
BGU I 142	159	Alexandria	Certificate.
BGU I 241	177	Karanis	Court case.
Römer	179	Koptos	Diploma.
P. Coll. Youtie I 53			Private letter.
ILS 8867	II	Bithynia	Prefect.

There is some doubt as to the numeral of this unit. The inscription from Bithynia clearly mentions the I *Ulpia* as does the diploma of 179, but the other non-reconstructed numeral is in a certificate of examination of 159 which points to II *Ulpia*. The 179 diploma seems to be preferable since the examination certificate identifies the unit as II *Ulpia* not II *Ulpia Afrorum*. *P. Coll. Youtie* I 53 has been discussed above with reference to the *ala Thracum Mauretana* and dated to 145–52.

I *Apamenorum*

Document	Date	Origin	Description
BGU III 729	144	Karanis	Iulius Apollinarius archive.
P. Lond. II, p. 207, 177	145	Karanis	Iulius Apollinarius archive.
CIL XVI 184	156–61	Karanis	Diploma.
BGU III 888	159/60	Karanis	Iulius Apollinarius archive.
Römer	179		Diploma.
BGU II 423; *Sel. Pap.* II 112	II	Philadelphia	Letter sent via unit *librarius*.
BGU II 462		Karanis	Iulius Apollinarius archive.
P. Mich. VII 446; *CPL* 226	II		Soldiers associated with II *Traiana*.
CPL 310	II	Kasr el Banat	Ostrakon.
P. Brooklyn 24	215		Attestation of unit.
P. Panop. 1	298		Account.
P. Mich. IX 542	III	Karanis	Veteran buys house.
P. Oxy. XII 1511; *RMR* 102	III	Oxyrhynchus	Account with legionaries.
Outside Egypt:			
CIL III 600	*c.* 163	Macedonia	Vexillation in Mesopotamia.
CIL XIV 171		Ostia	Prefect.

There are numerous attestations of this unit but few are very informative. A lot of the documents are undated. The unit does appear in the *Notitia Dignitatum* (*Or.* xxxi 60) stationed in the Thebaid and is clearly attested in the third century. The first clearly dated documents come from a small archive relating to C. Iulius Apollinarius and concern his marital problems and land holdings in Karanis.

The *cohors* I *Apamenorum* is attested on an ostrakon of the second century from the Wadi Hammamat (*CPL* 310). It is possible that the unit was stationed in Philadelphia where a letter was sent through the *librarius* of the unit (*BGU* II 423 = *Sel. Pap.* II 112). Associations with legionaries in accounts might suggest that the unit was stationed at Nikopolis (*P. Mich.* VII 446 = *CPL* 226, *P. Oxy.* XII 1511).

I *Augusta Praetoria Lusitanorum equitata*

Document	Date	Origin	Description
RMD 9	105		Diploma.
CIL III 13582	110	Talmis	Dedication.
SB I 3919	111	Nubia	Prefect.
SB I 4608	98–117	Talmis	Dedication.
PSI IX 1063; *RMR* 74	117		Receipts for *viaticum* for recruits.
BGU II 696; *CPL* 118; *RMR* 64	156	Contrapollonos-polis Magna	Strength report.
SB IV 9227/9228	160	Syene	*Epikrisis.*
CIL XVI 184	156–61	Karanis	Diploma.
Römer	179		Diploma.
SB V 8828	180–92	Contrapollonos-polis Magna	Dedication to Serapis.
ChLA IV 264	II	Oxyrhynchus	Tax receipts.
CIL III 22	288	Hierakonpolis	Camp rebuilt.
SB I 4564		Talmis	Dedication.
SB I 4572		Talmis	Dedication.
SB I 4566		Talmis	Dedication.
Outside Egypt:			
RMD 2	75	Moesia	Diploma.
CIL XVI 33	86	Judaea	Diploma.
RMD 6	96	Moesia Superior	Diploma.
CIL V 7425	*c.* 100	Italy	Prefect.
CIL XVI 164	110	Pannonia Inferior	Diploma.
CIL XVI 179/180	148	Pannonia Inferior	Diploma.
RMD 102	157	Pannonia Inferior	Diploma.
RMD 55	161	Moesia Superior	Diploma.
CIL III 14214		Moesia Inferior	Veteran's tombstone.

This cohort is clearly not the same unit as served in Moesia. The unit arrived in Egypt from Judaea prior to 105 and then stayed through the second and third centuries. The unit is well attested during the second century and many of the references come from Upper Egypt. *BGU* II 696 of 156 gives us the full name of the unit and its strength.

There is a series of references from Nubia and the border of Egypt. Talmis (Kalabsha) contained a temple to Mandoulis on which the Roman soldiers inscribed their prayers and names (*SB* I 4608, 4564, 4566, 4572, *CIL* III 13582). Soldiers from the cohort formed part of the garrison at

Syene (*SB* IV 9227, 9228). The most informative document is *BGU* II 696 = *CPL* 118 = *RMR* 64, the account of the strength of the unit mentioned above, from Contrapollonsopolis Magna (Ridisiya) from where a road ran across to Marsa Alam on the Red Sea coast. The unit had been stationed there since 131. A soldier made a dedication to Serapis in the same town between 180 and 192. In 288, the camp of the unit at Hierakonpolis, ten miles north of Contrapollonospolis Magna but on the east bank, was rebuilt (*CIL* III 22).

I *Flavia Cilicia equitata*

Document	Date	Origin	Description
CIL XVI 29	83	Koptos	Diploma.
SB V 8587	81–96	Hammamat	Dedication to Pan.
RMD 9	105		Diploma.
SB V 8324	118	Mons Claudianus	Dedication.
CPR I 18	124	Arsinoite	Prefect acts as judge.
CIL III 14147[3]	117–38	Syene	Honorific inscription.
CIL III 6025	*c.* 140	Syene	Building dedication.
BGU II 696; *CPL* 118; *RMR* 64	156	Contrapollonos-polis Magna	Soldier transfers to I *Augusta Lusitanorum*.
SB V 8911	158	Alexandria	Building dedication.
P. Phil. 16	161	Philadelphia	Veteran.
CIL III 14147[4]	162	Syene	Inscription.
AE 1974 No. 664	166	Syene	Imperial dedication.
Römer	179	Koptos	Diploma.
P. Mich. III 435; *CPL* 219	II		Accounts with legions II and III.
ChLA IV 264	II	Oxyrhynchus	Account of taxes.
AE 1905 No. 54	217–18	Elephantine	Inscription for commander.
P. Oxy. XLI 2978	III	Oxyrhynchus	Prefect.
P. Mich. VII 455	III		Possible attestation.
P. Hamb. I 103	III		Possible attestation.
SB V 8537		Hierasykaminos	Dedication.
AE 1956 No. 54		Mons Claudianus	Tombstone of *eques*.

This unit is comparatively well attested from the first century through to the third, though the third-century reference is to a former prefect of the unit and not good evidence of the unit's presence. The name of the unit suggests that it was a Flavian creation. The lack of a *cognomen* for the dead horseman in *AE* 1956 No. 54 suggests that the inscription was of an early date.

The *cohors* I *Flavia Cilicia* appears at various places all over Egypt: in 81–96 and 118 in the Eastern Desert (*SB* V 8587, 8324, *cf. AE* (1956) No. 54), at Syene under Hadrian in *c.* 140, 162, 166 and 217–18

(*CIL* III 14147³, 6025, 14147⁴, *AE* (1974) No. 664, *AE* (1905) No. 54), at Alexandria in 158 (*SB* V 8911), and at Hierasykaminos, about 120 km south of Syene (*SB* V 8537). The unit is thus well attested. It seems possible that the unit moved to Syene under Hadrian.

In all three inscriptions from Syene and in the Elephantine inscription, the unit was commanded by a legionary centurion. This was standard practice in the Syene garrison and only one of the three cohorts stationed at Syene would normally be commanded by a prefect.

I *Hispanorum equitata*

Document	Date	Origin	Description
CIL XVI 29	83		Diploma.
CIL III 50; *I.*	83	Thebes	Dedication by prefect to
Memnon 9			Memnon.
SB V 8515	85	Talmis	Dedication.
CIL III 14147²	99	Syene	Honorific inscription.
RMD 9	105	Koptos	Diploma. Unit in Judaea.
SB V 8518		Talmis	Dedication.
SB I 4124		Talmis	Dedication.
SB I 4126		Talmis	Dedication.
SB 4591		Talmis	Dedication.

Outside Egypt:

Because of the large number of references to units of this name, I have grouped the references by region rather than by date.

Document	Date	Origin	Description
P. Lond. 2851; *RMR* 63; *CPL* 112; *ChLA* III 219	105	Stobii, Macedonia	Strength report.
CIL XVI 163	110	Dacia	Diploma.
RMD 35	133	Dacia Porolissensis	Diploma.
RMD 47	154	Dacia Porolissensis	Diploma.
CIL XVI 110; *RMD* 64; 66; 65; 115	164	Dacia Porolissensis	Diploma.
CIL XVI 185	164	Dacia Porolissensis	Diploma.
CIL III 6450		Pannonia Inferior	Dedication.
CIL III 14430		Moesia Inferior	Unit called *Gordiana*.
CIL XVI 43	98	Britain	Diploma.
CIL XVI 48	103	Britain	Diploma.
CIL XVI 51	105	Britain	Diploma.
CIL XVI 69	122	Britain	Diploma.
CIL XVI 70	124	Britain	Diploma.
CIL XVI 93	146	Britain	Diploma.

Document	Date	Origin	Description
CIL VII 371		Britain	Commanded by a centurion of X *Fretensis.*
CIL VII 372		Britain	Altar.
CIL VII 373		Britain	Prefect.
CIL VII 374		Britain	Prefect.
CIL VII 377		Britain	Prefect.
CIL VII 378		Britain	Prefect.
CIL VII 379		Britain	Prefect.
CIL VII 380		Britain	Prefect.
CIL VII 1232		Britain	Prefect.
CIL VII 1146		Britain	Tombstone.
CIL VIII 853	*c.* 140	Provincia Proconsularis	Retired centurion.
CIL VIII 9360		Mauretania Caesarensis	Retired prefect.
CIL VIII 1769/2226		Numidia	Dedication.
CIL V 7425		Italy	Prefect.
CIL XIII 7769	158	Germania Inferior	Dedication by prefect.
CIL XIII 4030		Belgica	Prefect of cohort and *ala Vocontiorum.*
CIL XIII 11982		Germania	Tombstone of veteran.

This unit has an unusually clear date of departure from Egypt. It had arrived in the province by 83 and left prior to 105. In the diploma of that date, the unit was serving in Judaea but was still under the command of the prefect of Egypt and was, therefore, still listed. It probably never returned to Egypt. A different unit of the same name was in Britain in the second century. The unit went to the Danube after Judaea. This is confirmed by Hunt's *pridianum* from Stobii which found its way back to Egypt, probably with a returning veteran. The unit served with II *Ituraeorum equitata* and I *Thebaeorum equitata* at Syene in 99.

II *Ituraeorum equitata*

Document	Date	Origin	Description
CIL III 14147[1]	28	Syene	Inscription put up by a *cohors Ituraeorum*.
SB V 8336; *I. Memnon* 5	75/6	Thebes	Dedication to Memnon.
CIL XVI 29	83	Koptos	Diploma.
CIL III 14147[2]	99	Syene	Honorific inscription.
I. Memnon 63	I?	Thebes	Memnon dedication.
ChLA XI 500	I		Mentions unit with *legio* III.
RMD 9	105	Koptos	Diploma.
SEG XXXI (1981) 1532	135	Philae	Dedication to Isis.
SB V 7912	136	Pselchis	Dedication.
SB I 4601	144	Talmis	Dedication.
SB I 4616	144	Talmis	Dedication.
SB I 4603	144	Talmis	Dedication.
SB V 8521	146/7	Talmis	Dedication.
CIL XVI 184	156–61	Karanis	Diploma.
Römer	179	Koptos	Diploma.
SB IV 7362	188	Arsinoite	*Epikrisis.*
ChLA IV 264	II	Oxyrhynchus	Tax receipts.
CIL XI 3101	post-218	Italy	Prefect who served in Egypt.
BGU XI 2024	224	Thebaid	Requisition of supplies.
SB V 8537		Hierasykaminos	Dedication.
CIL III 14147[7]		Pselchis	Tombstone of decurion.
SB I 4570		Talmis	Dedication.
SB V 8671		Philae	Dedication. Unit at Syene.

This unit is attested throughout the period, first appearing in 75, if not 28, and it is attested in the *Notitia Dignitatum* (*Or.* xxviii 44). The doubt over the first reference is caused by the absence of a numeral in the inscription. This same problem throws doubt on the identification of the unit attested in *SB* V 8671 from Philae. The III *Ituraeorum* was also based in Egypt and so confusion is possible.

In almost every document, the *cohors* appears on the border of Upper Egypt either at Syene, Pselchis (Dakke), or Hierasykaminos. The unit gathered supplies from the Thebaid in 224 (*BGU* XI 2024) and other references from Lower and Middle Egypt involve veterans.

III *Ituraeorum*

Document	Date	Origin	Description
CIL XVI 29	83	Koptos	Diploma.
P. Mich. IX 568 & 569	90	Karanis	Legal document.
P.Oxy. VII 1022	103	Oxyrhynchus	List of recruits.
RMD 9	105	Koptos	Diploma.
AE 1952 No. 249	138–61	Euniko, Wadi Semna	Building dedication.
CIL XVI 184	156–61	Karanis	Diploma.
Römer	179		Diploma.
P. Mich. III 164; *CPL* 143; *RMR* 20	243–4		List of promotions.
ChLA X 445	III		Fragment attesting I *Pannoniorum*.
SB I 1020		Talmis	Dedication.
SB I 1021		Talmis	Dedication.
CIL III 12069		Ptolemais Hormou	Greetings left for the next garrison.
Outside Egypt:			
CIL IX 1619	117–38	Beneventum	Former prefect.
CIL VIII 2394/2395		Numidia	Former prefect.

This unit appears to have been in Egypt throughout the period, though it does not appear in the *Notitia Dignitatum*. The appearance of the unit in the diploma of 156–61 depends upon an emendation of the text. The first editor restored IIIETV[to read 'III et V [Ituraeorum' when the more natural reading must surely be 'III Etu[raeorum'. Given the length of time that the unit spent in Egypt, it is poorly attested. The legal text from Karanis of 90 is the record of M. Anthestius Gemellus' attempt to straighten out business of his mother's.[21]

Most of the documents give us very little information about the station of the unit. Two dedications from Talmis, both undated (*SB* I 1020, 1021) involve C. Iulius Aminnaius which might suggest a more personal visit to the temple than is suggested by the inscriptions of other soldiers at the site. A list of recruits has been preserved at Oxyrhynchus (*P.Oxy.* VII 1022) but it may have been preserved amongst the papers of a veteran of the unit and does not suggest that the unit was stationed there. *CIL* III 12069 was a message left by members of the *cohors scutata civium Romanorum* to soldiers of this unit who were about to take over the garrison of Ptolemais Hormou (El-Lahun, at the entrance to the Fayum, opposite Hawara).

I *Pannoniorum*

Document	Date	Origin	Description
CIL XVI 29	83	Koptos	Diploma.
RMD 9	105	Koptos	Diploma.
CIL XVI 184	156–61	Karanis	Diploma.
Römer	179		Diploma.
CPR VI 76	II/III		Mentioned in will.
ChLA X 445	III		Fragment mentions III *Ituraeorum*.
Outside Egypt:			
CIL XVI 53	107	Mauretania Caesarensis	Diploma.
Smallwood, 246★	98–117	Ephesus	Former prefect.
CIL VIII 20144	*c.* 160	Oran	Former prefect.
CIL V 885		Aquilea	Tombstone of soldier.
CIL XIII 7510		Germania Superior	Tombstone of soldier.
CIL XIII 7511		Germania Superior	Tombstone of soldier.
CIL XIII 7582		Germania Superior	Tombstone of soldier.

Like the last unit, this cohort is poorly attested. It is mentioned in all four diplomas but does not appear in the *Notitia Dignitatum*. It must be assumed that the attestations from outside Egypt refer to different units.

Scutata civium Romanorum

Document	Date	Origin	Description
BGU III 741	143/4	Arsinoite	Contract.
P.Mich. VII 455	III		Possible attestation.
CIL III 6610		Alexandria	Tombstone of soldier.
CIL III 12069		Ptolemais Hormou	Greetings left by III *Ituraeorum*.
AE 1906 No. 35		Cyrenaica	Prefect of unit at Alexandria.
Outside Egypt:			
CIL XI 3801	I	Veii	Former prefect.

★ E.M. Smallwood, *Documents Illustrating the Principates of Nerva, Trajan and Hadrian*, Cambridge, Cambridge University Press, 1966.

As a citizen unit, this cohort never appears on the diplomas which leads to problems in dating its arrival. The first dated inscription comes from 143/4 but it is likely that the unit was based in Egypt during the first century since *CIL* XI 3801 details the career of a former prefect, telling us that he had been *primus pilus* of *legio* XXII and had followed that up by being military tribune in both *legio* XXII and III. As both these legions were based in Egypt in the first century, it is probable that this officer spent his entire military career in the same province. The unit appears in the *Notitia Dignitatum* stationed at Mutheos (*Or.* xxxi 59) in the Thebaid.

I *Thebaeorum equitata*

Document	Date	Origin	Description
CIL XVI 29	83	Koptos	Diploma.
CIL III 14147[2]	99	Syene	Honorific inscription.
CIL III 6627;	I	Koptos	Inscription commemorating
I.Portes 56			fort construction.
RMD 9	105	Koptos	Diploma.
BGU I 114	115		Legal cases.
SB I 1018		Talmis	Dedication.
SB I 1019		Talmis	Dedication.
SB V 8524		Talmis	Dedication.
SB I 4614		Talmis	Dedication.
SB V 8523		Talmis	Dedication.
SB V 8525		Talmis	Dedication.
SB V 8541		Talmis	Dedication.
SB I 4600		Talmis	Dedication.
SB I 4561		Talmis	Dedication.

This unit is attested in Egypt in the first century and disappears in the early second century. In 105, the unit was in Judaea. As the legal case of 115 involved a veteran, it is possible that the unit never returned to Egypt.

The cohort appears in *CIL* III 6627 of the mid-first century, an inscription from Koptos attesting the building of forts in the Eastern Desert, but since most units contributed soldiers to the work party, the unit need not have been stationed in the area. A series of undated dedications from Talmis and an inscription from Syene (*CIL* III 14147[2]) strongly suggest that the unit was stationed in that region.

II *Thebaeorum*

Document	Date	Origin	Description
CIL XVI 29	83	Koptos	Diploma.
CIL III 37; *I.Memnon* 13	92	Thebes	Dedication to Memnon by prefect.
RMD 9	105	Koptos	Diploma.
BGU VII 1690	131	Philadelphia	Contract.
CIL XVI 184	156–61	Karanis	Diploma.
BGU VII 1574	176/7	Philadelphia	Official letters.
Römer	179	Koptos	Diploma.

The numeral of this unit is not preserved in the 156–61 diploma.

I *Thracum equitata*

Document	Date	Origin	Description
P.Mil.Vogl. I 25	127	Tebtunis	Former prefect.
CPL 159	127	Contrapollonos-polis Magna	Birth certificate.
SB I 4552		Talmis	Dedication.
SB I 4553		Talmis	Dedication.
SB I 4607		Talmis	Dedication.
Outside Egypt:			
CIL XVI 33	86	Judaea	Diploma.
CIL III 600	*c.* 163	Macedonia	Unit serving in Mesopotamia.
AE 1951 No. 254		Ismir	Dedication to Isis and Serapis.
IGRR III 1015; *OGIS* 586; *CIG* 4356		Syria	Inscription honouring prefect.
CIL III 4316		Pannonia Superior	Unit attested.
CIL III 151385		Pannonia Inferior	Tombstone.
CIL VII 273/274		Britain	Prefect.
CIL VIII 7803		Germania Inferior	Tombstone.
CIL VIII 8318		Germania Inferior	Tombstone.
CIL VIII 8099		Germania Inferior	Tombstone.
CIL VIII 8319		Germania Inferior	Tombstone.
CIL VIII 6213		Germania Superior	Tombstone.
CIL VIII 6286		Germania Superior	Tombstone.

Only a few references connect this unit with Egypt. The unit was stationed at the camp at Contrapollonospolis Magna which was occupied after 132 by *cohors* I *Augusta Praetoria Lusitanorum*. The unit may have left Egypt at this date.

II *Thracum*

Document	Date	Origin	Description
P. Turner 18	84–96		Letter.
RMD 9	105	Koptos	Diploma.
P. Wisc. I 14	131	Syene	Legal case.
SB X 10530	143	Thebes	Legal agreement.
WO 927	167	Thebes	Receipt.
Römer	179		Diploma.
WO 1015		Thebes	Receipt.
SB I 4593		Talmis	Dedication.
Outside Egypt:			
RMD 79	65	Germania	Diploma.
CIL XVI 158	80	Germania Inferior	Diploma.
CIL XVI 33	86	Judaea	Diploma.
CIL XVI 48	103	Britain	Diploma.
CIL XVI 69	122	Britain	Diploma.
CIL VII 1091		Britain	Tombstone.

This unit does not appear in the 156–61 diploma but must surely be one of the units lost in various *lacunae* of the text. The unit does not appear in the diploma of 83. It arrived in Egypt sometime between 84 and 96. The unit appears in the *Notitia Dignitatum* (*Or.* xxviii 45). References from elsewhere may refer to different units.

A soldier of the cohort died in the camp at Syene in 131 (*P. Wisc.* I 14) and there is one dedication from Talmis (*SB* I 4593). There are two ostraka from Thebes suggesting that the unit was in that area in the mid-to late second century (*WO* 927, 1015). *SB* X 10530 is a legal agreement over the property of a deceased quarry-man of this unit suggesting that the unit was involved in the exploitation of the mines of the Eastern Desert.

VII *Ituraeorum*

Document	Date	Origin	Description
CIL III 59; *I. Memnon* 26		Thebes	Dedication.
CIL XVI 184	156–61	Karanis	Diploma.

This unit almost certainly did not exist. There are only these two possible references to the unit and its inclusion in the diploma is a misreading (see III *Ituraeorum* above). Bernand publishes a photograph of the inscription together with his transcription. The photograph is clear and the numeral cannot be read any other way. The perfect appears to have been called C. Cornelius Jucrpetianus. This should be read as Lucretianus which leaves a 'p', possibly a rho, to make Lucr<i>etianus. The inscriber was careless and possibly inexperienced in Latin and this is the most economical explanation for this phantom unit.

Nigri

There are a number of units which bear slightly unusual names. The *cohortes Nigri, Facundi, M. Flori, Aelii Habeti* and the *ala Paullini* all appear to be named after men rather than after tribes or regions as was the standard practice. The *cohors Nigri* carries in *O. Tait I: Petrie* 245 the designation *Camerensiana* which suggests an Italian origin for the unit. All these units are attested in the first half of the first century AD and do not appear in the later period. It is possible that the units were carrying the name of the person who initially raised them but perhaps it is more likely that they took the name of their commanding officer. The name of the unit would, therefore, change with a change of commander which would have caused administrative problems. This form of nomenclature suggests an early, irregular system.[22] The *cohortes Nigri* and *M. Flori* both appear in the Wadi Hammamat. *Cohors Facundi* was at Pselchis and troops of the *Aelii Habeti* and *ala Paullini* were at Alexandria.

Document	Date	Origin	Description
SB V 8580	19	Hammamat	Dedication to Ammon.
O. Tait I: *Petrie* 245	15–36	Apollonis Hydreuma	Receipt.

In the dedication to Ammon the unit is known simply as the *speiras Nigrou* but in the ostrakon the cohort is *Nigri Camerensiana*. In AD 19, the soldier who was assisting the man in charge of the mines was Mammogais, son of Bataios, a distinctly non-Italian name.

Facundi

Document	Date	Origin	Description
SB V 7959	28	Pselchis	Dedication to Hermes
SB V 8622		Wadi Fawakhir	Dedication

M. Flori (Frori)

Document	Date	Origin	Description
SB I 4401		Hammamat	Dedication.

Aelii Habeti

Document	Date	Origin	Description
SB XVI 12069	27	Alexandria	Loan.

II Hispanorum

Document	Date	Origin	Description
BGU I 114	134	Koptos	Marriage dispute.
P. Hamb. I 103	III		Contract.
Outside Egypt:			
ILS 8867	II	Bithynia	Prefect.

This unit was probably never in Egypt since, apart from a reference to a prefect of the unit appearing as judge in a legal dispute, the unit does not appear elsewhere. The Bithynian inscription records the career of a former prefect who had been prefect of I *Ulpia Afrorum* in Alexandria and then went on to command the II *Hispanorum pia Flavia*. The Hamburg papyrus refers to a horseman of the cohort or *ala pia Flavia*. The connection is not strong enough to place the unit in Egypt.

Ma..an

Document	Date	Origin	Description
SB V 8529		Talmis	Dedication

This dedication defies analysis.

I Nom

Document	Date	Origin	Description
P. Mich VII 455; CPL 133	III		Mentioned in military records.

This unit is possibly to be identified with the I *Numidiarum* active in Syria during the first century but the reference is such that it is possible that the unit was never in Egypt.[23]

Equitum Singularium

Document	Date	Origin	Description
P. Oxy. VII 1022	103		Letter delivered by *eques.*
P. Oxy. XX 2284	258		*Eques* renting land.
P. Freib. IV 66	II/III	Theadelphia	Receipt.
SPP XXII 92	III	Soknopaiou Nesos	Receipt.
P. Ross. Georg. III 1			Mentions *singulares* and legionaries.

The interpretation of SPP XXII 92 is dependent upon a reading of P. Freib. IV 66 and is republished with it. The first reference to a horseman of this type comes in a letter sent by the prefect to his brother who was at the time commanding forces at Oxyrhynchus. It must be doubted whether the *singulares* were formally constituted as a unit in this period rather than the term being used to designate guards of the prefect. The documents dated to the early third century mentioning an officer of the unit suggest that there was a formal organisation.[24]

I *Damascenorum*

Document	Date	Origin	Description
P.Oxy. III 477	132/3		Prefect.
BGU I 73	135	Arsinoite	Prefect.
BGU I 136	135	Arsinoite	Prefect.

This unit is only attested through the perfect. It suggests that the perfect and not the unit was in Egypt.

NUMERI

Cataphracti

Document	Date	Origin	Description
P.Oxy. XLI 2951	267	Alexandria	Sale of female slave.

This was a unit of heavy cavalry.

Hadrianorum Palmyrenorum Sagittorum

Document	Date	Origin	Description
SB V 8810	216	Koptos	Dedication.
P.Oxy. XLIII 3115	271	Oxyrhynchus	Supplies delivered to unit.

The unit may have been involved in policing the desert roads, a duty to which, since Palmyra was a caravan city, Palmyrenes would have brought considerable experience.

Hemesenorum

Document	Date	Origin	Description
P.Mich. VII 454; *RMR* 30	II/III		A transfer from unit to an unknown unit.

Orientalum

Document	Date	Origin	Description
P.Mich. VII 454; *RMR* 30	II/III		Mention of unit.

Salatorum

Document	Date	Origin	Description
P.Oxy. XLI 2951	267	Alexandria	Sale of female slave.

Anatoliorum

Document	Date	Origin	Description
P.Flor. II 278 V 1			Mention in a collection of military letters.

The name of the unit has been restored in a lacuna and the restoration must be regarded as unlikely.

Table A1.1 Units and stations in the Notitia Dignitatum[1]

Units	Stations
1. Legions	
V Macedonica	Memphis
XIII Gemina	Babylon
III Diocletiana	Andron/Ombos/Praesentia/Thebes
II Traiana	Parembole/Apollonospolis Magna
II Flavia Constantia Thebaeorum	Kusas
I Valentiana	Koptos
I Maximiana	Philae
II Valentiana	Hermonthis
2. Alae	
Theodosiana	—
Arcadiana	—
II Armeniorum	Small Oasis
III Araborum	Terenuthis
VIII Vandilorum	Arsinoe?
VII Sarmatorum	Scenae Mandrae
I Aegyptiorum	Gerra
veterana Gallorum	Rhinocolura
I Herculia	Outside Gerasa
V Raetorum	Scenas Veteranorum
I Tingitana	Thinunepsi
Apriana	Hipponos
II Assyriorum	Sosteos
V Praelectorum	Dionysias
II Ulpia Afrorum	Thaubastos
II Aegyptiorum	Tacasarta
I Abasgorum	Ibeon
II Hispanorum	Peos Artemidos
Germanorum	Pesla
IV Britanorum	Ision
I Hiberiorum	Thmou
Neptunia	Chenoboscia
III dromedariorum	Maximianopolis
VIII Palmyrenorum	Poenicion
VII Herculia volontaria	Contra Latopolis
I Francorum	Contra Apollonospolis
I Iovia catafractariorum	Pampane
VIII [ ]	Abydos/Abocedo
II Herculia dromedariorum	Psinabla
I Abasgorum	Large Oasis
I Quadorum	Small Oasis
I Valeria dromedariorum	Precteos
3. Cohorts	
III Galatorum	Kephro
II Astarum	Busiris
I sagittariorum	Naithu
I Augusta Pannoniorum	Th(m)ouis?

Units	Stations
I Epireorum	Castra Iudaeorum
IV Iuthungorum	Aphrodito
II Ituraeorum	Aiy
II Thracum	Muson
IV Numidiarum	Narmuthis
I Lusitanorum	Hieracon
scutata civium Romanorum	Mutheos
I Apamenorum	Silsili
XI Chamauorum	Peamu
IX Tzanorum	Nitnu
IX Alamannorum	Burgo Severi
I Felix Theodosiana	Elephantine
V Syentium	Syene
VI saginarum	Castris Lapidariorum
VII Francorum	Diospolis
4. Equites	
Stablesiani	Pelusium
Saraceni Thamudeni	Scenas Veteranorum
sagitarii indigenae	Tentyra
sagitarii indigenae	Koptos
sagitarii indigenae	Diospolis
sagitarii indigenae	Latopolis
sagitarii indigenae	Maximianopolis
Promoti indigenae	—
felices Honoriani	Asfunis
5. Cunei equitum	
Maurorum scutariorum	Lycopolis
scutariorum	Hermopolis
6. Milites	
Milites Miliarenses Syene	

Note: 1. *Not. Dig. Or.* XXVIII, XXXI. Units are given in each section in order of appearance in the *Notitia*. The spelling of stations has been normalised only in cases in which the station meant is clear.

APPENDIX 2
The archaeology of the army

Archaeology is the basis of much conventional military history of the Roman Empire but there has been no collection of archaeological material relating to the army in Egypt. This appendix is a brief discussion of the remains of military architecture from Roman Egypt.

The camp at Nikopolis, about two and a half miles east of Alexandria, was the most important Roman military site. The fort was more or less complete until the late nineteenth century when the Khedive's palace was built on the site. Breccia could only find a mosaic depicting Bacchus remaining.[1] There had been no excavation nor was there a plan made before the fort's destruction. The fullest description is in Murray's *Handbook for Travellers in Lower and Upper Egypt*.

About 2 miles beyond the French lines or 2½ from the Rosetta Gate is a Roman station, called *Caesar's* or the *Roman Camp*. It marks the site of *Nicopolis*, or Juliopolis, where Augustus defeated the partisans of Antony; . . . The camp now almost obliterated by the immense palace of the Khedive, resembled the Myos Hormos, and the fortified stations, or *hydreumas* in the desert; but was stronger, larger and better built. It was nearly square, measuring 291 paces, by 266 within, the walls being from 5 to 5½ paces thick. It had four entrances, one in the centre of each face, 15 paces wide and defended by round or semi-circular towers, 18 paces in diameter or twelve within. On each face were 6 towers distant from each other 33 paces; those of the doorway excepted which are only 15 paces apart. Those at the 4 corners were larger than the others having a diameter of 22 paces. Its NW face stood very near the sea in the present gardens of the palace, where a mosaic pavement was recently visible; and a short way from the SW gate are the remains of an aqueduct that supplied it with water. . . . The Praetorium, or commandant's house, had a large mosaic, now almost totally destroyed, with various ornamental devices, and a half figure of Bacchus, holding in one hand a bunch of grapes, in the other a crook, the attribute of Osiris. Near the sea, outside the NW corner of the station, is another bath. . . . The walls of the station were of stone, with the courses of flat bricks or tiles, at intervals, usual in Roman buildings; and the whole was constructed on a scale worthy of the grandeur of the early part of the empire.[2]

Nikopolis was a first-century fort, occupied from the earliest period of Roman control. The inscriptions *CIL* III 13 and 14 were found inside the camp and date to the late second century. An inscription dating from 174 relating to the rebuilding of a camp was probably found in or near Alexandria.[3] The remains of the camp described above need not have been of that date since these inscriptions could have been incorporated in a later development. The style of construction, as far as can be ascertained, is similar to the fort at el-Lejjun in Arabia which was built in the late third century, and the fort at Luxor which was constructed c. 301.[4]

The fort of Kysis near the modern village of Dush, in the Khargeh oasis in the Western Desert has been excavated by the Institut Français d'archéologie Orientale (IFAO). The first remains on the fort site are possibly Ptolemaic but there is little evidence of any change in the material culture of the area in the Ptolemaic period. The major development of the area came with the building of a temple on the site under Domitian. In this period, Greek became the dominant language. There is comparatively little material dating from the first two centuries of Roman rule. The bulk of the archaeological material, the pottery, ostraka, a few papyri and the coins, comes from the fourth century. The temple was converted into a fort at the beginning of the fourth century. Other fortifications in the Western Desert have been dated to the fourth or the fifth centuries AD. The function of these fortifications is unclear since the evidence for contact between these oases and the peoples to the south and the south-west is slight.[5]

There is a great deal of archaeological and epigraphic material of a military nature from the roads across the Eastern Desert. In the Roman period, there were three main ports on the Red Sea. The oldest of these was Berenike, a Ptolemaic foundation. The temple of the town has inscriptions honouring Tiberius and perhaps Marcus Aurelius. It flourished in the first century AD.[6] The next port north, Quseir, probably the ancient Leukos Limen, has recently been excavated.[7] The excavators thought that the site could have had a Ptolemaic foundation but was not an important site until the Roman period. Most of the evidence from the site dates to the first or early second centuries but the excavators thought that the final stage of Roman occupation might just have been in the early third century.[8] Further north, there is the small port of Philoteras and then Abu Sha'r (Myos Hormos).

The fort at Abu Sha'r has also recently been excavated. This fort, 77.5 m × 64 m, with twelve or thirteen small towers on the walls, was the first building on the site and was constructed between 306 and 337.[9] It is unlikely that the fort represents the first use of the port site for the Eastern trade. The trade was seasonal and although it was extremely profitable, it is conceivable that traders left few archaeological remains.

There are five main routes across the Eastern Desert. The most southerly route runs from Edfu (Apollonospolis Magna) to Berenike. Two routes both run from Koptos to El Laqeita, the ancient station of Phoenikon. The southerly route heads to the south-east to join the road from Edfu. The other road heads along the Wadi Hammamat to Quseir. A fourth route heads out to the north-east from Qena, past the quarry at Mons Porphyrites and, with a branch out to Mons Claudianus, on to Abu Sha'r. The fifth route is the *Via Hadriana*, the exact course of which is unknown, but which ran from Antinoopolis to the Red Sea. It probably reached the sea at Abu Sha'r before running along the coast towards Berenike. All the roads, with the exception of the *Via Hadriana*, are comparatively well known from epigraphic studies and from archaeological explorations.[10]

The most southerly route, from Edfu, seems to have been mainly exploited during the Ptolemaic period. There is some archaeological evidence for Roman fortifications along the route.[11] In the Roman period, the focus of trade shifted to the routes across from Koptos. Both routes from Koptos passed through Phoenikon (El Laqeita), a small oasis about thirty-four kilometres from Koptos. There are no remains there today. Two inscriptions from the site date to the first century. One is a dedication to Pan of Claudian date and the other attests the presence of the centurion C. Papirius Aequus of III *Cyrenaica*.[12] The road to Berenike then passed through Didyme to Aphrodito where there is a small fort, 65 × 55 paces. There are Latin and Greek inscriptions here from as early as 2 BC, showing official Roman involvement in the trade to the East, but the first dated military inscription comes from AD 78–9, attesting the building of the fort to secure the well. Another inscription from the first century attests the presence of a centurion of the XXII *Deiotariana*.[13] The road went through Compasi, Iovis, Aristonis, to Falacro. Here, the road from Edfu met this route. There is a fort of 38 × 33 paces. The road continues to Apollonos, Cabalsi or Caban, Kainon Hydreuma (New Well), and Vetus Hydreuma where there are a series of fortifications. The next place was Berenike.

The road from Koptos to Quseir has more inscriptions and better-preserved archaeological sites. Qasr el Banat (Figure 1), the first fort after Phoenikon, 40 m × 33 m, has inscriptions nearby dated to the Augustan and Hadrianic periods.[14] Only one fragmentary inscription is necessarily military, since it is on the fort itself.[15] El Moueh fort, 55 m × 55 m,

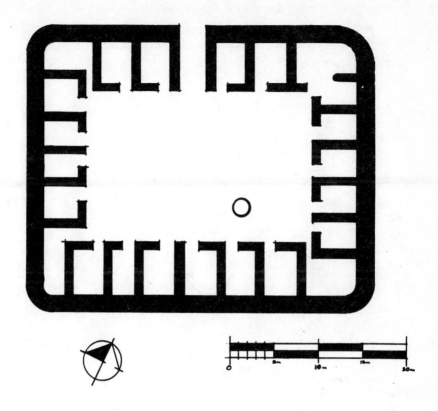

Figure 1 The fort at Qasr el Banat

has an undated inscription erected by Dida, son of Damana, a Volquian serving with the *ala Vocontiorum*.[16] The next fort, 50 m × 50 m, was at Bir Hammamat (Figure 2) where there was a temple to Pan. Inscriptions date from the late first century BC to the third century AD. Soldiers appear in AD 18, 20, 64/5, 79, under Domitian, and in 91.[17] There is also mention in these inscriptions of a *dekanos* and watchtower guards.[18] No fort has been found at Fawakhir which is nine kilometres on from Hammamat but there are the remains of a civilian settlement and a Ptolemaic temple.[19] It was here that the Guéraud ostraka were found. The next fort is at El Zerqa (Figure 3), 60 m × 60 m. El Homra is another square fort, just smaller than El Zerqa. There was a fort at Bir Seyala which has now decayed. The last fort before Quseir is at El Duwi, 153 km from Koptos. This fort is also square, with sides of between 56 m and 57 m. Meredith found thirty-four towers, Reddé and Golvin thirty-seven, placed at high points along the road. They were square,

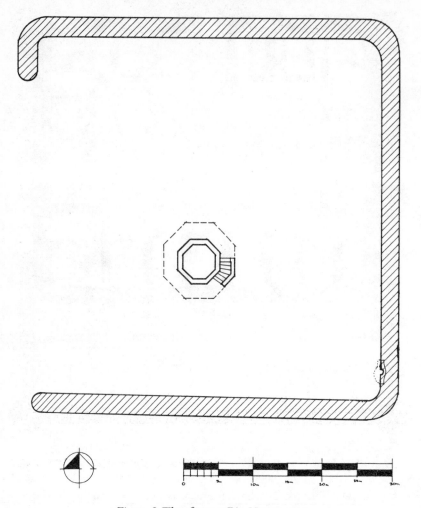

Figure 2 The fort at Bir Hammamat

with sides of about 3 m and some still stand to 3 m in height. The distances between the towers vary considerably.

The road from Kaenopolis (Qena) to Myos Hormos (Abu Sha'r) ran past the quarries at Mons Porphyrites and Mons Claudianus. The route came first to the fort at Bir Aras, then to El Heila where coins of the tetrarchic period were found. At El Saquia, there is a fort of 31 m × 34 m but also the remains of a much larger, square fortification with sides of about 130 m. Constantinian coinage has been found here. There is a large fort at Deir el Atrash, sides of 90 m. At Qattar the fort has sides of around 40 m. At Badi, the fort is about 45 m × 37 m. There are two large

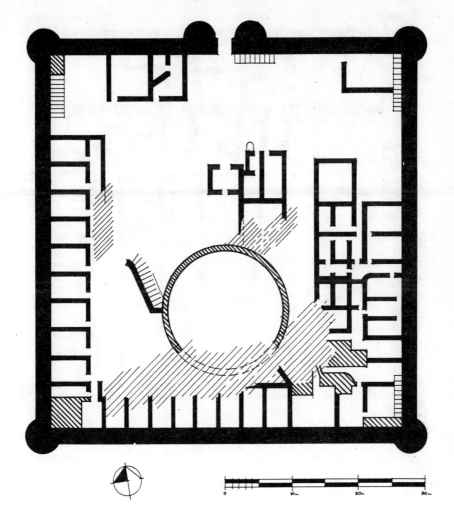

Figure 3 The fort at Tell el Zerqa

forts attached to the quarry at Mons Porphyrites and Wadi Umm Sidri. Beyond these is Wadi Belih, 48.5 m × 38 m, the last fort before Myos Hormos.

There is a branch off this road to the quarries at Mons Claudianus. The branch comes off at Aras and the first fort is Qreya, a square fort with sides of 50 m. The next fort is El Zarga and then, just five kilometres on from El Zarga, there is the fort of Abu Zawal, 75 m × 50 m. After Mons Claudianus, there is the fort at Wadi Umm el Barud (Figure 4) which is a square fort with sides of only 33 m. A cross-wall in the fort suggests that at one time the fort was even smaller than this. The two

197

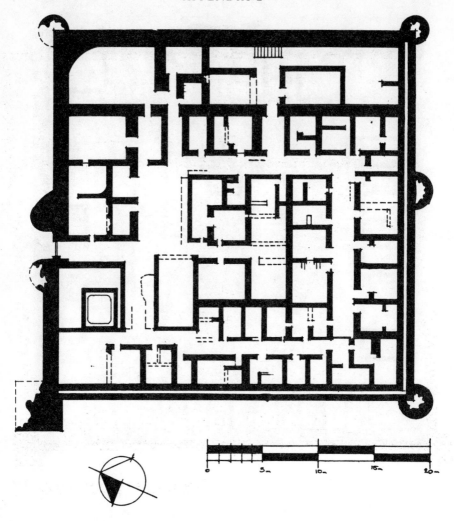

Figure 4 The fort at Wadi Umm el Barud

best-known forts of the sector are Mons Claudianus and Mons Porphyrites. Mons Porphyrites was 85 m × 55 m, larger than the majority of the forts on the route, and had a bath complex. The first inscriptions from the site date to the reign of Trajan and there is an inscription dating from the reign of Hadrian. Some of the epigraphic material dates from the fourth century, or even later, when there was a church on the site.[20] Mons Claudianus (Figure 5) is currently being excavated. A very large number of ostraka have been found. The inscriptions at the site date to the reigns of Trajan and Hadrian.[21] The fort had two stages of construction. There is an internal cross-wall within the fort, as at Umm el Barud,

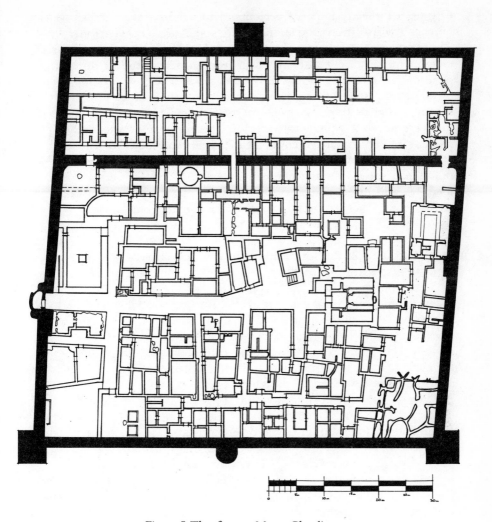

Figure 5 The fort at Mons Claudianus

which was at one time an outer wall. The fort measures 75 m × 52 m or 75 m × 70 m.[22]

The forts or resting points were comparatively close together and a traveller could easily pass more than one in a night's journey.[23] It has been assumed that these forts and towers were erected to protect the trade from India passing along the roads. The cargoes were extremely valuable and brought in a great deal of revenue in customs duties.[24] There are, however, difficulties in seeing the desert fortifications as a single planned system of defence.

It is a truism of Roman military archaeology that forts without towers date from the early imperial period and that there was a gradual development towards more and more bastions and smaller and smaller forts. The development culminated in the abandonment of the square or rectangular fort in favour of forts which were shaped according to the topography of the site. It is reasonable to assume that contemporary fortifications, is one province, according to some central plan, will be similar in construction and style. The forts of the Eastern Desert, however, show considerable typological variation. It is not just the sizes and shapes of the forts which vary, even along the same road, but also the number and types of towers attached to these forts. Some forts had no towers; others had towers on the corners; others had angle towers and intermediate wall towers and gate towers. Some towers were circular; some were square. There was considerable variation not only in the style of the fortification and, therefore, in the date of the forts' construction.

This does not accord with the epigraphy. The epigraphic record would lead us to date all the fortifications to the first century AD. The epigraphy, however, does not illustrate the full chronological range of the occupation of these sites. This can most easily be seen at Mons Claudianus where all the epigraphy dates from the Trajanic and Hadrianic periods. The exploitation of the quarries of the Eastern Desert had been underway since before the beginning of the Roman period and continued well into it. The Romans exercised some control of the mines throughout the period. There is no obvious explanation for the outburst of epigraphic activity in the first third of the second century.

There were some fortifications in the Eastern Desert from the first century. *CIL* III 6627 commemorates the completion of a programme of building and renovation of the desert fortifications which implies that there had been some prior fortification in the area. Not all the water points were, however, fortified. The most heavily fortified road, Koptos to Quseir, passed through an unfortified civilian settlement at Wadi Fawakhir. As this was the find-spot of the Guéraud ostraka, it is likely that soldiers were stationed there. Soldiers in the desert needed water but they did not necessarily need forts. The extant archaeological remains appear to reflect later periods of occupation, perhaps third or fourth century. The fort at El Saquia demonstrates the evolution of the forts. The best-preserved fortifications are 31 m × 34 m. There are no angular towers shown on the plan. There are, however, portal bastions which may have been late additions to the fort and would suggest a late date. Coinage found at the site is Constantinian. Yet, around this site are the remains of much larger fortifications with sides of 130 m. This must be an earlier fortress, again without bastions.

The forts may be difficult to date archaeologically but the watchtowers are impossible. The ostraka which mention them are dated to the second century. There is epigraphic evidence for watchtower guards but the inscriptions are, unfortunately, undated. From the mid-second century at the latest, there were manned watchtowers in the Eastern Desert.

There was a considerable military presence in the Desert from the beginning of the Roman period and possibly even before. Many of the sites along the roads were occupied from this period and there was some fortification of the *hydreumata* from the mid-first century at the latest. Some of the surviving fortifications in the desert show signs of modification and probably represent third-century, or later, constructions. The remains represent multi-period occupation and use of the roads. Many of the fortifications considerably post-date the initial military occupation.

The north-eastern frontier was protected by a fort at Pelusium. The extant fort was badly damaged during an Arab-Israeli war when the Israelis turned the site into a military base. The discoveries of modern excavation include a bath house, a mosaic and a fortress. The fort was 400 m × 200 m and was made of brick. The smaller walls had six towers, while the north and south walls had ten towers. There were Islamic inscriptions on the site but there was also a lot of Graeco-Roman pottery. There is a suggestion that this fort dates to the third century.[25] An excavation at the beginning of the century described a second fort in the same area, 100 m × 100 m, in an area known as Tell Makhzan.[26]

There were further fortifications near the border town of Qantara, the second town along the road from Palestine after Pelusium. There is a very brief description of the site by the Flinders Petrie team who visited when excavating Tanis. An inscription, recording the building of the fort in 288, was found.[27] Just beyond the site is the fort of Qasr Gheit or Oqtahieh. The site was occupied by Nabataeans in the first century AD but was taken over by the Romans and there is a Roman necropolis 100 m from the fort. The excavator remarked that 'le camp ne semble pas avoir été défendu par des murailles'. It is not entirely clear what led the excavator to identify the structure as a Roman fort.[28] There was a camp, unexcavated, at Tell el-Maskhuta (Heroonopolis), controlling the Wadi Tumilat exit from Egypt.[29] Also on this frontier is a late Roman or Byzantine camp at Tell el-Herr. The fort is square with sides of 90 m. The gate is in the east wall and leads onto a colonnaded street. Recent excavations have pointed to there being several distinct periods in the life of the fort. Beneath the 90 m square fort, there was a 140 m square fort, possibly of the fifth century. Beneath this structure there was another fort, though the ground-plan is not clear, which, on numismatic evidence, probably dates to the late third-century.[30]

A possible parallel to Qasr Gheit was to be found on the borders of Upper Egypt. At Shellal, near Philae, to the south of Aswan, there was a series of Roman fortifications including an entrenched camp with mud brick walls. Inside the fort, the north gate was protected by an internal bastion. There was also an entrenched building within the fort. To the east of these structures were the remains of another camp. This appears to have been an entrenched camp with four gates. There were no remains of walls. There were no buildings within these camps but there were two mass graves containing 100 bodies all of whom had neck cords and many of whom had fractured skulls, suggesting execution or death by violence.[31]

Excavations at the Nubian site of Qasr Ibrim have produced less Roman material than might have been expected. A survey of the remains suggests that the Romans withdrew from the site *c.* AD 100. This is shown by a decline in the number of Egyptian amphorae fragments, a decrease in the use of wool, the preferred Roman fabric, with a corresponding increase in the number of cotton and linen fragments, and a decline in the number of Latin and Greek texts. The large number of Latin texts shows that the Roman army formed a significant proportion of the text-producing population, though, after the initial conquest, Latin was soon replaced by Greek as the dominant language.[32]

The retreat from Qasr Ibrim would probably have made the fortress at Mehendi, to the south of Hierasykaminos, the most southerly Roman fort. The site was described by Lepsius.

'Mehendi – which name probably only signifies the structure, the camp in Arabic, is the best preserved Roman encampment that I have ever seen. It lies at a steep height and thence commands the river and a little valley extending on the south side of the camp from the Nile, and turns the caravan road into the desert, which comes back again at Medile. The wall of the town encloses a square running down the hill a little to the east and measuring one hundred and seventy-five paces from south to north and one hundred and twenty-five paces from east to west. From the walls there rise regularly four corner and four middle towers; of the latter the south and north formed also the gates which, for the sake of better security, led into the city with a bend and not a direct line. The southern gate, and the whole southerly part of the fortress, which comprehended about one hundred and twenty houses are excellently preserved. Immediately behind the gate one enters a straight street sixty-seven paces long, which is even now, with but little interruption, vaulted: several narrow by streets lead off on both sides and are covered, like all the houses of the district, with vaults of Nile bricks. The street leads to a great open place in the middle of the city, by which lay, on the highest point of the hill, the largest and best built house – no doubt belonging to the Roman commander – with a semi-circular niche at the eastern end. The city walls are built of unhewn stone; the gateway only, which has a well-turned Roman arch, is erected of well-cut freestone, among the blocks of which several are built in, bearing sculptures of pure Egyptian.[33]

The fort was clearly an impressive building even when Lepsius visited it. The vaulting comes as a surprise but the general design appears to be similar to the fort at Dionysias, to be discussed below.

The next garrison north was at Pselchis, modern Dakke. Although many ostraka have been found in the camp there, there is no full description of the fortifications. The camp was clearly occupied in the first century.[34] Five miles north of Dakke was the Roman or Byzantine fort of Kostamreh.[35] There was also a Byzantine fortified town at Sabaqura, about twelve miles north of Dakke.[36]

There was a wall between the towns of Aswan and Philae. The wall is 5.25 m thick at the base and may have been as high as 10 m. The function of the wall is unclear but the excavator, on very little evidence, thought that it was probably part of the tetrarchic defences.[37] Syene (Aswan) was a major centre for the Roman military in Upper Egypt, though no archaeological evidence of the fort(s) has been discovered.

There is considerably less archaeological data from the Egyptian Nile valley. Thirty miles north of Aswan are the remains of a fort at Nag' el Hagar. The site has not been fully excavated but the fort appears to have been about 150 m × 150 m. The fort contains a large granite bath tub and several columns, many of which were reused in a nearby mosque. At least one corner was fortified by a tower and the gate had certain ornamental qualities. The columns appear to have been arranged so as to form a colonnaded approach to a central building which, like the fort at Mehendi, had a niche at the far end. The excavators suggested that the building was a church. This building reused blocks which originated in a Vespasianic temple and other blocks were either Trajanic or Hadrianic. The visible remains suggest that the fort was erected in the late third century at the earliest and may well have been a fourth-century construction. It was certainly in use for some considerable time and in a later report the excavators identified a structure in one corner of the fort as a 'palace', though it may be a religious structure.[38]

A possible fort at El Kab also reused Pharaonic temple blocks. The fort was square and there were no towers on the gates. The coinage recovered suggests that the fort was used mainly in the fourth century.[39]

The fort at Luxor was similar to Nikopolis in having numerous towers and fortified gates. It was built next to the river and some of the remains have been washed away as the Nile has moved slowly towards the east. The fort incorporated a large section of the temple to Amun–Min erected by Amenhotep III and Ramesses II. The fort's construction is dated to 301.[40]

There was also a Roman fort near the site of Akhenaten's city at Amarna, probably to guard the alabaster quarries that lie in the hills behind the city. The only attestation of the fort at this much studied site is decidedly cryptic. Pendlebury concluded his historical introduction to the site with 'For the city of the Horizon was to have no successor save for a Roman fort or two'. His map shows the position of the fort but gives no other details.[41]

The fort of Babylon, Old Cairo, is one of the most famous of Egyptian forts. This was a large fort but, unlike the other forts we have looked at, was not regular in shape. The south wall was 300 feet long and had four bastions. The north wall was 660 feet, without visible towers but this was the most badly damaged section of the fort. The fort stretched north to south for about 1,225 feet. The east wall had at least two bastions. The west wall followed the line of the Nile and had two large towers to protect the gateway. The walls were 8 feet thick. A late source dates the fort to c. 100 AD and associates it with Trajan. Trajan certainly helped develop Babylon and was associated with the construction of the nearby canal which ran along the Wadi Tumilat to the Suez isthmus and the Red Sea. It is quite possible that Trajan placed a fort here to control the traffic along the canal. The typology of the fort, however, differs very markedly from Trajanic forts elsewhere and the remains, as observed by modern travellers, are probably much later.[42]

The fort at Dionysias in the Fayum (Figure 6) was excavated by a joint French–Swiss expedition 1948–1950. The fort was 94.4 m × 80 m. It was built from brick. It had square towers on each corner and semi-circular towers on the sides. On the west face the intermediate tower was square. The single gate was protected by round towers. Inside the fort was a colonnaded road leading to a large central building which had the same niche as has been noticed at several other forts. There is no material from the fort prior to 290 and the excavators thought that the fort was Diocletianic or very slightly later, though Carrié argues, unconvincingly, for a slightly earlier date.[43]

In addition to the forts known through archaeology, there are many sites which appear in the documentary material. We know that there were forts, as opposed to places where soldiers were stationed, at Koptos in AD 85 and at Contrapollonospolis Magna in the early second century.[44] The fort at Syene was rebuilt under Diocletian.[45] In AD 288, the camp at Hierakonpolis was built, the same year as the dedication of the camp at Qantara.[46]

The camps at Dionysias, Myos Hormos and Luxor were built within twenty years. There are notable similarities between Dionysias, Tell el-Herr and Mehendi and between Luxor and Nikopolis. At the same time, there was increased activity on the Myos Hormos road and, in roughly the same period, we have building works attested at Syene, Hierakonpolis

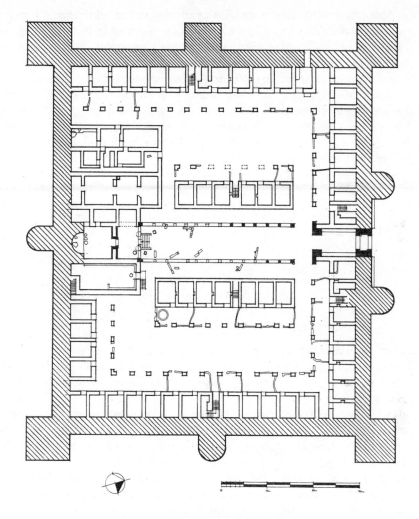

Figure 6 The fort at Dionysias

and Qantara. It is notable that many of the forts seem to have reused blocks from temple structures or were sited in disused temples, pointing to a late third-century date at the earliest. Many of the fortifications seem to be of fairly similar style and a lot of the dated material from this type of fort converges on a date for foundation of *c.* 300.

There were earlier fortifications but most of the extant remains date from the late Empire. This may be because of the current state of excavation and, as investigations continue, more early Roman fortifications may be found, since later forts may have been built on earlier sites, obliterating the earlier remains. Pelusium and Shellal show multi-period occupation. The surviving remains of the forts at Nikopolis and Babylon must also conceal earlier forts. Certain sites show adaptation over several centuries and a continuity of military interest from the Principate to the late empire. Some forts, however, were clearly the first forts on the site. Myos Hormos was built on virgin sand. Dush was converted from a temple in the late third or early fourth century. Luxor was built in 301 from a temple. Dionysias was a completely new construction. No known military site preceded the fort at Nag' el-Hagar. We may safely conclude that there was a considerable increase in fortifications in Egypt in the period from 280 to 320.

This is not an isolated phenomenon. Parker summed up the position in the neighbouring province of Arabia:

> Three salient points emerged. First, it appeared that few of the extant forts along the Arabian frontier dated to the second or third centuries and that, therefore, the frontier seems to have been only lightly defended in this period. Second, it appeared that a major military build up occurred in the late third and early fourth centuries when a number of forts appear to have been erected or reoccupied. Third, many of the same forts were abandoned in the beginning of the late fifth and early sixth centuries.[47]

Parker saw the development as a response to the increasing problems Rome was having with the Saracens after the collapse of the old order in the desert regions in the East following the destruction of the caravan city of Palmyra.[48]

Troubles in Arabia could have affected Egypt since Egypt had a substantial number of Arabs on the eastern side of the country. The Nile was a dividing line between Arabia and Africa and the tribes east of the Nile were seen as Arabic by classical writers. We also see the emergence of a threat to the security of Egypt in this period from the Blemmyes and Axumites. These threats cannot, however, have been very serious. Egypt had been troubled with raiders since time immemorial and the Romans had had some success in restricting their activities. It is historically unlikely that the sparsely populated regions bordering Egypt suddenly became a threat. The fortification programme on the eastern frontier was part of a general policy of fort building, a policy that may have been a response to the political insecurity of the third century but was probably not related to a specific new threat.

The fortifications were very impressive. A village like Dionysias must have been dominated by the nearby fort. Similarly, the fort at Nikopolis was an imposing structure, with its multiple towers, mosaics and baths. Lepsius' description of Mehendi allows us to assess the architectural impact of the fort. The architecture draws the attention of the visitor to the central building and especially to the alcove within the building which must surely have housed something of religious or symbolic significance. Such features have no clear military significance and it seems that many of the architectural features of the late Roman fort were meant to impress the communities in which the forts were placed. The positioning of some forts in central locations within the villages or towns cannot be a coincidence. This was not simply functional architecture. The forts were meant to impress.

NOTES

INTRODUCTION

1 M.P. Speidel, 'Work to be done on the organization of the Roman army', *Bulletin of the Institute of Archaeology*, 1989, vol. 26, pp. 99–106, reprinted in M.P. Speidel, *Roman Army Studies* II, Stuttgart, Steiner, 1992, pp. 13–20.

2 E. Birley, 'Introduction', in E. Birley, *Roman Army Papers 1929–1986*, Amsterdam, Gieben, 1988; E. Birley, 'The epigraphy of the Roman army', *Actes du deuxième congrès internationale d'epigraphie grecque et latine*, Paris, Maisonneuve, 1953, pp. 226–38, reprinted in Birley, *Roman Army Papers*, pp. 3–11. See also E. Birley, 'Senators in the emperors' service', *PBA*, 1954, vol. 39, pp. 197–214, reprinted in Birley, *Roman Army Papers*, pp. 75–92.

3 E.N. Luttwak, *The Grand Strategy of the Roman Empire From the First Century AD to the Third*, Baltimore, John Hopkins, 1976.

4 B. Isaac, *The Limits of Empire: The Roman Army in the East*, Oxford, Clarendon, 1993; F.G.B. Millar, 'Emperors, frontiers and foreign relations', *Britannia*, 1982, vol. 13, pp. 1–24; F.G.B. Millar, *The Emperor in the Roman World*, London, Duckworth, 1977; J.C. Mann, 'Power, force and the frontiers of the empire', *JRS*, 1979, vol. 69, pp. 175–83; J.C. Mann, 'The frontiers of the Principate', *ANRW*, 1974, vol. 2.1, pp. 508–31.

5 The issues raised by the military treatises are complex. See C.M. Gilliver, *The Roman Art of War: Military Theory and Practice. A study of the Roman military writers*, unpublished Ph.D. thesis, University of London, 1993.

6 D.J. Breeze and B. Dobson, *Hadrian's Wall*, London, Penguin, 1987, pp. 39–43; E. Birley, 'Hadrianic frontier policy', *Carnuntia*, 1956, vol. 3, pp. 25–33.

7 N. Lewis, 'The Romanity of Roman Egypt: a growing consensus', *Atti del XVII Congresso Internazionale di Papirologia*, Naples, Centro internazionale per lo studio dei papiri Ercolanesi, 1984, pp. 1077–84.

2 THE ARMY AND THE PROVINCE

1 *Baedeker's Guide to Egypt*, Norwich, Automobile Association, c. 1987, pp. 12–13.

2 H.E. Hurst, *The Nile*, London, Constable, 1969, pp. 18–19. K.W. Butzer, *Early Hydraulic Civilization in Egypt: A Study in Cultural Ecology*, Chicago and London, University of Chicago Press, 1976, p. 13: 'Rainfall in the Libyan desert and the Red Sea Hills has been insufficient to sustain any appreciable population, except in the vicinity of springs or wadis with high watertables, since at least 30,000–50,000 years ago.'

3 *Baedeker's Guide to Egypt* produces figures based on a 1978 census giving population figures for the varius oases of the Western Desert: Bahriya: 6,000; Khargeh: 15,000; Siwa: 5,000; Farafra: 1,000. This was out of a total Egyptian population of 39,640,000.

4 Butzer, *Early Hydraulic Civilization*, p. 97.

5 Butzer, *Early Hydraulic Civilization*, p. 97, estimated the nomadic population at a few thousand.

6 D.S. Whitcomb and J.H. Johnson, *Quseir Al–Qadim 1980: Preliminary Report*, Malibu, Udena, 1982, depict the harshness of the environment at Quseir Al–Qadim which flourished in the first century AD as a port for the Indian trade and then had a renaissance in the medieval period as a port for the *hajj*.

7 Hadrian also built a road which ran from Antinoopolis to Myos Hormos but it is unclear what precise route this followed. Another wadi, the Wadi Gasus, may have been exploited in the Pharaonic period. A. Nibbi, 'The two stelae from the Wadi Gasus', *JEA*, 1976, vol. 62, pp. 45–56.

8 Balthasar de Monconys, *Voyage en Egypte*, Cairo, IFAO, 1973 (1st ed. 1695), p. 186 (pp. 52–3). Monconys visited Egypt between 1646 and 1647.

9 Butzer, *Early Hydraulic Civilization*, pp. 74–7, has attempted to solve these problems by collecting the evidence for settlements in each nome and then combined this data by giving each settlement a point score according to function. He then relates the total point score to population. There are, however, serious methodological problems since the original data is drawn from a 2,000 year period. Butzer is well aware of this: 'the reader is fore-warned that none of the numerical data are to be taken literally' (p. 76).

10 Strabo, 17.1.35.

11 *Baedeker's Guide to Egypt*, p. 8.

12 *Genesis* 47; *Exodus* 12.38; H. Kees, *Ancient Egypt: A Cultural Topography*, Chicago and London, University of Chicago Press, 1961, p. 30, p. 88. Butzer, *Early Hydraulic Civilization*, pp. 94–5.

13 D.J. Thompson, *Memphis under the Ptolemies*, Princeton, Princeton University Press, 1988, p. 10.

14 Hurst, *The Nile*, p. 19.

15 In the Napoleonic wars British forces invaded Egypt from the Red Sea but the major expedition landed on the Mediterranean coast to meet the French forces near Alexandria.

16 Kees, *Ancient Egypt*, p. 183.

17 The route is from the *Itinerarium Antonini* and probably dates to *c.* AD 400.

18 *CIL* III 14147[5].

19 There is some disagreement about this and the double first cohort may be a Flavian innovation. See C.M. Gilliver, *The Roman Art of War: Military Theory and Practice. A study of the Roman military writers*, unpublished Ph.D. thesis, University of London, 1993.

20 L.J.F. Keppie, *The Making of the Roman Army*, London, Batsford, 1984; P.Holder, *Studies in the Auxilia of the Roman Army from Augustus to Trajan* (*BAR* 70), Oxford, 1980; D.B.Saddington, *The Development of the Roman Auxiliary Forces from Caesar to Vespasian (49 BC – AD 79)*, Harare, University of Zimbabwe, 1982. The evidence seems to point to a gradual change from the Republican model to the imperial model and is shown by the existence of units departing from later patterns of nomenclature in being named after their commanders. See M.P. Speidel, 'Auxiliary units named after their commanders: four new examples from Egypt', Aeg., 1982, vol. 62, pp. 165–72, reprinted in M.P. Speidel, *Roman Army Studies* I, Amsterdam, Gieben, 1984, pp. 101–8; M.P. Speidel, 'The Eastern Desert garrisons under

Augustus and Tiberius', *Studien zu dem Militärgrenzen Roms II 1977. X Int. Limes Congress in Germania Inferior*, Bonn, Habelt, 1977, pp. 511–15, reprinted in Speidel, *Roman Army Studies* I, pp. 323–8; E. Birley, 'Units named after their commanders', *Ancient Society*, 1978, vol. 9, pp. 257–73, reprinted in E. Birley, *Roman Army Papers 1929–1986*, Amsterdam, Gieben, 1988, pp. 268–84.

21 *RMR* 63 = *CPL* 112.

22 *RMR* 64 = *BGU* II 696.

23 *P. Dura* 89 = *RMR* 50; *P. Dura* 82 = *RMR* 47.

24 A.K. Bowman and J.D. Thomas, 'A military strength report from Vindolanda', *JRS*, 1991, vol. 81, pp. 62–73.

25 J. Lesquier, *L'armée romaine de l'Egypte d'Auguste à Dioclétien*, Cairo, IFAO, 1918, pp. 40–72.

26 Lesquier, *L'armée romaine*, p. 56.

27 Lesquier, *L'armée romaine*, pp. 40–50.

28 Lesquier, *L'armée romaine*, pp. 54–5. K. Strobel, 'Zu Fragen der frühen Geschichte der römischen Provinz Arabia und zu einigen Problemen der Legionsdislokation im Osten des Imperium romanum zu Beginn des 2 Jh.n.Chr.', *ZPE*, 1988, vol. 71, pp. 251–80, suggests that the legion disappeared in the Jewish uprising in Egypt, AD 115–17.

29 C. Römer, 'Diplom für einen Fussoldaten aus Koptos vom 23. März 179', *ZPE*, 1990, vol. 82, pp. 137–53.

30 The *ala Commagenorum* may have been replaced by the *ala Vocontiorum* which, in turn, was replaced, some eighty years or more later, by the *Heracliana*, and the *ala Augusta* may have been replaced by the *veterana Gallica*. The *Thracum Mauretana* reinforced the garrison. For the cohorts, the task is more difficult. The *cohors Hispanorum* is last attested in the Egyptian evidence in 105, just as the *Augusta praetoria Lusitanorum* is first attested. The I *Thebaeorum equitata* last appears in 115 which would initially suggest replacement by either the *Ulpia Afrorum equitata* or the *Apamenorum* but the 115 attestation is to a veteran which does not necessarily prove that the unit returned from Judaea where it was serving, though still attached to the Egyptian command, in 105. There does not appear to have been a replacement for the II *Thebaeorum*.

31 Strabo, 17.1.12.

32 Strabo, 17.1.30; Strabo, 17.1.41.

33 M.P. Speidel, 'Augustus' deployment of the legions in Egypt', *CE*, 1982, vol. 47, pp. 120–4, reprinted in Speidel, *Roman Army Studies* I, pp. 317–21.

34 Tac., *Ann.* IV 5.

35 Tac., *Hist.* I 70.

36 Tac., *Ann.* XV 36.

37 Tac., *Hist.* II 6.

38 Jos., *BJ* II 66–9. Josephus lists the assembled forces, including three legions, twenty-three cohorts and five *alae*. Of these cohorts, ten were made up of 1,000 foot and the remaining thirteen were mixed cavalry and infantry; 600 foot and 120 horsemen. This was supplemented by 15,000 troops levied by the client-kings. Josephus adds this up as being an army of 60,000 men when the catalogue gives nearly 10,000 less than that. Of the forces listed, there were only 15,000 legionaries.

39 Jos., *BJ* II 385–7.

40 Jos., *BJ* VII 1–19. Some cohorts and *alae* remained at Jerusalem but this passing reference contrasts with the much fuller treatment of the subsequent legionary deployments. Historians did realise that the auxiliary units were an important part of the Roman army (Tac., *Hist.* IV 12 f.). Writers from

Strabo onwards acknowledge the importance of the auxiliary units as a numerical and military component of the army, yet, when considering the numbers and dispositions of the *auxilia*, they appear badly informed or uninterested. To Tacitus and Josephus the Roman army was synonymous with the Roman legions. The legion was still, in theory at least, the Roman citizen unit and had provided Rome with her empire so that although to the modern historian the difference between the two types of unit may appear to be more one of size than function, to Tacitus and to Josephus the differences were of tradition.

41 Strabo, 16.4.22. For discussion of this expedition see S. Jameson, 'Chronology of the campaigns of Aelius Gallus and C. Petronius' *JRS*, 1968, vol. 58, pp. 71–84.
42 Strabo, 17.1.54.
43 The Koptos inscription is discussed by D.L. Kennedy, 'The composition of a military work party in Roman Egypt (*ILS* 2483: Coptos)', *JEA*, 1985, vol. 71, pp. 156–60.
44 *PSI* IX 1063 = *RMR* 74.
45 M. Reddé and J.-C. Golvin, 'Du Nil à la Mer Rouge: documents anciens et nouveaux sur les routes du désert oriental d'Egypte', *Karthago*, 1987, vol. 21, pp. 5–64.
46 Strabo, 16.4.24; Pliny, *NH* VI 101.
47 Strabo, 17.1.45.
48 *Periplus* 1. M.G. Raschke, 'New studies in Roman commerce with the East', *ANRW*, 1978, vol. 2.9.2, pp. 605–1363, details the evidence for the date which depends upon numismatic evidence from India. The *Periplus* refers to silver coinage being exchanged in India rather than bullion and all the silver coins in India are of Julio-Claudian date. The dating evidence is thus not good. L. Casson, *The Periplus Maris Erythraei*, Princeton, Princeton University Press, 1989, pp. 6–7, agrees with Raschke's date. A. Fuks, 'Notes on the archive of Nicanor', *JJP*, 1951, vol. 5, pp. 207–16, reprinted in A. Fuks, *Social Conflicts in Ancient Greece*, Jerusalem and Leiden, Brill, 1984, pp. 312–21, looks at the archive of Nikanor which covers the business of the family from AD 6 onwards.
49 See Appendix 2.
50 *RMR* 11 = P. *Vindob.* L 112 = *CPL* 116 = *Doc. Eser. Rom.* 17.
51 *RMR* 51 = *CPL* 322 = *Doc. Eser. Rom.* 25.
52 *BGU* VII 1612.
53 *CIL* III 12048. The find-spot is unknown.
54 *AE* (1952) No. 249.
55 *CIL* III 13578; *CIL* III 22.
56 *CPL* 122 = *RMR* 70.
57 *SB* XVI 12069.
58 *P. Oxy.* XIV 1666.
59 *P. Mich.* VIII 502; III 203.
60 *SB* III 7959 of AD 14/15, *SB* III 7926, 7948, *SB* III 7912 of 136.
61 *SB* XVI 13030.

3 RECRUITMENT AND VETERAN SETTLEMENT

1 I. Biezunska-Malowist, 'Les citoyens romains à Oxyrhynchos aux deux premiers siècles de l'empire', in *Le monde grec. Hommages à Claire Préaux*, Brussels, Université de Bruxelles, 1975, pp. 741–7, and E.G. Turner, 'Roman

Oxyrhynchus', *JEA*, 1952, vol. 38, pp. 78–93, discuss Oxyrhynchus. The discrepancy in the numbers of veterans settled in each district was noted by C. Wessely, *Karanis und Soknopaiu Nesos (Denkschriften der kaiserlichen Akadamie der Wissenschaften in Wien. Philosophisch-historische Klasse*, vol. 47), Vienna, 1902. This has been further elaborated by D.H. Samuel, 'Greeks and Romans at Socnopaiou Nesos', *Proceedings of the XVIth International Congress of Papyrologists*, Chico, Scholars Press, 1981, pp. 389–403. Samuel notes that those Romans attested at Soknopaiou Nesos were either officials or non-residents.

2   G. Forni, *Il reclutamento delle legioni da Augusto a Diocleziano*, Rome, Facultà di lettere e filosofia, Università di Pavia, 1953; J.C. Mann, *Legionary Recruitment and Veteran Settlement during the Principate*, London, Institute of Archaeology, 1983.

3   G. Webster, *The Roman Imperial Army of the First and Second Centuries AD*, London, Black, 1962, p. 90: 'Recruitment became more and more dependent upon the frontier peoples, until the army forming the frontier garrisons became almost a hereditary caste.'

4   See pp. 29–30.

5   The reading was revised by R.P. Wright, 'New readings of a Severan inscription from Alexandria', *JRS*, 1941, vol. 31, pp. 33–52.

6   J.F. Gilliam, 'The veterans and the *Praefectus Castrorum* of the II *Traiana*, AD 157', *AJPh*, 1956, vol. 77, pp. 359–75, reprinted in J.F. Gilliam, *Roman Army Papers*, Amsterdam, Gieben, 1986, pp. 145–61.

7   J.F. Gilliam, 'The plague under Marcus Aurelius', *AJPh*, 1961, vol. 73, pp. 225–51, reprinted in Gilliam, *Roman Army Papers*, pp. 227–53, discusses these documents and produces a similar table to Table 3.3. *CIL* VIII 18067 has over ninety surviving names of soldiers discharged in 166, having been recruited in 140 and 141, but we are unable to assess how many of the soldiers were discharged from the legion that year. *CIL* VIII 18068 has a similar number of troops who were discharged in 198, having been recruited in 173. Only one of the ten cohorts has a completely preserved list of discharged troops. Cohort seven discharged thirty-four men, whilst cohort ten discharged thirty-two or more men. The legion may have discharged 370 men in that year. *CIL* III 14507 of 195 records the discharge of recruits of 169. The inscription is not completely preserved but it is possible to see that over forty-three men were discharged from the double strength first cohort, twenty plus from the second and eighteen from the third. This would suggest that about 220 men were discharged from the legion. *CIL* III 8110 from Moesia does not record many of the names of the men but does record the total numbers discharged, 239, from the recruits of 134 and 135. Also from Moesia, *CIL* III 6178, dated to 134/5, contains a complete list of the discharged for three cohorts, including the double strength first cohort. From these cohorts it is possible to estimate the total numbers discharged at 198 and the stone is large enough to have about 210 names inscribed on it. *AE* (1955) No. 238 + *AE* (1969) No. 633 of 157 gives 133 names. *CIL* III 6580 of 194 gives us three complete cohorts, the second with ten men, the fifth with twelve, and the sixth with six. The seventh cohort had at least eleven men discharged and the third at least six. From the one century of the first cohort which appears on the inscription three men were discharged. This would suggest that about one hundred men were discharged from the ten cohorts of the legion.

8   A.R. Burn, '*Hic Breve Vivitur*', *Past & Present*, 1953, vol. 4, pp. 2–31, based his study of mortality patterns on the epigraphic evidence but K. Hopkins,

'On the probable age structure of the Roman population', *Population Studies*, 1966, vol. 20, pp. 245–64, shows that there are irregularities in the evidence. The material is shaped by cultural values which might either stress the very old, ensuring more inscriptions were put up to honour them, or youths, cut off before their prime. In most cases, the very young have few monuments. In some cases, the age of the deceased may be approximated. The epigraphically attested population structure is frequently demographically unlikely or impossible. Soldiers, however, joined the army between the ages of 15 and 25 and there is little reason to believe that the above factors will have applied to troops above the age of 20. We may also use non-epigraphic material. B.W. Frier, 'Roman life expectancy: Ulpian's evidence', *HSCP*, 1982, vol. 86, pp. 213–51 and B.W. Frier, 'Roman life expectancy: the Pannonian evidence', *Phoenix*, 1983, vol. 37, pp. 328–44 has produced a further set of figures. Both sources present some difficulties. Ulpian's researches may not have been accurate and the ageing of skeletal remains is not a precise science. We can also use modern populations as a comparison and T.G. Parkin, *Demography and Roman Society*, Baltimore, John Hopkins, 1992, Table 9, selects the Coale-Demeny Model West Level 3 Female from A.J. Coale *et al., Regional Model Life Tables and Stable Populations*, New York, Academic Press, 1983, as representative of the ancient world. Egyptian census documents as collected by R.S. Bagnall and B.W. Frier, *The Demography of Roman Egypt*, Cambridge, Cambridge University Press, 1994, record the ages of the registered persons.

9   The material for Rome, Italy and Lambaesis is taken from Hopkins, 'On the probable age structure of the Roman population', pp. 245–64. The Egyptian evidence is taken from Bagnall and Frier, *The Demography of Roman Egypt*, p. 100. The Pannonian material comes from Frier, 'Roman life expectancy: the Pannonian evidence', pp. 328–44. The Coale-Demeny model is as used by Parkin, *Demography and Roman Society*, Table 9.

10 A.E. Samuel *et al., Death and Taxes: Ostraka in the Royal Ontario Museum* I (*ASP* 10), Toronto, Hakkert, 1971, analyse the tax receipts to produce an extremely pessimistic view of the demographics of Upper Egypt but the epigraphic material collected by B. Boyoval, 'Tableau général des indications d'âge de l'Egypte romaine', *CE*, 1977, vol. 52, pp. 345–51, is more positive, suggesting a life expectancy somewhere between 26 and 34 years, though Boyoval argues that the material is fundamentally skewed by cultural factors.

11 *ILS* 2747; R. Cagnat, *L'armée romaine d'Afrique*, Paris, Impremie Nationale, 1913, pp. 52–3.

12 Tac., *Ann.* XII 32.5 states that the Roman colony at Colchester was created to protect the country against revolt and present the locals with an example of ordered Roman government. Mann, *Legionary Recruitment and Veteran Settlement*, pp. 60–62, shows that colonies were often created in areas which had recently been vacated by sizeable Roman forces.

13 See pp. 61–3.

14 *P.Giss.* I 60.

15 *BGU* II 587.

16 M.*Chr.* I 461.

17 *P.Oxy.* III 653.

18 *P.Oxy.* XII 1508, verso 1536.

19 The auxiliary diploma does not normally make any mention of possible settlement procedures. Two diplomas, however, do mention settlement: *CIL* X 867 and *CIL* X 3335. Both deal with veterans from the fleet at Misenum who were assigned to the colony at Paestum.

20 See pp. 216–7, n. 23.
21 Strabo, XVII 35; E.M.Husselman, *Karanis. Excavations of the University of Michigan in Egypt 1929–1935: Topography and Architecture,* Ann Arbor, University of Michigan, 1979, pp. 55–6. Although one building in the village has been identified as a barrack block, the extremely tentative identification is almost certainly wrong. The building was large and contained a number of ostraka relating to the shipment of grain. There was military involvement in this activity but civilians were also involved and it is best to see the building as a large house which perhaps served as an office for the grain supply.
22 *SB* VI 9636. N. Lewis, 'A veteran in quest of a home', *TAPA,* 1959, vol. 90, pp. 139–46.
23 *RMR* 74 = *PSI* IX 1063.
24 See pp. 135–7.
25 D.W. Rathbone, 'Villages, land and population in Graeco–Roman Egypt', *PCPhS,* 1990, vol. 36, pp. 103–42, shows the traditionally accepted figures for the population of Egypt are far too high.

4 THE LEGAL STATUS OF SOLDIERS AND VETERANS

1 Apuleius, *Metam.* IX 39.
2 J.B. Campbell, *The Emperor and the Roman Army,* Oxford, Clarendon, 1984, p. 253.
3 Campbell, *Emperor and the Roman Army,* p. 207.
4 Campbell, *Emperor and the Roman Army,* p. 228.
5 Herodian's view is decidedly negative. Herodian, III 8.4–5: 'The soldiers too were given a substantial sum of money and with this many other privileges that they had not had before such as an increase in pay (which Severus was the first to give), permission to wear a gold ring and the right to live at home with their wives.'
6 J.B. Campbell, 'The marriage of Roman soldiers under the Empire', *JRS,* 1978, vol. 68, pp. 153–67.
7 Dio, LX 24.3.
8 P. Garnsey, 'Septimius Severus and the marriage of Roman soldiers', *CSCA,* 1970, vol. 3, pp. 45–73; Herodian, III 8.4–5.
9 M.*Chr.* I 372 = *FIRA*^{2} III 19.
10 *Dig.* XXIX 1.1; Gaius, *Institutes,* II 109; *CJ* VI 21.3.
11 *Dig.* XXIX 1.24.
12 Jos., *BJ* VI 188–9.
13 *Dig.* XXIX 1.1 tells us which emperors granted privileges; *CJ* VI 21; Campbell, *Emperor and the Roman Army,* pp. 207–29.
14 Gaius, *Institutes,* II 110–11; *BGU* I 140.
15 *BGU* V 1020 gives an almost complete text of the second century AD and a small extract is preserved in the first-century text *P.Oxy.* XLII 3014.
16 *Dig.* XXVIII 2.26.
17 *Dig.* IV 6.45; IV 6.7; IV 6.17; IV 6.34; IV 6.35.9; IV 6.40; *CJ* II 51; II 51.3 limits the privilege to one year after the discharge of the soldier.
18 *CJ* II 51.1. Campbell, *Emperor and the Roman Army,* pp. 236–42.
19 *Dig.* XLIX 16.9; XLIX 16.13; *BGU* V 1020.111.
20 S. Mitchell, 'A new inscription from Pisidia: requisitioned transport in the Roman empire', *JRS,* 1976, vol. 66, pp. 106–32.

21 *BGU* I 140.

22 Aelius Aristides, *Oration* XXVI: *Regarding Rome*, 73. This is taken from the start of a long section dealing with military affairs. He is more interested in the physical isolation of the army than its legal status at this stage, but he does discuss citizenship with regard to the army later in the section.

23 In legal commentaries, with one exception (*Dig.* L 2.9 distinguishes between veterans of the fleet and the rest), there is no differentiation between legionaries and soldiers of other units. There is, however, some evidence for the grant of differing privileges:

(i) Bronze diplomas were given to auxiliary veterans following their discharge. These attest a grant of citizenship to the veteran and also grant *conubium* with either the wife the veteran had when citizenship was given or with a future wife, provided that there was only one. Citizenship was granted to the children and descendants of the veteran in documents issued before 140. After this date, the children are not mentioned. Legionaries did not receive diplomas (*P. Mich.* VII 432 is a text of a supposed military diploma granted to a legionary but although the wording is remarkably similar to the auxiliary diploma, there is no mention of the privileges granted (cf. *P.Ryl.* IV 611 (AD 87/8)). J.C. Mann and M.M. Roxan, 'Discharge certificates of the Roman army', *Britannia*, 1988, vol. 19, pp. 341–9, cast doubt on the traditional view that the diploma was a discharge certificate and proof of citizenship status. They point to *ILS* 9060 which shows a veteran gaining citizenship without producing a diploma. Diplomas were important, however, and veterans without a diploma could have problems establishing status (*P. Hamb.* I 89 shows a veteran having problems proving his citizenship status because he only had an *idiograph*). Veterans without bronze diplomas were registered as Roman citizens but did not receive *conubium* (*BGU* I 113; 265), and the children of C. Veturius Gemellus proclaimed that their deceased mother was recorded on a bronze inscription in Rome as if the diploma was important in establishing the status of their mother rather than their father (*P. Oxy.* LV 3798). Although diplomas could be used to establish citizenship, veterans could prove their status through other means. Diplomas appear to have been more important for securing the grant of *conubium*. Since legionary veterans did not receive a diploma, we must assume that they did not receive this privilege.

(ii) In AD 63, veterans of various units complained to Tuscus, the prefect. (*P. Fouad* 21; *SB* V 8247. This text is discussed by C.B. Welles, 'The *immunitas* of the Roman legionaries in Egypt', *JRS*, 1938, vol. 28, pp. 41–9; A. Segre, '*P. Yale* 1528 and *P. Fouad* 21', *JRS*, 1940, vol. 30, pp. 153–4; W.L. Westermann, 'Tuscus the prefect and the veterans in Egypt' *Class. Phil.*, 1941, vol. 36, pp. 21–9; S. Daris, 'Sul papiro Osloense inv.1451', *Aeg.*, 1962, vol. 42, pp. 123–7; G. Chalon, *L'édit de Tiberius Iulius Alexander*, Olten, Bibliotheca Helvetica Romana 5, 1964, pp. 64–6.) Tuscus instructed the veterans to return home as matters were in hand since he had written to the *strategoi* of the nomes to instruct them to abide by the terms of the imperial constitution and, angrily rebuking them for wasting time, he informed them that not all their positions were the same: 'I said to you before that the basis of complaint is not similar or the same for each of you. For some of you are legionary veterans and some from the cohorts, some from the *alae*, some from the oarsmen group so that the legal right is not the same for all.' We have no details as to the cause of the dispute between the *strategoi* and the veterans but can point to an analogous situation in which a *strategos* complained that the higher status groups did not recognise his authority over them when they were acting as tax collectors (*BGU* III 747 = W. *Chr.* 35). Tuscus, faced with a similar problem, may have exaggerated the differences between the various veterans but it seems likely that there was some difference in legal status between veterans of the legions and veterans of other units at this period, but the exact nature of the difference is obscure. Nevertheless, the veterans were similar enough in legal position to make common cause.

(iii) In AD 150, prospective veterans of *legio* X *Fretensis*, serving in Judaea, petitioned the legate (*PSI* IX 1026 = *CPL* 117). These men had been transferred from the fleet at Misenum to serve with this legion and now wished appropriate documentation to be issued to show that they had been discharged from the legion and not the fleet. The legate replied stating that '*veterani ex legionibus instrumentum accipere non solent*' (veterans from the legion do not normally receive a certificate) but the prefect of Egypt would be informed so that any necessary documentation could be issued on their return. The *instrumenta* referred to are normally assumed to be diplomas. The specific request of the veterans was, however, for documentation to be issued by the legate attesting the completion of service in the legion and there is no mention of citizenship or *conubium*. The reply of the legate also does not mention the privileges normally associated with diplomas but the reply in itself, together with the notification to be sent to the prefect of Egypt would have been enough to prove that the men were discharged from the legion. Thus, the men received what they had requested but no more and it would be unreasonable to believe that *conubium* or citizenship was at stake given the failure of all parties to mention either privilege. There are two possible explanations for the need for this documentation on the part of the veterans of X *Fretensis*, the first and most obvious being that the documentation would enable them to claim greater privileges on their return to Egypt. The second is that since the soldiers left Egypt to join the fleet at Misenum and there were regulations, see (iv), designed to prevent Egyptians joining the legions, our veterans may have simply wanted further documentation to secure their position on return to their native land.

(iv) *Epikrisis* documents (*P.Hamb.* I 30; 31a; *BGU* I 113; 265; III 780; 847; *SB* IV 7362; VI 9228 discussed in A. Aly, *The Roman Veterans in Egypt*, unpublished Ph.D. thesis, University of Michigan, 1947, p. 67; J. Lesquier, *L'armée romaine de l'Egypte d'Auguste à Dioclétien*, Cairo, IFAO, 1918, pp. 163–203; P. Schubert, *Les archives de Marcus Lucretius Diogenes*, Bonn, Habelt, 1990, Papyri 6 and 7; C.A. Nelson, *Status Declarations in Roman Egypt* (*ASP* 19), Amsterdam, Hakkert, 1979) also distinguish between veterans of various units. These documents are copies from the day book of the prefect which record hearings to determine civil status. Typically, these documents list the various groups whose status was being examined: Alexandrians, Romans, the freedmen of Roman citizens, and the veterans of the *alae*, cohorts, and fleets, but there is no mention of legionary veterans. In theory, all legionaries were citizens before enlistment and Egyptians were not allowed to enter a legion (*CPL* 102; *Gnomon of the Idios Logos* = *BGU* V 1020, 55). The reality was a little more confused since men with Roman names were recruited into auxiliary units and non-citizens joined the legions, suggesting that there was little real difference in the relative status of auxiliary and legionary units. It does appear, though, that virtually all serving legionaries carried a Roman name and, probably, Roman citizenship. If non-citizens were recruited, they received the citizenship upon enlistment. In this case, the citizenship status of legionaries would be established before service in the legions and, there-fore, when they were discharged, there would be no need for them to undergo an examination to determine that status, thus explaining their absence from the list of types of person being examined in the *epikrisis* docu-mentation. If a problem did arise and the status of a former legionary was questioned, status could be established at an *epikrisis* and the veteran would be entered under the rubric of 'Roman'. Certain veterans identified in the *epikrisis* texts as 'those without the bronze' have been identified with legionaries on the basis of the legate's reply discussed in (iii) above, but, as A. Degrassi, 'ΟΥΕΤΡΑΝΟΙ ΟΙ ΧΩΡΙΣ ΧΑΛΚΩΝ', *RFIC*, 1934, vol. 12, pp. 194–200, pointed out, it would have been far more in keeping with the linguistic forms of the texts to simply refer to 'those who had served in the legions'. See also W. Seston, 'Les vétérans sans diplômes des légions romaines', *Revue de Philologie*, 1933, vol. 59, pp. 375–99; R. Cavenaile, 'Le P. Mich. VII 432 et l'*honesta missio* des légionnaires', *Studi in Onore di Aristide Calderini e Roberto Paribeni*, Milan, Editrice Ceschina, 1953, vol. 2, pp. 243–51.

(v) Two documents attest privileges granted to legionaries on discharge. *BGU* II 628 = *CPL* 103 = W.*Chr.* 462 preserves an edict of the triumvir Octavian copied for Manius Valens, veteran of a legion. This gives immunity from cer-tain forms of duty on goods to the veteran and his parents, children and wife and immunity from the billeting of magistrates upon them. Certain privileges were granted regarding registering in Rome for the census, even if the family was absent, which suggest that the family would be Roman citizens. *CPL* 104 = W.*Chr.* 463, a wooden tablet, is a better-preserved but more complex document. The document is a request for the registration of the children of M. Valerius Quadratus as Roman citizens. On the exterior of the tablet Quadratus included a copy of an edict of Domitian. Domitian granted veterans immunity from customs duties, and Roman citizenship to children and parents. The parents and children received similar immunities to the veterans. Wives appear to have received all the same privileges as parents and children. The decree was copied from a bronze tablet erected in Caesarea but it appears to be a general edict and not just related to veterans of the *X Fretensis*. On the interior there is a copy of a decree which relates directly to veterans of *legio* X *Fretensis*. It is probable that there was another wooden tablet which went with this surviving one which would contain the end of the edict of Domitian and the beginning of this second document. The second document looks very much like an auxiliary diploma. It is a copy of a grant of certain unknown privileges to the veteran, his wife and children. The third part of the dossier moves the scene to Egypt and is a sworn statement for M. Iunius Rufus, prefect of Egypt, that the children of Quadratus, there listed, were due the privilege of citizenship granted by the emperor. Quadratus did not attempt to register his wife as a Roman citizen in Egypt but this is not a problem. His wife may have died or have been a Roman citizen in her own right. The decree shows that wives of legionary veterans would not be granted *conubium* but citizenship, making the grant of *conubium* unnecessary.

The only area in which the difference can be seen is in the privileges relating to the status of the wife of the veteran since the wives of legionaries appear to receive citizenship whilst those of auxiliaries were covered by a grant of *conubium*.

24 Pliny, *Ep.* X 5, 6, and 7.
25 N. Lewis, *Life in Egypt under Roman Rule*, Oxford, Clarendon, 1983, pp. 18–19.

26 E. Kühn, *Antinoopolis: ein Beitrag zur Geschichte des Hellenismus im römischen Ägypten. Gründung und Verfassung*, Göttingen, Kaestiner, 1913, p. 19; M. Zahrnt, 'Antinoopolis in Ägypten: die hadrianische Gründung und ihre Privilegien in der neueren Forschung' *ANRW*, 1988, vol. 2 10.1, pp. 669–706; J. de M. Johnson, 'Antinoe and its Papyri', *JEA*, 1914, vol. 1, pp. 168–81; Schubert, *Les archives de Marcus Lucretius Diogenes*, pp. 26–9.

27 Kühn, *Antinoopolis*, pp. 86–8. *W.Chr.* I 26.

28 R. Taubenschlag, *The Law of Greco-Roman Egypt in the Light of the Papyri*, Milan, Cisalpino Goliardico, 1972, p. 596; *W.Chr.* I 29.

29 Taubenschlag, *The Law of Greco-Roman Egypt*, p. 604.

30 H.I. Bell, 'Diplomata Antinoitica', *JEA*, 1933, vol. 33, pp. 514–28.

31 *W.Chr.* 27.

32 *BGU* I 265 is a Roman/Alexandrian *epikrisis* document, headed 'Antinoites', which Kühn thought might mean that Antinoites were included as an equivalent group. This is, however, an isolated occurrence and the mention of Antinoites is not in the main body of the document but precedes it. It is probably only a scribal note as to where the examination took place. The Antinoopolites were not on a par with the Alexandrians or the Romans but did have substantial legal privileges.

33 H.I. Bell, 'Antinoopolis: a Hadrianic foundation in Egypt', *JRS*, 1940, vol. 30, pp. 133–49, wrote that 'those [veterans] at present known as Antinoites did not become citizens until the reign of Antoninus Pius and it seems likely that about that time an attempt was made to increase the population of the city.' They did not form part of Hadrian's original allocation of settlers for his city since the city was meant to give a focus for non-Alexandrian, Hellenic elements within Egypt and veterans were not necessarily of Greek origins. The point is essentially a negative one since scholars have not been able to find any veteran Antinoopolites before the reign of Pius. It is worth, however, a brief examination of the evidence. In 148, the veteran and Antinoopolite C. Valerius Chairemonianus appears in the evidence from Karanis (*BGU* I 300). Longinus Priscus appears as an Antinoopolite during the reign of Pius (*BGU* I 179). In 133, the son of Chairemonianus raised a loan with the help of two veterans, Longinus Priscus and L. Octavius (*BGU* I 581). This suggests that Longinus Priscus, L. Octavius and C. Valerius Chairemonianus were all veterans and it is this connection which the son used when he needed sureties for his loan. As two of these were Antinoopolites during the reign of Pius, it must suggest either that Pius recruited veterans discharged before his reign or that they were already Antinoopolites in 133. C. Domitius Clemens, veteran, witnessed the opening of a will at Karanis in 131 (*CPL* 220). In 155, Domitius Clemens appeared in a list of witnesses for a declaration of status involving C. Iulius Niger and his son C. Iulius Longinus. All the witnesses were Antinoopolites (*SB* XII 11103). These cases are by no means conclusive but the most economical explanation of the material is that veterans were enrolled as Antinoopolites in the years 130–8 as part of the initial citizenship body.

34 *Dig.* XLIX 18.1; 18.3.

35 P. Garnsey, *Social Status and Legal Privilege in the Roman Empire*, Cambridge, Cambridge University Press, 1970.

36 *SB* V 7523. This is a witnessed statement that C. Maevius Apella, veteran of *ala Apriana*, had been beaten on the order of the *strategos*.

37 Tac., *Ann.* XIII.51.

38 See note 23 (v) above.

39 *Dig.* L 4.18, L 4.1 the division between *munera* and *honores*; L 4.12 magis-

terial positions are not *munera*; L 4.18.24 veterans must meet patrimonial expenses; L 5.7, L 4.3, XLIX 18.2 veterans excused *munera*.

40 V.B. Schuman, 'The income of the office of πϱάκτοϱες ἀϱγυϱικῶν of Karanis', *BASP*, 1975, vol. 12, pp. 23–66.

41 N. Lewis, *The Compulsory Public Services of Roman Egypt*, Florence, Papyrologica Florentina, 1982, pp. 144–5; F. Oertel, *Die Liturgie*, Leipzig, Teubner, 1917, pp. 392, 396.

42 *P. Phil.* 1.

43 H.C. Youtie, 'ΑΠΑΤΟΡΕΣ: Law vs. custom in Roman Egypt', *Le monde grec. Hommages à Claire Préaux*, Brussels, Université de Bruxelles, 1975, pp. 723–40, reprinted in H.C. Youtie, *Scriptiunculae Posteriores*, Bonn, Habelt, 1981–2, pp. 17–35.

44 *BGU* II 423 = *Sel.Pap.* I 112.

45 See pp. 130–1.

46 *BGU* V 1020; 43; 53; 56.

47 *CPL* 148–57; H. A. Sanders, 'Two fragmentary birth-certificates from the Michigan collection', *MAAR*, 1931, vol. 9, pp. 61–80.

48 Watson argues that the development of law is an historic practice. The law of every country is very often created in specific historical circumstances and does not necessarily bear any relationship to contemporary society. A. Watson, *The Making of the Civil Law*, Cambridge, Mass., Harvard University Press, 1981, p. 1, writes that

The Western legal tradition is basically unitary, and much of the same historical, legal elements have gone into the creation of the law of each nation state: Roman law, Germanic customs, canon law, feudal law, and so on. Yet the great bulk of modern Western systems are divided into common law systems that derive from English law, civil law systems that have an important historical connection – though not always easy to define – with Roman law, and mixtures of the two. This truth remains despite, on the one hand, overwhelming joint social and economic circumstances, such as the industrial revolution, in civil law and common law countries alike, and on the other hand, disparate political regimes, ranging from democracy to despotism, within a group of systems. As a result the similarities between any two civil systems are greater than between civil law systems and common law systems.

In *The Evolution of Law*, Oxford, Blackwell, 1985, p. 42, Watson argues that in developed systems, with specialist lawyers, law develops without 'too much concern with the concerns of society'. We may doubt whether the law of the Roman empire was quite so remote from the concerns of society. Watson is most convincing when looking at modern, professionalised systems but the ancient respect for law and perceptions of unchanging rules points to a similar conservatism within law in Rome. Augustus' legislation would have a moral force which would encourage subsequent emperors to maintain his rules even if the situation with which they dealt had long since ceased to be relevant and they themselves were unaware of the reasoning behind the legislation.

5 THE ARMY IN ACTION

1 R. Macmullen, *Soldier and Civilian in the Later Roman Empire*, Cambridge, Mass., Harvard University Press, 1963, presents a rather pessimistic picture of relations between soldiers and civilians. This has become the dominant

view of that relationship.

2   Strabo, 16.4.10–14. L. Terok, 'Geschichte Meroes. Ein Beitrag über die Quellenlage und den Forschungsstand', *ANRW*, 1988, vol. 2 10.1, pp. 107–341, constructs a king list for Meroe which is almost complete from *c.* 760 BC to AD 360.

3   Pliny, *NH* VI 195.

4   Strabo, 17.1.54; Pliny, *NH* VI 184–6.

5   *CIL* III 14147[5]; Strabo, 17.1.53.

6   Strabo, 16.4.23; S. Jameson, 'Chronology of the campaigns of Aelius Gallus and C. Petronius', *JRS*, 1968, vol. 58, pp. 71–84.

7   Strabo, 17.1.54; Dio, LIII 3.29.

8   Pliny, *NH* VI 181; *Res Gestae* 26 5. 'At my command and under my auspices two armies were led at almost the same time into Aethiopia and Arabia, which is called the Blessed, and many hostile forces of both peoples were cut down in battle and many towns captured. In Aethiopia, the troops advanced as far as the town of Nabata, which is next to Meroe; in Arabia to the borders of the Sabaeans, to the town of Mariba'.

9   Jos., *BJ* III 8; Tac., *Hist.* I 70; Jos., *BJ* II 494.

10 Dio, LXII 18; Tac., *Ann.* XV 36. Nero thought of fleeing to Egypt as the armies of his enemies closed in and this must be related to his preparations for a campaign.

11 Seneca, *Quaestiones Naturales* VI 8 3–5.

12 Pliny, *NH* VI 181. There are some worrying differences between Pliny's and Seneca's accounts which might suggest that these were two different expeditions. The texts are fully discussed by A.M. Demicheli, *Rapporti di pace e di guerra dell' Egitto romano con le populazioni dei deserti africani*, Milan, Università di Genoa, 1976, p. 94.

13 *IGRR* I 1207. The inscription was found at Thebes.

14 Strabo, 17.1.53.

15 Aelius Aristeides, *Oratio* XXVI, *On Rome* 70.

16 Pliny, *NH* VI 176; Strabo, 16.4.18.

17 The most southerly outpost of the empire, Qasr Ibrim, has recently been excavated. The evidence for a Roman military presence is slight but discussed by W.Y. Adams, 'Ptolemaic and Roman occupation at Qasr Ibrim', in F. Geus and F. Thill (eds), *Mélanges offerts à Jean Vercoutter*, Paris, Editions recherches sur les civilizations, 1988, pp. 9–17.

18 HA, *Aurelian* 33.

19 Zosimus, I 17; HA, *Probus* 17, 19; *Firmus, Proculus and Bonosus* 3; Procopius, I 19; R.T. Updegraff, 'The Blemmyes I: the rise of the Blemmyes and the Roman withdrawal from Nubia under Diocletian', *ANRW*, 1988, vol. 2 10.1, pp. 44–106.

20 Tac., *Ann.* XV 26.

21 Suet., *Vesp.* 6.

22 Tac., *Hist.* V 1; Jos., *BJ* IV 658; V 44.

23 Jos., *BJ* VII 117.

24 There is a high level of continuity in the auxiliary garrison between the first and second centuries. See pp. 24–7.

25 *RMD* 9.

26 *P. Mich.* VIII 465; 466. Iulius Apollinarius is known to be a soldier of III *Cyrenaica* from *P. Mich.* IX 562. See pp. 134–5.

27 *BGU* I 140 = M. *Chr.* 373; *P.Mich.* IX 562; P.V.C. Bauer *et al.*, *The Excavations at Dura-Europos. Preliminary Report of the Fourth Season of Work, October 1930 – March 1931*, New Haven and London, Yale University Press

and Oxford University Press, 1933, p. 57. The crucial fragment was not published until Fink re-examined the stone M.I. Rostovtzeff *et al., The Excavations at Dura-Europos. Preliminary Report of the Sixth Season of Work, October 1930 – March 1931*, New Haven and London, Yale University Press and Oxford University Press, 1936, p. 480.

28 HA, *Had*. 12.

29 *ILS* 1071. B. Isaac and I. Roll, 'Legio II Traiana in Judaea', *ZPE*, 1979, vol. 33, pp. 149–55; J.R. Rea, 'The Legio II Traiana in Judaea', *ZPE*, 1980, vol. 38, pp. 220–1, threw doubt on the reading. B. Isaac and I. Roll, 'Legio II Traiana in Judaea – A reply', *ZPE*, 1982, vol. 47, pp. 131–2, reasserted the readings of their earlier article.

30 M.P. Speidel, 'The Roman army in Arabia', *ANRW*, 1977, vol. 28, pp. 687–730, reprinted in M.P. Speidel, *Roman Army Studies* I, Amsterdam, Gieben, 1984, pp. 229–72.

31 B. Isaac and I. Roll, 'Judaea in the early years of Hadrian's reign', *Latomus*, 1979, vol. 38, pp. 54–66. For the problems of the movements of various legions in this period see also M. Mor, 'The Roman legions and the Bar–Kochba revolt (132–135 AD)', *Der römischen Limes in Österreich. Akten des 14 int. Limeskongresses 1986 in Carnuntum*, Vienna, Österreiches Akademie des Wissenschaften, 1990, pp. 163–77; K. Strobel, 'Zu Fragen der frühen Geschichte der römischen Provinz Arabia und zu einigen Problemen der Legionsdislokation im Osten des Imperium romanum zu Beginn des 2 Jh.n.Chr.', *ZPE*, 1988, vol. 71, pp. 251–80; D.L. Kennedy, 'Legio VI Ferrata: the annexation and early garrison of Arabia', *HSCP*, 1980, vol. 84, pp. 283–309; L.J.F. Keppie, 'The legionary garrison of Judaea under Hadrian', *Latomus*, 1973, vol. 32, pp. 859–64; L.J.F. Keppie, 'Legions in the East from Augustus to Trajan', in P. Freedman and D. Kennedy (eds), *The Defence of the Roman and Byzantine East (BAR 297)*, Oxford, 1986, pp. 411–29.

32 HA, *Antoninus Pius*, 5; Pausanias, VIII 43.3; *CIL* VI 1208.

33 Herodian, VI 4 7; HA, *Sev. Alex*. 53.

34 Zosimus, *Nova Historia* I 44.

35 Zosimus, *Nova Historia* I 50; HA, *Claudius* 11; *Aurelian* 32; *Firmus, Bonosius, Proculus and Saturninus* 3.

36 Strabo, 17.1.53.

37 Suet., *Vesp*. 19, provides a clear example of the impudence of the Alexandrian mob. Another reference to these disturbances is discussed by C.P. Jones, 'The date of Dio of Prusa's Alexandrian Oration', *Historia*, 1973, vol. 22, pp. 302–39.

38 Philo, *In Flaccum* 27–8. Philo, who was determined to deflect criticism from Agrippa, emphasised that Agrippa visited Alexandria on the instructions of Gaius.

39 Philo, *In Flaccum* 36–9, procession of Karabas; 53–72, actions against the Jews; 73–80, assault on the elders.

40 Philo, *In Flaccum* 86–94; 109–15.

41 Jos., *BJ* II 487ff. After the defeat of the Judaean rebels in AD 70, action was taken against the Temple of Onias in Egypt which was developing as a centre for disaffected elements fleeing Judaea. The temple was destroyed and the Jewish community of Egypt handed over anyone they suspected of involvement with the rebels to the Roman authorities (*BJ* VII 420–5).

42 The widespread destruction in Cyrenaica is well attested. Cyrene itself was extensively rebuilt during the second century and some of the work was specifically associated with the *tumultus Iudaicus*. The main Cyrene-Apollonia road was destroyed in the conflict and rebuilt in 119 (*SEG* IX 252). Damage

due to the revolt necessitated repairs at the temples of Hecate (*SEG* IX 168) and Apollo (*SEG* IX 189). The destruction in Cyrenaica obviously encouraged a building programme. The archaeological record of the revolt is described by Sh. Applebaum, 'The Jewish revolt in Cyrene in 115–117 and the subsequent recolonisation', *JJS*, 1951, vol. 2, pp. 177–86, who lists the building work at Cyrene in the second century. There is a temptation to associate all the building and rebuilding of the mid-second century with imperial beneficence due to the Jewish revolt but a certain amount of the work may have been the gradual improvement or repair of the cities. Cyrene was also part of the Panhellenic league created by Hadrian which was a means by which Hadrian distributed favours and money. A.J. Spawforth and S. Walker, 'The World of the Panhellion. I. Athens and Eleusis', *JRS*, 1985, vol. 75, pp. 78–104; A.J. Spawforth and S. Walker, 'The World of the Panhellion. II. Three Dorian cities', *JRS*, 1986, vol. 76, pp. 88–103. There can, however, be no doubt that the revolt was a major and destructive event in the history of Cyrenaica. The Jewish community is attested by *SEG* XVI 931 and *SEG* XVII 823.

43 Eusebius, *HE* IV 2.

44 Dio, LXVIII 32. There is a discrepancy between Eusebius and Dio as to the name of the leader of the revolt. This is especially worrying as it is exactly this kind of detail that lends credence to the historical account.

45 Orosius, *Adv. Pag.* VII 12.6.

46 Appian, BC II 90; Appian, *Fragment* 19.

47 *BGU* III 889 = *CPJ* II 449.

48 *P.Brem.* II = *CPJ* II 444; *P.Oxy.* III 707 = *CPJ* II 447; *P.Oxy.* III 705 = *CPJ* II 450.

49 *CPJ* II 443 = *P.Giss.* I 41 = *W.Chr.* 18; *CPJ* II 446 = *P.Brem.* 15.

50 *CPJ* II, Section IX, pp. 108–77.

51 *CPJ* II 436 = *P.Giss.* I 19.

52 *CPJ* II 437 = *P.Giss.* I 24.

53 *P.Brem.* 1 = *CPJ* II 438 = *W.Chr.* 16.

54 *CPJ* II 440 = *P.Bad.* 36. This document ends almost immediately after these words which makes restoration difficult; an abbreviated form of *grammateis* might be suggested but the meaning of the end of the document is obscure.

55 *CPJ* II 439 = *W.Chr.* 17 = *P.Giss.* I 27.

56 *P.Brem.* 15 = *CPJ* II 446.

57 E.M. Smallwood, *The Jews under Roman Rule*, Leiden, Brill, 1976, p. 399; A. Rowe, 'The discovery of the famous temple and enclosure of Serapis at Alexandria', *ASAE*, 1946, suppl. II, p. 62, presents some evidence for repairs at the Serapeum in Alexandria but the association of Hadrian with these repairs may not be related to any destruction of the temple during the revolt.

58 HA, *Had.* 12 1 attests a dispute concerning the place of residence of an Apis bull. The date of the affair appears to be 122–3. Dio, LXIX 8 1, tells us that Hadrian wrote to Alexandria to stop a disturbance. It is tempting to connect these two reports especially as Dio is epitomated and of uncertain date. It is likely that Hadrian adjudicated on the issue of the Apis bull, a decision that was treated as final, and so ended the rioting.

59 John Malalas, *Chron.* XI 23; HA, *Anton. Pius* V 5. S. Strassi Zaccaria, *L'editto di M. Sempronius Liberalis*, Trieste, Bernardo, 1988, points to further evidence of an uprising in an issue of coins in Rome which suggested that the corn supply had been secured. The evidence is hardly sufficient, however, to suggest a major rebellion.

60 Dio, LXXII 24.

61 HA, *M.Ant.* XXI 2; cf. *Avidius Cassius* VI 7. The wording in both is virtually identical. The involvement of Avidius Cassius with Egypt is detailed by
A.K. Bowman, 'A letter of Avidius Cassius', *JRS*, 1970, vol. 60, pp. 20–6.

62 Dio, LXXVIII 21–3; cf. HA, *Anton. Caracalla* 6; Herodian, IV 9.
A. Lukaszewicz, 'Alexandria sous les Sévères et l'historiographie', in
L. Criscuolo and G. Geraci (eds), *Egitto e storia antica dell' ellenismo all' età
araba*, Bologna, CLUEB, 1989, pp. 491–6, deals with the chronological
problems of Caracalla's trip to Egypt.

63 Dio, LXXIX 35.

64 Eusebius, *HE* VII 21.

65 Suet., *Aug.* 18; Dio, LI 18.1.

66 *P.Wash.Univ.* I 7 is the only parallel for the use of soldiers on the canals and
is dated to the fifth or sixth century.

67 *P.Ryl.* IV 603.

68 *BGU* II 597.

69 *BGU* IV 1188.

70 *P.Oxy.* XLII 3028.

71 *ChLA* IV 264; see pp. 24–6.

72 *BGU* III 802.

73 *SB* VI 9223; *P.Oxy.Hel.* 14.

74 *P.Oxy.* III 522.

75 *O.Guéraud* 14.

76 *OGIS* II 660 = *I.Koptos* 41 = *CIG* 4716 = *SB* V 8580.

77 *CIL* III 25.

78 *CIG* 4713e = *Inscr. Mus. Cairo*, p. 34, No. 9277.

79 *OGIS* II 678.

80 *SB* X 10530.

81 *CIL* III 6627. See pp. 29–30.

82 *IGRR* I 1142.

83 *CIL* III 13580.

84 HA, *Probus* 9.

85 *AE* (1974) No. 664.

86 *CIL* III 13578.

87 *CIL* III 12048.

88 *CIL* III 22; 13578.

89 H. Cuvigny, 'Un ostracon inédit du désert orientale et la provenance de
O.Amst.9', *Proceedings of the XXth International Congress of papyrologists,
Copenhagen, 23–29 August 1992*, Copenhagen, Museum Tusculanum Press,
1994, pp. 229–30; W. Clarysse and P.J. Sijpesteijn, 'A military roster on a
vase in Amsterdam', *Ancient Society*, 1988, vol. 19, pp. 71–96.

90 O. Guéraud, 'Ostraka grecs et latins de l'Wâdi Fawâkhir', *BIFAO*, 1942,
vol. 41, pp. 141–96; the Greek ostraka were republished as *SB* VI 9017.
P.J. Sijpesteijn, 'Letters or ostraka', *TAΛANTA*, 1973, vol. 5, pp. 72–84;
J.F. Gilliam, 'Three ostraka from Latopolis', *BASP*, 1976, vol. 13, pp. 55–61,
reprinted in J.F. Gilliam, *Roman Army Papers*, Amsterdam, Gieben, 1986,
pp. 379–86; R.S. Bagnall, 'The Roman garrison of Latopolis', *BASP*, 1975,
vol. 12, pp. 135–44. O. *Barns* = R. Coles, 'The Barns Ostraka', *ZPE*, 1980,
vol. 39, pp. 126–31 = *SB* XVI 12649–12655. See also H.C. Youtie, 'Greek
ostraka from Egypt', *TAPA*, 1950, vol. 81, pp. 99–116, where No. 11 appears
to be quite similar to the Latopolis, and Florida/Amsterdam/Barns finds.

91 O. *Amst.* 8, 9, 10, 11, 12, 13, 14.

92 R.S. Bagnall, 'Upper and lower guard posts', *CE*, 1982, vol. 57, pp. 125–8:
R.S. Bagnall, 'Army and police in Roman Upper Egypt', *JARCE*, 1977,

vol. 14, pp. 67–86; M. Reddé and J.-C. Golvin, 'Du Nil à la Mer Rouge: documents anciens et nouveaux sur les routes du désert orientale d'Egypte', *Karthago*, 1987, vol. 21, pp. 5–64; M. Reddé and J.-C. Golvin, 'Quelques recherches récentes sur l'archéologie militaire romaine en Egypte', *CRAI*, 1986, vol. 29, pp. 172–96; S.E. Sidebotham, *Roman Economic Policy in the Erythraea Thalassa 30* BC–AD 217 (Mnemosyne Suppl. 91), Leiden, Brill, 1986; R.E. Zitterkopf and S.E. Sidebotham, 'Stations and towers on the Quseir-Nile road', *JEA*, 1989, vol. 75, pp. 155–89; S.E. Sidebotham *et al.*, 'Fieldwork on the Red Sea coast: the 1987 season', *JARCE*, 1989, vol. 26, pp. 127–66.

93 *O. Florida* 2.
94 Bagnall, 'Army and police in Roman Upper Egypt', pp. 67–86.
95 *I. Koptos* 41, 43, 50, 51, 52, 53. Cf. 60, 62, 64, 77, 92, 115, 133, 86 = *SB* V 8580, 8581, 8585–8, 8593, 8633, 8630, 8615, 8620h, 8591, 8622, *CIL* III 28.
96 *I. Koptos* 60, 63, 75, 105 = *SB* V 8593, 8631, 8611.
97 *P. Fay.* 38 = *Doc. Eser. Rom.* 70 = *ChLA* III 207.
98 *P. Fay.* 108.
99 *BGU* IX 1891; 1892; 1894; XV 2512; 2537; 2539; *P.Berl. Frisk* 1: *P.Berl. Leigh.* I 6; *P.Bour.* 32; *P.Col.* II 1; V 1; *P.Fam. Tebt.* 23; *P.Mich.* IV 223; 224; 225; 362.
100 *P.Rein.* II 95.
101 Achilles Tatius, III and IV; Heliodoros, *Aithiopika*.
102 Xenophon of Ephesus IV 1.
103 Philo, *In Flaccum* 86–93.
104 Eusebius, *HE* VI 40.
105 *P.Thmouis* 98.
106 *P.Thmouis* 104.
107 *P.Thmouis* 116.
108 *BGU* I 372 = *W. Chr.* 19. Zaccaria, *L'editto di M. Sempronius Liberalis; P.Fay.* 24.
109 *P.Oxy.* XII 1408.
110 *P.Oxy.* XLVII 3364 = J.D. Thomas, 'A petition to the prefect of Egypt and related imperial edicts', *JEA*, 1975, vol. 61, pp. 201–21.
111 *BGU* I 325; *P.Ant.* II 87.
112 *P.Mich.* VI 425.
113 *P.Fay.* 38 = *Doc. Eser. Rom.* 70 = *ChLA* III 207.
114 A.E. Hanson, 'Village officials at Philadelphia: a model of Romanization in the Julio–Claudian period', in L. Criscuolo and G. Geraci (eds), *Egitto e storia antica dall' ellenismo all'età araba*, Bologna, CLUEB, 1989, pp. 429–40, details the career of Nemesion. The documents we are concerned with are *P.Corn.* inv.90 and *P.Mich.* X 582.
115 *SB* X 10270.
116 *P.Oxy.* IX 1185.
117 *P.Oxy.* XIV 1637.
118 Eusebius, *HE* VI 41.
119 *BGU* XIII 2352.
120 *P.Oxy.* IV 747.
121 *P.Oxy.* I 64; *P. Oxy.* I 65.
122 *PSI* III 184; 222.
123 *P.Wisc.* II 48.
124 *SB* I 5280.
125 *SB* V 7687 = *I. Fayoum* I 24.
126 These village officers are frequently attested. *Archephodoi* appear at least

seventy times in the first three centuries AD. Sword-bearers are attested about fifteen times including, on one occasion, a chief sword-bearer: *P.Mich.* XII 656.

127 *P.Wisc.* II 70.

128 *SB* X 10619 = *P.Alex & Giss* 3. See also *CIL* III 6581 and *P.Hamb.* I 39.

129 There are few cases of soldiers attested in contexts that would associate them with these centurions. *P. Wisc.* I 24 is an order to arrest from Philadelphia from either the second or third century, issued by Sarapion to the *archephodoi*, the village policemen, stating that a soldier would collect the accused in due course.

130 P.A. Brunt, 'Princeps and equites', *JRS*, 1983, vol. 73, pp. 42–75; P.A. Brunt, 'The administrators of Roman Egypt', *JRS*, 1975, vol. 65, pp. 124–47, reprinted in P.A. Brunt, *Roman Imperial Themes*, Oxford, Clarendon, 1990, pp. 215–54.

131 *RMR* 58; *RMR* 9 = *Doc. Eser. Rom. 10* = ChLA I 7 = *CPL* 106. Other documents on this piece of papyrus are *RMR* 10; 37; 68 all of which are edited as *CPL* 106 = *Doc. Eser. Rom. 10* = *ChLA* I 7.

132 *Ballio* may mean 'to the ballista' or 'to the baths'.

133 The entry is 'harena'.

134 The normal translation of the entry *pagano cultus* would be 'in plain clothes' but 'to the local cult' appears more comprehensible. The syntax is unclear.

135 Guéraud, 'Ostraka grecs et latins de l'Wâdi Fawâkhir', pp. 141–96 = *O. Guéraud.*

136 *O. Guéraud* 1.

137 *O. Guéraud* 2.

138 *O. Guéraud* 8.

139 *O. Guéraud* 9.

140 *O. Guéraud* 10.

141 *O. Guéraud* 11.

142 *O. Guéraud* 13.

143 *O. Guéraud* 14.

144 *O. Guéraud* 15.

145 *O. Guéraud* 18.

146 *O. Guéraud* 20.

147 *O. Guéraud* 21.

148 *O. Guéraud* 22.

149 *O. Guéraud* 26.

150 *O. Guéraud* 19, 24, 41.

151 *O. Guéraud* 23, 24, 34, 31.

152 *O. Florida* 7.

153 *O. Florida* 14.

154 *O. Florida* 20.

155 C. Préaux, 'Ostraca de Pselkis de la bibliothèque Bodléenne', *CE*, 1951, vol. 26, pp. 121–155; *O.Bodl. inv.* 2950–3017; *WO* 1128–1146; H.G. Evelyn White, 'Graeco-Roman ostraka from Dakke, Nubia', *CR* 1919, vol. 33, pp. 49–53.

6 THE ARMY AND THE ECONOMY

1 M.H. Crawford, 'Money and exchange in the Roman world', *JRS*, 1970, vol. 60, pp. 40–8; K. Hopkins, 'Taxes and trade in the Roman Empire, 200

BC–AD 400', *JRS*, 1980, vol. 70, pp. 101–25; J. Wacher, *The Towns of Roman Britain*, Berkeley, University of California Press, 1975.

2 This is a standard view of the decline of the Roman world and was a theme of many ancient historians who stressed the militarisation of the empire after the Severan period. See A.H.M. Jones, *The Later Roman Empire*, Oxford, Blackwell, 1964, vol. 2, pp. 1038–45, and, for a more cautious view, A. Cameron, *The Later Roman Empire*, London, Fontana, 1993, pp. 145–7.

3 R. Alston, 'Roman military pay from Caesar to Diocletian', *JRS*, 1994, vol. 84, pp. 113–23.

4 Suet., *Div. Iul.* 36.3.

5 Cassius Dio, LXVII 3; Suet., *Dom.* 7.3.

6 Herodian, VI 8.8.

7 Dio, LV 23.

8 Hopkins, 'Taxes and trade', pp. 101–25, suggests that the retirement bonus was paid to auxiliaries: 'Incidentally, are we sure that auxiliaries received no retirement gratuity? No source says so. Was it really possible to recruit equal numbers of troops to each branch of the army ... with marked discrepancies of reward especially in the second century AD, when many auxiliary recruits were already Roman citizens.'

9 *Dig.* XXXIV 1.20; XXXIV 1.20.3; X 2.39.2. R.P. Duncan-Jones, *The Economy of the Roman Empire: Quantitative Studies*, Cambridge, Cambridge University Press, 1974, pp. 29–30. The rates for children in Trajan's alimentary scheme were considerably lower than this.

10 Martial, III 7, gives this as a standard gift from patrons at the morning levée. He may well be exaggerating for effect. Duncan-Jones, *The Economy of the Roman Empire*, p. 138.

11 Duncan-Jones, *The Economy of the Roman Empire*, pp. 145–6.

12 *CIL* V 5262.

13 Duncan-Jones, *The Economy of the Roman Empire*, pp. 17–32.

14 Duncan-Jones, *The Economy of the Roman Empire*, pp. 365–6.

15 H.-J. Drexhage, *Preise, Mieten/Pachten, Kosten und Löhne im römischen Ägypten bis zum Regierungsantritt Diokletians (Vorarbeiten zu einer Wirtschaftsgeschichte des römischen Ägypten I)*, St Katherinen, Scripta Mercaturae, 1991, p. 453.

16 N. Lewis, *The Compulsory Public Services of Roman Egypt*, Florence, Papyrologica Florentina, 1982.

17 Drexhage, *Preise, Mieten/Pachten, Kosten und Löhne*, pp. 129–54. A.C. Johnson, *Roman Egypt to the Reign of Diocletian* = T. Frank (ed.), *An Economic Survey of the Roman World*, vol. II, Baltimore, Johns Hopkins Press, 1936, pp. 150–4, is an earlier collection of prices.

18 This is very difficult to assess since we know little about the basics of Egyptian agriculture. See D.W. Rathbone, 'The weight and measurement of Egyptian grain', *ZPE*, 1983, vol. 53, pp. 265–75. R.P. Duncan-Jones, 'Variations in Egyptian grain measures', *Chiron*, 1979, vol. 9, pp. 347–75. Egypt was more productive than other Mediterranean countries with a yield of eight or ten per unit of grain planted; see Jones, *The Later Roman Empire*, vol. 2, p. 767. It was standard to plant one *artaba* per *aroura* and so one *aroura* would produce seven *artabai* of grain. Although the *artaba* varies, we might assume a minimum subsistence level of 1.25 *artabai* per adult person per month. This means that a peasant would need just over two *arourai* to support himself and suggests, with taxation etc., that it would be difficult to survive on much less than five *arourai*. This would be the equivalent of 1,270 *drachmae* of property in the second century.

19 The literary evidence points to the bonus being paid in the first century to

legionaries and the first-century archive of the veteran Lucius Bellienus Gemellus (N. Hohlwein, 'Le vétéran Lucius Bellienus Gemellus', *Etudes de Papyrologie*, 1957, vol. 8, pp. 69–86) suggests a level of wealth greater than that of the ordinary villager. Gemellus had several estates in the Fayum but it is impossible to place an absolute value upon his land. He was born in AD 32 and so probably left the army around 77. We do not know the source of his wealth. In the second century, however, there is little obvious difference between the economic status of legionary veterans and that of auxiliary veterans and neither group appears to have enjoyed great wealth. Neither auxiliaries nor legionaries received the retirement gratuity in the second century.

20 Since a land owner with a small plot would save on labour costs by working the land himself, the return on investment on small plots of land was probably much higher than the return on large estates. It is also possible that land in Egypt was cheap, offering higher rates of return.

21 See n. 15 above.

22 *P. Panop.* 2.

23 D. van Berchem, 'L'annone militaire dans l'empire romain au IIIe. siècle', *Memoires de la société nationale des antiquaires de France*, 1936, vol. 10, pp. 117–202; D. van Berchem, 'L'annone militaire est-elle un mythe?' in A. Chastagnol *et al.* (eds), *Armées et fiscialité dans le monde antique* (*Colloque nationaux du CNRS 963*), Paris, CNRS, 1977, pp. 331–9; R. Develin, 'The army pay rises under Severus and Caracalla and the question of the *annona militaris*', *Latomus*, 1971, vol. 30, pp. 687–95.

24 *P. Amh.* II 107, 109; *P. Ryl.* II 85; *BGU* II 809.

25 *P. Grenf.* I 48; *PSI* VII 797.

26 *RMR* 78.

27 *O. Milne* 103; 104; *O. Strasb.* 445.

28 *P. Gen.* I 35 = *Doc. Eser. Rom.* 56; *BGU* I 266.

29 *BGU* II 665.

30 *SPP* XXII 92.

31 *P. Cair. Isid.* 54; 56.

32 *P. Ryl.* II 189.

33 *BGU* VII 1564.

34 A.H.M. Jones, 'The cloth industry under the Roman empire', *Economic History Review*, 1966, vol. 12, pp. 183–92, reprinted in A.H.M. Jones, *The Roman Economy*, Oxford, Blackwell, 1974, pp. 350–64, argues that the cloth industries of these provinces had been exhausted by the demands of the Roman military, but this seems distinctly unlikely.

35 *P. Dura* 56 = *RMR* 99; *P. Dura* 97 = *RMR* 83. *P. Oxy.* XII 1414.

36 D.W. Rathbone, 'Villages, land and population in Graeco–Roman Egypt', *PCPhS*, 1990, vol. 36, pp. 103–42.

37 J.M. Carrié, 'Le rôle économique de l'armée dans l'Egypte romaine', in A. Chastagnol *et al.* (eds), *Armées et fiscialité dans le monde antique* (*Colloques nationaux du CNRS 963*), Paris, CNRS, 1977, pp. 373–91.

38 A. Cerati, *Caractère annonaire et assiette de l'impot foncier au Bas–Empire*, Paris, Bibliotheque d'histoire du droit et droit romaine 20, 1975; van Berchem, 'L'annone militaire est-elle une mythe?', pp. 331–9.

39 A. Déléage, *La capitation du Bas–Empire*, Macon, Protat Frères, 1945, pp. 30–1, 78; J. Durliat, *Les finances publiques de Dioclétien aux Carolingiens* (284–889), Sigmaringen, Thorbecke, 1990, pp. 46–9.

40 S. Mitchell, 'A new inscription from Pisidia: requisitioned transport in the Roman empire', *JRS*, 1976, vol. 66, pp. 106–32.

41 Augustus set up the *aerarium militare* to pay retirement bonuses for soldiers. This institution continued into the third century which might suggest that the bonuses continued to be paid. There is, however, no mention of the payment of bonuses after AD 14, though veterans were, occasionally, given land. *Res Gestae* 17 explicitly states that Augustus funded the *aerarium* in order to supply the soldiers with bonuses. Dio, LV 24.9, and Suet., *Aug.* 49 4, both imply that the *aerarium* dealt with pay as well as with rewards. See M. Corbier, 'L'aerarium militare', in A. Chastagnol *et al.* (eds), *Armées et fiscialité dans le monde antique* (*Colloques nationaux du CNRS* 963), Paris, CNRS, 1977, pp. 197–234.

42 P.A. Brunt, 'Pay and superannuation in the Roman army', *PBSR*, 1950, vol. 18, pp. 50–75.

7 KARANIS: A VILLAGE IN EGYPT

1 B.P. Grenfell and A.S. Hunt, *Fayum Towns and their Papyri*, London, Egypt Exploration Society, 1900, pp. 20–1, 27–5.

2 A.E.R. Boak and E.E. Peterson, *Karanis: Topographical and Architectural Report of the Excavations during the Seasons 1924–28*, Ann Arbor, University of Michigan, 1931; A.E.R. Boak, *Karanis: The Temples, Coin Hoards, Botanical and Zoological Reports. Seasons 1924–31*, Ann Arbor, University of Michigan, 1933; D.B. Harden, *Roman Glass from Karanis found by the University of Michigan Expedition to Egypt 1924–29*, Ann Arbor, University of Michigan, 1936; E.M. Husselman, *Karanis. Excavations of the University of Michigan in Egypt 1928–1935: Topography and Architecture*, Ann Arbor, University of Michigan, 1979; L.A. Shier, *Karanis: Terracotta Lamps from Karanis, Egypt: Excavations of the University of Michigan*, Ann Arbor, University of Michigan, 1978; B. Johnson, *Pottery from Karanis: Excavations of the University of Michigan*, Ann Arbor, University of Michigan, 1981; R.E. Haatvedt and E.E. Peterson, *Coins from Karanis*, Ann Arbor, University of Michigan, 1964. In addition to these full length studies, there has also been an exhibition of the antiquities with catalogue, E.K. Gazda, *Karanis: An Egyptian Town in Roman Times*, Ann Arbor, University of Michigan, 1983, and numerous other studies of the archaeological and papyrological remains.

3 A.E.R. Boak, *Soknopaiou Nesos: The University of Michigan Excavations at Dime in 1931–32*, Ann Arbor, University of Michigan, 1935; *BGU* III 876; *P. Mich.* VI 380; 418.

4 Boak, *Karanis: The Temples, Coin Hoards, Botanical and Zoological Reports*, pp. 3, 20.

5 Husselman, *Karanis: Topography and Architecture*, p. 9.

6 H. Maehler, 'Häuser und ihre Bewöhner im Fayûm in der Kaiserzeit', in G. Grimm *et al.* (eds), *Das römisch-byzantinische Ägypten. Akten des internationalen Symposions 26–30 September 1978 in Trier*, Mainz, von Zabern, 1983, pp. 119–37.

7 C. Grande, review of Shier, *Karanis: Terracotta Lamps from Karanis, Egypt, JRS*, 1985, vol. 75, p. 284.

8 Haatvedt and Peterson, *Coins from Karanis*.

9 Harden, *Roman Glass from Karanis*.

10 Petrie inv. 1B/G2; *UC inv.* 31907. There are also *P. Hib.* II 212 of *c.* 250 BC, *P. Sorb.* I 56 of 215 BC, *SB* III 7222 of 229 BC. The last major dated group of papyri from the village come from *c.* AD 340 though *P. Col.* VIII 242 of the fifth century mentions the village.

11 Boak, *Karanis: The Temples, Coin Hoards, Botanical and Zoological Reports*, pp. 29–30.

12 Boak, *Karanis: The Temples, Coin Hoards, Botanical and Zoological Reports*, pp. 41–3. See the collection of the inscriptions made by E. Bernand, *Recueil des inscriptions grecques du Fayoum, Vol. I*, Leiden, Brill, 1975, No. 83–90, including republications of *SB* VIII 9817, 10167, 10168, 10169.

13 Boak, *Karanis: The Temples, Coin Hoards, Botanical and Zoological Reports*, p. 21.

14 Boak, *Karanis: The Temples, Coin Hoards, Botanical and Zoological Reports*, p. 5: 'The ground plan of the temple . . . is distinctly Egyptian and presents many points of similarity with that of other local shrines.'

15 Boak, *Karanis: The Temples, Coin Hoards, Botanical and Zoological Reports*, p. 14.

16 S. Sauneron, 'Les travaux de l'Institut Français d'Archéologie Orientale en 1974–1975', *BIFAO*, 1975, vol. 75, p. 461; S.A.A. el-Nassery *et al.*, 'Un grand bain gréco-romain à Karanis', *BIFAO*, 1976, vol. 76, pp. 231–75.

17 *BGU* II 379.

18 Husselman, *Karanis: Topography and Architecture*, p. 12.

19 P. Viereck, *Philadelphia (Morgenland 16)*, Leipzig, Heinrichs, 1928.

20 The Rylands papyrus gives a total amount of poll tax for the village of six talents, 2,312 *drachmae* or 38,312 *drachmae* and, since the poll tax was levied in the Arsinoite at 40 *drachmae*, this suggests 957.8 poll tax payers. Privileged groups paid poll tax at reduced rates and so we can estimate the total poll tax paying population at about 1,000. A.E.R. Boak, 'The population of Roman and Byzantine Karanis', *Historia*, 1955, vol. 4, pp. 157–62, estimates from the tax rolls that the number of poll tax payers in 171–4 was 575–644. Poll tax was levied on all male Egyptians over 14 but Roman and Alexandrian citizens, women and children were exempted. The likely total population of ordinary Graeco-Egyptians can be estimated using a multiple of 2.909 derived from R.S. Bagnall and B.W. Frier, *The Demography of Roman Egypt*, Cambridge, Cambridge University Press, 1994, p. 103, n. 35. I estimate the Roman population of the village to be about 14 per cent of the total in 171–4 and see no reason to suppose any difference in levels in 145–6. I, therefore, estimate the population to have been about 3,316 people in 145–6 and 1,907–2,135 in 171–4. We may note that the population fell in the space of one generation by 35.5 per cent to 42.5 per cent.

21 R. Alston, 'Houses and households in Roman Egypt', in R. Laurence and A. Wallace–Hadrill (eds), *Domestic Space in the Roman World (JRA Suppl.)*, forthcoming.

22 Shier, *Karanis: Terracotta Lamps from Karanis*, describes the patterns of distribution of the most common lamps from the Roman period at Karanis, in Shier's typology B2.1, B2.2, B2.3, and B2.4. B2.3 was spread all over Egypt. B2.1 was connected with the North Fayum and the Delta. B2.2 mainly comes from around Alexandria. B2.4 lamps are found in sites from the Delta and the Fayum. The earlier Roman types (B1.1 and B1.2) also show distinct connections with the Delta region. There is no evidence of the lamps of Upper Egypt reaching Karanis. The pattern points to strong links between Karanis and the Delta which are further attested by a number of receipts from the Karanis gate for goods travelling to Memphis (*BGU* III 764–6; *P. Lond.* II, p. 6, 469). The pottery is overwhelmingly Egyptian in origin and much of it was locally manufactured. There is very little fine ware preserved for the first two centuries AD but there are a number of African red slip pots probably of third-century origin. There are also few *amphorae*,

suggesting that there was little trade. Johnson, *Pottery from Karanis*, Fine ware No. 203–207; Red Slip No. 213–54.

23 Husselman, *Karanis: Topography and Architecture*, p. 54; E.M. Husselman, 'The granaries of Karanis', *TAPA*, 1952, vol. 83, pp. 56–73; Gazda, *Karanis: An Egyptian Town in Roman Times*, p. 11.

24 R.K. Enders, 'The remains of wild and domestic animals', in Boak, *Karanis: The Temples, Coin Hoards, Botanical and Zoological Reports*; H. Kees, *Ancient Egypt: A Cultural Topography*, trans. I.F.D. Morrow, Chicago and London, Chicago University Press, 1961, p. 226, notes that the Fayum was the finest hunting ground in the whole of Egypt.

25 *BGU* I 34.

26 R.S. Bagnall, 'Agricultural productivity and taxation in later Roman Egypt', *TAPA*, 1985, vol. 115, pp. 289–305.

27 *P.Mich.* VI 372 is undated and so could refer to the earlier or later position. It is possible that the fall in population was related to a significant decline in available land.

28 O.M. Pearl, 'The 94 klerouchies at Karanis', *Akten des XIII int. Papyrologenkongresses: 1971*, Munich, Beck, 1974, pp. 325–30. With an average of thirty persons per klerouchy, Pearl notes that this would suggest an enormous population but men could be members of more than one klerouchy and perhaps not all klerouchies would function simultaneously.

29 *P.Cair.Isid.* 10; 11.

30 H. Geremek, *Karanis: Communauté rurale de l'Egypte romaine au IIᵉ–IIIᵉ siècles de notre ère*, Warsaw, Archiwum filologiczne 17, 1969, pp. 56–7.

31 J.F. Oates, 'Landholding in Philadelphia in the Fayum (AD 216)', *Proceedings of the XII International Congress of Papyrology (ASP 7)*, Toronto, Hakkert, 1970, pp. 385–7.

32 R.S. Bagnall, 'Landholding in late Roman Egypt: the distribution of wealth', *JRS*, 1992, vol. 82, pp. 128–49.

33 *BGU* II 647; *SB* XII 11124.

34 *P.Gen.* II 100–2; *P.Gen.* II 97. Another Minucius, Minucius Nepos, appears in *P.Mich.* IX 571, a document preserved at Karanis, but is only mentioned since he was the centurion of a soldier of III *Cyrenaica* who was in the village and there is no reason to believe that this Minucius ever visited Karanis.

35 *P.Oxy.* VII 1022; *SB* V 7605; *P.Oslo.* III 124.

36 *BGU* I 326.

37 *BGU* I 327.

38 *P.Mich.* IV 224, 4130; VI 370; cf. *BGU* Iı 696.

39 *CPL* 215, cf. 240.

40 *P.Ryl.* 160; *BGU* VII 1574; *P.Col.Youtie* I 64.

41 *P.Mich.* IV 224, 3931.

42 *SB* IV 7362.

43 *BGU* I 71.

44 This survey has produced a large number of Longini and it is tempting to propose some connection but Longinus is an extremely common name and over 180 separate people are attested in Egypt. A disproportionate number of documents of known provenance which mention Longini come from Karanis.

45 J.F. Gilliam, 'Some Roman elements in Roman Egypt', *ICS*, 1978, vol. 3, pp. 115–31. H.A. Sanders, 'Two fragmentary birth certificates from the Michigan collection', *MAAR*, 1931, vol. 9, pp. 61–80. See also now P. van Minnen, 'House to house enquiries: an interdisciplinary approach to Roman Karanis', *ZPE*, 1994, vol. 100, pp. 227–51.

46 For other connections between the names see H.I. Bell, 'A happy family', *Aus Antike und Orient: Festschrift Wilhelm Schubart*, Leipzig, Harassowitz, 1950, pp. 38–47; P.J. Sijpesteijn, 'A happy family?', *ZPE*, 1976, vol. 21, pp. 169–81.

47

Date	Reference	Description
154	*P.Mich.* VI 428	Sale of house.
155	*SB* XII 11103	Birth certificate.
172	*P.Mich.* VI 384	Receipt.
172/3	*SB* V 7558	Relief from guardianship.
177/8–182/3	*BGU* III 782	Iulius Longinus' dealings.
179	*P.Mich.* VI 364	Land registration.
182-5	*P.Mich.* VI 385	Garden taxes receipt book.
183	*P.Mich.* VI 395	Tax receipt.
185	*P.Mich.* VI 386	Tax receipt.
186	*P.Mich.* VI 396	Tax receipt.
188	*P.Mich.* VI 387	Tax receipt.
189	*P.Mich.* VI 370	Census declaration.
197	*P.Mich.* VI 422	Petition to the prefect.
197	*P.Mich.* VI 423–4	Petition to the *strategos*.
198	*P.Mich.* VI 425	Petition to the *epistrategos*.
199/200	*P.Mich.* VI 426	Petition to the *epistrategos*.
206	*P.Mich.* VI 397	Tax receipt.
207	*P.Mich.* VI 398	Tax receipt.
211/12	*SB* IV 7361	Petition to the *epistrategos*.
214	*SB* IV 7360	Land registration.
	SB XII 11114	Complaint of Iulius Niger.

48 *SB* XII 11103. Of the witnesses, only C.Domitius Clemens appears elsewhere. In *CPL* 220 of 131, a veteran of the same name was a witness to a will from the Arsinoite.

49 *P.Mich.* IX 554, division of property (Domitianic); *BGU* II 472, receipt for final payment in deed of sale (139); *P.Mich.* VI 428, deed of sale of house (154).

50 The neighbouring property in the deed of sale also belonged to Valeria Diodora and consisted of a house and a dovecote. The property, however, had been divided between Aquila and his sisters.

51

Date	Reference	Description
90	*P.Mich.* IX 568–9	M.Anthestius Gemellus. Loan arrangement.
117–18	*P.Fam.Tebt.* 18	Anthestius Gemellus appointed to liturgic post.
122	*P.Mich.* III 185	M.Anthestius Gemellus. Rental of land.
128	*P.Mich.* III 166	M.Anthestius Longus. Birth certificate.
138–161	*BGU* III 709	M.Anthestius Cap[ ]. Sale of land.
141	*P.Phil.* 11	C.Anthestius Numisianus. Division of land.

Date	Reference	Description
150/173	*P.Phil.* 12	L.Anthestius Germanus. Lease of property.
162/3	*P.Amh.* II 92	M.Anthestius Capitolinus. Lease of oil retail rights.
166/9	*P.Mich.* XII 629	M.Anthestius Gemellus. Request to remain in Karanis.
172	*SB* V 7558	Anthestius Gemellus. Petition to escape guardianship.
172	*P.Mich.* VI 384	M.Anthestius Tertaianus. Tax receipt.
172–3	*P.Mich.* IV 223, 2814; 224, 3533	M.Anthestius Capitolinus.
172–3	*P.Mich.* IV 224, 3752; 5140; 5423	M.Anthestius Gemellus.
174	*P.Gen.* II 108	Tax payment.
176	*BGU* II 666	Anthestius Capitolinus. Owner of olive grove.
194	*BGU* I 326	M.Anthestius Petronianus. Opening of will.
II (mid)	*BGU* II 613	Anthestius Gemellus. Dispute over land.
II	*PSI* VI 704	M.Anthestius.
II	*P.Ryl.* IV 612 = *P.Mich.* VII 434	C.Anthestius Numisianus. Marriage contract.

52

Date	Reference	Description
96	*P.Mich.* IX 571	Sabinus. Deposit receipt.
107	*P.Mich.* VIII 465	Apollinarius. Letter to Tasoucharion.
107	*P.Mich.* VIII 466	Apollinarius. Letter to Sabinus.
117/18	*P.Mich.* IX 549	Will of Sambathion.
117–138	*P.Mich.* inv.5849 (IX 549 n.3)	Census document.
119	*P.Mich.* IX 562	Apollinarius. Land rental.
131	*P.Mich.* IX 572	Apollinarius. Tax receipt.
Post-130	*P.Mich.* VIII 493	Sabinus. About legal dealings.
	P.Mich. VIII 485	Sabinus. Letter about promotion.
	P.Mich. VIII 486	Apollinarius. Complaint from Sempronius.
	P.Mich. VIII 496	Apollinarius. Invitation to visit.
	P.Mich. VIII 497	Apollinarius. About building works.
	P.Mich. VIII 498	Apollinarius. Thank you letter for recommendation.
	P.Mich. VIII 499	Apollinarius. Request for the use of influence.
	P.Mich. VIII 500	Apollinarius. Letter about the non-delivery of cotton.

53 J.C. Mann, 'The organization of the *Frumentarii*', *ZPE*, 1988, vol. 74, pp.

149–50. N.B. Rankov, '*Frumentarii*, the *Castra Peregrina* and the provincial *Officia*', *ZPE*, 1990, vol. 80, pp. 176–82.

54 Sambathion raises the interesting, if unlikely, possibility that the family had a semitic origin. *CPJ* III, pp. 43–87 lists the known occurrences of Sambathions in Egypt.

55 The Latin of these texts has caused some comment. G.B. Pighi, *Lettere Latine d'un soldato di Traiano, P. Mich. 467–472*, Bologna, Facultà di lettere e filosofia degli studi di Bologna, 1964; J.N. Adams, *The Vulgar Latin of the letters of Claudius Terentianus*, Manchester, Faculty of Arts, Manchester University, 1977. All the documents in this series are undated.

> *P.Mich*. VIII 467 Terentianus to Tiberianus. Terentianus has joined the fleet.
> *P.Mich*. VIII 468 Terentianus to Tiberianus. Terentianus ill while at sea.
> *P.Mich*. VIII 469 Terentianus to Tiberianus. Tiberianus called *speculator*.
> *P.Mich*. VIII 470 Fragment in Latin; similar hand to above.
> *P.Mich*. VIII 471 Terentianus to Tiberianus. Account of quarrel.
> *P.Mich*. VIII 472 Tiberianus to Longinus Priscus.
> *P.Mich*. VIII 473 Tabetheus to Tiberianus. Account of murder.
> *P.Mich*. VIII 474 Tiberianus. Family matters in Alexandria.
> *P.Mich*. VIII 475 To Tiberianus. Family news from Papirus.
> *P.Mich*. VIII 476 Terentianus to Tiberianus. Asking permission to buy a slave.
> *P.Mich*. VIII 477 Terentianus to Tiberianus. Riots in Alexandria.
> *P.Mich*. VIII 478 Terentianus to Tiberianus. Terentianus wounded and confined to camp.
> *P.Mich*. VIII 479 Terentianus to Tiberianus. Legal matters involving Tabetheus.
> *P.Mich*. VIII 480 Terentianus. Petition to the archidikastes.
> *P.Mich*. VIII 481 Terentianus to Tasoucharion.
> *ChLA* V 229 Terentianus. Fragment in Latin.

56 One could envisage circumstances such as divorce and remarriage or a close emotional tie between the 'father' and 'son' which led to the relationship being given the status of a father-son relationship with could explain the rather complex family structure here suggested. Familial designations are frequently used in correspondence between people who do not appear to have been related which suggests that Romano–Egyptians were far less restrictive in their use of such designations than is common in modern Western society.

57 Boak and Peterson, *Karanis: Topographical and Architectural Report*, Fig. 48.

58 Boak, *Soknopaiou Nesos*, p. 9; E. Will, 'Heron', *LIMC*, 1990, vol. 5.1, pp. 391–4.

59 Geremek, *Karanis: Communauté rurale*, pp. 56–7.

60 See pp. 45–6.

61 H. Ammar, *Growing up in an Egyptian Village*, London, Routledge & K. Paul, 1954, pp. 26–33, shows the importance of children as part of the labour force in contemporary Egypt.

62 J.F. Oates, 'Philadelphia in the Fayum during the Roman Empire', *Atti XI Congresso internazionale di papirologia, Milano, 1965*, Milan, Instituto Lombardo di scienze e lettere, 1966, pp. 454–7; J.F. Oates, 'Landholding in Philadelphia in the Fayum (A.D. 216)', pp. 385–7. Oates analyses a tax register from 216 listing the land holders of the village and was able to calculate from this the average land holdings of the majority of the villagers. The average veteran

grain land holding was nearly 13 *arourai* whilst soldiers had 9½ *arourai*. For orchard land the veterans had less than one *aroura* but the soldiers had four. This was virtually the same as the averages for the other land holders of the village. The veteran community of Philadelphia resembled the Karanis group in many ways. The veterans arrived at about the same time, *c.* AD 86, and Philadelphia seems to have had a Roman population of around 20 per cent. The main difference between Karanis and Philadelphia for our purposes is the relative paucity of archaeological data from the latter village.

8 DIOCLETIAN AND AFTER

1 A.J. Butler, *The Arab Conquest of Egypt and the Last Thirty Years of Roman Dominion*, Oxford, Clarendon, 1978 (1st ed., 1902), p. 229.

2 J. Maspero, *Organisation militaire de l'Égypte byzantine*, Paris, Libraire ancienne Honoré Champion, 1912, argues that the army of the fifth and sixth century differed in many respects from that of the fourth century.

3 There is some difficulty in dating this division. T.D. Barnes, *The New Empire of Diocletian and Constantine*, Cambridge, Mass., Harvard University Press, 1982, pp. 201–8, argues that the papyrological evidence suggests no division before 314/15 but the names of the new provinces which reflect the patron deities of the Tetrarchs, would suggest a division under Diocletian, perhaps *c.* 297–8 when Diocletian was in Egypt.

4 There are a vast number of works on this issue. The best introductions are P. Brown, *The World of Late Antiquity: From Marcus Aurelius to Muhammad*, London, Thames and Hudson, 1971, and A. Cameron, *The Later Roman Empire*, London, Fontana, 1993.

5 R.S. Bagnall, 'Landholding in late Roman Egypt: the distribution of wealth', *JRS*, 1992, vol. 82, pp. 128–49.

6 The chronology of these events has been the subject of much scholarly debate. J. Schwartz, *L.Domitius Domitianus (Papyrologica Bruxellensia 12)*, Brussels, Fondation Egyptologique Reine Elisabeth, 1975; J.D. Thomas, 'The date of the revolt of L.Domitius Domitianus', *ZPE*, 1976, vol. 22, pp. 253–79; A. Geissen, 'Numismatische Bemerkung zu dem Aufstand des L.Domitius Domitianus', *ZPE*, 1976, vol. 22, pp. 280–6; J.D. Thomas, 'A family archive from Karanis and the revolt of Domitius Domitianus', *ZPE*, 1977, vol. 24, pp. 233–40.

7 R.P. Duncan–Jones, 'Pay and numbers in Diocletian's army', *Chiron*, 1978, vol. 8, pp. 541–60, reprinted in R.P. Duncan–Jones, *Structure and Scale in the Roman Economy*, Cambridge, Cambridge University Press, 1990, pp. 105–17, assesses the size of various units from the contributions made to the units in *P. Panop.* 2. The difficulty in using this material is that we cannot know whether all the troops of the unit were stationed at the fort which was supplied or whether all the supplies for the unit came from Panopolis.

8 *CIL* III 13578; 22.

9 The archaeological material is collected in Appendix 2.

10 Libanius, *Or.* XLVII 33.

11 J.M. Carrié, 'Patronage et propriété militaires au IVᵉ s. Objet rhétorique et objet réel du discours sur les patronages de Libanius', *BCH*, 1976, vol. 100, pp. 159–76; J.M. Carrié, 'L'esercito: transformazioni funzionali ed economie locale', in A. Giardina (ed.), *Società romana e impero tardoantico. Instituzioni, ceti, economie*, Bari, Laterza, 1986, pp. 449–88; R.S. Bagnall, 'Military

officers as landowners in fourth century Egypt', *Chiron*, 1992, vol. 22, pp. 47–54.
12 *P. Abinn.* 44–47; 49–52.
13 *P. Abinn.* 18, 28, 48.
14 *P. Abinn.* 35.
15 The most easily available text is in H. Musirillo, *The Acts of the Early Christian Martyrs*, Oxford, Clarendon, 1972. The procedures for joining the Roman army are outlined by R.W. Davies, 'Joining the Roman Army', *BJ*, 1969, vol. 169, pp. 208–32, reprinted in R.W. Davies, *Service in the Roman Army*, Edinburgh, University Press, 1989, pp. 3–30.
16 C.P. Jones, '*Stigma*: Tattooing and branding in antiquity', *JRS*, 1987, vol. 77, pp. 139–55.
17 Libanius, *Or.* XLVII 32.
18 R. Remondon, 'Soldats de Byzance d'après un papyrus trouvé à Edfou', *Recherches de Papyrologie*, 1961, vol. 1, pp. 41–93.
19 O.F.A. Meinardus, 'An examination of the traditions of the Theban legion', *Bull. de la Soc. d'arch. Copte*, 1976–8, vol. 23, pp. 5–32; D.F. O'Reilly, 'The Theban legion of St Maurice', *Vigiliae Christianae*, 1978, vol. 32, pp. 195–207. Both these writers believe that there is some truth in the legends though the evidence they produce is unconvincing.
20 D. van Berchem, *L'armée de Dioclétien et la réforme constantinienne*, Paris, Imprimerie Nationale and P. Geuthner, 1952; Maspero, *Organisation militaire*; Butler, *The Arab Conquest of Egypt*.
21 R.M. Price, 'The *limes* of Lower Egypt', in R. Goodburn and P. Bartholomew (eds), *Aspects of the Notitia Dignitatum: Papers presented to a conference in Oxford, December 13 to 15, 1974* (BAR 15), Oxford, 1976, pp. 143–55.
22 A.K. Bowman, 'The military occupation of Upper Egypt in the reign of Diocletian', *BASP*, 1978, vol. 15, pp. 25–38, notes that the changes in military disposition were connected with a radical overhaul of taxation and the supply of the army.

9 CONCLUSION

1 A.K. Bowman and D.W. Rathbone, 'Cities and administration in Roman Egypt', *JRS*, 1992, vol. 82, pp. 107–27.
2 A.K. Bowman and J.D. Thomas, *Vindolanda: The Latin Writing Tablets*, London, *Britannia Monographs* 4, 1983; A.K. Bowman and J.D. Thomas, *The Vindolanda Writing Tablets*, London, British Museum Press, 1994; A.K. Bowman and J.D. Thomas, 'A military strength report from Vindolanda', *JRS*, 1991, vol. 81, pp. 62–73.
3 *RMR* 1–4, 6–8 = *P. Dura* 100, 101, 104, 105, 98, 99, 102.
4 *RMR* 63 = *CPL* 112.
5 Apuleius, *Met.* IX 39.
6 M. Sasel Kos, 'A Latin epitaph of a Roman legionary from Corinth', *JRS*, 1978, vol. 68, pp. 22–6. This was further discussed by F.G.B. Millar, 'The world of the Golden Ass', *JRS*, 1981, vol. 71, pp. 63–75. There are examples from Britain of soldiers and centurions being portrayed in identical fashion. *RIB* 17 refers to a soldier, *RIB* 492 to an *optio* and *RIB* 491 to a centurion.
7 *RIB* 152.
8 Tac., *Ann.* XIV 31.

APPENDIX 1: MILITARY UNITS

1 A.E. Hanson, 'Juliopolis, Nicopolis, and the Roman camp', *ZPE*, 1980, vol. 37, pp. 249–54. The archaeological remains of the camp are considerably later than our period and were largely destroyed in the early twentieth century. See pp. 192–3.

2 The standard prosopographies for the Roman army in Egypt also note the provenance of the evidence, clearly showing the preponderance of the Alexandrian evidence. R. Cavenaile, 'Prosopographie de l'*armée romaine* d'Egypte d'Auguste à Dioclétien', *Aeg.*, 1970, vol. 50, pp. 213–320. N. Critini, 'Supplemento alla prosopografia dell' esercito romano d'Egitto da Augusto a Diocleziano', *Aeg.*, 1973, vol. 53, pp. 93–158.

3 *SB* I 1023. See also *SB* I 4594, 4597, 4610.

4 *OGIS* 205; *CIL* III 79; *SB* V 7908; *SB* V 7932; H.G. Evelyn White, 'Graeco–Roman ostraka from Dakke, Nubia', *CR*, 1919, vol. 33, pp. 49–53.

5 *CIL* III 6627; *CIL* III 13580. *I. Portes* 95. *CIL* III 13574 = *I. Portes* 93.

6 *P. Oxy. Hel.* 14; *BGU* III 802; *SB* VI 9223; *P. Lond.* II 261; *SB* VI 9223; *P. Oxy.* II 276.

7 *CIL* III 14147[4]; *CIL* III 14147[3]; *AE* (1974) No. 664; *CIL* III 6025.

8 *I. Memnon* 2, 7, 10, 44, 46, 47, 74.

9 *SB* V 8386; *SB* V 8806.

10 *AE* (1956) No. 8 = *I. Pan* 67.

11 E. Bernand, *Inscriptions Grecques et Latines d'Akoris*, Cairo, IFAO, 1988, No. 172; 3; 21; 19 = *SEG* XXIX (1979) 1622. It is also probable that a detachment of the fleet was stationed here, No. 12 = *AE* (1971) No. 481; No. 16; No. 19.

12 Jos., *BJ* III 8; *CIL* III 25.

13 Jos., *BJ* VII 19; VI 418; VII 117.

14 D. Braund, 'The Caucasian frontier: myth, exploration, and the dynamics of imperialism', in P. Freedman and D. Kennedy (eds), *The Defence of the Roman and Byzantine East* (*BAR* 297), Oxford, 1986, pp. 31–49; J. Kolendo, 'Le projet et l'expédition de Néron dans le Caucase', *Neronia*, 1977, pp. 23–7; M.T. Griffin, *Nero: The End of a Dynasty*, London, Batsford, 1984, p. 229; A.M. Demicheli, *Rapporti di pace e di guerra dell' Egitto romano con le populazioni dei deserti africani*, Milan, Università di Genoa, 1976, p. 94.

15 Centurions could be sent out of the provinces in which they were serving and they were used for many different tasks.

16 Jos., *BJ* II 385–7; IV 606.

17 *BGU* I 9; *BGU* XI 2070; *BGU* II 378 = M. *Chr.* 88; *SB* IV 7367; *P. Lond.* p. 152 II 196.

18 *CIL* XVI 1; 2. See *ala Paullini* and the M. *Frori, Aelii Habeti*, and *Nigri* cohorts. E. Birley, 'Units named after their commanders', *Ancient Society*, 1978, vol. 9, pp. 257–73, reprinted in E. Birley, *Roman Army Papers 1929–1986*, Amsterdam, Gieben, 1988, pp. 268–84; M.P. Speidel, 'Auxiliary units named after their commanders: four new examples from Egypt', *Aeg.*, 1982, vol. 62, pp. 165–72, reprinted in M.P. Speidel, *Roman Army Studies* I, Amsterdam, Gieben, 1984, pp. 101–8; M.P. Speidel, 'The Eastern Desert garrisons under Augustus and Tiberius', *Studien zu dem Militärgrenzen Roms II 1977. X Internationalen Limes Congress in Germania Inferior*, Bonn, Habelt, 1977, pp. 511–15, reprinted in Speidel, *Roman Army Studies* I, pp. 323–8.

19 P.A. Holder, *Studies in the Auxilia of the Roman Army from Augustus to Trajan* (*BAR* 70), Oxford, 1980, p. 209.

20 HA, *Ant. Pius.* V 4; Pausanias, VIII 43.3; *CIL* VI 1208.

21 See pp. 133–4.
22 See n. 18.
23 *CIL* XVI 35.
24 M.P. Speidel, 'The prefect's horse-guards and the supply of weapons to the Roman army', *Proceedings of the XVI International Congress of Papyrologists (ASP 23)*, Chico, Scholars Press, 1981, pp. 405–9, reprinted in Speidel, *Roman Army Studies* I, pp. 329–31, details the evidence for the existence of this unit but does not discuss the possibility of the development of the unit over time.

APPENDIX 2: THE ARCHAEOLOGY OF THE ARMY

1 E. Breccia, *Alexandria ad Aegyptum: A Guide to the Ancient and Modern Town and its Graeco-Roman Museum*, Bergamo, Instituto Italiano d'Arti Grafiche, 1922, p. 86.
2 J. Murray, *A Handbook for Travellers in Lower and Upper Egypt*, London, Murray, 1880, p. 141.
3 *CIL* III 12048.
4 S.T. Parker, *Romans and Saracens: A History of the Arabian Frontier*, Philadelphia, American Schools of Oriental Research, 1986, pp. 58–72.
5 A full excavation report is expected. A. Poesner–Krieger, 'Les travaux de l'Institut Français d'Archéologie Orientale en 1982–1983', *BIFAO*, 1983, vol. 83, pp. 343–63; A. Poesner–Krieger, 'Les travaux de l'Institut Français d'Archéologie Orientale en 1986–1987', *BIFAO*, 1987, vol. 87, pp. 299–336; A. Poesner–Krieger, 'Les travaux de l'Institut Français d'Archéologie Orientale en 1987–1988', *BIFAO*, 1988, vol. 88, pp. 181–237; C. Gautier, 'Monnaies trouvées à Douch', *BIFAO*, 1981, vol. 81, pp. 111–14; J. Gascou, 'Douch: rapport préliminaire des campagnes de fouilles de l'hiver 1978/1979 et de l'automne 1979', *BIFAO*, 1980, vol. 80, pp. 287–345; M. Reddé, 'Les oasis d'Egypte', *JRA*, 1989, vol. 2, pp. 281–90; M. Reddé and J.–C. Golvin, 'Quelques recherches récentes sur l'archéologie militaire romaine en Egypte', *CRAI*, 1986, vol. 29, pp. 172–96; A. Fakhry, 'Bahia and Farafra Oases', *ASAE*, 1939, vol. 39, pp. 627–42; R. Naumann, 'Bauwerke der Oase Khargeh', *MDAIK*, 1939, vol. 8, pp. 1–16; G. Wagner, 'Le camp romaine de Doush (Oasis de Khargeh-Egypte)', *Studien zu den Militärgrenzen Roms III. 13 int. Limeskongress. Aalen 1983*, Stuttgart, K. Theis, 1986, pp. 671–2; M. Reddé, 'A l'ouest du Nil: une frontière sans soldats, des soldats sans frontière', *Roman Frontier Studies 1989: Proceedings of the XVth International Congress of Roman Frontier Studies*, Exeter, Exeter University Press, 1991, pp. 485–93.
6 D. Meredith, 'Berenice Troglodytica', *JEA*, 1957, vol. 43, pp. 56–70.
7 Strabo, 16.4.24; Pliny, *NH* VI 101; A. Fuks, 'Notes on the archive of Nicanor', *JJP*, 1951, vol. 5, pp. 207–16, reprinted in A. Fuks, *Social Conflicts in Ancient Greece*, Jerusalem and Leiden, Brill, 1984, pp. 312–21; M. Reddé and J.–C. Golvin, 'Du Nil à la Mer Rouge: documents anciens et nouveaux sur les routes du désert orientale d'Egypte', *Karthago*, 1987, vol. 21, pp. 5–64; D.S. Whitcomb and J.H. Johnson, *Quseir Al–Qadim 1980: Preliminary Report*, Malibu, Udena, 1982.
8 Whitcomb and Johnson, *Quseir Al-Qadim 1980*, p. 3 (pre-Roman site), p. 7. The pottery is of first- and second-century date. 'The occupation lasted from perhaps early in the first century of our era into the early third century at the latest.' A large central building has pottery from the first century only (pp. 64–5).

NOTES

9 S.E. Sidebotham *et al.*, 'Fieldwork on the Red Sea coast: the 1987 season', *JARCE*, 1989, vol. 26, pp. 127–66; S.E. Sidebotham, 'A limes in the Eastern Desert of Egypt: myth or reality', *Roman Frontier Studies 1989: Proceedings of the XVth International Congress of Roman Frontier Studies*, Exeter, Exeter University Press, 1991, pp. 494–7.

10 D. Meredith, 'The Roman remains in the Eastern Desert of Egypt', *JEA*, 1952, vol. 38, pp. 94–111; D. Meredith, 'The Roman remains in the Eastern Desert of Egypt', *JEA*, 1953, vol. 39, pp. 45–106; D. Meredith, 'Inscriptions from the Berenice Road', *CE*, 1954, vol. 29, p. 282; D. Meredith, 'The Myos Hormos Road', *CE*, 1956, vol. 31, pp. 356–62; C.H.O. Scaife, 'Two inscriptions at Mons Porphyrites (Gebel Dokhan). Also a description with plans of stations between Kainopolis and Myos Hormos together with some other ruins in the neighbourhood of Gebel Dokhan', *Bulletin of the Faculty of Arts. Fouad I University*, 1935, vol. 3, pp. 58–104; J. Couyat, 'Ports gréco-romain de la Mer Rouge et grandes routes du désert arabique', *CRAI*, 1910, pp. 525–42; G.W. Murray, 'The Roman roads and stations in the Eastern Desert of Egypt', *JEA*, 1925, vol. 11, pp. 138–50; A. Bernand, *De Koptos à Kosseir*, Leiden, Brill, 1972; A. Bernand, *Pan du Désert*, Leiden, Brill, 1977; A. Bernand, *Les portes du désert: recueil des inscriptions grecques d'Antinooupolis, Tentyris, Koptos, Apollonopolis Parva et Apollonopolis Magna*, Paris, CNRS, 1984; Reddé and Golvin, 'Quelques recherches récentes sur l'archéologie militaire romaine en Egypte', pp. 172–96; Reddé and Golvin, 'Du Nil à la Mer Rouge', pp. 5–64; R.E. Zitterkopf and S.E. Sidebotham, 'Stations and towers on the Quseir-Nile Road', *JEA*, 1989, vol. 75, pp. 155–89. This bibliography does not include works on specific sites or those which are primarily discursive rather than accounts of archaeological or epigraphic explorations.

11 See Reddé and Golvin, 'Du Nil à la Mer Rouge', on Wadi Abbad, Wadi Abu Middrik, Wadi Samut. I am reliant throughout this section on Reddé and Golvin's work.

12 *I. Koptos* 1 = *SB* I 1006; *I. Koptos* 2 = *CIL* III 6628.

13 *I. Pan* 64–8 esp. 67, 68.

14 *I. Koptos* 3, 4, 5 = *SB* I 4380, 4374, 4381.

15 *I. Koptos* 8.

16 *I. Koptos* 19 = *AE* (1911) No 121.

17 *I. Koptos* 41, 43, 50, 51, 52, 53. cf. 60, 62, 64, 77, 92, 115, 133, 86 = *SB* V 8580, 8581, 8585–7, 8593, 8633, 8630, 8615, 8620h, 8622, *CIL* III 28.

18 *I. Koptos* 60, 63, 75, 105 = *SB* V 8593, 8631, 8611.

19 Zitterkopf and Sidebotham, 'Stations and towers on the Quseir–Nile Road', pp. 155–89.

20 *I. Pan* 20, 21, 22, 27, 28, 29 = *SB* I 4383, V 8320, 8321, 8162, 8163.

21 *I. Pan* 37–47 = *CIL* III 24, 25, *SB* V 8323, 8322, 8324, *AE* (1956) No. 54.

22 *O. Mons Claudianus*; J. Bingen, 'Première campagne de fouille au Mons Claudianus: rapport préliminaire', *BIFAO*, 1987, vol. 87, pp. 45–52; J. Bingen, 'Quatrième campagne de fouille au Mons Claudianus: rapport préliminaire', *BIFAO*, 1990, vol. 90, pp. 63–81; J. Bingen, 'Mons Claudianus: rapport préliminaire sur les cinquième et sixième campagnes de fouille (1991–1992)', *BIFAO*, 1992, vol. 92, pp. 15–36; J. Bingen and W. Van Rengen, 'Sur quelques inscriptions du Mons Claudianus', *CE*, 1986, vol. 61, pp. 139–46; H. Cuvigny, 'Nouveaux ostraca grecs du Mons Claudianus', *CE*, 1986, vol. 61, pp. 271–86. In the 1960s, both Claudianus and Porphyrites were surveyed by a German team. T. Kraus *et al.*, 'Mons Claudianus – Mons Porphyrites: Bericht über die zweite Forschungsreise 1964', *MDAIK*, 1967,

vol. 22, pp. 108–205; T. Kraus and J. Röder, 'Mons Claudianus: Bericht über eine erste Erkundungsfahrt im März 1961', *MDAIK*, 1962, vol. 18, pp. 80–120.

23 S.E. Sidebotham, *Roman Economic Policy in Erythraea Thalassa 30 BC – AD 217* (*Mnemosyne* Suppl. 91), Leiden, Brill, 1986, p. 62. 'There were no fixed distances between the water points in the Eastern Desert. Their locations did not necessarily represent the distances one could travel in a single day. Most water points were so close together that a fast traveller could visit two or three in a day's journey.'

24 H. Harrauer and P.J. Sijpesteijn, 'Ein neues Dokument zu Roms Indienhandel. P. Vindob. G.40822', *Anz. der Phil.-hist. Klasse der Osterr. Akad. der Wissenschaft*, 1985, vol. 122, pp. 124–55. *I.Portes 67 = SEG* XX (1964) No. 688.

25 M. Abd. el-Maqsoud, 'Preliminary report on the excavations at Tell El-Farama (Pelusium): first two seasons (1983/4 and 1984/5)', *ASAE*, 1984/5, vol. 70, pp. 3–8; M. Abd. el-Maqsoud and J.Y. Carriez-Maratray, 'Une inscription grecque de la forteresse de Péluse', in *Sociétés urbaines en Egypte et au Soudan (Cahiers de Recherches de l'Institut de Papyrologie en Lille 10)*, Lille, 1991, pp. 97–103.

26 M. Clédat, 'Le temple de Zeus Cassius à Peluse', *ASAE*, 1913, vol. 13, pp. 79–85.

27 *CIL* III 13578; W.M. Flinders Petrie *et al.*, *Tanis II: Nebesheh (Am) and Defenneh (Tahpanhes)*, London, Egypt Exploration Fund, 1888, p. 99.

28 M. Clédat, 'Fouilles à Qasr Gheit', *ASAE*, 1912, vol. 12, pp. 145–68.

29 *CIL* III 6633.

30 J. Leclant and G. Clerc, 'Fouilles et travaux en Egypte et au Soudan, 1986–1987', *Orientalia*, 1988, vol. 57, pp. 307–404; E. Louis and D. Valbelle, 'Les trois dernières forteresses de Tell el-Herr', in *Sociétés urbaines en Egypte et au Soudan (Cahiers de Recherches de l'Institut de Papyrologie en Lille 10)*, Lille, 1991, pp. 61–71.

31 G.A. Reisner, *The Archaeological Survey of Nubia: Bulletin* 1, Cairo, National Printing Department, 1908, pp. 20–1.

32 W.Y. Adams, 'Ptolemaic and Roman occupation at Qasr Ibrim', in F. Geus and F. Thill (eds), *Mélanges offerts à Jean Vercoutter*, Paris, Editions recherches sur les civilizations, 1988, pp. 9–17: 'Recent work has shed almost no new light on the period of Ptolemaic and Roman occupation in Lower Nubia between about 300 BC and 300 AD.' See also W.Y. Adams, 'Primis and the "Aethiopian" Frontier', *JARCE*, 1983, vol. 20, pp. 93–104.

33 R. Lepsius, *Discoveries in Egypt, Ethiopia and the Peninsula of Sinai*, London, Bohn, 1853, pp. 126–7.

34 C.M. Firth, *The Archaeological Survey of Nubia: Bulletin 5*, Cairo, National Printing Department, 1909, p. 8.

35 J. Garstang, 'Excavations at Hierakonpolis, at Esna, and in Nubia', *ASAE*, 1907, vol. 8, pp. 132–48.

36 C.M. Firth, *The Archaeological Survey of Nubia: Bulletin 4*, Cairo, National Printing Department, 1909, p. 17.

37 H. Jaritz, 'The investigation of the ancient wall extending from Aswan to Philae', *MDAIK*, 1987, vol. 43, pp. 67–74.

38 M. el Din Mustafa and H. Jaritz, 'A Roman fortress at Nag' el-Hagar: first preliminary report', *ASAE*, 1984/5, vol. 70, pp. 21–31; U.A. Wareth, 'Nag al-Hagar, a Roman fortress with a palace of the late Roman Empire: second preliminary report', *BIFAO*, 1992, vol. 92, pp. 185–95.

39 J. Capart, 'Troisième rapport sommaire sur les fouilles de la fondation Egyptologique Reine Elisabeth à El Kab: Novembre 1945 à Fevrier 1946',

ASAE, 1947, vol. 46, pp. 337–55; [El Kab], 'Exposition des fouilles d'El Kab', *CE*, 1952, vol. 27, pp. 332–6; there is some doubt as to whether this is a military structure.

40 M. el-Saghir *et al., Le camp romain de Louqsor* (*IFAO* 83), Cairo, IFAO, 1986; J.-C. Golvin and M. Reddé, 'L'enceinte du camp militaire romain de Louqsor', *Studien zu den Militärgrenzen Roms III. 13 Int. Limeskongress. Aalen 1983* (*Forschungen und Berichte zur verund Frühgeschichte in Baden-Würtemburg* 20), Stuttgart, 1986, pp. 594–9; P. Lacau, 'Inscriptions latines du temple de Louxor', *ASAE*, 1934, vol. 34, pp. 17–46.

41 J.S. Pendlebury, *Tell el-Amarna*, London, Louvat Dickson and Thompson, 1935, pp. 31, 36. J. Samson, *Amarna*, London, University College London, 1972, merely notes that the fort is unexcavated.

42 A.J. Butler, *The Arab Conquest of Egypt and the Last Thirty Years of Roman Dominion*, Oxford, Clarendon, 1978 [1st ed., 1902], pp. 238–44.

43 J. Schwartz and H. Wild, *Qasr Qârûn/ Dionysias 1948. Fouilles Franco-Suisses. Rapports I*, Cairo, IFAO, 1950, p. 63; J. Schwartz *et al., Fouilles Franco-Suisses. Rapports II. Qasr Qârûn/Dionysias 1950*, Cairo, IFAO, 1969, p. 1. J.M. Carrié, 'Les *Castra Dionysiados* et l'évolution de l'architecture militaire romaine tardive', *MEFRA*, 1974, vol. 86, pp. 819–50. The archive of the commander of the unit stationed at the fort has been published as *P. Abinn.* and is discussed on pp. 149–153.

44 *P. Wisc.* II 53; *RMR* 64 = *BGU* II 696 = *CPL* 118.

45 Procopius, I 19.

46 *CIL* III 22.

47 S.T. Parker, 'The nature of Rome's Arabian frontier', *Roman Frontier Studies 1989: Proceedings of the XVth International Congress of Roman Frontier Studies*, Exeter, Exeter University Press, 1991, pp. 498–504; Parker, *Romans and Saracens*.

48 Contrary to this D.F. Graf, 'Rome and the Saracens', in T. Fahd (ed.), *Arabie préislamique et son environnement historique et culturel*, Leiden, Brill, 1989, pp. 341–400.

BIBLIOGRAPHY

Adams, J.N., *The Vulgar Latin of the Letters of Claudius Terentianus*, Manchester, Faculty of Arts, Manchester University, 1977.

Adams, W.Y., 'Primis and the "Aethiopian" frontier', *JARCE*, 1983, vol. 20, pp. 93–104.

——, 'Ptolemaic and Roman occupation at Qasr Ibrim', in F. Geus and F. Thill (eds), *Mélanges offerts à Jean Vercoutter*, Paris, Editions recherches sur les civilizations, 1988, pp. 9–17.

Adriani, A., 'Scavi della missione dell' istituto Papirologica Fiorentino ad Antinoe', *ASAE*, 1939, vol. 39, pp. 659–63.

Alston, R., 'Roman military pay from Caesar to Diocletian', *JRS*, 1994, vol. 84, pp. 113–23.

——, 'Violence and social control in Roman Egypt', *Proceedings of the XXth International Congress of papyrologists, Copenhagen, 23–29 August, 1992*, Copenhagen, Museum Tusculanum Press, 1994, pp. 517–21.

——, 'Houses and households in Roman Egypt', in R. Laurence and A. Wallace–Hadrill (eds), *Domestic Space in the Roman World (JRA* Suppl.), forthcoming.

Aly, A.A., *The Roman Veterans in Egypt*, unpublished Ph.D. thesis, University of Michigan, 1947.

Amelotti, M., *Il testamento romano attraverso la prassi documentale. I. Le forme classiche di testamento*, Florence, Le Monnier, 1966.

Ammar, H., *Growing up in an Egyptian Village*, London, Routledge & K. Paul, 1954.

Anderson, W.S., 'Juvenal Satire 15: cannibals and culture', in A.J. Boyle (ed.), *The Imperial Muse; Ramus essays in Roman Literature of the Empire: To Juvenal through Ovid*, Clayton, Victoria, Aureal, 1988, pp. 203–14.

Applebaum, Sh., 'The Jewish revolt in Cyrene in 115–117 and the subsequent recolonisation', *JJS*, 1951, vol. 2, pp. 177–86.

Arens, W., *The Man-Eating Myth: Anthropology and Anthropophagy*, New York, Oxford University Press, 1979.

Badawy, A., *A History of Egyptian Architecture II*, Berkeley, University of California Press, 1966.

Baedeker's Guide to Egypt, Norwich, Automobile Association, *c.* 1987.

Bagnall, R.S., 'The Roman garrison of Latopolis', *BASP*, 1975, vol. 12, pp. 135–44.

——, 'Army and police in Roman Upper Egypt', *JARCE*, 1977, vol. 14, pp. 67–86.

——, 'Property holdings of the liturgists in fourth-century Karanis', *BASP*, 1978, vol. 15, pp. 9–16.

241

——, 'Upper and lower guard posts', *CE*, 1982, vol. 57, pp. 125–8.

——, 'Agricultural productivity and taxation in later Roman Egypt', *TAPA*, 1985, vol. 115, pp. 289–305.

——, 'Combat ou vide: Christianisme et paganisme dans l'Egypte romaine tardive', *Ktema*, 1988, vol. 13, pp. 285–96.

——, 'Landholding in late Roman Egypt: the distribution of wealth', *JRS*, 1992, vol. 82, pp. 128–49.

——, 'Military officers as landowners in fourth century Egypt', *Chiron*, 1992, vol. 22, pp. 47–54.

Bagnall, R.S., and Frier, B.W., *The Demography of Roman Egypt*, Cambridge, Cambridge University Press, 1994.

Baines, J. and Malek, J., *Atlas of Ancient Egypt*, Phaidon, Oxford, 1984.

Baldini, A., 'La rivolta Bucolica e l'usurpazione di Avidio Cassio', *Latomus*, 1978, vol. 37, pp. 634–78.

Baldwin, B., 'Crime and criminals in Roman Egypt', *Aeg.*, 1963, vol. 43, pp. 250–63.

Barnes, T.D., *The New Empire of Diocletian and Constantine*, Cambridge, Mass., Harvard University Press, 1982.

Bauer, P.V.C., Rostovtzeff, M.I. and Bellinger, A.R., *The Excavations at Dura-Europos. Preliminary Report of the Fourth Season of Work, October 1930 – March 1931*, New Haven and London, Yale University Press and Oxford University Press, 1933.

Bell, H.I., 'Diplomata Antinoitica', *JEA*, 1933, vol. 33, pp. 514–28.

——, 'The economic crisis in Egypt under Nero', *JRS*, 1938, vol. 28, pp. 1–8.

——, 'Antinoopolis: a Hadrianic foundation in Egypt', *JRS*, 1940, vol. 30, pp. 133–49.

——, 'A happy family', *Aus Antike und Orient: Festschrift Wilhelm Schubart*, Leipzig, Harassowitz, 1950, pp. 38–47.

Bell, H.I., Martin, V., Turner, E.G. and van Berchem, D., *The Abinnaeus Archive: Papers of a Roman Military Official in the Reign of Constantius II*, Oxford, Clarendon, 1962.

Berchem, D. van, 'L'annone militaire dans l'empire romain au IIIe. siècle', *Memoires de la société nationale des Antiquaires de France*, 1936, vol. 10, pp. 117–202.

——, *L'armée de Dioclétien et la réforme constantinienne*, Paris, Imprimerie Nationale and P. Geuthner, 1952.

——, 'L'annone militaire est-elle un mythe?', in A. Chastagnol, C. Nicolet and H. van Effenterre (eds), *Armées et fiscalité dans le monde antique (Colloques nationaux du CNRS 963)*, Paris, CNRS, 1977, pp. 331–9.

Bernand, A., *De Koptos à Kosseir*, Leiden, Brill, 1972.

——, *Pan du Désert*, Leiden, Brill, 1977.

——, *Les portes du désert: recueil des inscriptions grecques d'Antinooupolis, Tentyris, Koptos, Apollonopolis Parva et Apollonopolis Magna*, Paris, CNRS, 1984.

Bernand, A. and Bernand, E., *Les inscriptions grecques et latines du colosse de Memnon*, Cairo, IFAO, 1960.

Bernand, E., *Recueil des inscriptions grecques du Fayoum*, Vols. I–III, Leiden, Brill, 1975–84.

——, *Inscriptions Grecques et Latines d'Akoris*, Cairo, IFAO, 1988.

Biezunska–Malowist, I., 'La famille du vétéran romain C.Iulius Niger de Karanis', *Eos*, 1957–8, vol. 49, pp. 155–64.

——, 'Les citoyens romains à Oxyrhynchos aux deux premiers siècles de l'empire', in *Le monde grec. Hommages à Claire Préaux*, Brussels, Université de Bruxelles, 1975, pp. 741–7.

Bingen, J., 'Un dédicace de marchands palmyréniens à Coptos', *CE*, 1964, vol. 59, pp. 355–8.

——, 'Première campagne de fouille au Mons Claudianus: rapport préliminaire', *BIFAO*, 1987, vol. 87, pp. 45–52.

——, 'Quatrième campagne de fouille au Mons Claudianus: rapport préliminaire', *BIFAO*, 1990, vol. 90, pp. 63–81.

——, 'Mons Claudianus: rapport préliminaire sur les cinquième et sixième campagnes de fouille (1991–1992)', *BIFAO*, 1992, vol. 92, pp. 15–36.

Bingen, J. and Van Rengen, W., 'Sur quelques inscriptions du Mons Claudianus', *CE*, 1986, vol. 61, pp. 139–46.

Birley, E., 'The epigraphy of the Roman army', *Actes du deuxième congrès internationale d'epigraphie grecque et latine (1952)*, Paris, Maisonneuve, 1953, pp. 226–38, reprinted in E. Birley, *Roman Army Papers 1929-1986*, Amsterdam, Gieben, 1988, pp. 3–11.

——, 'Senators in the emperors' service', *PBA*, 1954, vol. 39, pp. 197–214, reprinted in E. Birley, *Roman Army Papers 1929–1986*, Amsterdam, Gieben, 1988, pp. 75–92.

——, 'Hadrianic frontier policy', *Carnuntia*, 1956, vol. 3, pp. 25–33.

——, 'Units named after their commanders', *Ancient Society*, 1978, vol. 9, pp. 257–73, reprinted in E. Birley, *Roman Army Papers 1929–1986*, Amsterdam, Gieben, 1988, pp. 268–84.

——, *Roman Britain and the Roman Army*, Kendal, Wilson, 1983.

——, *Roman Army Papers 1929–1986*, Amsterdam, Gieben, 1988.

Blok, A., 'The peasant and the brigand: social banditry reconsidered', *CSSH*, 1972, vol. 14, pp. 494–502.

——, *The Mafia of a Sicilian Village 1860–1960*, Oxford, Blackwell, 1974.

Boak, A.E.R., *Karanis: The Temples, Coin Hoards, Botanical and Zoological Reports. Seasons 1924–31*, Ann Arbor, University of Michigan, 1933.

——, *Soknopaiou Nesos: The University of Michigan Excavations at Dime in 1931–32*, Ann Arbor, University of Michigan, 1935.

——, 'The population of Roman and Byzantine Karanis', *Historia*, 1955, vol. 4, pp. 157–62.

Boak, A.E.R. and Peterson, E.E., *Karanis: Topographical and Architectural Report of the Excavations during the Seasons 1924–28*, Ann Arbor, University of Michigan, 1931.

Boren, H.C., 'Studies relating to the *stipendium militium*', *Historia*, 1983, vol. 32, pp. 427–60.

Bowersock, G.W., *Roman Arabia*, Cambridge, Mass. and London, Harvard University Press, 1983.

Bowman, A.K., 'A letter of Avidius Cassius', *JRS*, 1970, vol. 60, pp. 20–6.

——, *The Town Councils of Roman Egypt (ASP 11)*, Toronto, Hakkert, 1971.

——, 'Papyri and Roman imperial history', *JRS*, 1976, vol. 66, pp. 153–73.

——, 'The military occupation of Upper Egypt in the reign of Diocletian', *BASP*, 1978, vol. 15, pp. 25–38.

——, *Egypt after the Pharaohs 332 BC – AD 642: From Alexander the Great to the Arab Conquest*, Oxford, Oxford University Press, 1986.

Bowman, A.K. and Rathbone, D.W., 'Cities and administration in Roman Egypt', *JRS*, 1992, vol. 82, pp. 107–27.

Bowman, A.K. and Thomas, J.D., *Vindolanda: The Latin Writing Tablets*, London, Britannia Monographs 4, 1983.

——, 'A military strength report from Vindolanda', *JRS*, 1991, vol. 81, pp. 62–73.

——, *The Vindolanda Writing Tablets*, London, British Museum Press, 1994.

Boyoval, B., 'Tableau général des indications d'âge de l'Egypte romaine', *CE*, 1977, vol. 52, pp. 345–51.

Braund, D., 'The Caucasian frontier: myth, exploration, and the dynamics of imperialism', in P. Freedman and D. Kennedy (eds), *The Defence of the Roman and Byzantine East* (*BAR* 297), Oxford, 1986, pp. 31–49.

Braunert, H., 'Griechische und römische Komponenten im Stadtrecht von Antinoopolis', *JJP*, 1962, vol. 14, p. 73.

Breccia, E., 'Osiris = Apis in abito militare romano', *BSSA*, 1918, vol. 16, pp. 184–7.

——, *Alexandria ad Aegyptum: A Guide to the Ancient and Modern Town and its Graeco–Roman Museum*, Bergamo, Instituto Italiano d'Arti Grafiche, 1922.

Breeze, D.J., 'Pay grades and ranks below the centurionate', *JRS*, 1971, vol. 61, pp. 130–5.

Breeze, D.J. and Dobson, B., *Hadrian's Wall*, London, Penguin, 1987.

Brown, P., *The World of Late Antiquity: From Marcus Aurelius to Muhammad*, London, Thames and Hudson, 1971.

——, *The Body and Society: Men, Women and Sexual Renunciation in Early Christianity*, New York, Columbia University Press, 1988.

Brunt, P.A., 'Pay and superannuation in the Roman army', *PBSR*, 1950, vol. 18, pp. 50–75.

——, 'Conscription and volunteering in the Roman imperial army', *Scripta Classica Israelica*, 1974, vol. 1, pp. 90–115.

——, 'The administrators of Roman Egypt', *JRS*, 1975, vol. 65, pp. 124–47, reprinted in P.A. Brunt, *Roman Imperial Themes*, Oxford, Clarendon, 1990, pp. 215–54.

——, 'Did imperial Rome disarm her subjects', *Phoenix*, 1975, vol. 29, pp. 260–70, reprinted in P.A. Brunt, *Roman Imperial Themes*, Oxford, Clarendon, 1990, pp. 255–66.

——, 'Princeps and equites', *JRS*, 1983, vol. 73, pp. 42–75.

——, *Roman Imperial Themes*, Oxford, Clarendon, 1990.

Bülow–Jacobsen, A., 'Mons Claudianus: Roman granite quarry and station on the road to the Red Sea', *Acta Hyperborea*, 1988, vol. 1, pp. 159–65.

——, 'The excavation and ostraka of Mons Claudianus', *Proceedings of the XIXth International Congress of Papyrologists*, Cairo, Center of Papyrological Studies, Ain Shams University, 1992, pp. 49–63.

Burn, A.R., '*Hic Breve Vivitur*', *Past & Present*, 1953, vol. 4, pp. 2–31.

Butler, A.J., *The Arab Conquest of Egypt and the Last Thirty Years of Roman Dominion*, Oxford, Clarendon, 1978 [1st ed., 1902].

Butzer, K.W., *Early Hydraulic Civilization in Egypt: A Study in Cultural Ecology*, Chicago and London, University of Chicago Press, 1976.

Cagnat, R., *L'armée romaine d'Afrique*, Paris, Imprimerie Nationale, 1913.

Cameron, A., *The Later Roman Empire*, London, Fontana, 1993.

Campbell, J.B., 'The marriage of Roman soldiers under the Empire', *JRS*, 1978, vol. 68, pp. 153–67.

——, *The Emperor and the Roman Army*, Oxford, Clarendon, 1984.

Capart, J., 'Troisième rapport sommaire sur les fouilles de la fondation Egyptologique Reine Elisabeth à El Kab: Novembre 1945 à Fevrier 1946', *ASAE*, 1947, vol. 46, pp. 337–55.

Carrié, J.M., 'Les *Castra Dionysiados* et l'évolution de l'architecture militaire romaine tardive', *MEFRA*, 1974, vol. 86, pp. 819–50.

——, 'Patronage et propriété militaires au IVe s. Objet rhétorique et objet réel du discours sur les patronages de Libanius', *BCH*, 1976, vol. 100, pp. 159–76.

——, 'Le rôle économique de l'armée dans l'Egypte romaine', in A. Chastagnol, C. Nicolet and H. van Effenterre (eds), *Armées et fiscalité dans le monde antique* (*Colloques nationaux du CNRS 963*), Paris, CNRS, 1977, pp. 373–93.

——, 'L'esercito: transformazioni funzionali ed economie locale', in A Giardina (ed.), *Società romana e impero tardoantico. Instituzioni, ceti, economie*, Bari, Laterza, 1986, pp. 449–88.

——, 'Le soldat', in A. Giardina (ed.), *L'homme romain*, Rome and Bari, Laterza, 1992, pp. 127–72.

Casson, L., *The Periplus Maris Erythraei*, Princeton, Princeton University Press, 1989.

Cavenaile, R., 'Le P. Mich. VII 432 et *l'honesta missio* des légionnaires', *Studi in Onore di Aristide Calderini e Roberto Paribeni*, Milan, Editrice Ceschina, 1953, vol. 2, pp. 243–51.

——, 'Prosopographie de l'armée romaine d'Egypte d'Auguste à Dioclétien', *Aeg.*, 1970, vol. 50, pp. 213–320.

Cerati, A., *Caractère annonaire et assiette de l'impot foncier au Bas-Empire*, Paris, Bibliotheque d'histoire du droit et droit romaine 20, 1975.

Chalon, G., *L'édit de Tiberius Iulius Alexander*, Olten, Bibliotheca Helvetica Romana 5, 1964.

Cheesman, G.L., *The Auxilia of the Roman Imperial Army*, Oxford, Clarendon,1914.

Clarysse, W. and Sijpesteijn, P.J., 'A military roster on a vase in Amsterdam', *Ancient Society*, 1988, vol. 19, pp. 71–96.

Clédat, M., 'Fouilles à Qasr Gheit', *ASAE*, 1912, vol. 12, pp. 145–68.

——, 'Le temple de Zeus Cassius à Peluse', *ASAE*, 1913, vol. 13, pp. 79–85.

Coale, A.J., Demeny, P. and Vaughan, B., *Regional Model Life Tables and stable populations*, New York, Academic Press, 1983.

Coles, R., 'The Barns Ostraka', *ZPE*, 1980, vol. 39, pp. 126–31.

Corbier, M., 'L'aerarium militare', in A. Chastagnol, C. Nicolet and H. van Effenterre (eds), *Armées et fiscalité dans le monde antique (Colloques nationaux du CNRS 963)*, Paris, CNRS, 1977, pp. 197–234.

Cotton, H.M. and Geiger, J., *Masada II. The Yigael Yadin Excavations 1963–65: Final Reports*, Jerusalem, Israel Exploration Society, 1989.

Couyat, J., 'Ports gréco-romains de la Mer Rouge et grandes routes du désert arabique', *CRAI*, 1910, pp. 525–42.

Crawford, M.H., 'Money and exchange in the Roman world', *JRS*, 1970, vol. 60, pp. 40–8.

Critini, N., 'Supplemento alla prosopografia dell'esercito romano d'Egitto da Augusto a Diocleziano', *Aeg.*, 1973, vol. 53, pp. 93–158.

Cuvigny, H., 'Nouveaux ostraca grecs du Mons Claudianus', *CE*, 1986, vol. 61, pp. 271–86.

——, 'Un ostracon inédit du désert orientale et la provenance de O.Amst.9', *Proceedings of the XXth International Congress of papyrologists, Copenhagen, 23–29 August 1992*, Copenhagen, Museum Tusculanum Press, 1994, pp. 229–30.

Daoud, A. and Wagner, G., 'Inscriptions latines et grecques de la Société Archéologique de Alexandrie', *ZPE*, 1985, vol. 61, pp. 209–14.

Daris, S., 'Sul papiro Osloense inv.1451', *Aeg.*, 1962, vol. 42, pp. 123–7.

——, 'Documenti minori dell'esercito romano in Egitto', *ANRW*, 1988, vol. 2 10.1, pp. 724–42.

——, 'Le truppe ausiliarie romane in Egitto', *ANRW*, 1988, vol. 2 10.1, pp. 743–66.

Davies, R.W., 'Joining the Roman army', *BJ*, 1969, vol. 169, pp. 208–32, reprinted in R.W. Davies, *Service in the Roman Army*, Edinburgh, University Press, 1989, pp. 3–30.

——, 'The enlistment of Claudius Terentianus', *BASP*, 1973, vol. 10, pp. 21–5.

——, 'The investigation of some crimes in Roman Egypt', *Ancient Society*, 1973, vol. 4, pp. 199–212, reprinted in R.W. Davies, *Service in the Roman Army*,

Edinburgh, University Press, 1989, pp. 175–86.

——, 'The daily life of the Roman soldier under the Principate', *ANRW*, 1974, vol. 2.1, pp. 229–338, reprinted in R.W. Davies, *Service in the Roman Army*, Edinburgh, University Press, 1989, pp. 33–70.

——, *Service in the Roman Army*, Edinburgh, University Press, 1989.

Degrassi, A., 'ΟΥΕΤΡΑΝΟΙ ΟΙ ΧΩΡΙΣ ΧΑΛΚΩΝ', *RFIC*, 1934, vol. 12, pp. 194–200.

Déléage, A., *La capitation du Bas-Empire*, Macon, Protat Frères, 1945.

Delia, D., *Alexandrian Citizenship during the Roman Period*, Atlanta, Scholars Press, 1991.

Demicheli, A.M., *Rapporti di pace e di guerra dell' Egitto romano con le populazioni dei deserti africani*, Milan, Università di Genoa, 1976.

Desanges, J., 'Arabes et Arabie en terre d'Afrique dans la géographie antique', in T. Fahd (ed.), *Arabie préislamique et son environnement historique et culturel*, Leiden, Brill, 1989, pp. 416–20.

Develin, R., 'The army pay rises under Severus and Caracalla and the question of the *annona militaris*', *Latomus*, 1971, vol. 30, pp. 687–95.

Devijver, H., 'The Roman army in Egypt with special reference to the *Militiae Equestres*', *ANRW*, 1974, vol. 2.1, pp. 452–92.

Dobson, B., '*Praefectus Castrorum Aegypti* – a reconsideration', *CE*, 1982, vol. 57, pp. 332–7.

Domaszewski, A. von, 'Der Truppensold der Kaiserzeit', *Neue Heidelberger Jahrbücher*, 1900, vol. 10, pp. 218–41.

Donadoni, S., *Antinoe (1965–1968). Missione archeologica in Egitto dell' Universiti di Roma*, Rome, Instituto di studi del vicino Oriente, 1974.

Drexhage, H.-J., *Preise, Mieten/Pachten, Kosten und Löhne im römischen Ägypten bis zum Regierungsantritt Diokletians* (*Vorarbeiten zu einer Wirtschaftsgeschichte des römischen Ägypten* I), St Katherinen, Scripta Mercaturae, 1991.

Duncan-Jones, R.P., *The Economy of the Roman Empire: Quantitative Studies*, Cambridge, Cambridge University Press, 1974.

——, 'Pay and numbers in Diocletian's army', *Chiron*, 1978, vol. 8, pp. 541–60, reprinted in R.P. Duncan-Jones, *Structure and Scale in the Roman Economy*, Cambridge, Cambridge University Press, 1990, pp. 105–17.

——, 'Variations in Egyptian grain measures', *Chiron*, 1979, vol. 9, pp. 347–75.

——, *Structure and Scale in the Roman Economy*, Cambridge, Cambridge University Press, 1990.

Durliat, J., *Les finances publiques de Dioclétien aux Carolingiens (284–889)*, Sigmaringen, Thorbecke, 1990.

Eck, W. and Wolff, H., *Heer und Integrationspolitik: Die römischen Militärdiplome als historische Quelle*, Vienna, Passauer historische Forschungen 2, 1986.

[El Kab], 'Exposition des fouilles d'El Kab', *CE*, 1952, vol. 27, pp. 332–6.

Fakhry, A., 'Bahia and Farafra Oases', *ASAE*, 1939, vol. 39, pp. 627–42.

Fentress, E., *Numidia and the Roman Army* (*BAR* 53), Oxford, 1979.

Ferrill, A., *The Fall of the Roman Empire: The Military Explanation*, London, Thames and Hudson, 1986.

Fikhman, I.F., 'Quelques données sur la genèse de la grande propriété foncière à Oxyrhynchus', in *Le monde grec. Hommages à Claire Préaux*, Brussels, Université de Bruxelles, 1975, pp. 784–90.

Finley, M.I., *The Ancient Economy*, London, Penguin, 1973.

Firth, C.M., *The Archaeological Survey of Nubia: Bulletin 4*, Cairo, National Printing Department, 1909.

——, *The Archaeological Survey of Nubia: Bulletin 5*, Cairo, National Printing Department, 1909.

BIBLIOGRAPHY

Forni, G., *Il recluctamento delle legioni da Augusto a Diocleziano*, Rome, Facultà di lettere e filosofia, Università di Pavia, 1953.

Frank, T., *Roman Imperialism*, New York, Macmillan, 1929.

Fraser, P.M., *Ptolemaic Alexandria*, Oxford, Clarendon, 1972.

Frend, W.H.C., 'Augustus' Egyptian frontier Qasr Ibrim?', *Roman Frontier Studies 1979 (BAR* 71) Oxford, 1980, pp. 927–30.

Frere, S., *Britannia*, London, Routledge & Kegan Paul, 1978.

Frier, B.W., 'Roman life expectancy: Ulpian's evidence', *HSCP*, 1982, vol. 86, pp. 213–51.

——, 'Roman life expectancy: the Pannonian evidence', *Phoenix*, 1983, vol. 37, pp. 328–44.

Fuks, A., 'Notes on the archive of Nicanor', *JJP*, 1951, vol. 5, pp. 207–16, reprinted in A. Fuks, *Social Conflicts in Ancient Greece*, Jerusalem and Leiden, Brill, 1984, pp. 312–21.

——, 'The Jewish revolt in Egypt (AD 115–117) in the light of the papyri', *Aeg.*, 1953, vol. 33, pp. 131–58, reprinted in A. Fuks, *Social Conflicts in Ancient Greece*, Jerusalem and Leiden, Brill, 1984, pp. 322–49.

——, 'Aspects of the Jewish revolt in AD 115–117', *JRS*, vol. 51, pp. 98–104, reprinted in A. Fuks, *Social Conflicts in Ancient Greece*, Jerusalem and Leiden, Brill, 1984, pp. 350–56.

——, *Social Conflicts in Ancient Greece*, Jerusalem and Leiden, Brill, 1984.

Gallant, T.W., 'Greek bandits: lone wolves or a family affair', *Journal of Modern Greek Studies*, 1989, vol. 6, pp. 269–90.

Garnsey, P., *Social Status and Legal Privilege in the Roman Empire*, Cambridge, Cambridge University Press, 1970.

——, 'Septimius Severus and the marriage of Roman soldiers', *CSCA*, 1970, vol. 3, pp. 45–73.

Garstang, J., 'Excavations at Hierakonpolis, at Esna, and in Nubia', *ASAE*, 1907, vol. 8, pp. 132–48.

Gascou, J., 'Douch: rapport préliminaire des campagnes de fouilles de l'hiver 1978/1979 et de l'automne 1979', *BIFAO*, 1980, vol. 80, pp. 287–345.

Gautier, C., 'Monnaies trouvées à Douch', *BIFAO*, 1981, vol. 81, pp. 111–14.

Gazda, E.K., *Karanis: An Egyptian Town in Roman Times*, Ann Arbor, University of Michigan, 1983.

Geissen, A., 'Numismatische Bemerkung zu dem Aufstand des L. Domitius Domitianus', *ZPE*, 1976, vol. 22, pp. 280–6.

Geraci, G., *Genesi della provincia romana d'Egitto*, Bologna, CLUEB, 1983.

Geremek, H., *Karanis: Communauté rurale de l'Egypte romaine au IIe–IIIe siècles de notre ère*, Warsaw, Archiwum filologiczne 17, 1969.

Gilliam, J.F., 'The Roman military *feriale*', *HThR*, 1954, vol. 47, pp. 183–96.

——, 'The veterans and the *Praefectus Castrorum* of the II *Traiana*, AD 157', *AJPh*, 1956, vol. 77, pp. 359–75, reprinted in J.F. Gilliam, *Roman Army Papers*, Amsterdam, Gieben, 1986, pp. 145–61.

——, 'The plague under Marcus Aurelius', *AJPh*, 1961, vol. 73, pp. 225–51, reprinted in J.F. Gilliam, *Roman Army Papers*, Amsterdam, Gieben, 1986, pp. 227–53.

——, 'Romanization of the Greek East: the role of the army', *BASP*, 1965, vol. 2, pp. 65–73, reprinted in J.F. Gilliam, *Roman Army Papers*, Amsterdam, Gieben, 1986, pp. 281–7.

——, 'A legionary veteran and his family', *BASP*, 1971, vol. 8, pp. 39–44.

——, 'Notes on Latin texts from Egypt', in *Le monde grec. Hommages à Claire Préaux*, Brussels, Université de Bruxelles, 1975, pp. 766–74, reprinted in J.F. Gilliam, *Roman Army Papers*, Amsterdam, Gieben, 1986, pp. 363–72.

——, 'Three ostraka from Latopolis', *BASP*, 1976, vol. 13, pp. 55–61, reprinted in J.F. Gilliam, *Roman Army Papers*, Amsterdam, Gieben, 1986, pp. 379–86.

——, 'Some Roman elements in Roman Egypt', *ICS*, 1978, vol. 3, pp. 115–31.

——, *Roman Army Papers*, Amsterdam, Gieben, 1986.

Gilliver, C.M., *The Roman Art of War: Military Theory and Practice. A study of the Roman military writers*, unpublished Ph.D. thesis, University of London, 1993.

Golvin, J.-C. and Reddé, M., 'L'enceinte du camp militaire romain de Louqsor', *Studien zu den Militärgrenzen Roms III. 13 Int. Limeskongress. Aalen 1983*, (*Forschungen und Berichte zur verund Frühgeschichte in Baden–Würtemburg* 20), Stuttgart, 1986, pp. 594–9.

Goodman, M., *The Ruling Class of Judaea: The Origins of the Jewish Revolt against Rome*, Cambridge, Cambridge University Press, 1987.

Graf, D.F., 'Rome and the Saracens', in T. Fahd (ed.), *Arabie préislamique et son environnement historique et culturel*, Leiden, Brill, 1989, pp. 341–400.

Grande, C., review of Shier, *Karanis: Terracotta Lamps from Karanis, Egypt, JRS*, 1985, vol. 75, p. 284.

Grenfell, B.P. and Hunt, A.S., *Fayum Towns and their Papyri*, London, Egypt Exploration Society, 1900.

Griffin, M.T., *Nero: The End of a Dynasty*, London, Batsford, 1984.

Griffiths, J.G., 'Human sacrifice in Egypt: the Classical evidence', *ASAE*, 1948, vol. 48, pp. 409–23.

Guéraud, O., 'Ostraka grecs et latins de l'Wâdi Fawâkhir', *BIFAO*, 1942, vol. 41, pp. 141–96.

Haatvedt, R.E. and Peterson, E.E., *Coins from Karanis*, Ann Arbor, University of Michigan, 1964.

Hanson, A.E., 'Juliopolis, Nicopolis, and the Roman camp', *ZPE*, 1980, vol. 37, pp. 249–54.

——, 'Private letter', *BASP*, 1985, vol. 22, pp. 87–96.

——, 'The keeping of records at Philadelphia', *Proceedings of the XVIIIth International Congress of Papyrology*, Athens, Greek Papyrological Society, 1988, pp. 261–77.

——, 'Village officials at Philadelphia: a model of Romanization in the Julio–Claudian period', in L. Criscuolo and G. Geraci (eds), *Egitto e storia antica dall'ellenismo all'età araba*, Bologna, CLUEB, 1989, pp. 429–40.

Harden, D.B., *Roman Glass from Karanis found by the University of Michigan Expedition to Egypt 1924–1929*, Ann Arbor, University of Michigan, 1936.

Harrauer, H. and Sijpesteijn, P.J., 'Ein neues Dokument zu Roms Indienhandel. P. Vindob.G.40822', *Anz. der Phil.-hist. Klasse der Osterr. Akad. der Wissenschaft.* 1985, vol. 122, pp. 124–55.

Harris, W.V., *War and Imperialism in Republican Rome 327–70 BC*, Oxford, Clarendon, 1979.

Heinen, H., 'Zwei neue römische Soldatengrabsteine aus Ägypten', *ZPE*, 1980, vol. 38, pp. 115–24.

Helgeland, J. 'Roman army religion', *ANRW*, 1978, vol. 2 16.2, pp. 1470–505.

Hobsbawm, E.J., *Bandits*, London, Weidenfeld and Nicolson, 1969.

Hobson, D.W., 'House and household in Roman Egypt', *YCS*, 1985, vol. 28, pp. 211–19.

——, 'Naming practices in Roman Egypt', *BASP*, 1990, vol. 26, pp. 157–74.

Hohlwein, N., 'Le vétéran Lucius Bellienus Gemellus', *Etudes de Papyrologie*, 1957, vol. 8, pp. 69–86.

Holder, P.A., *Studies in the Auxilia of the Roman Army from Augustus to Trajan* (*BAR* 70), Oxford, 1980.

Hombert, M. and Préaux, C., *Recherches sur le recensement dans l'Egypte romaine* (*Pap.Lugd.Bat.* V), Leiden, Brill, 1952.

Hopkins, K., 'On the probable age structure of the Roman population', *Population Studies*, 1966, vol. 20, pp. 245–64.

——, *Conquerors and Slaves*, Cambridge, Cambridge University Press, 1978.

——, 'Taxes and trade in the Roman Empire, 200 BC – AD 400', *JRS*, 1980, vol. 70, pp. 101–25.

——, *Death and Renewal*, Cambridge, Cambridge University Press, 1983.

Hurst, H.E., *The Nile*, London, Constable, 1969.

Husselman, E.M., 'The granaries of Karanis', *TAPA*, 1952, vol. 83, pp. 56–73.

——, *Karanis. Excavations of the University of Michigan in Egypt 1928–1935: Topography and Architecture*, Ann Arbor, University of Michigan, 1979.

Huzar, E.G., 'Augustus, heir of the Ptolemies', *ANRW*, 1988, vol. 2 10.2, pp. 343–82.

Isaac, B., 'The meaning of *limes* and *limitanei* in ancient sources', *JRS*, 1988, vol. 78, pp. 123–47.

——, *The Limits of Empire: The Roman Army in the East*, Oxford, Clarendon, 1993.

Isaac, B. and Roll, I., 'Legio II Traiana in Judaea', *ZPE*, 1979, vol. 33, pp. 149–55.

——, 'Judaea in the early years of Hadrian's reign', *Latomus*, 1979, vol. 38, pp. 54–66.

——, 'Legio II Traiana in Judaea – A reply', *ZPE*, 1982, vol. 47, pp. 131–2.

Jahn, J., 'Zur Entwicklung römischer Soldzahlungen von Augustus bis auf Diocletian', *Studien zu Fundmünzen der Antike*, 1984, vol. 2, pp. 53–74.

——, 'Der Sold römischer Soldaten im 3 Jh.n.Chr.: Bemerkungen zu *ChLA* 446, 473 und 495', *ZPE*, 1985, vol. 53, p. 217–27.

Jameson, S., 'Chronology of the campaigns of Aelius Gallus and C.Petronius', *JRS*, 1968, vol. 58, pp. 71–84.

Jaritz, H., 'The investigation of the ancient wall extending from Aswan to Philae', *MDAIK* 1987, vol. 43, pp. 67–74.

Johnson, A.C., *Roman Egypt to the Reign of Diocletian* = T. Frank (ed.), *An Economic Survey of the Roman World*, vol. II, Baltimore, Johns Hopkins Press, 1936.

Johnson, B., *Pottery from Karanis: Excavations of the University of Michigan*, Ann Arbor, University of Michigan, 1981.

Johnson, J. de M., 'Antinoe and its papyri', *JEA*, 1914, vol. 1, pp. 168–81.

Johnson, S., *Late Roman Fortifications*, London, Batsford, 1983.

Jones, A.H.M., *The Later Roman Empire*, Oxford, Blackwell, 1964.

——, 'The cloth industry under the Roman empire', *Economic History Review*, 1966, vol. 12, pp. 183–92, reprinted in A.H.M. Jones, *The Roman Economy*, Oxford, Blackwell, 1974, pp. 350–64.

——, *The Roman Economy*, Oxford, Blackwell, 1974.

Jones, C.P., 'The date of Dio of Prusa's Alexandrian oration', *Historia*, 1973, vol. 22, pp. 302–39.

——, '*Stigma*: tattooing and branding in antiquity', *JRS*, 1987, vol. 77, pp. 139–55.

Kaimio, J., 'Notes on the pay of Roman soldiers', *Arctos*, 1975, vol. 9, pp. 39–46.

Keenan, J.G., 'Evidence for the Byzantine army in the Syene papyri', *BASP*, 1990, vol. 27, pp. 139–50.

Kees, H., *Ancient Egypt: A Cultural Topography*, trans. I.F.D. Morrow, Chicago and London, Chicago University Press, 1961.

Kennedy, D.L., 'Legio VI Ferrata: the annexation and early garrison of Arabia', *HSCP*, 1980, vol. 84, pp. 283–309.

——, 'The composition of a military work party in Roman Egypt (*ILS* 2483: Coptos)', *JEA*, 1985, vol. 71, pp. 156–60.

Keppie, L.J.F., 'The legionary garrison of Judaea under Hadrian', *Latomus*, 1973, vol. 32, pp. 859–64.

——, *Colonisation and Veteran Settlement in Italy 47–14 B.C.*, London, British School in Rome, 1983.

——, *The Making of the Roman Army*, London, Batsford, 1984.

——, 'Legions in the East from Augustus to Trajan', in P. Freedman and D. Kennedy (eds), *The Defence of the Roman and Byzantine East* (BAR 297), Oxford, 1986, pp. 411–29.

Kirwan, L.P., 'Rome beyond the Southern Egyptian frontier', *PBA*, 1977, vol. 63, pp. 13–31.

Klein, M.J., *Untersuchungen zu den kaiserlichen Steinbrüchen an Mons Porphyrites und Mons Claudianus in der östlichen Wüste Ägyptens*, Bonn, Habelt, 1988.

Kolendo, J., 'Le projet et l'expédition de Néron dans le Caucase', *Neronia*, 1977, pp. 23–7.

Koliopoulos, J.S., *Brigands with a Cause: Brigandage and Irredentism in Modern Greece 1821–1912*, Oxford, Clarendon, 1987.

——, 'Brigandage and irredentism in nineteenth-century Greece', *European History Quarterly*, 1989, vol. 19.2, pp. 193–228.

Kraus, T. and Röder, J., 'Mons Claudianus: Bericht über eine erste Erkundungsfahrt im März 1961', *MDAIK*, 1962, vol. 18, pp. 80–120.

Kraus, T., Röder, J. and Müller–Wiener, W., 'Mons Claudianus – Mons Porphyrites: Bericht über die zweite Forschungsreise 1964', *MDAIK*, 1967, vol. 22, pp. 108–205.

Kühn, E., *Antinoopolis: ein Beitrag zur Geschichte des Hellenismus im römischen Ägypten. Gründung und Verfassung*, Göttingen, Kaestiner, 1913.

Lacau, P., 'Inscriptions latines du temple de Louxor', *ASAE*, 1934, vol. 34, pp. 17–46.

Lander, J., *Roman Stone Fortifications: Variation and Change from the First Century AD to the Fourth* (BAR 206), Oxford, 1984.

——, 'Did Hadrian abandon Arabia?' in P. Freedman and D. Kennedy (eds), *The Defence of the Roman and Byzantine East* (BAR 297), Oxford, 1986, pp. 447–61.

Leclant, J. and Clerc, G., 'Fouilles et travaux en Egypte et au Soudan, 1986–1987', *Orientalia*, 1988, vol. 57, pp. 307–404.

Lepsius, R., *Discoveries in Egypt, Ethiopia and the Peninsula of Sinai*, London, Bohn, 1853.

Lesquier, J., *L'armée romaine de l'Egypte d'Auguste à Dioclétien*, Cairo, IFAO, 1918.

Lewin, L., 'The oligarchical limitations of social banditry in Brazil: the case of the good thief Antonio Silvano', *Past & Present*, 1979, vol. 82, pp. 116–41.

Lewis, N., 'A veteran in quest of a home', *TAPA*, 1959, vol. 90, pp. 139–46.

——, *The Compulsory Public Services of Roman Egypt*, Florence, Papyrologica Florentina, 1982.

——, 'Soldiers permitted to own provincial land', *BASP*, 1982, vol. 19, pp. 143–8.

——, *Life in Egypt under Roman Rule*, Oxford, Clarendon, 1983.

——, 'The Romanity of Roman Egypt: a growing consensus', *Atti del XVII Congresso Internazionale di Papirologia*, Naples, Centro internazionale per lo studio dei papiri Ercolanesi, 1984, pp. 1077–84.

Liebeschuetz, J.H.G.W., *Barbarians and Bishops: Army, Church and State in the Age of Arcadius and Constantine*, Oxford, Clarendon, 1990.

Lloyd, J.A., Reece, R., Reynolds, J.M. and Sear, F.B., *Excavations at Sidi Khrebish, Benghazi (Berenice) I: Buildings, Coins, Inscriptions, Architectural Decoration, Tripoli, Libya Antiqua* Suppl. 5, 1982.

Louis, E. and Valbelle, D., 'Les trois dernières forteresses de Tell el-Herr', in *Sociétés urbaines en Egypte et au Soudan (Cahiers de Recherches de l'Institut de Papyrologie en Lille 10)* Lille, 1991, pp. 61–71.

Lukaszewicz, A., 'Alexandria sous les Sévères et l'historiographie', in L. Criscuolo and G. Geraci (eds), *Egitto e storia antica dell'ellenismo all'età araba*, Bologna, CLUEB, 1989, pp. 491–6.

Luttwak, E.N., *The Grand Strategy of the Roman Empire from the First Century AD to the Third*, Baltimore, Johns Hopkins Press, 1976.

Macmullen, R., *Soldier and Civilian in the Later Roman Empire*, Cambridge, Mass., Harvard University Press, 1963.

——, 'Nationalism in Roman Egypt', *Aeg.*, 1964, vol. 44, pp. 179–99.

——, 'How big was the Roman imperial army?' *Klio*, 1980, vol. 62, pp. 451–60.

——, 'The legion as society', *Historia*, 1984, vol. 33, pp. 440–59.

——, 'The Roman emperor's army costs', *Latomus*, 1984, vol. 43, pp. 571–80.

Maehler, H., 'Häuser und ihre Bewöhner im Fayûm in der Kaiserzeit', in G. Grimm, H. Heinen and E. Winter (eds), *Das römisch-byzantinische Ägypten. Akten des internationalen Symposions 26–30 September 1978 in Trier*, Mainz, von Zabern, 1983, pp. 119–37.

Mann, J.C., 'The raising of new legions during the Principate', *Hermes*, 1963, vol. 91, pp. 483–9.

——, 'The frontiers of the Principate', *ANRW*, 1974, vol. 2.1, pp. 508–31.

——, 'Power, force and the frontiers of the empire', *JRS*, 1979, vol. 69, pp. 175–83.

——, *Legionary Recruitment and Veteran Settlement during the Principate*, London, Institute of Archaeology, 1983.

——, 'The organization of the *Frumentarii*', *ZPE*, 1988, vol. 74, pp. 149–50.

Mann, J.C. and Roxan, M.M., 'Discharge certificates of the Roman army', *Britannia*, 1988, vol. 19, pp. 341–9.

el-Maqsoud, M. Abd., 'Preliminary report on the excavations at Tell El-Farama (Pelusium): first two seasons (1983/4 and 1984/5)', *ASAE*, 1984/5, vol. 70, pp. 3–8.

el-Maqsoud, M. Abd. and Carriez-Maratray, J.Y., 'Une inscription grecque de la forteresse de Péluse', *in Sociétés urbaines en Egypte et au Soudan (Cahiers de Recherches de l'Institut de Papyrologie en Lille 10)*, Lille, 1991, pp. 97–103.

Marichal, R., *L'occupation romaine de la basse Egypte: le statut des Auxilia. P. Berlin 6,866 et P. Lond. 1196*, Paris, E. Droz, 1945.

——, 'Le solde des armées romaines d'Auguste à Septime-Sévère d'après les P. Gen. Lat. 1 et 4 et le P.Berlin 6.866', *Annuaire de l'Institut de Philologie et d'histoire Orientales et Slaves*, 1953, vol. 13 *(Mélanges Isidore Lévy)*, pp. 399–421.

Maspero, J., *Organisation militaire de l'Egypte byzantine*, Paris, Libraire ancienne Honoré Champion, 1912.

Meinardus, O.F.A., 'An examination of the traditions of the Theban legion', *Bull. de la Soc. d'arch. Copte*, 1976–8, vol. 23, pp. 5–32.

Meredith, D., 'The Roman remains in the Eastern Desert of Egypt', *JEA*, 1952, vol. 38, pp. 94–111.

——, 'The Roman remains in the Eastern Desert of Egypt', *JEA*, 1953, vol. 39, pp. 45–106.

——, 'Inscriptions from the Berenice Road', *CE*, 1954, vol. 29, p. 282.

——, 'The Myos Hormos Road', *CE*, 1956, vol. 31, pp. 356–62.

——, 'Berenice Troglodytica', *JEA*, 1957, vol. 43, pp. 56–70.

Millar, F.G.B., *The Emperor in the Roman World*, London, Duckworth, 1977.

——, 'The world of the Golden Ass', *JRS*, 1981, vol. 71, pp. 63–75.

——, *The Roman Empire and its Neighbours*, London, Duckworth, 1981.

——, 'Emperors, frontiers and foreign relations', *Britannia*, 1982, vol. 13, pp. 1–24.

Milne, J.G., *A History of Egypt under Roman Rule*, London, Methuen, 1924.

Minnen, P. van, 'House to house enquiries: an interdisciplinary approach to Roman Karanis', *ZPE*, 1994, vol. 100, pp. 227–51.

Mitchell, S., 'A new inscription from Pisidia: requisitioned transport in the Roman empire', *JRS*, 1976, vol. 66, pp. 106–32.

Balthasar de Monconys, *Voyage en Egypte*, Cairo, IFAO, 1973 [1st ed. 1695].

Mor, M., 'The Roman legions and the Bar-Kochba revolt (132–135 AD)', *Der römischen Limes in Österreich. Akten des 14 int. Limeskongresses 1986 in Carnuntum, Vienna, Österreiches Akadamie des Wissenschaften*, 1990, pp. 163–77.

Murray, G.W., 'The Roman roads and stations in the Eastern Desert of Egypt', *JEA*, 1925, vol. 11, pp. 138–50.

Murray, J., *A Handbook for Travellers in Lower and Upper Egypt*, London, Murray, 1880.

Musirillo, H., *The Acts of the Early Christian Martyrs*, Oxford, Clarendon, 1972.

Mustafa, M. el Din and Jaritz, H., 'A Roman fortress at Nag' el-Hagar: first preliminary report', *ASAE*, 1984/5, vol. 70, pp. 21–31.

el-Nassery, S.A.A., Wagner, G. and Castel, G., 'Un grand bain gréco-romain à Karanis', *BIFAO*, 1976, vol. 76, pp. 231–75.

Naumann, R., 'Bauwerke der Oase Khargeh', *MDAIK*, 1939, vol. 8, pp. 1–16.

Nelson, C.A., *Status Declarations in Roman Egypt (ASP 19)*, Amsterdam, Hakkert, 1979.

Nibbi, A., 'The two stelae from the Wadi Gasus', *JEA*, 1976, vol. 62, pp. 45–56.

Nicole, J. and Morel, Ch., *Archives militaires du Ier siècle. Texte inédit du papyrus de Genève*, Geneva, 1900.

Nock, A.D., 'The Roman army and the Roman religious year', *HThR*, 1952, vol. 45, pp. 187–252, reprinted in A.D. Nock, *Essays on Religion in the Ancient World*, Oxford, Clarendon, 1972, pp. 736–90.

Oates, J.F., 'Philadelphia in the Fayum during the Roman empire', *Atti XI Congresso internazionale di papirologia, Milano, 1965*, Milan, Instituto Lombardo di scienze e lettere, 1966, pp. 454–7.

——, 'Fugitives from Philadelphia', *Essays in Honor of C. Bradford Welles (ASP 1)*, New Haven, American Society of Papyrologists, 1966, pp. 87–95.

——, 'Landholding in Philadelphia in the Fayum (A.D. 216)', *Proceedings of the XIIth International Congress of Papyrology (ASP 7)*, Toronto, Hakkert, 1970, pp. 385–7.

——, *Checklist of Editions of Greek Papyri and Ostraca (BASP Suppl. 4)*, Atlanta, 1985.

Oertel, F., *Die Liturgie*, Leipzig, Teubner, 1917.

Oliver, J.H., 'Teamed together in Death', *Hesperia*, 1965, vol. 34, pp. 252–3.

O'Malley, P., 'Social bandits, modern capitalism and the traditional peasantry: a critique of Hobsbawm', *Journal of Peasant Studies*, 1979, vol. 6.4, pp. 489–501.

O'Reilly, D.F., 'The Theban legion of St Maurice', *Vigiliae Christianae*, 1978, vol. 32, pp. 195–207.

Parassoglou, G.M., 'Property records of L. Pompeius Niger, legionary veteran', *BASP*, 1970, vol. 7, pp. 87–98.

Parker, H.M.D., *The Roman Legions*, Cambridge, Heffer, 1958.

Parker, S.T., *Romans and Saracens: A History of the Arabian Frontier*, Philadelphia, American Schools of Oriental Research, 1986.

——, 'The nature of Rome's Arabian frontier', *Roman Frontier Studies 1989: Proceedings of the XVth International Congress of Roman Frontier Studies*, Exeter, Exeter University Press, 1991, pp. 498–504.

Parkin, T.G., *Demography and Roman Society*, Baltimore, Johns Hopkins Press, 1992.

Passerini, A., 'Gli aumenti del soldo militare da Commodo a Maximino', *Athenaeum*, 1946, vol. 24, pp. 145–59.

Peacock, D.P.S., *Rome in the Desert: A symbol of power*, Southampton, University of Southampton, 1992.

Pearl, O.M., 'The 94 klerouchies at Karanis', *Akten des XIII int. Papyrologenkongresses: 1971*, Munich, Beck, 1974, pp. 325–30.

Pendlebury, J.S., *Tell el-Amarna*, London, Louvat Dickson and Thompson, 1935.

Flinders Petrie, W.M. Murray, A.S. and Griffiths, F.LL., *Tanis II: Nebesheh (Am) and Defenneh (Tahpanhes)*, London, Egypt Exploration Fund, 1888.

Pflaum, H.-G., 'Un nouveau diplome militaire d'un soldat de l'armée d'Egypte', *Syria*, 1967, vol. 44, pp. 339–62.

Pighi, G.B., *Lettere Latine d'un soldato di Traiano, P. Mich. 467–472*, Bologna, Facultà di lettere e filosofia degli studi di Bologna, 1964.

Poesner-Krieger, A., 'Les travaux de l'Institut Français d'Archéologie Orientale en 1982–1983', *BIFAO*, 1983, vol. 83, pp. 343–63.

——, 'Les travaux de l'Institut Français d'Archéologie Orientale en 1986–1987', *BIFAO*, 1987, vol. 87, pp. 299–336.

——, 'Les travaux de l'Institut Français d'Archéologie Orientale en 1987–1988', *BIFAO*, 1988, vol. 88, pp. 181–237.

Préaux, C., 'Ostraca de Pselkis de la bibliothèque Bodléenne', *CE*, 1951, vol. 26, pp. 121–55.

Price, R.M., 'The *limes* of Lower Egypt', in R. Goodburn and P. Bartholomew (eds), *Aspects of the Notitia Dignitatum: Papers presented to a conference in Oxford, December 13 to 15, 1974 (BAR 15)*, Oxford, 1976, pp. 143–54.

Priest, N., 'A loan of money with some notes on the *ala Mauretana*', *ZPE*, 1983, vol. 51, pp. 65–70.

Rankov, N.B., '*Singulares Legati Legionis*: a problem in the interpretation of the Ti.Claudius Maximus inscription from Philippi', *ZPE*, 1990, vol. 80, pp. 165–75.

——, '*Frumentarii*, the *Castra Peregrina* and the provincial *Officia*', *ZPE*, 1990, vol. 80, pp. 176–82.

Raschke, M.G., 'New studies in Roman commerce with the East', *ANRW*, 1978, vol. 2.9.2, pp. 605–1363.

Rathbone, D.W., 'The weight and measurement of Egyptian grain', *ZPE*, 1983, vol. 53, pp. 265–75.

——, 'Villages, land and population in Graeco-Roman Egypt', *PCPhS*, 1990, vol. 36, pp. 103–42.

Rea, J., 'The Legio II Traiana in Judaea', *ZPE*, 1980, vol. 38, pp. 220–1.

Reddé, M., 'Les oasis d'Egypte', *JRA*, 1989, vol. 2, pp. 281–90.

——, 'A l'ouest du Nil: une frontière sans soldats, des soldats sans frontière', *Roman Frontier Studies 1989: Proceedings of the XVth International Congress of Roman Frontier Studies*, Exeter, Exeter University Press, 1991, pp. 485–93.

——, *Le Tresor de Douch*, Cairo, IFAO, 1992.

Reddé, M. and Golvin, J.-C., 'Quelques recherches récentes sur l'archéologie militaire romaine en Egypte', *CRAI*, 1986, vol. 29, pp. 172–96.

——, 'Du Nil à la Mer Rouge: documents anciens et nouveaux sur les routes du désert orientale d'Egypte', *Karthago*, 1987, vol. 21, pp. 5–64.

Reisner, G.A., *The Archaeological Survey of Nubia: Bulletin* 1, Cairo, National Printing Department, 1908.

Remondon, R., 'Soldats de Byzance d'après un papyrus trouvé à Edfou', *Recherches de Papyrologie*, 1961, vol. 1, pp. 41–93.

Rich, J. and Shipley, G. (eds.), *War and Society in the Roman World*, London and New York, Routledge, 1993.

Römer, C., 'Diplom für einen Fusssoldaten aus Koptos vom 23. März 179', *ZPE*, 1990, vol. 82, pp. 137–53.

Rostovtzeff, M.I., Bellinger, A.R., Hopkins, C. and Welles, C.B., *The Excavations at Dura-Europos. Preliminary Report of the Sixth Season of Work, October 1930 – March 1931*, New Haven and London, Yale Univeristy Press and Oxford University Press, 1936.

Rowe, A., 'The discovery of the famous temple and enclosure of Serapis at Alexandria', *ASAE*, 1946, suppl. II.

Rowlandson, J., 'Freedom and subordination in ancient agriculture: the case of the *Basilikoi Georgoi* of Ptolemaic Egypt', *Crux: Essays presented to G.E.M. de Ste Croix*, Exeter, Imprint Academic, 1985, pp. 327–47.

Roxan, M.M., *Roman Military Diplomas 1954–1977*, London, Institute of Archaeology, 1978.

——, 'The distribution of Roman military diplomas', *Epigraphische Studien*, 1984, vol. 12, pp. 265–87.

——, *Roman Military Diplomas 1978–1984*, London, Institute of Archaeology, 1985.

——, 'Findspots of Roman military diplomas of the Roman auxiliary army', *Institute of Archaeology Bulletin*, 1992, vol. 26, pp. 127–81.

Saddington, D.B., *The Development of the Roman Auxiliary Forces from Caesar to Vespasian (49 BC–AD 79)*, Harare, University of Zimbabwe, 1982.

el-Saghir, M., Golvin, J.-C., Reddé, M., Hagazy, El-S. and Wagner, G., *Le camp romain de Louqsor (IFAO 83)*, Cairo, IFAO, 1986.

Salmon, E.T., *Roman Colonization under the Republic*, London, Thames and Hudson, 1969.

Salway, P., *Roman Britain,* Oxford, Oxford University Press, 1981.

Samson, J., *Amarna*, London, University College London, 1972.

Samuel, A.E., Hastings, W.K., Bowman, A.K. and Bagnall, R.S., *Death and Taxes: Ostraka in the Royal Ontario Museum I (ASP 10)*, Toronto, Hakkert, 1971.

Samuel, D.H., 'Greeks and Romans at Socnopaiou Nesos', *Proceedings of the XVIth International Congress of Papyrologists*, Chico, Scholars Press, 1981, pp. 389–403.

Sander, E., 'Das Recht des römischen Soldaten', *Rh.M.,* 1958, vol. 101, pp. 152–91 and pp. 193–234.

Sanders, H.A., 'Two fragmentary birth certificates from the Michigan collection', *MAAR*, 1931, vol. 9, pp. 61–80.

Sasel Kos, M., 'A Latin epitaph of a Roman legionary from Corinth', *JRS*, 1978, vol. 68, pp. 22–6.

Sauneron, S., 'Les travaux de l'Institut Français d'Archéologie Orientale en 1974–1975', *BIFAO*, 1975, vol. 75, pp. 447–78.

Scaife, C.H.O., 'Two inscriptions at Mons Porphyrites (Gebel Dokhan). Also a description with plans of stations between Kainopolis and Myos Hormos together with some other ruins in the neighbourhood of Gebel Dokhan', *Bulletin of the Faculty of Arts. Fouad I University*, 1935, vol. 3, pp. 58–104.

Schubert, P., *Les archives de Marcus Lucretius Diogenes*, Bonn, Habelt, 1990.

Schuman, V.B., 'The income of the office of πράκτορες ἀργυρικῶν of Karanis', *BASP*, 1975, vol. 12, pp. 23–66.

Schwartz, J., *L.Domitius Domitianus (Papyrologica Bruxellensia 12)*, Brussels, Fondation Egyptologique Reine Elisabeth, 1975.

Schwart, J. and Wild, H., *Qasr Qârûn/Dionysias 1948. Fouilles Franco-Suisses. Rapports I*, Cairo, IFAO, 1950.

Schwartz, J., Badawy, A., Smith, R. and Wild, H., *Fouilles Franco-Suisses. Rapports II. Qasr Qârûn/Dionysias 1950*, Cairo, IFAO, 1969.

Segre, A., 'P. Yale 1528 and P. Fouad 21', *JRS*, 1940, vol. 30, pp. 153–4.

Seston, W., 'Les vétérans sans diplômes des légions romaines', *Revue de Philologie*, 1933, vol. 59, pp. 375–99.

Shaw, B.D., 'Soldiers and society: the army in Numidia', *Opus*, 1983, vol. 2, pp. 133–64.

——, 'Bandits in the Roman empire', *Past & Present*, 1984, vol. 105, pp. 3–52.

Shier, L.A., *Karanis: Terracotta Lamps from Karanis, Egypt: Excavations of the University of Michigan*, Ann Arbor, University of Michigan, 1978.

Sidebotham, S. E., *Roman Economic Policy in the Erythraea Thalassa 30 BC – AD 217 (Mnemosyne Suppl. 91)*, Leiden, Brill, 1986.

——, 'Aelius Gallus and Arabia', *Latomus*, 1986, vol. 45, pp. 590–602.

——, 'A limes in the Eastern Desert of Egypt: myth or reality', *Roman Frontier Studies 1989: Proceedings of the XVth International Congress of Roman Frontier Studies*, Exeter, Exeter University Press, 1991, pp. 494–7.

Sidebotham, S.E., Riley, J.A., Hamroush, H.A. and Barakat, H., 'Fieldwork on the Red Sea coast: the 1987 season', *JARCE*, 1989, vol. 26, pp. 127–66.

Sijpesteijn, P.J., 'Edict of Calvisius Statianus', *ZPE*, 1971, vol. 8, pp. 186–92.

——, 'Letters on ostraka', *TAΛANTA*, 1973, vol. 5, pp. 72–84.

——, 'A happy family?', *ZPE*, 1976, vol. 21, pp. 169–81.

——, 'Der Veteran Aelius Syrion', *BASP*, 1984, vol. 21, pp. 211–20.

——, 'P. Princeton II 50 and the number of soldiers in Roman Egypt', *ZPE*, 1986, vol. 65, p. 168.

Smallwood, E.M., *Documents Illustrating the Principates of Nerva, Trajan and Hadrian*, Cambridge, Cambridge University Press, 1966.

——, *The Jews under Roman Rule*, Leiden, Brill, 1976.

Smith, E.B., *Egyptian Architecture as Cultural Expression*, New York, Appleton-Century, 1938.

Smith, R.E., 'The army reforms of Septimius Severus', *Historia*, 1972, vol. 21, pp. 481–500.

Spawforth, A.J. and Walker, S., 'The World of the Panhellion. I. Athens and Eleusis', *JRS*, 1985, vol. 75, pp. 78–104.

——, 'The World of the Panhellion. II. Three Dorian cities', *JRS*, 1986, vol. 76, pp. 88–103.

Speidel, M.A., 'Roman army pay scales', *JRS*, 1992, vol. 82, pp. 87–106.

Speidel, M.P., 'The captor of Decebalus, a new inscription from Philippi', *JRS*, 1970, vol. 60, pp. 142–53, reprinted in M.P. Speidel, *Roman Army Studies* I, Amsterdam, Gieben, 1984, pp. 173–87.

——, 'The pay of the auxilia', *JRS*, 1973, vol. 63, pp. 141–7, reprinted in M.P. Speidel, *Roman Army Studies* I, Amsterdam, Gieben, 1984, pp. 83–9.

——, 'The Eastern Desert garrisons under Augustus and Tiberius', *Studien zu dem Militärgrenzen Roms II 1977. X Internationalen Limes Congress in Germania Inferior*, Bonn, Habelt, 1977, pp. 511–15, reprinted in M.P. Speidel, *Roman Army Studies* I, Amsterdam, Gieben, 1984, pp. 323–8.

——, 'The Roman army in Arabia', *ANRW*, 1977, vol. 28, pp. 687–730, reprinted in M.P. Speidel, *Roman Army Studies* I, Amsterdam, Gieben, 1984, pp. 229–72.

——, 'The prefect's horse-guards and the supply of weapons to the Roman army', *Proceedings of the XVI th International Congress of Papyrologists (ASP 23)*, Chico, Scholars Press, 1981, pp. 405–9, reprinted in M.P. Speidel, *Roman Army Studies* I, Amsterdam, Gieben, 1984, pp. 329–31.

———, 'Thracian horsemen in Egypt's *ala veterana Gallica* (*P.Lond.* 482)', *BASP*, 1982, vol. 19, pp. 167–70, reprinted in M.P. Speidel, *Roman Army Studies* I, Amsterdam, Gieben, 1984, pp. 333–6.

———, 'Augustus' deployment of the legions in Egypt', *CE*, 1982, vol. 47, pp. 120–4, reprinted in M.P. Speidel, *Roman Army Studies* I, Amsterdam, Gieben, 1984, pp. 317–21.

———, 'Auxiliary units named after their commanders: four new examples from Egypt', *Aeg.*, 1982, vol. 62, pp. 165–72, reprinted in M.P. Speidel, *Roman Army Studies* I, Amsterdam, Gieben, 1984, pp. 101–8.

———, *Roman Army Studies* I, Amsterdam, Gieben, 1984.

———, 'Palmyrenian irregulars at Koptos', *BASP*, 1984, vol. 21, pp. 221–4, reprinted in M.P. Speidel, *Roman Army Studies* II, Stuttgart, Steiner, 1992, pp. 82–5.

———, 'Centurions and horsemen of legio II Traiana', *Aeg.*, 1986, vol. 66, pp. 163–8, reprinted in M.P. Speidel, *Roman Army Studies* II, Stuttgart, Steiner, 1992, pp. 233–9.

———, 'Nubia's Roman garrison', *ANRW*, 1988, vol. 2 10.1, pp. 767–98, reprinted in M.P. Speidel, *Roman Army Studies* II, Stuttgart, Steiner, 1992, pp. 240–74.

———, 'The soldiers' servants', *Ancient Society*, 1988, vol. 20, pp. 239–47, reprinted in M.P. Speidel, *Roman Army Studies* II, Stuttgart, Steiner, 1992, pp. 342–52.

———, 'Work to be done on the organization of the Roman army', *Bulletin of the Institute of Archaeology*, 1989, vol. 26, pp. 99–106, reprinted in M.P. Speidel, *Roman Army Studies* II, Stuttgart, Steiner, 1992, pp. 13–20.

———, *Roman Army Studies* II, Stuttgart, Steiner, 1992.

Speidel, M.P. and Seider, R., 'A Latin papyrus with a recruit's request for service in the auxiliary cohorts', *JEA*, 1988, vol. 74, pp. 242–4, reprinted in M.P. Speidel, *Roman Army Studies* II, Stuttgart, Steiner, 1992, pp. 306–9.

Sperber, D., 'The centurion as tax collector', *Latomus*, 1969, vol. 28, pp. 186–9.

Strobel, K., 'Zu Fragen der frühen Geschichte der römischen Provinz Arabia und zu einigen Problemen der Legionsdislokation im Osten des Imperium romanum zu Beginn des 2 Jh.n.Chr.', *ZPE*, 1988, vol. 71, pp. 251–80.

Syme, R., 'The Lower Danube under Trajan', *JRS*, 1959, vol. 49, pp. 26–53.

Taubenschlag, R., *The Law of Greco–Roman Egypt in the Light of the Papyri*, Milan, Cisalpino Goliardico, 1972.

Terok, L., 'Geschichte Meroes. Ein Beitrag über die Quellenlage und den Forschungsstand', *ANRW*, 1988, vol. 2 10.1, pp. 107–341.

Thomas, J.D., 'A petition to the prefect of Egypt and related imperial edicts', *JEA*, 1975, vol. 61, pp. 201–21.

———, 'The date of the revolt of L. Domitius Domitianus', *ZPE*, 1976, vol. 22, pp. 253–79.

———, 'A family archive from Karanis and the revolt of L. Domitius Domitianus', *ZPE*, 1977, vol. 24, pp. 233–40.

Thompson, D.J., *Memphis under the Ptolemies*, Princeton, Princeton University Press, 1988.

———, 'The high priests of Memphis under Ptolemaic rule', in M. Beard and J. North (eds), *Pagan Priests: Religion and Power in the Ancient World*, London, Duckworth, 1989, pp. 95–116.

Trigger, B.G. Kemp, B.J., O'Connor, D. and Lloyd, A.B., *Ancient Egypt: A Social History*, Cambridge, Cambridge University Press, 1983.

Turner, E.G., 'Roman Oxyrhynchus', *JEA*, 1952, vol. 38, pp. 78–93.

———, 'Oxyrhynchus and Rome', *HSCP*, 1975, vol. 79, pp. 1–24.

Updegraff, R.T., 'The Blemmyes I: the rise of the Blemmyes and the Roman withdrawal from Nubia under Diocletian', *ANRW*, 1988, vol. 2 10.1, pp. 44–106.

Van Hooff, A.J.L., 'Ancient robbers: reflections behind the facts', *Ancient Society*, 1988, vol. 19, pp. 105–24.

Van 't Dack, E., 'L'Armée romaine d'Egypte de 55 à 30 av. J.C.', in G. Grimm, H. Herier and E. Winter (eds), *Das römische-byzantinische Ägypten. Akten des internationalen Symposions 26–30 September in Trier*, Mainz, von Zabern, 1983, pp. 19–29.

——, 'Notes de lecture', *Miscellània papirològica Ramon Roca-Puig*, Barcelona, Fundació Salvador Vires Casajuna, 1987, pp. 327–35.

Viereck, P., *Philadelphia (Morgenland 16)*, Leipzig, Heinrichs, 1928.

Wacher, J., *The Towns of Roman Britain*, Berkeley, University of California Press, 1975.

Wagner, G., 'Le camp romaine de Doush (Oasis de Khargeh – Egypte)', *Studien zu den Militärgrenzen Roms III. 13 int. Limeskongress. Aalen 1983*, Stuttgart, K. Theis, 1986, pp. 671–2.

——, *Les oasis d'Egypte à l'époque grecque, romaine et byzantine d'après les documents grecs*, Cairo, IFAO, 1987.

Wallace, S.L., *Taxation in Egypt from Augustus to Diocletian*, Princeton, Princeton University Press, 1938.

Wareth, U.A., 'Nag al-Hagar, a Roman fortress with a palace of the late Roman empire: second preliminary report', *BIFAO*, 1992, vol. 92, pp. 185–95.

Watson, A., *The Making of the Civil Law*, Cambridge, Mass., Harvard University Press, 1981.

——, *The Evolution of Law*, Oxford, Blackwell, 1985.

Watson, G.R., 'The pay of the Roman army: Suetonius, Dio, and the *quartum stipendium*', *Historia*, 1956, vol. 5, pp. 332–40.

——, 'The pay of the Roman army: the auxiliary forces', *Historia*, 1959, vol. 8, pp. 372–8.

——, *The Roman Soldier*, Thames and Hudson, London, 1964.

——, 'Documentation in the Roman army', *ANRW*, 1974, vol. 2.1, pp. 493–507.

Webster, G., *The Roman Imperial Army of the First and Second Centuries AD*, London, Black, 1962.

Weinstein, M.E. and Turner, E.G., 'Greek and Latin papyri from Qasr Ibrim', *JEA*, 1976, vol. 62, pp. 115–30.

Welles, C.B., 'The *immunitas* of the Roman legionaries in Egypt', *JRS*, 1938, vol. 28, pp. 41–9.

Wells, C.M., *The German Policy of Augustus*, Oxford, Clarendon, 1972.

Wessely, C., *Karanis und Soknopaiu Nesos (Denkschriften der kaiserlichen Akadamie der Wissenschaften in Wien. Philosophisch-historische Klasse*, vol. 47), Vienna, 1902.

Westermann, W.L., 'Tuscus the prefect and the veterans in Egypt', *Class. Phil.*, 1941, vol. 36, pp. 21–9.

Whitcomb, D.S. and Johnson, J.H., *Quseir Al-Qadim 1980: Preliminary Report*, Malibu, Udena, 1982.

Evelyn White, H.G., 'Graeco-Roman ostraka from Dakke, Nubia', *CR*, 1919, vol. 33, pp. 49–53.

Whitehorne, J.E.G., 'More about L. Pompeius Niger, legionary veteran', *Proceedings of the XVIIIth International Congress of Papyrology*, Athens, Greek Papyrological Society, 1988, pp. 445–50.

——, 'Soldiers and veterans in the local economy of first-century Oxyrhynchus', in M. Capasso, G.M. Savorelli and R. Pintaudi (eds), *Miscellanea Papyrologica (Papyrologica Florentina 19)*, Florence, Gonnelli, 1990, pp. 543–57.

Wierschowski, L., *Heer und Wirtschaft: das römische Heer der Prinzipatszeit als Wirtschaftsfaktor*, Bonn, Habelts Disertationsdrucke, 1984.

Will, E., 'Heron', *LIMC*, 1990, vol. 5.1, pp. 391–4.

Winkler, J., 'Lollianus and the Desperadoes', *JHS*, 1980, vol. 100, pp. 155–81.

Wright, R.P., 'New readings of a Severan inscription from Alexandria', *JRS*, 1941, vol. 31, pp. 33–52.

Yeivin, S., 'Notes on the northern temple at Karanis', *Aeg.*, 1934, vol. 14, pp. 71–9.

Youtie, H.C., 'Greek ostraka from Egypt', *TAPA*, 1950, vol. 81, pp. 99–116.

——, 'ΑΠΑΤΟΡΕΣ: Law vs. custom in Roman Egypt', *Le monde grec. Hommages à Claire Préaux*, Brussels, Université de Bruxelles, 1975, pp. 723–40, reprinted in H.C. Youtie, *Scriptiunculae Posteriores*, Bonn, Habelt, 1981–2, pp. 17–35.

——, *Scriptiunculae*, Amsterdam, Hakkert, 1971–5.

——, *Scriptiunculae Posteriores*, Bonn, Habelt, 1981–2.

Zaccaria, S. Strassi, *L'editto di M. Sempronius Liberalis*, Trieste, Bernardo, 1988.

Zahrnt, M., 'Antinoopolis in Ägypten: die hadrianische Gründung und ihre Privilegien in der neueren Forschung', *ANRW*, 1988, vol. 2 10.1, pp. 669–706.

Zitterkopf, R.E. and Sidebotham, S.E., 'Stations and towers on the Quseir-Nile Road', *JEA*, 1989, vol. 75, pp. 155–89.

INDEX

259